stated in the Preface, this volume offers a wide range of responses to the problem. Part I covers U.S. student unrest and Part II, foreign student unrest (in Latin America, France, Germany, Italy, and Japan).

Forty eminent specialists have contributed to the book, including Margaret Mead, David Riesman, Sidney Hook, former U.S. Commissioner of Education James E. Allen, Jr., CBS President William S. Paley, and nationally syndicated columnist Art Buchwald. The student point of view is represented especially by the former president of the U.S. National Student Association.

The book's comprehensiveness is enhanced by a special section (Part III) of official statements, letters, and addresses concerning student unrest in the U.S. Included are statements from government officials, such as Pres. Richard M. Nixon, Sen. Edward M. Kennedy, Congresswoman Shirley Chisholm, and Attorney General John N. Mitchell; educational leaders; national organizations; and faculty groups.

The unique combination of U.S. and foreign coverage and the broad spectrum of solutions offered by the contributors make this book indispensable for high school, college, and university administrators, faculty, libraries, and others who are concerned with the future of education.

The Editors

WILLIAM W. BRICKMAN is Professor of Educational History and Comparative Education, Graduate School of Education, University of Pennsylvania. He also serves as Editor of School & Society, *published by the Society for the Advancement of Education, of which he is Secretary. He is the author of* Guide to Research in Educational History *and is co-editor and co-author of* The Changing Soviet School.

STANLEY LEHRER is President and Publisher of School & Society, *as well as President and Treasurer of the Society for the Advancement of Education. He also is Publisher of the organization's book publishing division. His book,* Leaders, Teachers, and Learners in Academe: Partners in the Educational Process, *was published in 1970 by Appleton-Century-Crofts.*

CONFLICT AND CHANGE ON THE CAMPUS:

The Response to Student Hyperactivism

BOOKS BY WILLIAM W. BRICKMAN AND STANLEY LEHRER

John Dewey: Master Educator

The Countdown on Segregated Education

Religion, Government, and Education

A Century of Higher Education:
Classical Citadel to Collegiate Colossus

Automation, Education, and Human Values

CONFLICT AND CHANGE ON THE CAMPUS:

The Response to Student Hyperactivism

EDITED BY

WILLIAM W. BRICKMAN

Professor of Educational History and Comparative Education,
Graduate School of Education, University of Pennsylvania;
Editor of School & Society

AND

STANLEY LEHRER

President, Society for the Advancement of Education;
Publisher of School & Society and School & Society Books

SCHOOL & SOCIETY BOOKS

NEW YORK, 1970

Copyright © 1970 by School & Society Books,
1860 Broadway, New York, N. Y. 10023

FIRST EDITION

LIBRARY OF CONGRESS CATALOG CARD NUMBER 75-115102

Printed in the United States of America

To

ELAYNE and BERNARD LEVY

*sincere friends with the deep conviction that reason
must pervade the changing values of today's students*

and

ADOLPHE ERICH MEYER

teacher, colleague, and friend

Contents

PART II. FOREIGN STUDENT ACTIVISM

PART III. DOCUMENTS ON STUDENT UNREST:
A NATIONAL DIALOGUE

COMPILED BY STANLEY LEHRER

Preface

~~~~~~

TYPICAL, PARK-LIKE college and university campuses are deceptively tranquil. Behind the façades of old and new buildings, from Columbia University in the East to San Francisco State College in the West, throb the restlessness and rebelliousness of recalcitrant groups of students. Periodic student protests and strikes, imbued with strong convictions to change academic policies and procedures and frequently exhibiting savage destructiveness and disregard of the desires of others to study uninterruptedly, have dispelled the usual collegiate calm. The story of campus conflict is being written occasionally in blood as policemen clash with student activists. Police assistance sometimes has been requested by institutions to help restore order by lifting a state of siege imposed by students. Most college and university administrators prefer, however, to resolve campus conflicts without depending upon the sheer strength of the police. Some administrators have sought injunctions in the courts to restrain campus activists. For the sake of survival, the academic world is struggling desperately to find appropriate solutions to the battle of lawlessness vs. learning. Amidst the broken glass of vandalized campuses are the shattered dreams of educators who want to teach, of students who want to learn, of colleges and universities that want to advance the cause of higher education in a peaceful and dignified manner.

Riots, revolts, and acts of violence are neither current phenomena nor the tools of only American students. History reveals many confrontations between students and their schools. And countries in Europe, Asia, Africa, and Latin America have felt the thrust of student revolt.

The tempo of discontent has quickened, with more and more institutions experiencing disruptive flare-ups. Many student dissidents are determined to overturn the collegiate establishment as an alternative to their unmet, militant demands for changes in the plans, programs, and practices of several colleges and universities. While some schools have accepted the belief that certain changes should be made in response to justifiable demands, others have refused to give an inch in their confrontation with extremists. The times call for reason and resolution in meeting the challenge of student hyperactivism.

This book examines the nature and scope of student unrest in the U. S. The essays in Part I probe the sensitive issues that have caused the students and the collegiate establishment to split apart. Various sources were consulted in an attempt to gather suggestions for easing or eliminating the widespread incidences of student disenchantment with, and disorder at, the nation's colleges and universities. A cross section of professional opinion was obtained from specialists in educational administration, secondary and higher education, history, philosophy, social and political science, religion, anthropology, psychology, psychiatry, law, government, journalism, book publishing, and broadcasting. Among the many writers is the past president of the U. S. National Student Association. Since student unrest has rippled from the colleges to secondary schools, the book provides an essay on this dimension of the problem. Serious disturbances by students in foreign countries are given attention in Part II. At the end of the volume (Part III) is a collection of several significant U.S. documents on student unrest, including historic pronouncements by President Richard M. Nixon; Robert H. Finch, Secretary of Health, Education, and Welfare; Attorney General John N. Mitchell; Senator Edward M. Kennedy; and a variety of national organizations.

The book will be useful to college and university administrators, faculty members, and students as well as general readers who are—and should be—concerned about the issues involved in student activism and who are committed, by virtue of professional dedication or genuine regard for higher education, to finding suitable remedies for the explosive dilemma confronting academia. The contents also offer a base for serious and constructive study in such courses as educational sociology, educational administration, and higher education. If the volume's subject matter is helpful in generating equitable solutions to the question of student unrest, then the editors have achieved their purpose.

The cooperation of all writers is appreciated. They kindly granted permission to reprint their essays in this book. The editors are equally grateful to the many publications and organizations which have approved of our use of their material. In addition to the reprinted papers, there are essays which are being published for the first time, and the editors are indebted to the thoughtful contributors. Special thanks to Robert S. Rothenberg of the Society for the Advancement of Education for his very capable assistance every step of the way during the creation of the book. To my wife, Laurel, belongs the distinction of being helpful whenever possible. Her suggestions concerning the book were invaluable, and even her moral support aided in the volume's completion.

STANLEY LEHRER

New Hyde Park, N. Y.
July, 1969

Introduction

STUDENT ACTIVISM AND ACADEMIC
APATHY SINCE 1963

~~~~~~

FROM THE TIME of the higher institution of learning at Athens, through the universities founded during the Middle Ages, down to the multiversities of the present decade, the student has constituted a problem to the scholastic, governmental, or ecclesiastical authorities. These problems involved not only academic issues, but also misbehavior in college and community and participation in political demonstrations and revolutions. It is not at all difficult to recall the bloody town vs. gown riots in medieval Paris, the student resistance to totalitarian tyrannies in 19th-century Germany and Russia, the demonstrations and riots in colleges of colonial America, the panty raids in mid-20th-century American citadels of higher learning, and other incidents.

It seems impossible to make any sound generalization covering all the instances of student activism. Some seem trivial, others significant; some beneficial, others destructive. Distinctions might be made between those based on justice and injustice, on reason and unreason, but these may be based on particular value systems and may not reflect objective criteria of judgment. Such is the difficulty in appraising the situation of student unrest in our time.

We witness wanton destruction and complete disregard of human rights in some student demonstrations. On the other hand, student action has resulted in the reconsideration and reform of inflexible academic procedures, as well as changes for the betterment of society.

In an effort to clarify this issue to some extent, the writer reprints with minor variations the texts of four editorials on this theme published in *School & Society* between 1963 and 1968. They illustrate the fact of the escalation of student activism from the simple to the complex, from challenges of regulations to the assault upon the structure of society itself. They also indicate a growing impatience with the indifference and lassitude often shown by the majority of students and staff toward the catastrophic events on college campuses.

November, 1963

A wave of riots shattered the American academic calm in the spring of 1963. First at Princeton University and subsequently at Brown and Yale universities, many students transformed their intellectual environment into an area ruled by a rampaging and destructive mob of irresponsible and immature individuals. Fortunately, this situation proved to be temporary and wiser heads brought about calm and a return to reason and dignity.

It does no one any good, least of all the participating students themselves, to raise the question, as some have done, about the shortcomings of our society or the slow process of maturation. No doubt, explanations and excuses may be found in American life, mores, and values to account for the lapses by the learners in the colleges and universities. The observer of the native scene might also mention the restlessness of youth as evidenced by the racial and other demonstrations. Those who are aware of the developments taking place in other countries might call attention to the political demonstrations and riots carried out by students all over the world. Moreover, in England students have become increasingly vocal with regard to such issues as curfew hours and the entertainment of visitors of another sex in their dormitory rooms. From some Dutch universities, there have come disturbing and extremely shocking reports concerning sadistic practices of initiation of new students.

Clearly, then, the problem of student behavior is one that is not peculiar to the U.S. Yet, this fact cannot and should not be used as an extenuating circumstance. There is no reason why American higher education should not strive—and attain—the highest possible standards in scholarship *and* in human behavior.

From this standpoint, it becomes evident that everyone connected with a college and university—president, professor, and pupil alike—must exert himself to make certain that higher education remains an intellectual process. Let all of these insist that each member of the collegiate community subject himself to self-discipline and restraint. Hazing, panty raids, and other forms of intemperate or riotous action in group form should not be tolerated in an academic atmosphere. Anyone who is acceptable as a student in an institution of higher learning must show that he is capable of higher levels of behavioral performance. This principle applies to individual as to collective behavior. It may be true that *errare est humanum;* yet, it does not follow that the recognition of the possibility of individual frailty should be extended to individuals in the mass.

The number of aspirants to a higher education is expected to exceed the facilities. Serious consideration should be given by administrators and faculty to the question of the retention of those who are not sufficiently mature to take seriously the privilege of obtaining an advanced education.

College is a place for learning, not for larks.

January, 1967

One of the striking developments in higher education in recent years has been the constantly increasing pressure by college and university students on faculty, administration, society, and government. Students have openly expressed demands for radical and rapid change, and demonstrated, sat in, and lay in for them. They have called for modified or no examinations, removal of restrictions to entertaining the opposite sex in dormitories, active participation in policy-making in higher education, grading the professors, the fundamental freedom of orating obscenities, and more and more. Demonstrations of one type or another for or against one cause or another are a commonplace in the colleges and universities.

Anyone who is familiar with the history of higher education, especially since the Middle Ages, knows that student actions, with and without violence, have taken place in all centuries and in all countries, including the U.S.A. In recent years, students have been activistic, particularly in Asian, African, and Latin American universities, so that it can be said with confidence that manifestations of student unrest occur on a global scale.

With these facts as background, let us turn to the events of the post-Berkeley period in American higher education. In 1966, students at Harvard and Brown Universities made efforts to prevent physically government officials from expressing viewpoints with which they were in disagreement. Such individuals insisted on academic freedom to curtail the freedom of others. There were official apologies, of course, and it is most unlikely that the strong-arm students were more than a mere minority. On the other hand, one might also be aware of the attitude of the academic apologists that opposition to the Vietnam war is a legitimate excuse for any type of behavior by students.

Faculties and administrations—and students, as well—have remained too long silent, foot-dragging, pussyfooting, and otherwise inactive in the face of student invective, demonstrations, and violence. It should be clear that sociological apologetics and an excessively broad, one-sided conception of academic freedom constitute a danger to the collegiate community and its educational objectives. Students who demand freedom from responsibility and who deprive others of their freedom are immature at best and totalitarian-minded at worst.

Academia is the institution for instruction, inquiry, discussion, debate, and deliberation. It is not, in and of itself, a place for political activism or for the propagating by force of social and other doctrines. It is time for all those who wish to advance education in the college and university to resolve to act. Appeasement and mollycoddling, as many have suspected all the time, did not serve to satisfy the activistic students. Let the advocates of higher education apply the reasonable rules of administration which are designed to develop an intellectual atmosphere on the campus.

In our world there is already too much intolerance and force. The university should remain a realm where reason should reign.

January, 1968

The year 1967 may well be referred to as the Year of Violence, not only in international affairs, but also in domestic matters, both in the U.S. and in the rest of the world. On the educational scene, demonstrations, interference with the rights of others, and riots have become the order of the day, an established fact that permits no contradiction—all in the name of academic freedom, civil rights, and liberalism. Respect for authority and tradition, discussion, and patience seem to have been discarded in favor of pressure and violence in order to gain one's ends. In the U.S., this type of behavior, which has roots as far back as the 17th century, has been gaining momentum from the beginning of Berkeley-itis in 1964 and has spread to campuses all over the country.

In point of fact, the disdain for orderly procedures has become manifest even in secondary schools. There have been instances of disruptive and violent action by adolescents aware of the impact of flexed muscles. With an abundance of academic apologists in higher and secondary education, one can foresee an increasing number of incidents in which student power will make itself felt and will force changes in policy and personnel in educational institutions.

It is all too easy for a writer, teacher, parent, or a citizen at large to criticize and denounce the nonaction and the ill-action by boards of trustees, school boards, and administrative officials. No doubt a great deal of such criticism is justifiable. There does not seem to be any rational basis for the coddling of criminals and dillydallying with delinquents. Yet, one must appreciate the fact that we are not in the position of those who are under the constant pressure of the mumbo-jumbo artists who uphold the civil and constitutional rights of young people to deny the same rights to others. Also, we cannot overlook the *Zeitgeist* which is the context of the student power movement.

What seems to be called for, at this time, is a determination on the part of the responsible elements in education, society, and government to insist upon the integrity of the educational institution and upon orderly processes of discussion, debate, and dissent. Where there are no rules, no laws, there is bound to be anarchy—whether on the campus or in the community.

Consequently, all those involved in the administration and process of education on all levels must resolve to practice reasonable patience, fairness, and consideration toward all who pass through the doors of schools and colleges. There must be an effective insistence upon standards of tolerance and behavior so that the work of education can go on with a minimum of disruption and delay. Administrators and faculty should be willing to cooperate to put teeth into reasonable regulations for admission, retention, and graduation. The factor of character needs to be given more attention than it has received until now.

It is well known that there are some faculty members and administrators who sympathize with student activists, and at times incite, comfort, and defend them. What is necessary is constant cooperation by determined members of the academic community, a hitherto

silent but hopefully strong majority, to make the university a center
of scholarly and intellectual activity where the principles of good
human relations are perennially practiced. How this can be accomplished cannot be delineated here and now. The various institutions, singly and in concert, can find suitable procedures to put into
operation the basic objective of maintaining educational integrity so
that the university can perform its functions properly. Under such
circumstances, the university would not bend in the direction of any
doctrine or any form of duress, however camouflaged by specious
language.

Without academic law and order, academic anarchy is inevitable.

October, 1968

The student movement, activism, power, unrest, revolution, or
whatever word one wishes to describe the recent disruptions of the
work of colleges and universities all over the world, is no longer a
phenomenon; it is an established fact, a reality of the times. Relatively few are shocked any more by the happenings which bring
universities to a sudden stop. The expectation for the future seems
to be more of the same activity that characterized the academic year
1967-68. The turmoil and turbulence of the town has been transferred to the territory of the gown. Neo-nihilism threatens to become the norm.

It is all too easy to mention institutions and countries invidiously,
but this simply recapitulates the overfamiliar. The fact of the matter
is that large numbers of what were once called institutions of
higher learning are in danger of demise through the revolutionary
tactics of some student and faculty personnel. It appears unlikely
that any college or university is safe—unless something substantial is
done by the responsible elements of the institution.

In too many instances, administrators, faculty, and students have
been immobilized by indecision, paralyzed by propaganda, and fro-
zen by fear, while those bent on ruining the university as an agency
of scholarship and society literally ran riot. Too many persons
associated with higher education either kept silent or overtly or
covertly supported the extremists. Such an attitude stemmed possibly
from the conviction that any counteraction against violence toward
university personnel or property was an infringement upon the
students' academic freedom. Some professors, indeed, do not express

disapproval of the hyperactivists because of their belief that they would not be considered "liberal."

The history of student unrest and rioting in the university goes back to the beginnings of the institution in the Middle Ages. Students have protested through the centuries, on and off the campus, for good and for bad causes, for and against freedom. Without considering the off-campus activity by the students at this time, it is pertinent to assert that the closing down of the universities constitutes anti-intellectualist tyranny. As such, it is necessary that this be prevented in advance or counteracted after the occurrence.

Students have incontrovertible rights in the educational process. These rights pertain to a good education, equality and fairness of treatment, petition and hearing of grievances, and representation to give voice to their views on various matters of policy. They do not have the right to deprive other students of their right to an education or faculty and administrators of their right to do their work. They certainly do not have any right to seize and destroy property (including research materials) and to jeopardize the life and health of university personnel. Nor is there any justification in attacking an administration which seeks to restore some semblance of sanity on the academic scene.

Another point should be given attention. One should not dismiss the probability that nihilistic students are less concerned with the university than with the destruction of social institutions in the large. Appeasement, compromise, and near-capitulation never will satisfy them. They will not quiet down until the university as such ceases to exist. Once the university is no more, they will then assault society.

The students, professors, administrators, and trustees who are concerned about the existence of higher education must determine to act together to remove the clot from the campus. This can be done by consistent cooperation in meeting the nihilistic onslaught. There must be an application of the principles of reason, enforcement of fair regulations, change based on mutual respect and understanding, and a forthrightness in matters affecting all associated with higher educational institutions. A careful, realistic policy of admission and retention of students is crucially necessary. Those who are not real students in the full sense of the word do not have the constitutional or any other right to a place on the campus.

Academic freedom for the professor, student, and administrator is a *sine qua non* of higher education. It does not include the freedom to deprive anyone else from his exercise of academic freedom. When members of a university do not act to ensure universal academic freedom—to study, teach, do research, and administer—they are contributing to the withering away of their institution.

Silence does not imply simple assent—it is a guarantee of destruction. *Vivat Academia!*

Conclusion

Solutions do not come easily, even those committed to paper. The problem of student activism seems likely to remain a perennial one. Consequently, something needs to be said—and done—if the university is to exist as an institution.

There must be a cooperative effort to apply the rule of reason and goodwill to the disagreements on the academic scene. The university trustees, administrators, and faculty should be willing to reexamine their functions in the interest of serving to the fullest the interrelated needs of students and the demands of scholarship. Service to society and the state, however important, is secondary to the fundamental nature and purpose of the university as university.

Grievances and dissatisfactions abound in any institution. The very character of the university fosters debate and dissent. The resolution of conflicts must be accomplished on the basis of the full realization of the freedom of all persons involved. Equitable procedures exist or can be adopted to redress wrongs and to prevent injustice.

Academic justice requires reason, and restraint, and respect for the rights of others. Also necessary is a firm resolve to uphold the integrity of the university against those who misuse the principles of freedom in guaranteeing their own and in curtailing or destroying the freedom of others. What is needed is the exercise of the courage of one's conviction in maintaining the existence of the university as an institution dedicated to the intellectual advancement of students in an atmosphere of sound, objective scholarship practiced by a fairminded faculty and administration. Academic lethargy is a luxury of the past.

Compromise with, or concession to, extremism is an open invitation to graduated repetition. The inevitable result is institutional decline and fall.

WILLIAM W. BRICKMAN

PART I

Student Activism in America

1

THE NEW BREED IN SEARCH
OF A NEW MORALITY

JACK F. PADGETT

THE COLLEGE CAMPUS TODAY is witnessing the rise of a "new breed" in search of a "new morality." College students are openly defiant of certain aspects of the world as they find it. No longer merely on the defensive for their beliefs and behavior, the present student generation has taken the offensive in criticizing the attitudes and actions of anyone over thirty. However apropos the charge of "silent generation" was of students in the '50s, the label is ludicrous today.

Students today are speaking and acting as they have not done in the recent past and it is important to try to discover what the talk and the action are all about. Specifically, I want to examine and to evaluate three concrete criticisms of middle-class America levied by some members of the younger generation: (1) the depersonalization of life; (2) the phoniness and lack of authenticity of so much of life today; (3) social complacency and the failure to act to bring about needed social reform.

The System: Agent of Depersonalization of Life

First is the contention that individual freedom and self-fulfillment are seriously endangered by the over-organization of life, or what is

From *Liberal Education*, October, 1968. Reprinted by permission of the author and the editor of *Liberal Education*. Jack F. Padgett is Professor of Philosophy, Albion College, Albion, Mich.

known simply as "The System" or "The Establishment." Whatever may have been true in frontier days, the vision of the lone individual making his place in the world has for most of us faded, except for occasional Walter Mitty fantasies or nocturnal exploits on TV. Nor is it the big plains that the individual must fight against; he must rather fight against being swallowed up in the immensity of big government, big business, big unions, big debts, and big educational institutions. Education, too, has taken on immense proportions and students are complaining about the bigness and impersonality of the educational enterprise. Though the complexity of current campus crises defy simple explanation, surely they dramatize the disastrous and disruptive effects on the educational process of the depersonalization and the dehumanization of the campus.

If a student is to grow as a human being and not merely as a symbol manipulator, then there is no substitute in the learning process for direct and personal confrontation among students and between student and teacher. Students attending the National Conference on Student Stress held in Washington, D. C. (June, 1966), emphasized the point when they expressed a "yearning to talk with professors on terms of equality, to have them 'level with us,' and to 'know what they really think.' "[1]

The villain, then, for the new breed is the present prevailing system of organization which substitutes mechanized communication for meaningful dialogue and false familiarity of the salesman to his client for deeply personal relationships. How can one hope to live authentically in such a society?

Phoniness and Lack of Authenticity

Thus, the second criticism by the new breed focuses on phoniness and the lack of authenticity of so much of life in America. Is it foolish idealism to expect people in positions of power to speak honestly; to give real reasons for an action rather than devious ones, even when this evasion is done supposedly in the name of personal or national security? Some things we cannot and should not protect another person from facing, for to do so is to deny him the opportunity to mature.

I recently talked with the parents of a student of mine about their son's plans for a special study project abroad that sounded stimulat-

---

[1] Reported in *The National Observer,* June 20, 1966.

ing and which I had encouraged him to pursue further. In the course of the conversation it became evident that the parents did not think they could afford the financial expense entailed but had not told this to their son. In their desire not to discourage his enthusiasm they were nevertheless keeping from him some vital information necessary for him to make a responsible choice.

To put the issue this way, of course, is being too generous. Too much of the generation gap is due to intentionally communicated misinformation. Nothing is more devastating to good morale in an organization or in a democratic society than to discover that your leaders are not leveling with you. The college campus has not escaped this credibility gap.

Student complaints do not, however, focus on dishonesty alone or merely on the non-curricular aspects of education; they are also directed to the academic enterprise itself. Educators are challenged to make learning relevant to living, to provide teachers who really teach, and to find a way between dogmatism and indifference in helping students to cope with fundamental problems of human existence in a nuclear age. Students at Berkeley make it quite clear that "their search is for identity, meaning, community and, by no means least, a response from the adult world."[2]

The most serious charge of lack of authenticity is directed to the gap between the professed American way of life and how we actually live. It is the failure of those in power (The Establishment), "to translate educational, political, and social ideals into realities"[3] that leads to the greatest disillusionment with the traditional values of the past.

Social Complacency

The third criticism is, perhaps, most significant of all; it is also inseparable from and really underlies the other two. Faced with "The Organization" as the agent of depersonalization and with obstacles in society that prevent one from living authentically, the natural question is: What are we going to do about it? It is the answer to this question that most clearly separates the new radicals from the rest of society. For what astonishes and infuriates the new

---

[2] Joseph Katz and Nevitt Sanford, "Cause of the Student Revolution," *Saturday Review,* December 18, 1965, p. 79.

[3] Charles B. Ketchum, "The Search for the New Morality," *The Christian Century,* October 12, 1966, p. 1236.

breed most of all is the inaction and the passive acceptance of the status quo by most members of society. Unwilling to accept the pet slogans of the past such as, "You can't fight city hall," and, "Don't sweat it," the new activists are determined to *do* something about civil rights, Vietnam, poverty in the midst of plenty, the power structure on the campus. The action advocated and taken by the new activists is direct and highly personal; personal involvement at times even outweighs the practical results attained. Thus the younger generation is not willing to be depersonalized in the name of efficiency or to sacrifice self at the altar of the god of physical comfort.

What then, does the new breed want? What they profess to want most of all, and claim as a right, is a say in what affects them. "Participatory democracy" has become the political slogan and not until it replaces "paternalistic democracy" in all facets of our society will the new breed rest content. Paternalism, whether in public or private life, must end and a new era of sharing power and responsibility must begin.

How is one to reply to these criticisms? That something should be said by members of my generation can hardly be in doubt. Perhaps the place to begin is by admitting that ready-made solutions are not available although recognizing that solutions are nonetheless urgently needed. If the old values and the old methods for knowing them are no longer adequate, then it behooves us to admit it and to begin the search for a new morality that is adequate for our times.

Confusion of Legitimate and Illegitimate Demands

First, what about the claim that "The System" or "The Organization" is the villain of the college campus? Like most of us, student attitudes are ambivalent and their views ambiguous. They want the opportunity for close contact with professors, but readily transfer to larger institutions because they feel stifled by the smaller campus; they want personal attention and the unity in academic life of a small campus along with the anonymity and the diversity of social life of the larger groups; they want their gripes listened to by administrators, but cry to be let alone in the non-academic aspects of their lives; they want freedom and privacy to develop truly meaningful interpersonal relations, but interpret this to mean that college facilities should be made available for couple privacy.

Can this be done? Aren't students asking for the best of both worlds? Yes, they are; but why not, they argue? A confusion of legitimate and illegitimate demands is evident. For example, when students say that the university is designed primarily for their enlightenment and, therefore, they should have a voice in its operation, they are both correct and justified; but when they also want the right to live a private life apart from any institutional demands, while enjoying the benefit of the institution, they are both incorrect and unjustified. We have for too long preached critical inquiry into all areas of life in our classrooms and practiced *in loco parentis* when it came to the rules governing campus life. We do need to be as concerned for providing the conditions and the context in which human freedom and responsibility may be exercised outside the classroom as we have been concerned to provide for academic freedom and intellectual responsibility in the classroom. What can be questioned, however, is a model of behavior sometimes advocated that portrays individuals and the various segments of the college community as atomistically related to each other—*i.e.,* related as separate and distinct entities—hence devoid of any cooperative ties that bind them together in a common enterprise. No one can both choose to belong to an organization, enjoying the benefits of cooperative effort, and at the same time choose to act as if he were entirely independent of that organization. The development of free and responsible individuals is the end that justifies an educational institution (students are right in reminding us of this point); nonetheless social cooperation is the essential means to that end. Merely because group living is at times inconvenient or occasionally makes demands on individual members for the sake of the cohesion of the group does not justify incitement to riot or advocacy of anarchy.

Thus the attempt to devise legitimate patterns of behavior for those living in institutional housing and thereby part of the social organization of the college cannot in truth be modeled after a code of behavior appropriate for the same individuals who rent rooms or apartments on their own, independent of the college. Hence, student demands for complete and uninterrupted couple privacy in a social living unit operated by the college, is not legitimate in the same sense as the demand to be a participating member of the decision-making process by which campus rules and regulations are formulated.

Abuse vs. Legitimate Use of Authority

Second, let's examine the ideal of "participatory democracy." The use and abuse of power is a perennial problem, but it takes on a special urgency today. To ask the younger members of society to be silent while their elders proceed to pollute the air and water necessary for life, overpopulate the lands on which life must be lived, ignore the rights of minorities and the pleas of the poor, conduct wars which may lead to atomic annihilation, or administer educational institutions in which students do not learn what is necessary for a meaningful life in the twentieth century is to foster apathy, cynicism, or open rebellion. Surely a sane society organized on democratic principles with the aim of promoting the general welfare can and must offer better options than these. If our words and deeds in dealing with major social upheavals amount to a counsel of despair, then we should not be surprised that young people take us seriously and do despair over the legacy they have inherited. Nevertheless some things must be said to the advocates of action with integrity. The complexity of some of the problems we face do defy simple solution; some problems do resist direct and immediate action; and still others can best be solved only through arduous arbitration carried on quietly and in private. Somehow we need to share power and responsibility with those affected without endless debate and undue delay, and without dissipating the power to act. However, someone or some group must have the authority finally to decide and to implement policy and be able to expect that the policy will receive respectful consideration. Furthermore, there *is* a difference between dogmatic appeal to authority and rational appeal to authority, just as there is between abuse and legitimate use of authority. No one can be competent in everything, so that appeal to the expertise of specialists is inevitable and legitimate. In this case, confidence is placed in the competency of the person in light of knowledge he has and skills he has developed; the assumption is that he would be willing to correct, modify, or abandon his views if the evidence warranted. Such an appeal to authority is part of life today and should not be confused with a dogmatic appeal to authority which holds that what the authority states is true because he says so. Repudiation of any and all authority is not a mark of maturity or a stride toward freedom, but a mark of immaturity and a giant step toward anarchy.

If we take "participatory democracy" seriously, then it follows that no *one* segment of the community can dictate policy. Let us not confuse the right to participate in the *formulation* of policy with the right to *determine* policy. Also, when a joint decision is reached then it should carry the respect of the diverse groups represented. Some students interpret any arbitration of grievances as a sell-out unless all they submitted is accepted as submitted; but does this not reflect their own "hang-up" on a kind of paternalism in reverse? To arbitrate differences entails uncertainty of outcome or the arbitration is a farce. Similarly, students in rejecting the unwarranted dogmatism of teachers and administrators sometimes fall into the same trap by claiming that they know what is best in dealing with difficult and delicate problems.

For example, take the current issue on college campuses concerning the role that students should play in the decision-making process of the institution. Should students have a direct voice in administrative affairs or should student involvement be through the formation of student committees paralleling faculty and administrative committees, with provision made for communication and consultation among the various committees? I confess that I do not know the absolute answer to this important question; but neither do students have the answer, though claims to this effect are sometimes made. Rather than endless debate, it would be more in keeping with the tenor of the new morality to acknowledge our mutual ignorance and then to proceed to initiate some experiments—preferably at a variety of institutions—with the aim of testing different approaches to student participation in the administration of the college and university. Here is honest and thoughtful action that provides a procedure for checking on the value of the action taken. We are currently engaged in this process at Albion College and I hope that we can share our results with other colleges.

The temptation to play god and to abuse the use of power is not reserved for deans and presidents alone. The poignant message of Orwell's *Animal Farm* applies to students as well.

Ideals Proclaimed vs. Values Attained

Finally, what about the problem of authenticity today? To live authentically demands the kind of critical reflection on self and society that is a rare achievement in any age. Our age tends to discourage thinking at all; "respond, don't reflect" is the motto. Any evidence that people are exercising judgment in the selection of values is welcomed.

The present generation is certainly correct in insisting on greater honesty among the various segments of the college community. Students should not be treated like children who must be protected from the hard facts of life on a college campus: faculty politics, pressures from irate parents and members of the board of trustees, community pressure, and the economic problems of academic institutions. Their naïveté on these matters is too often due to the failure of the faculty and of the administration to inform them of the real issues at stake in the decision-making process of the campus. What students have no right to expect is to know everything; not because of an inherent inability of administrators to be honest, but because of the inherent inability of anyone to be completely honest even with himself, let alone when one is dealing with diverse interest groups. What is at issue, therefore, is not the realization of an impossible ideal of honesty, but the willingness to discuss openly problems of college policy and to explore openly possible solutions with those segments of the campus, including students, who are directly affected by the decisions to be made.

At the national level the problem is immensely complex and the security of the nation cannot be sacrificed at the altar of naive honesty; but the responsibility at this point clearly rests with our leaders, who must be willing to risk much for the sake of a well-informed populace. The credibility gap over Vietnam and the resulting divisions of our people into opposing and hostile camps is one of the most disturbing illustrations of this kind of deception.

Authenticity requires unusual honesty and perceptivity in regard to one's own values. The "new breed" shows much-needed insight when it claims that something is not really valuable to me if I have not experienced it as valuable. It may be that there is something of value there for me once I appropriate it, in which case it is a potential value for me; or it may be the kind of experience which I conceive to be a valuable one and choose to be guided toward its realization, in which case it is an ideal for me. But potential values and ideals are not actual experiences of value, though we constantly confuse them. Indeed it is the gap between ideals proclaimed and values attained that is at the root of most of the current protest. Whereas the older members of society tend to accept the profession of the ideal as guarantee of its future realization, some members of the younger generation won't wait and they are setting about to realize the values themselves; they are determined to cash in on the promissory notes society has been issuing for so long: equality, peace with justice, quality education, for example.

Life is precarious at best and offers no guarantee that our ideals will be realized; we can't even be sure that they should be realized. In all candor we must relinquish any claim to knowledge of universal truth and of absolute values; instead we must accept and act on the basis of human truths and human values, ever open to new insights and new dimensions of experience. Think and act in this world we must; we can choose to act blindly and irresponsibly or we can choose to act on the basis of the best critical reflection of our day, recognizing our own limited and partial visions and accepting the risk and the responsibility for our words and our deeds. Because we can't live by reason alone is no excuse for not living by reason at all.

2

WHAT'S BUGGING THE STUDENTS

IRVING KRISTOL

No ONE, except perhaps a few college administrators, mourns the passing of "the silent generation." But it must be said in its favor that at least one knew what the American university students of the 1950s were silent about, and why. They were conformists for plain, indeed, obvious and traditional, conformist reasons. We may have been distressed and vexed by this conformism; we were not mystified by it; whereas we are very much mystified by the nonconformism of the students of the sixties.

Many of the same middle-aged critics who so fervently and eloquently condemned the silent generation are now considerably upset and puzzled at the way students are "misbehaving" these days. One wanted the young to be idealistic, perhaps even somewhat radical, possibly even a bit militant—but not like this! It used to be said that the revolution devours its children. It now appears that these children have devoured this revolution.

What is it all about? One thing is fairly clear: the teach-ins, the sit-ins, the lay-downs, the mass picketing, and all the rest are not *merely* about Vietnam, or civil rights, or the size of classes at Berkeley, or the recognition of Red China. They are about these issues surely, and most sincerely. But there is, transparently, a pas-

From *The Atlantic Monthly*, November, 1965. Reprinted by permission of the author and the publisher. Copyright © 1965 by The Atlantic Monthly Company, Boston, Mass. Irving Kristol is Executive Vice President and Senior Editor, Basic Books, Inc., and Luce Professor of Urban Values, New York University.

sion behind the protests that refuses to be satisfied by the various topics which incite it. This passion reaches far beyond politics, as we ordinarily understand that term. Anyone who believes the turbulence will subside once we reach a settlement in Vietnam is in for a rude surprise. Similarly, anyone who thinks of present-day campus radicalism as a kind of over-zealous political liberalism, whose extremism derives from nothing more than youthful high spirits, is deceiving himself. What we are witnessing is an event *in* American politics, but not *of* it.

Indeed, one of the most striking features of the new radicalism on the campus is that it is, in one sense, so apolitical. It is a strange experience to see a radical mood in search of a radical program; it is usually very much the other way around. These young American radicals are in the historically unique position of not being able to demand *a single piece of legislation* from their government—their "platform" is literally without one legislative plank. Their passion for "freedom now" coexists with a remarkable indifference to everything the United States government is doing, or might do, in this direction.

If one read every campus leaflet published these past two years and attended every campus or off-campus demonstration, and knew only what one learned from these sources, one would hardly be aware that the Johnson Administration had enacted in the area of civil rights the most far-reaching reforms in a century of legislative history. There has been no campus meeting to celebrate the passage of the Civil Rights Act or the Voting Rights Act. There has not even been any meeting criticizing these laws for "not going far enough." It's as if nothing had happened—or, to put it more precisely, as if whatever happens in Washington has nothing to do with the world the students live and act in.

The same sort of thing is to be seen with regard to the war on poverty, a topic upon which students will declaim passionately and with unquestionable sincerity. But it seems that their passion is so pure, their sensibility so fine, that these would be violated by a consideration of anything so vulgar as how to get more money into poor people's pockets. The recent increase in social security and the medicare bill made their way through Congress without the benefit of so much as a benevolent nod from the campuses. Whenever I have mentioned this legislation in conversation, I have received an icy stare of incomprehension and disdain, as if I were some kind of political idiot who actually believed what he read in the *New York Times*.

Even in the single area where one would most expect specific and tangible proposals of reform, the organization of the multiversity, these have not made their appearance. For an entire year the students of the University of California at Berkeley have given dramatic evidence of dissatisfaction with their university experience—and does anyone know specifically what they would like, by way of improvement? The university officials certainly don't know, nor do the regents, nor do the faculty. Some outsiders *think* they know. Berkeley is too large, they say, too anonymous; there is no possibility of a face-to-face community of scholars, young and old. This is true enough. But the Riverside branch of this same university is a small liberal arts college, with great intimacy and comfort, and for the past decade it has had much difficulty in attracting enough students. They all want to go to Berkeley, and the reason, they will explain, is: "That is where the action is."

The denunciations of the multiversity suspiciously resemble the way New Yorkers excoriate "megalopolis"—having come there in the first place, and determinedly remaining there, for no other reason than that New York *is* a megalopolis. All Americans will always insist that they adore small towns and detest great cities, but the movement of population from towns to cities remains strangely unaffected. And Berkeley, even today, has far more student applications than it can handle; one might even say, *especially* today, for I understand that the number of applications has, in fact, slightly increased.

No, the upsurge of left-wing sentiment and left-wing opinion on the American campus today is not the sort of thing progressive parents and educators had in mind ten years ago when they benevolently urged students to become "socially committed" and "more idealistic." They naively wished them to have intelligent discussions of Vietnam, not to hurl insults and epithets at Averell Harriman (as happened at Cornell), or tear up their draft cards, or laud the Viet Cong. They wished them to be urbane and tolerant about sex, not to carry placards with dirty words, or demand the sale of contraceptives in the college bookstore. They wished them to be concerned for civic and social equality for the Negro, not to denounce "white America" as a pious fraud, whose "integration" did not differ essentially from South Africa's apartheid, or express sympathy with a mindless (if occasionally eloquent) black nationalism. They wished—they wished, in short, that their children be just like them, only a wee bit bolder and more enlightened. Instead, these children are making it very clear that being just like their parents, progressive or not, is the fate they wish most desperately to avoid.

And this, I think, is the crux of the matter. The new student radicalism is so fundamentally at odds with our conventional political categories because it is, above all, an *existentialist* revolt. The term is unfortunately chic, and ambiguous, too. But in this context it has a fairly definite meaning: the students are in rebellion, not so much because things are bad for them, or for others, but because things are what they are for them and for others.

Clues to the meaning of this rebellion may be found in two phrases that now appear ever more commonly in the left-wing campus vocabulary. The first is "organized America." The second is "participatory democracy."

"Organized America" is, quite simply, America, and not, as one might think, some transient bureaucratic excrescence on the body of America. As a matter of fact, today's students are immensely skillful in coping with bureaucracies and their paper work. They fill out forms and applications with a briskness and competence that startle the middle-aged observer. (I would guess that no one over the age of forty could properly fill out a college application form unless he received guidance from some kindly youngster.) What bugs the students is not these trivia but the society they emanate from—the affluent society, welfare state and all. The liberalism (and the radicalism, too) of the 1930s and 1940s has borne its fruit, and it tastes bitter to the children, setting their teeth on edge. That is why American students, amidst reasonably general prosperity and under a liberal Administration that is expanding the welfare state more aggressively and successfully than anyone had thought possible, feel more "alienated" than ever before. So many college students "go left" for the same reason that so many high school students "go delinquent." *They are bored.* They see their lives laid out neatly before them; they see themselves moving ahead sedately and more or less inexorably in their professional careers; they know that with a college degree even "failure" in their careers will represent no harsh punishment; they know "it's all laid on"—and they react against this bourgeois utopia their parents so ardently strove for.

One of the unforeseen consequences of the welfare state is that it leaves so little room for personal idealism; another is that it mutes the challenge to self-definition. All this is but another way of saying that it satisfies the anxieties of the middle-aged while stifling the creative energies of the young. Practically every college student these days understands what is meant by an "identity crisis": it is one of the clichés of the sixties. It is not, perhaps, too much to say that mass picketing on the campus is one of the last, convulsive twitches of a slowly expiring American individualism.

American youth, however, has had one grand idealistic experience: the civil rights movement. This has been the formative experience for the activists of the 1960s; it is this movement that gave them a sense of personal power and personal purpose; and it is the civil rights movement which instructed them in the tactics of civil disobedience that are now resorted to at the drop of a hat. Unfortunately, the civil rights movement has had one great drawback: so far from being a proper "dissenting" movement, it has behind it the President, Congress, the courts, the laws of the land, and a majority of public opinion. This fact helps explain why the younger militants have constantly pushed the movement toward "extremes"—for example, demanding utter, complete, and immediate *equality of condition* for the Negro, as against mere equality of opportunity.

Such equality of condition is what "freedom now" has come to mean. And since this demand cannot be fulfilled without repealing three centuries of history, and since even Lyndon Johnson hasn't figured out a way to do this, there is some satisfaction in such a maneuver. The trouble is that the students do not know how to fulfill this demand either, and are even running out of extremist slogans; which is why so many of them are receptive to the idea of switching their attention to Vietnam, where they can be more splendidly, less ambiguously, in "the opposition."

A second theme of student radicalism today, and a polar twin to the concept of "organized America," is the idea of "participatory democracy." This is a vague notion, but a dynamic one. It expresses a profound hostility toward, and proposes an alternative to, everything that is impersonal, manipulative, "organized" in the American political process. Indeed, many of these students simply dismiss American democracy as a sham, a game played by the "power structure" for its own amusement and in its own interests. *True* democracy, they insist, can only mean direct democracy, where the people's will is expressed and legislated by the people themselves rather than by elected representatives, most of whom achieve office by deceit and retain office through the substantial support offered them by the vested interests.

One is reminded by this of nothing so much as the Russian Narodniki ("populists," our textbooks call them) of the end of the nineteenth century. They, too, were largely middle-class students who selflessly turned their backs on the careers the Czarist bureaucracy offered them. They, too, "returned to the people," leaving the fleshpots of Petrograd for the villages of the interior, much as our students leave their comfortable homes in New York or Chicago for Southern ghettos and slums. And they, too, were hostile to the nascent liberal institutions of their day, seeing political salvation only in a transformed and redeemed people rather than in improvements in any kind of system of representative government. It is also interesting to recall that, though they were as individuals the gentlest and most humane of their time, they nevertheless believed in the justice and efficacy of terrorism against the status quo and assassination against its spokesmen.

The analogy is, of course, very superficial: the United States today is not Czarist Russia of yesterday. But it is nevertheless illuminating, because it helps reveal the inner logic of the idea of "participatory democracy," a logic which proceeds from the most exemplary democratic premises to the most illiberal conclusions. Though few students these days learn it in their social studies course, the Founding Fathers of the American republic were exceedingly familiar with the idea of "participatory democracy"; as a matter of fact, this was what the word "democracy" usually meant prior to 1789. They rejected "participatory democracy" (they called it "direct democracy") in favor of "representative government" for two reasons. First, they didn't see how it could work in so large and complex a nation, as against a small city-state. Second, and more important, they thought it inconsistent with the idea of free government—that is, a government that respected the liberties of the individual. For participatory democracy requires that all people be fit to govern; and this in turn requires that all people *be made* fit to govern, by rigid and uniform educational training, constant public indoctrination, close supervision of private morals and beliefs, and so forth. No legislator can be as free as a private citizen, and to make all the people legislators is willy-nilly to abolish the category of private citizen altogether.

This, of course, is exactly what the Communists do, after their own fashion. They claim to exemplify a truer, more "direct," more "participatory," more "popular" democracy than is to be found in the representative institutions of the bourgeois West. The claim has a certain plausibility, in that regimes established by mass movements and mass revolutions certainly "involve the people" more than does any merely elected government. The semblance of "involvement" is perpetuated, as we know, through the mass organizations of the Communist state, and the fact that it is done under compulsion, and becomes more of a farce with every passing Communist year, is one of the inner contradictions both of the Communist system and of the myth of direct democracy itself.

These contradictions our left-wing students are not entirely unaware of. Though many of them are, to one degree or another, either pro-Communist or belligerently "neutralist," theirs is a very qualified and unconventional version of this attitude; which is why conventional anti-Communist propaganda tends to pass them by. They are, for instance, extraordinarily uninterested in the Soviet Union, and they become ever less interested to the degree that the Soviet Union liberalizes its regime—that is to say, to the extent that the Soviet Union becomes merely another "organized" system of rule.

What they seek is a pure and self-perpetuating popular revolution, not a "planned economy" or anything like that. And this is why they are so attracted to Castro's Cuba and Mao's China, countries where the popular revolution has not yet become "bourgeoisified." As for mass terror in Cuba and China—well, this actually may be taken as a kind of testimony to the ardor and authenticity of the regime's revolutionary fervor. Our radical students, like other radical students before them, find it possible to be genuinely heartsick at the injustices and brutalities of American society, while blandly approving of injustice and brutality committed elsewhere in the name of "the revolution."

Like other radical student generations before them, they are going to discover one day that their revolution, too, has been betrayed, that "organized society" is what revolutions establish as well as destroy. One hopes they will not be made too miserable by their disillusionment. One also hopes, it must be added, that they won't make *us* too miserable before that day arrives.

3

THE NEW STUDENT AND HIS
ROLE IN AMERICAN COLLEGES

EDWARD J. BLOUSTEIN

IN HIS STUDY OF LIFE in the France of Louis XIV, entitled *The Splendid Century*,[1] W. H. Lewis describes with a fine irony the growing revolutionary sentiment of the French peasantry:

> And then there was a nasty spirit abroad in the village; the people were getting impudent, slacker about paying their feudal dues, and sulking about the performance of Manorial Corvées. In some districts peasants have begun "to stare proudly and insolently" at their lord, and are "putting their hands in their pockets instead of saluting him. . . . A noble has been executed for squeezing his peasants a little too hard; it is becoming quite common for peasants to go to law with their seigneur. Things have come to a pretty pass in France.

And so too have things come to a pretty pass in American higher education! There is a nasty spirit abroad on the college campus; students are growing impudent: sulking and unwilling simply to

---

[1] Doubleday (Anchor paperback), New York, 1957.

From *Liberal Education*, October, 1968, and included in *Dimensions of Academic Freedom*, by Walter P. Metzger, Sanford H. Kadish, Arthur DeBardeleben, and Edward J. Bloustein (Urbana: University of Illinois Press, 1969). Copyright, 1969, by the Board of Trustees of the University of Illinois. Based on an address delivered at the University of Illinois Law School, May 9, 1968. Reprinted by permission of the author, the editor of *Liberal Education*, and the University of Illinois Press. Edward J. Bloustein is President, Bennington College, Bennington, Vt.

attend classes and take notes, they are protesting, striking, sitting-in, demanding a voice in the governance of their colleges, staring proudly and insolently at college presidents and professors alike.

American colleges and universities are undergoing a constitutional crisis. Students are seeking a new role in academic life. The purpose of this paper is to inquire into the causes and the nature of student assertion of a right to share in the management of the American college and university.

The classical American college, against which the ire of students is directed, was a place of serene social relationships and scholarly detachment. Trustees, presidents, faculty and students each had a well-established place in a well-ordered hierarchy. Self-appointed trustees, acting as representatives of the general public or some specialized religious community, determined the goals of the college and hired a president to implement these chosen goals. The president then hired a faculty to teach what he believed had to be taught, and he admitted students to the college to learn what he believed had to be learned.

President, faculty and students lived together in the bucolic isolation of their campus, each fulfilling a pre-established role in a universe ordered by the trustees' vision. Students were responsible to the faculty for fulfilling their academic duties and to the president and his staff for living the life of gentlemen. Faculty were responsible to the president for fulfilling their teaching duties and comporting themselves as scholars and men of good breeding. And, finally, the president was responsible to the trustees for maintaining the internal harmony of the system and directing it towards its ordained ends.

The congruity and consistency of this classical academic community was assured as much by its system of educational values as it was by its hierarchical structure. The intention and unifying purpose of the institution was to transmit a received system of learning and culture. The knowledge to be transmitted was considered to be relatively fixed and it was systematically arranged into convenient and appropriate subject matter areas, one relating to another in the same harmonious order which was found in nature. The social tradition which was to be inculcated was likewise characterized by its fixity and its conformity to well-established social expectations.

The student's role in this classical college is simple to describe. A college education was available to and important for a relatively small segment of the population; learning the liberal arts was considered a costly luxury. The student was thus doubly privileged: privileged to be among those chosen to attend college at all, and in attendance at college because he was privileged to be among those who could afford to do so. And, of course, the one privilege reinforced the other.

The privileged student did not go to college, he was sent. His relationship to the college was a contractual one, and the contract concerned was what lawyers term a third-party beneficiary contract. Under such a contractual scheme, one party obliges himself to another to have that other party provide a benefit in goods or services to some third party. In this instance, parents paid tuition to the college in consideration of the college's providing a benefit for their child in the way of educating him.

Since they carried somewhat the sense of a charitable relationship, the early history of such third-party beneficiary contracts—the history relevant for our purposes in this paper—left no room to the beneficiary, the object of charity, to have a voice over any incidents of the contract. Appropriate to this tradition of the law of contracts as well as to his status as a privileged person, the student was in no position to require anything of his college or to enforce obligations against it; he simply accepted the education given to him.

Still another factor explains the passivity and docility of the traditional student. He was young in an age in which youth was not in fashion and at a time when parents took an assertive and autocratic stance towards their children. It is, I know, difficult for us to any longer evoke the sense of that day when parents were true "parents" and when being young, although not a disease was still considered an incapacity. There can be no legitimate doubt, however, that this facet of the cultural climate underlay and reinforced the traditional student's sense of his servile, child-like status in his relationship to his college.

It is not difficult to understand how, under these circumstances, the doctrine of *in loco parentis* grew, flourished and came to embody the college's conception of its relation to its students. Dealing with young people in a day when it still rang true to say "children are to be seen, but not heard," educating them under a third-party beneficiary contract enforcible only by a parent, and recognizing them as among a class privileged to be in college at all, it seemed natural, appropriate and just to look on the college as the student's substitute parent. The parent having given over his child to the college authorities for the purpose of his education, these authorities came to act in lieu of parents, empowered by law, custom and usage to direct and control student conduct to the same extent a parent could.

The fitting image is of the college president as the academic father and students as the dutiful children of learning: wise in his choice of what the young ones were to study; dedicated and enlightened in his mission as moral guardian over them; stern but just as their disciplinarian; and yet a man sufficiently attached to life's joy, to provide his young with wholesome and healthy—necessarily non-sexual—outlets for fun and games.

This is the picture of the "classical" college president and his academic wards. Students either had to fit into this picture or else they left the sacred academic precincts. They had no other choice than, in the words of the Illinois Supreme Court written in the dark era, to "yield obedience to those who, for the time being, are their master."

There are those, I am certain, who look back longingly to the classical American college in which trustees, president, faculty and students, each knowing their own place, revolved about the central sun of certain knowledge in orbital harmony. My own evocation of the past of our colleges serves an entirely different need, however. For one thing, I have no regret over the old order having passed; what praise it merits for its stability and fixity of purpose is surely overbalanced by its intellectual anemia, its myopic vision of its social function and its insufferable class bias. For another thing, however, for good or for ill, the winds of change have blown; and we must look to what is past not to savor it or forswear it, but to learn what we can from it.

To be sure, the view which I have presented of what I have called the classical American college is incomplete and wanting; it is a kind of historical caricature. Like other caricatures, however, it is intended to grasp and emphasize what is essential, even if it does so at the expense of some distortion. What marked the classical college was an hierarchical structure of authority, a fixed and ordered system of certain knowledge, a rigidly defined and severely limited set of educational functions, and a completely paternalistic relationship between student and college. The breakdown of the classical college system and the emergence of the new student may be traced, among other causes, to weaknesses in each of these characteristic elements of it.

This is not the place, of course, to discuss all of the causes of the dissolution of the classical system and the emergence of modern colleges and universities. It is enough for my purposes here to examine three of the chief engines of change: expansion in and transformation of the character of the body of knowledge the university is called upon to nurture and transmit, the development of the social function education is called upon to perform, and the emergence of the new student. Each of these changes has profoundly affected the organizational structure of the academic community and the student's role in it.

Contemporary knowledge is more a congeries of discrete and specialized truths than a unified system; and the congeries keeps growing and growing in size and complexity. Moreover, the extent of what we know is such that few men can profess anything but a relatively narrow segment of the body of our knowledge. Still further, we may say that, with the exception of mathematics and the subject areas it touches, deductive certainty has played a more and more insignificant role as a style of thought; tentative empirical hypotheses, shifting and changing explanations of observable facts, have come to typify our way of thinking. The final characteristic of contemporary knowledge which is significant in this context is that it has become increasingly useful to and important for us. Knowledge is a necessity of life in the intricate social, political and economic structure of the contemporary world.

Each of these characteristics of the corpus of our knowledge has had a marked effect on the college community. No longer can a board of trustees and a college president pretend to even a bare acquaintance with, much less a mastery over, the range of subjects the college teaches. Their attempts to manage and oversee what is taught necessarily reflect this fact. Under the circumstances, the faculty must look to their peers, within and without the college, for guidance and supervision in the performance of their teaching functions. And this, of course, represents a radical breach in the classical scheme of the organization of the college. Faculties can no longer be responsible, in any realistic sense, to presidents and lay boards for what they teach and how they teach it.

Still another consequence of the changed character of contemporary knowledge is that the curriculum has lost both its unity and what I might call its preemptive character. The complexity, diversity and specialization of contemporary thought make it impossible to fix upon any single set or even any small number of sets of subjects of study which can be considered basic or fundamental to higher education. Under these circumstances, method and the process of inquiry are bound to take on more importance than subject matter competence. And the varied interests, skills, capacities and inclinations of students come to be a more meaningful determinant of what they should study than any predetermined fixed order of universally prescribed courses.

The impact of this on the organization of the college is once again to impair the classical hierarchy of dominance and control. Those who would prescribe a course of study, whether boards, presidents or faculty, are increasingly at a loss to say what is to be prescribed. The very diversity and specialization of what we teach in the contemporary college makes it impossible to lay down with any assurance what anyone should learn.

This same influence on attempts to prescribe a settled curriculum arises from the empirical and non-deductive character of our knowledge. Instead of a single corpus of learning strictly ordered by the canons of logic and carrying the weight of an established tradition, we find discrete and shifting sets or families of theories, only loosely bound together and constantly shifting, as observation and new theoretical insight restructure entire fields of science. Who shall say, who can say, what is settled and enduring, what is fundamental to the educational process, in the face of this? Whoever has insight into this facet of the logic, the history and the sociology of knowledge must in modesty confess that attempts at prescribing a fixed and universal curricular organon are doomed to failure.

I suggest then, that the constitutional structure of the classical college has been impaired in two important respects by the development of our system of knowledge. The claim on the part of lay boards and presidents to exercise exclusive control over what is taught and how it is taught in the college has given way simply on account of obvious, though, of course, far from blameworthy, incompetence. And the boards' and presidents'—even the faculty's—claim to exercise exclusive control over what must be learned has given way because of the specialization, diversity and shifting empirical character of what is taught.

Although I shall develop this thought as I proceed, I might say in a preliminary fashion, at this point, that the constitutional role of students has been affected by each of these two revisions in the structure of the college community. Once the college faculty has successfully challenged the legitimacy of the board's and the president's exclusive role in determining educational policy, the whole classical structure of authority is threatened and students can begin to ask why boards and presidents should solely determine anything else. This same skeptical and corrosive doubt flows from the increasing weakness evidenced in authoritative attempts to prescribe a curriculum.

The final facet of the development of our system of knowledge which has affected the student's role in his college is directly related to the second major influence mentioned previously as having undermined the classical college. What we teach in colleges has come to have greater and greater utility for our society and this, in turn, has caused our society to look on the college in an entirely new light. Whereas formerly the function the college performed was limited, and of interest to a relatively small segment of the community, the contemporary college and university fulfills a multitude of social tasks which are of considerable importance to the society as a whole.

The traditional college prepared a privileged minority to take roles in society as members of a governing elite and as practitioners of a small number of the genteel professions; the research and scholarship which was done in it bore the mark of its origin in the ivory towers of academia. The burgeoning of knowledge in the physical and social sciences and its usefulness to society at large has now led to the appearance of a whole range of new professions and occupations which engage the interest and capacity of the broadest segments of our population. Moreover, academic research and scholarship now directly service our economy and our political and social life on a vast and unprecedented scale. Educational institutions have become a major and vital national resource rather than a peripheral upper-class luxury.

The transition in the importance of higher education in our national life is shown most graphically by comparison of enrollment figures and by examination of some financial data. The enrollment in colleges and universities in 1869 was 52,000, 0.1 per cent of our general population and 1.1 per cent of the 18-24 year olds; by 1910, it had grown to 355,000, 0.4 per cent of our general population and 2.9 per cent of the 18-24 year olds; by 1963, it had grown to 4,234,000, 2.2 per cent of the general population and 23.3 per cent of our 18-24 year olds.

In terms of public funding of education, the figures are no less dramatic. Up until this decade, federal funds expended for higher education were almost negligible. But in 1965, the federal government spent $1.9 billion and in 1966 it spent $2.6 billion directly on higher education. In addition to these funds, the federal government made grants of $3.2 billion in 1965 and $3.6 billion in 1966 to educational institutions for research activities. In these same years, 1965 and 1966, state governments expended $3.9 billion and $4.4 billion respectively for higher education. Combined state and federal expenditures in these two years represented some 58 per cent of the total cost of higher education in America.

It is plain that for good or for ill education has gone public. It is vested with a national interest and increasingly funded out of the public purse. There is every indication that the trend in this direction will increase rather than diminish in the coming years. The consequence of this development is to erode still further the structure of trustee and presidential authority.

Some of the erosion is quite direct, some of it indirect. Most federal funding is advanced for specified educational purposes, rather than general operating costs. In the case of research funds, the money most often goes directly to the academic researcher, and the college or university has virtually no control over its expenditure. In the case of other funds, the college can only say yea or nay to a grant for a specific purpose; very frequently, considering the penury of most academic budgets, there is really no choice. Thus, trustees and presidents have in good measure been forced to abdicate real control over the expenditure of their own funds to become bookkeepers of public funds.

The indirect effects of the widespread public interest in and support of higher education are even more important for our purposes. Even if federal funding did not limit the trustees' and presidents' available managerial options, it would still vastly diminish their power. Use of public funds in higher education calls for a degree and kind of public accountability, of responsibility to the public at large, which goes far beyond the vague and self-enforced sense which the traditional trustee and president had of representing the community interest. This change is reinforced by the fact that faculty and students alike—the low men on the traditional totem pole of academic power—are part of that public to which the trustee is accountable. Thus, the nature and extent of the trustees' and presidents' authority must necessarily be changed and diminished when they begin to expend and control funds which they do not themselves donate or generate.

Another aspect of the new public interest in education is that it gives college faculty a new sense of their social status, a sense which is at variance with their traditional subservient role in the collegiate hierarchy. They are no longer creatures of a benign alma mater's largesse. They are valued social operatives, sought after to fulfill important tasks in the economy and government and equally sought after by other academic institutions suffering from a faculty shortage caused by swollen enrollments.

No longer will a student look with awe and wonder at the college president and believe that the president controls the destiny of the great scholars with whom students study. Prestigious faculty now make and break colleges, buy and sell college presidents, as they say. Both faculty and students are well aware of this dramatic reversal of position and what its consequences are for the college power structure.

Still another facet of what we might call the nationalization of education is that members of the public in unprecedented numbers and coming from social strata and classes never before heard from in the halls of academia are now personally concerned with collegiate and academic affairs. Government officialdom, employers, professionals, workers, and parents of widely varying backgrounds all now feel a vital interest in a new found national resource and they expect it to meet their needs. No longer is the college the preserve of the few, to be watched over and nurtured by magnanimous and wealthy donors and wistful, teary-eyed alumni. The college is everyman's garden to be cared for and intended to suit everyman's taste and interest.

The last of the challenges to the classical college tradition is directed at the conception of the college serving *in loco parentis* directed at the paternalism embodied in the collegiate hierarchy of authority. This challenge arises from a number of causes: in the first place, the very conception of the rule and authority of parents has changed slowly over a period of time. Increasingly, parents have come to rely on reason and suggestion rather than status and command as the essential elements of their control over their children. Many parents, practicing the cult of permissiveness, have come to eschew any and all forms of discipline; even more have come to use discipline sparingly and only as a last resort. Finding one's self, self-expression and individual development have come to displace parental guidance and social standards of conformity as the molders of character and personality. All of these changes have contributed to the development of a generation of new students who instinctively react against authority, academic or otherwise.

The second cause of the breakdown of the paternalistic pattern of collegiate life is a changed attitude towards the nature of the learning process. The traditional student was a relatively more passive participant in the learning process than is the new student. Memory and deductive forms of reasoning were formerly more important student tools than imagination, observation and criticism. The new student is asked to learn by coping with his subject of study in the same way his teacher does; he is not asked so much to listen to his teacher as to do what his teacher does. He learns by doing and experiencing rather than remembering and deducing. Learning increasingly becomes a form of apprenticeship rather than a form of tutelage.

This changed conception of the learning process finds its way into the earliest school years and reaches its culmination, or should, in college study. Its impact on the constitutional organization of colleges is profound and in many respects similar to that, described above, of the changed character of knowledge systems. Just as the increasing complexity and specialization and the decreasing deductive unity and fixity of knowledge has weakened the authority of those who would pretend to prescribe curricula and otherwise control what is taught, so too the same result arises out of the changed conception of the learning process.

To the degree the student becomes an active and creative element in his own education, rather than a passive recipient in the process, he comes to resist and resent those who seek to determine for him what he should learn. The very intellectual independence and critical judgment which are fostered and desired as tools of learning are corrosive of the authority of faculty and academic administration. "It is so because the president and trustees say so" is no more an answer to be respected in fixing on a course of study or style of life on campus, than "it is so because Aristotle said so" is an answer to be respected in discussion of a philosophical or aesthetic problem in the classroom.

A third factor which tends to undermine the capacity of the college to act as a substitute parent is the new social attitude towards attending college. The traditional student was sent to college by his parents and felt it a privilege to be there. The new student goes to college because he knows it is necessary for him; his parent and, increasingly, his society, pays his way because, under the conditions of modern life, a college education is as much his right as a high school education is.

In these circumstances, the college must begin to regard its role as that of a social agent performing a socially valued function rather than merely that of a private agent of a parent undertaking an educational task the parent pays for. It is not the parent who puts the student into college but society, and in educating a student the college is not acting in the parent's name but in society's.

Moreover, although the student obviously benefits from his education, it is regarded as a necessity rather than a privilege by his society, which also derives benefit from it. The new student's attitude, even when a parent pays for his education, reflects the changed status of education as a social necessity rather than a private luxury in modern life. However thankful and appreciative of his education he may be, the student need not feel that anyone is doing him a remarkable favor for which he must be beholden and for which he must pay by adopting a respectful and deferential attitude towards authority.

Gone then is the older notion of a third-party beneficiary contract in favor of the privileged student who retained no right to control its incidence. In its place is a new status relationship in which the college performs a socially prescribed task in a manner over which the society generally, including the student, retains considerable control.

The private contract is now replaced by a public duty. In the transition, the paternalism of the older form of the relationship between student and college has become an anachronism.

The fourth and final cause of the breakdown of collegiate paternalism which I shall examine is the changed character of the student body itself. In the last century, we have experienced almost a hundredfold increase in the size of our collegiate student body; a change, as I have already indicated, from a student body comprised of 1 per cent of the 18-24 year olds 100 years ago, to 23.3 per cent of them today. These new students come from social classes and national and racial backgrounds never before present on college campuses in such numbers. They are bright and mature, alienated from traditional values, and newly aware of their political power. This adds up to a radical change in the character of the collegiate student body, and the purport of this change is to strain still further the traditional organization of collegiate authority.

The new student is not older than the traditional student, but he has had more experience of life. He comes from homes and family backgrounds which have been less isolated from the economic and social struggle. The very style of family life in which he has been brought up is more open and honest, has made him more aware of what life is really about. He is a product of a better primary and secondary education. And finally he shows the effect of the communications revolution, for he is a child of television and the film industry.

The sum of these influences has brought forth a generation of young people which is more sensitive to life in all its dimensions than any generation before it has been. These young people have vicariously experienced the whole range of human emotions and been witness to the whole play of political passions. Love and hatred; war, greed and bloodshed; discrimination, hunger and deprivation; electioneering and voting: they have seen it all in ways which were not possible before the advent of the television tube. These new students have gotten the message from the media and they exhibit its mark in their maturity of bearing and purpose.

The second characteristic of the new student which is important for our purposes is his alienation from traditional values and institutions. To be sure, there have been disaffected students before this time. The difference now is in the extent of the disillusion: it is more widespread and it bites more deeply into the range of life's values than it ever has before.

War, poverty, and racial discrimination all loom as fundamental and insurmountable political outrages. Infidelity, divorce, illegitimacy, bureaucratization, and mass conformity appear as poisonous and ineradicable social diseases. And the individual is thought to be inevitably threatened by increasing isolation, loneliness, and boredom. There is nothing to look forward to except losing one's soul in exchange for the dross of material wealth. The old values have failed and there are no new ones to take their place. All the ideologies, all the utopias—from democratic capitalism to Christian salvation to Marxist socialism—seem to have failed. The only heroes left are those who preach destruction, with no other vision of the social good.

This is indeed a generation of rebels without a cause, a generation of nihilists, a generation despairing of the life we live and set on remaking it, but without a vision of any alternative.

And yet the new student is a very political person. Again, of course, we can acknowledge the fact that student generations before this have played the political game. The difference here, as with this generation's alienation, is a difference of degree. Not small political cells, nor ineffectual weekly political discussion groups, but impressively large numbers of activists are dedicated with all their being to the pursuit of their political purposes.

In the struggle over the civil rights issue and over the Vietnam war they found a first taste of political success. No other generation of young people has had such political effect, none has been so heralded by journalists or so courted by politicians. They have quite suddenly achieved a sense of their own authority, a sense of the growing force of their own numbers, a sense of identification with the older European and Latin American tradition of student political power. Most important of all, they have developed a distinctive style of political action and a distinctive form of political tactics.

Thus, although the new student is alienated and lacks the conviction of an ideology, he is outraged by evil and thereby transformed into a political person. Disillusioned with traditional political programmatic goals, he stands and fights on limited particular issues. Disillusioned with traditional party and parliamentary politics, he confronts social wrongs directly, attempting limited and immediate remedies. Disillusioned with adult politicians, he has himself become a politician.

The impact of the three characteristics of the new student which I have described on the structure of collegiate authority has been extraordinary. No generation so bright and mature, so alienated from traditional values, and so political in its bearing could conceivably tolerate the paternalism of the classical collegiate system. The new student's maturity and his politicalization, combined with the influence of the other developments which I previously described, make attempts on the part of trustees and administration to authoritatively prescribe courses of study seem ever more illegitimate. The more mature student, seeking to have his education serve his new values and new political goals, wants and needs more of a voice in what he shall study and what the educational goals and values of the college shall be.

As for parietal rules, these seem ever more absurd. The values and style of life embodied in the campus rules of the "Old Coll" were born of a different time, a time which had not yet seen the unmasking of the sexual hypocrisy of the adult world, a time in which college students were tender and innocent young things who had to be protected from evil.

The new student, coming frequently from a different class and culture than the traditional student, is deeply impressed by the contrast in his values and those embodied in the rules of the traditional college. He is suspicious of the trustees and the college president because they are representatives of a value system and of a time he is in the act of rejecting. Under the circumstances, he sees no good reason to accept the authority of the trustees and college president over the conditions of his social life.

The intransigence of the classical collegiate system in the face of these student claims for new freedom and power has reinforced the strains of the underlying conflict. An unheeding structure of collegiate authority has caused the new student to begin to look upon college life as a replica of the wider world from which he is alienated. Trustees and presidents begin to assume the aspect of authoritarian oppressors, enforcing their own system of values on oppressed and powerless students, robbing them of their dignity and impairing their opportunity to pursue the true academic life. Faculty begin to appear to have sold out and abandoned their calling; instead of serving as prophets of a new and better world, they have been seduced to collaboration with the military-industrial establishment by the lure of lucrative contracts. The curriculum comes to seem empty and unimportant, out of tune with our times, irrelevant to our agonies and needs. The goals and purposes of colleges and universities seem to have been subverted from open-minded criticism of the established social order to authoritarian forms of protection and service of that conservative order. And underneath all these other appearances, there is the specter of the university as a bureaucratic machine controlled by irresponsible elites and as petty, inhuman, undemocratic and unresponsive as the world beyond the ivy-covered walls.

A structure of constitutional authority is a delicate thing. Compounded of force and implicit threats of force, of unquestioning acquiescence, habitual obedience, unresponsiveness to felt need, and an aura of moral fitness, it can only persist if each of these elements continues to contribute its saving balance. It now seems plain that the traditional hierarchical organization of collegiate power must either deliberately readjust to new realities or be transmuted by the impact of discontent.

Radical changes in the system of knowledge, in the social interest in knowledge, and in the student population have all combined to unhinge the delicate balance of academic authority. Acquiescence in, and habitual obedience to, the traditional structure have begun to dissolve under the actuality of a new relationship of faculty and students to presidents and trustees. The unresponsiveness of academic authority to the felt needs of students and to the changed conditions of academic life has slowly eroded the sense of that authority's moral fitness to govern. Under the circumstances, no matter how strong the force used or threatened, the college and university can never be the same again.

Student activists as well as apologists and defenders of the traditional order are both mistaken about the character of the constitutional revolution in academia. The activists, whether out of ignorance or assumed tactical necessity, conjure up images of the college more appropriate to a hundred years ago than today, and they urge political tactics as mistaken as their image of the college.

As with all revolutions, the seeds of this one were laid over a long period of time, and the foundations of the old order have long since been undermined by the growth of new sprouts of faculty and student authority. Trustees and presidents of a number of institutions have long since abandoned in fact, if not in law, any pretensions to absolute power and have been seeking diligently for a new form of order. Thus, what Riesman and Jencks call "the academic revolution" is proceeding apace. The need now is as much to consolidate and give structure to changes which have already taken place as it is to exert the pressure of opinion against enclaves of the old tradition. Deliberation about and thoughtful discussion of the new constitutional order should have as high a priority as strident demands and militant tactics against the old constitutional order.

Once it is agreed, as many would now agree, that trustees and presidents can no longer exercise absolute power over the academic world, once it is agreed that faculty and students must play a real and substantial role in academic government, a whole series of profound and complex problems arise. How precisely shall power be distributed among trustees, presidents, faculty and students? If the hierarchical structure of power is inappropriate, what should replace it? What is the appropriate sphere of each of the organs of power and how are the relationships between these organs and their various jurisdictions to be arranged?

Many colleges and universities are already deeply involved in addressing themselves to these issues and others like them. Some are doing this quite consciously; others as a facet of unconscious throes of change and transition, while still maintaining the fiction of the traditional structure.

Many a revolution has been lost after it had succeeded because those who favored and fought for change neglected to concern themselves with what was to follow the disappearance of the old order. It would be folly of the gravest character to undo the traditional academic structure only to have it replaced with one less just and more inadequate.

One of the most significant dangers we face in this regard is that some of the very tactics used to complete the work of reordering the structure of academic authority promise to prejudice the result unalterably. To be sure, there is still resistance in the academic world to abandoning the old forms of authority. And to be sure, this resistance must be overcome by organized political effort. But if there was ever a political struggle in which violence and illegality were unnecessary and inappropriate, this is one. If there was ever a political struggle in which violence and illegality were calculated to destroy the very fruits of victory which are sought, this is one.

The fact is that, for the reasons I have set forth at length, the traditional forms of power are already fast crumbling. The change is already in the works and its pace is quickening. Allies in the form of sympathetic trustees, presidents, and faculty are at hand. Tactics of violence are antithetical to deliberation, the very essence of the academic life. Under the circumstances, students with romantic, stereotyped, and anachronistic conceptions of revolution, students whose need to undertake violent political action is more a function of personal and emotional, rather than political, necessity should exercise restraint over their revolutionary fantasies. The violence they unleash may, on occasion, produce a temporary aura of success, but it threatens the long-range prospect for building the college and university we desire. As Paul Goodman put it in a slightly different context: "Out of the shambles can only come the same bad world."

Defenders of the old order also suffer under a number of illusions. The first and most important of these is that the whole "fuss," "the so-called revolt," is the work of a few ill-mannered, loud-mouthed radicals. The truth of the matter is, however, that revolutions call forth leaders; leaders never call forth revolutions. Leaders can never create social upheaval; they can only ride its crest.

As I have shown in the main body of this paper, the erosion of the traditional structure of academic authority which we are presently witnessing flows from developments in the character of knowledge, in the social uses to which knowledge is put, and in the psychology of our students. It is these underlying social facts which are responsible for transforming the academic world rather than any group of student leaders. Even if all our student activists were to disappear miraculously, the fundamental maladjustment in the organization of collegiate power would remain.

Too many of our academic leaders have mistaken the true nature of the student revolt. They are confused because at different times it appears to be addressed to one or another of different, relatively insignificant or, even when not insignificant, relatively isolated, facets of college life. First it is free speech on campus, then it is visitation hours in student rooms, then admissions and scholarships for black students, then recruitment of students by war industries, then the building of a gymnasium in an urban slum, then the contract relationship between the university and a defense research corporation. The connection between these seemingly isolated forays is that they all represent a testing of the academic decision process, they all go to challenge the legitimacy of the constitutional apparatus of the college or university.

These incidents are not only related to each other, but they are also related to the more profound challenges posed to the structure of the college which I have discussed above. In other words, the student activists have chosen to throw the gauntlet down, not only on issues which each have extraordinary immediate political appeal, but also on issues which each go to test the academic hierarchy and thereby reinforce and find reinforcement from the underlying causes of imbalance in the structure of academic authority. A failure to appreciate these relationships promises a failure to be able to cope successfully with the problems they present.

A related facet of the misunderstanding of the nature of the student revolt concerns an underestimation of the amount of support it finds on university campuses and elsewhere. It is significant and symbolic of this failure generally that the police, who had been called to cope with disturbances on the Columbia University campus and did a poor job of it, complained that their failure was attributable in part to the fact that the administration of the college had grossly underestimated the number of students who were "sitting-in" in their buildings.

I am certain that the experience at Columbia will turn out, after we have studied it, to be much like that at Berkeley in respect of the fact that—as the Muscatine Report demonstrates—the activists "succeeded" because they had wide support, not only among students generally, but among faculty and among the lay public as well. The reason for this support at Berkeley, Columbia, and elsewhere is not only traceable to the appeal of the particular political issues on which the ruckuses were raised, but also to the fact that the issues concerned evoked the support of all those—faculty, students, and laymen alike—who question the underlying structure of collegiate authority.

The second important illusion under which many defenders of the traditional college suffer concerns remedies. There are some "academic statesmen"—fortunately few in number—who insist that if the students do not appreciate what they have, let them leave or be "kicked out," and that this will represent a solution to the contemporary crisis. After all, they add, students do not attend college under coercion; if they do not choose to conform let them leave.

I believe that some students should indeed be disciplined and more generally that the order of the college community should be maintained during this difficult transition period. There are indeed a number of students who, because of political naïveté, political romanticism, or plain malevolence, are bent on destroying what most needs to be saved and rebuilt. And there are a greater number of other students who find in the contemporary situation of stress a rationalization for ill-mannered, selfish, and boorish disregard of the rights of others. But anyone who supposes that by disciplining such students we will have solved the crisis of academic authority is grossly mistaken. Its roots, as I have shown, go much deeper.

Nor do I believe—and I note my judgment is somewhat tentative on this score—we are very much nearer a solution by providing students "means to participate in the formulation and application of institutional policy affecting academic and student affairs," providing forms of due process in disciplinary proceedings, and removing all restraints on students' freedom to express themselves. These were the major recommendations of the *Joint Statement on Rights and Freedoms of Students,*[2] issued by the Association of American Colleges, the United States National Student Association, the American Association of University Professors and a number of other academic groups. As admirable and helpful as this statement is, and as strongly as I applaud the good judgment and diligence of those who produced it, I must conclude it is of peripheral interest in the context of the constitutional challenge American colleges and universities presently face.

The weakness of the *Joint Statement* resides in the vagueness of the language used to define the character of the student role and in the fact that even this obscure statement was further emasculated in the resolution of endorsement by the Association of American Colleges. A "means to participate in the formulation and application of institutional policy"—the language of the *Joint Statement*—is not the same as the assurance of some form of shared control or authority over institutional policy. In fact, it might be interpreted by some as more of the "let's pretend" theory of student government, more a form of "manipulated acquiescence," than a true grant of a significant share of power.

This appearance of weakness is underscored further by the fact that the resolution of endorsement of the Association of American Colleges limits the language of the *Joint Statement* by providing that the student participation concerned—and I quote the *Resolution of Endorsement*[3]—"may involve a variety of activities, under methods appropriate to each campus, ranging from student discussion of proposed policy in committees, in organized agencies of student government or through the student press to the more formal determination of policy by groups that include student members or, where and if delegated by appropriate authority, by groups that are

---

2 *Liberal Education,* LIV (March, 1968), pp. 152-158.
3 *Ibid.,* pp. 144-146.

composed only of students." Thus, it turns out that the colleges which endorsed the *Joint Statement* made little or no definitive commitment to the doctrine of shared power. In all probability the *Joint Statement* represents only a commitment to freedom of expression and opportunities for joint discussion; at most, it is a commitment, under some circumstances, to the joint or sole exercise by students of delegated power.

What the *Joint Statement* seems oblivious of is that the crucial issue before American colleges and universities is not due process, freedom of expression, or even forms of delegated representation, as important as these are. What is rather at issue is who shall retain ultimate control and sovereignty over the academic institution; what is at issue is whose goals, values, and objectives the college and university shall serve.

Due process in disciplinary proceedings and freedom of expression can help to assure that organs of power are responsive to the interests of those they serve. Representation on decision-making bodies whose authority is delegated by the ultimate organs of power can serve the same function even more effectively. But both of these political means fall short of reconstituting the organs of power themselves, fall short of changing the nature of ultimate sovereignty. As long as the power to be exercised by students—or faculty, for that matter—is solely delegated power rather than a share of ultimate power, the basic nature of their relationship to sovereign power remains untouched.

Thus, although the *Joint Statement* takes a significant step towards creating a more responsive academic government, it does not touch the problem of creating a more truly responsible academic government. In the long run, no institution can remain sufficiently responsive to those it serves, however well-intentioned and however well managed, unless it is responsible to them. And it can only be responsible to them if they share, in one way or another, in the ultimate disposition and control of power.

A share of delegated authority may assure responsiveness, but it is not to be confused with a share of the power to delegate authority, which is the reservoir of ultimate power. Only a share in that ultimate power can truly assure responsible government, rather than merely responsive government.

In conclusion, I would urge that student activists and protectors of the old order alike have mistaken the true nature of the student revolt: the student activists, because they do not sufficiently realize that the movement to reorganize the collegiate constitution had begun long before they came on the scene, that it has already progressed far beyond their wildest dreams, and that some of their tactics are inimical to its success. For their part, the protectors of the old order are mistaken about the true character of the revolt, its extent, and the kinds of remedies which are appropriate. Let us all get over our illusions and begin the difficult work of redefining the nature and character of ultimate authority in the academic world.

4

A CHANGING CAMPUS AND
A CHANGING SOCIETY

DAVID RIESMAN

IN ELECTIONS, as in student activism, the cumulative effect of relatively small shifts can be enormous, literally earthshaking. Most
educators must have read many articles on "new students," meaning
the visible activists; and on some campuses they almost must have
longed for some importation of such students as a sign that their
campuses have not been forsaken by modernity and that the world-
wide student presence—the presence of Paris and Columbia, of the
universities of Mexico and of Tokyo, of Dakar and of Prague—exists
on their shores also. For it is my impression that many college
administrators, contrary to the view of them held by faculty, students, and the media, like to live dangerously, just a little bit,
although if the seasoning of life becomes the main dish, that is
something else again. I have read somewhere that there were more-
than-momentary disorders on something like 200 campuses during
the 1967-68 academic year. Yet the institutions affected by any kind
of student turbulence are probably less than 10% of the total, and a
guess as to the number of students involved might be on the order of
300,000 out of a population of some 6,000,000.

I would like to share some of my fragmentary understanding of

Based on an address to the annual meeting, American Association of State Colleges and
Universities, Statler Hilton Hotel, Washington, D.C., Nov. 12, 1968. Used by permission of
the author and the association. David Riesman is Henry Ford II Professor of the Social
Sciences, Harvard University, Cambridge, Mass.

the attitudes of academic men, of students toward these men, and of the bearing on both of changes in our national life. It would be extremely interesting to know what the salient identifications of faculty members are. In the work of sociologists, a distinction has become common between the locals and the cosmopolitans. The cosmopolitans or the itinerants are those identified with an academic discipline. They define themselves first of all as historians or biologists, and indeed, within these broad specialties, with subspecialties. The colleagues that matter for them are those who share the same specialty, wherever they may be found, men with whom they are in touch through exchange of common readings, attendance at meetings, active correspondence, and sometimes through the students who move from one to the other. The locals are identified with the institution, with its particular fate, with its students. Their relation with students is less dependent upon the ability of the students to carry forward their particular specialty and more with other values they share with the students, such as a religious tie, or a regional one, or some other bond of particularity rather than universality. Likewise, the colleagues to whom they are bound are principally the men with whom they share loyalty to the institution, and only in lesser degree men who share loyalty to an academic guild.

Most dichotomies break down in individual instances, and this one is no exception. Consider the increasingly unionized faculties of the California state colleges. With what entities do these collective bargainers identify? Do they identify with the state college as such against its great rival for state funds, namely the branches of the University of California? To what extent are they identified with a particular state college and its local mission, and to what extent with biology, history, sociology? Do they have a cosmopolitan identity with the state colleges of New York, or a geographically localized one in opposition to Chancellor Dumke and the Trustees on Imperial Boulevard in Los Angeles? Or consider the faculty of a distinguished Ivy League university like Princeton. Many of these men are world-renowned in their disciplines, and are evidently cosmopolitans in that sense and in the more common meaning of the term. Yet they also may have a certain loyalty to Princeton; if they have tenure they are not likely to be using Princeton as a springboard to go somewhere else. Their mentality is not that of itinerants. They are truly home-guard cosmopolitans. Furthermore, in work that the sociologist Joseph Gusfield and I have been doing, we have found a number of men, and a very considerable number of women, who identify neither with the discipline nor with the institution. We have called them "job-holders"; they are people who are earning a living by teaching in a college or university, but their real interest is something else—such as raising a family, putting their husbands through the Ph.D., or doing work in the arts on the side—or rather, the job is what is on the side, although it may take a great deal of time and be done with conscientiousness. Our society is much less nepotistic than it once was. We do not make a man like Nathaniel Hawthorne a consul in a foreign post to give him a living, and few people enter religious orders now as a way to subsidize contemplation or writing. Teaching has become the most common form of patronage for people whose real interest lies elsewhere, and it is perhaps the form of patronage most suited to a society where corruption is diminished greatly and patronage is frowned upon.

Indeed, academic man no longer is to be patronized. Those men who have visibility in their discipline beyond their institution can not be exploited by virtue of their loyalty to that institution. As already suggested, this is clearly the case at a place like Princeton, where a professor of classics is likely to be paid almost as much as a professor of physics, and where neither is likely to be asked in a crude way, by a tyrannical department chairman, "What have you done lately to advertise our department?" However, as we have occasion to know every day, in many fields a man with a doctorate is a scarce resource, even if he is not visible as a scholar. The accrediting agencies and the ambitions of departments and institutions see to that.

It was not so long ago that academic men constituted an oppressed minority. There prevails a great deal of romanticism about the old-fashioned liberal arts college where a few scholars met in a leisurely way with each other and with students, where neither commercial values nor the mass media intruded, and where serenity prevailed. Student, faculty, and popular critics of contemporary higher education feel that they must paint the present situation as a fall from an earlier state of grace in order to justify their criticisms. I do not see why it is necessary to indulge in such mythology, no matter how critical one is.

The U.S. is almost certainly a more troubled country today than it was on Armistice Day in 1918. Yet it does not follow that we are worse off, but rather that we are more powerful in a more desperately armed world, and that we have higher expectations for equality and justice. I believe that we expect more of our educational institutions today. They are better than they were, in quality as well as quantity, but this only makes their customers more dissatisfied. In the old-fashioned college, faculty members earned a bare, if genteel, living—and subsidized the students. Before the rise of organized athletics, the students responded by rowdyism, far more mindless and even more violent than present-day student riots. Only a tiny proportion of the population had the sometimes doubtful benefit of post-secondary education, and neither the great robber barons nor the radicals who attacked them were likely to have attended college. Great pulpit orators had some influence, and a few college presidents belonged to this species, but, while there were islands of relative affluence, most lived a life of quiet desperation, trying to make ends meet and to stave off creditors; and, as we know, ever so many institutions failed.

Even in the period of the 1920's, when I was attending college, some of this feeling of deprivation survived. Faculty members were apt wryly to compare their mortgaged homes to the lavish fraternity houses; and graduate students and junior faculty, as well as many undergraduates, compared their pinched lives to the materialistic, but glamorous, collegians who came to college at parental expense to make contacts, in the pleasantest possible way, that would be useful on Wall Street, State Street, or Main Street. No one who has heard George Kennan describe the loneliness of Princeton in this period, as experienced by a reflective student, should look back in sorrow.

During all this time, the most influential faculty continued to feel that America was anti-intellectual and Philistine. As Richard Hofstadter has pointed out in his book, *Anti-Intellectualism in American Life*, one expression of the prevailing attitude was evident in many churchmen who thought *clever* people were unlikely to be *good* people, an outlook which we see in secular fundamentalist form in George Wallace's jeers against pseudo-intellectuals, by which he means an intellectual you disagree with.

More important, probably, in the general American culture, and related to this anti-intellectual outlook, has been the association of school with womenfolk, and of escape from school with masculinity. Huck Finn lighting out for the Territory is a symbol of the older America that is still, in part, with us. Girls seldom have reading blocks in school; boys often do. May this not reflect the fact that boys are taught in the elementary years by women, and of course they mostly are raised in the early years by their mothers; and also, in a culture that values masculine prowess and self-reliance, don't many feel the need to assert independence from school routines? If we can get more athletic men teaching English or the arts in elementary schools, and more attractive feminine women teaching the natural sciences and engineering in colleges and universities, we may begin to undo the somewhat arbitrary linkages that have associated attitudes toward school and toward school subjects with one's sexual identity. And in the U.S., since we are a democracy, one is not granted one's identity at birth, even one's sexual identity—it has to be achieved socially, like any other status. Indeed, at the university level, women often must prove that they are not brilliant and clever if they are to be thought properly feminine, while at that level men can come into their own and be fairly free, if they have not lost their minds and their courage as a result of having to prove their manliness at earlier points.

All this gets tied up with questions as to the supposed impracticality of learning and of learned men, a view that was easy to maintain when such men were underpaid and when college presidents could hire and fire them, rather than, as often at present, the other way around.

A dramatic break in the position of academic men came with World War II. Earlier wars had been fought with the benefit of the Corps of Engineers and other graduates of West Point and Annapolis, but World War II was the first to which academic scientists made decisive contributions. Radar in England, the atomic bomb in this country, later the DEW line, were contributions principally of academic scientists. Social scientists played a part, too, in studies of military morale, in analyses of the national character of enemies and allies, and in research on propaganda.

The industrial spinoff from defense also became clear after the war. Robert McNamara, a former Harvard Business School professor, went to the Ford Motor Co. with a group of his military colleagues. MIT scientists founded small companies along Route 128 around Boston. In fact, large business began to cultivate the academy as never before, and corporations began to take an interest in the educational level of the communities from which they recruited manpower or where their employees lived. The altered position of the university is illustrated by the remark a Dupont official made to me several years ago, namely that the university was unbeatable competition for Dupont—the universities could take their best chemists or chemical engineers away from them almost at will. Large companies like Dupont try to compete by making their laboratories as academic as possible and allowing a certain amount of justified bootlegging of private research on company time, like the private garden plots of a Soviet collective farmer.

More significant, though harder to document, is the infiltration of large, managerial business by academic styles of thought. These businessmen no longer regard culture as something to be left as occupational therapy for their wives, even though some still may regard membership on a board of trustees of a college as requiring no different talents from membership on the board of a local symphony or art museum. (In contrast, the owners of small businesses, although often extremely rich, have been influenced much less by academic styles of thought.)

Another great legacy of World War II was the G.I. Bill of Rights, which not only floated many previously anemic colleges which astonishingly managed to find room for the wave of students, but also forced them to adjust to their maturity. They doomed the collegiate in many places. The G.I.'s had seen San Francisco and Biarritz, Tokyo and Houston. The G.I. Bill allowed them to carry their tuition money anywhere and thus to begin to break down the geographic insularity which previously had protected colleges—a protection now again provided by the high tuitions imposed on out-of-state students and the quota on such students in many public institutions. State and local competition to put a public college in every sizable community or area exploded after World War II—one reason that many of the institutions broadened their scope and greatly enlarged their facilities.

Something new has happened when a high school begins to have so many of its students headed toward college as to tip the whole neighborhood toward college. In a study of Berkeley (Calif.) high schools a few years ago, Alan Wilson demonstrated that a high school senior of working-class origin in a middle-class high school where almost everybody went on to college would be likely to plan on college himself, even if people of the same aptitudes and family backgrounds as himself, in a predominantly working-class high school, would not attend college. And conversely, to show how democratic our society is, or how peer-oriented young people are, a young man of middle-class family background in a working-class high school would be less likely to plan on college than others like him in a prevailingly middle-class environment. Increasingly, of course, as more and more parents have attended college, the pressures on schools for college preparatory programs increase. The parents of working-class origin begin to believe that their own children can get ahead only by attending college, and they will tell the interviewer that a man now has to go to college if he is to make it in our society. Thus, more and more neighborhoods get tipped in that direction, so that college attendance has a cumulative quality, much as high school attendance did in the period before World War II.

All this, as one goes down the scale of socioeconomic status, is more true of young men than of young women, except among Negroes, where the situation is reversed. Among whites, barring the higher strata, a girl's education is not thought to matter so much as a boy's, even though in high school she is likely to do better, as we already have noticed. A girl is not sent away so far or kept in college so long, nor is as much money spent on her for tuition if the family has not ample means for all children. One consequence for many of the state colleges and universities is that they sometimes have very bright commuter girls who are academically and often socially superior to the men in the same institution, and, as happens at all levels of the academic enterprise, who find themselves going slumming when they go out with boys they meet at school; either that, or they sit at home waiting for callers.

It would be illuminating if we could overhear the often unspoken conversation that goes on between parents and children, in all social strata, about attending college and where to go. Among working-class parents who have had no college education, a study done by the sociologist, Joseph Kahl, a number of years ago, indicated some aspects of that conversation. He matched two samples of high school male seniors; matched them in terms of aptitude and family income, some of whom were going to college and some of whom were not. And to try to understand that decision, he talked both to the young men and to their fathers. Almost invariably, the fathers would say that they wanted their young people to go to college. But some also would say or mean something else: in effect, "Do you want to abandon me? Do you think I'm no good? Which do you want to be, a big shot, or a good guy?" Often, such young men would decide that they didn't have the money or the talent or the interest to attend college. In other cases, the father was genuinely eager for his son to attend college. Perhaps the home made provisions for study, rather than urging on the children the agenda that I once heard called "honey dew" days: "Honey, do this. Honey, do that." "Help me shingle the roof"—for a boy. "Give me a hand with the dishes"—for a girl. Indeed, these family pressures are such that it is not surprising that many of the college students hold part-time jobs which handicap their academic work and are not absolutely essential financially, but make sense humanly in the family context—more sense than returning to the campus in the evening, if one is a commuter, for some extracurricular event, or going to the library to get out that recommended reading for which one will not be held on the exam.

At the same time, the opportunity for college students to earn money on the side and the opportunity for their parents, under conditions of plentiful employment, to earn steady money has allowed families greater leeway in releasing their children from full-time employment for at least part-time higher education. Labor unions have had the power to keep the young out of the well-paying, full-time labor force, while the draft recently has operated in a similar way to channel people toward college as a temporarily deferable occupation.

And, as I already have indicated, the colleges and universities have been there to meet the demand and to help create it. It has taken an astonishingly long time for members of the Federal Congress and for state assemblymen and senators to discover that higher education is the new Rivers and Harbors pork barrel for poor landlocked communities. But this discovery has been made; and, for good reasons and not so good ones, states and areas compete to establish public colleges, so that each legislator will have at least one in his area. This is in fact an old American story, as Daniel Boorstin points out in the chapter, "The Booster College," in his volume, *The Americans: The National Experience*. Washington, D. C., was, until 1968, the only major city without a multi-purpose public college. But, in the fall of 1968, with the establishment of Federal City College, it has, at long last, joined the U.S.

The expansion of our colleges and their willingness to accommodate themselves to unanticipated students who turn up on their doorstep always have impressed me, but that impression was deepened when I spent an earlier sabbatical at the University of Sussex, one of the new British universities, which regards itself as quite "American" in its interdisciplinary programs and its general effort to be flexible and responsive to new social imperatives. But at Sussex, as at every other British university, there are places assigned in advance in every field, and if a single additional student turns up who had not been arranged for previously, he simply is turned away. He must wait at least another year. There is no such thing as overacceptance at a British university; nothing like our flexibility and willingness to improvise, to have students in trailers, as the University of California at Santa Cruz did in its first year—or to announce courses and then go find the faculty who may turn up to teach them at the last minute.

Indeed, the fluidity of the American student population reflects that of the society. Only in the more traditional, often private, liberal arts colleges do students suppose that they will follow a regular four-year sequence in the same institution; only in such places are freshmen marked at entry as members of the Class of 1973, who will be ready for their 25th reunions in 1998. More commonly, students go one term and not another; they drop in and they drop out; they transfer casually and without a feeling of being downgraded or upgraded on the basis of the time-honored liturgy of academic precedence. Bruce Eckland followed dropouts from the University of Illinois for 10 years, and found them eventually getting an A.B. somewhere. It may be only in such terms that we can explain the relative lack of hostility against academic institutions from those we term dropouts. While my Harvard colleague, Prof. S. M. Lipset, has some evidence that John Birch Society members and other right-wing fanatics are sometimes dropouts who resent the university which they were unable to complete, the little research we have on dropouts suggests that this kind of resentment is less common than one might suppose and that parents who have not finished college have not hindered their children from attending college; if anything, the contrary.

I mentioned earlier the obvious fact that, if the high schools had not expanded enormously, there would not be the cadres ready to go on to college. But the expansion of high schools has had another consequence, namely an enormous demand for college graduates to teach in secondary schools and a great need for people to teach the teachers—a kind of academic multiplier effect. Prosperity has meant, furthermore, that many corporations have been able to afford college graduates, whether or not anything they learned in college was relevant for what they would do in the company or whether the company might not teach it to them more economically than college could. It is a matter of prestige to have a receptionist who attended college. And by giving her a new job title, she even may be satisfied, or not aggressively dissatisfied, with her job. Furthermore, when the neighborhood becomes tipped in the direction of college, those who do not attend college begin to be psychologically deviant. A prospective employer may be right to fear that they lack the assiduity, the willingness to endure, and therefore, presumably, the willingness to learn rather than loaf on company time.

As if these pressures for the expansion of higher education were not enough, the Soviet Union provided an additional booster in 1958 in the form of Sputnik. There had developed before Sputnik a mood of self-criticism of American education at all levels. Why can't Johnny read? Why does he prefer football, fraternities, and frivolity to serious academic work? Why are our schools softer than those of the Swiss, the Russians, the Japanese? Sputnik contributed to a widening feeling that the country had gone soft in the international competition. I remember very well the founding of Oakland University as a branch of Michigan State University in 1958, and the approval it gained for announcing that it was to be a no-nonsense college with none of the collegiate or playboy fun and no concessions to Big Ten self-indulgence.

All these forces converged to heighten the power of the faculty and to lessen the relative power of the students, the administration, the local community, or the trustees. The faculty were the gatekeepers of the new American meritocracy, who decided how much further education a person could have, the level at which he was to be certified. A more just society accepted meritocracy as the alternative to favoritism, although the rich whose sons could not get into papa's college did so grudgingly, and the black and other disadvantaged minorities who could get into nobody's college now are objecting aggressively. Moreover, to the degree that we recognize the growing complexity of our society, we recognize the need for college-trained experts to advise, if not to manage, corporate and governmental affairs—though here again there are many who begrudge the need for experts and who, with terrifying simplicity, insist that it is all a plot to take America away from its traditional course. Students in college also may believe sometimes that affairs really would be simple if bad people didn't mess them up. But, more frequently, they turn to their professors in the hope of finding a meaning to their lives and an interpretation of the bewildering rate of change. This demand, of course, distributes itself unevenly over the curriculum, being especially pronounced in sociology, the more clinical sides of psychology, existential philosophy, and, sometimes, political science. (The experimental colleges have gotten some of this intellectual or, at times, anti-intellectual traffic, and so have the campus ministries which, in many institutions, have been a source of intellectual vitality or political activism, or occasionally both together.) Students or pastors have found it hard to maintain an underground curriculum because faculty have been talented at co-opting books or themes into the regular curriculum, and administrators have been inventive in finding room. Thus, the quest of many students and of many adults for better understanding has benefited the position of those faculty who seem to offer it—often faculty who earlier suffered from neglect at the hands of more fully collegiate or vocational student bodies.

This dramatic rise in the relative position of faculty members did not make most of us happier, nor did it rob us of feelings of underprivilege and deprivation. So far as I am aware, no rising group behaves that way. It continues to cherish its minority status as a basis for further claims on the general culture. Furthermore, the victory of academic values never has been anything like total. A few institutions have been turned into an academic version of a Marine boot camp, where the teaching assistants are the noncoms, the deans are the field-grade officers, and the senior faculty are the headquarters staff. Students may be proud to have survived, but seldom have formed enduring attachments to academic concerns. In the most academically selective institutions, those where three-quarters of the males go on to graduate or professional study, the faculty sometimes have been, until quite recently, cast in the role of models for a very large number of students for whom other models, such as ministers, businessmen, political leaders, accountants, insurance men, and so on, scarcely were visible. In fact, the decline in the status of the businessman, which began a good many years ago, was precipitate during the Depression and after World War II among the better students. The nonprofit sectors of society seemed to them somehow more pure. This now has changed among a small minority of students, who appear to regard all occupations as equally corrupt—which is a gain to the degree that it reduces snobbery, and a loss to the degree that it reduces everything to a common level of despair and disparagement.

There are still colleges to be found where undergraduates boast about how many bottles of beer they have consumed or how many bourbon shots they have downed, even while elsewhere officials worry that the next student they meet may be a narcotics agent, and look wistfully back to the days when sin took less pharmacological shape. In contrast, in the arts and sciences colleges and engineering schools of the great state universities, making the grade becomes increasingly more important than making the team. In their newly published book based on observations at the University of Kansas, Howard Becker, Blanche Geer, and Everett Hughes describe the way in which the fraternities have become, as it were, the shop stewards of the academic enterprise, encouraging their members to raise their grade-point average by a cooperative effort, although not to raise it astronomically. The power of the faculty and the need for good and adequate grades are recognized in such compromises, even while that power is resisted in marginal degree.

Such resistance is more difficult in a commuter college, where students have little chance to group together to decide what sort of effort the faculty is entitled to or how to beat the faculty at their own academic game. Here, as I have suggested before, it is often the family or the part-time job which competes with the curriculum and perhaps even more successfully with the extra-curriculum for the allegiance of students. Some commuter colleges are torn between the advantages of building dormitories to attract a wider-ranging, and perhaps somewhat more affluent, student body, while recognizing the troubles that resident students can create who will not necessarily devote the time spared from commuting to reading more books.

Still, it seems fair to say that what we now find the country over is rising faculty power *vis-à-vis* student collegiate life, at the very time when there is developing a new form of student power which is anti-collegiate, but also, in some ways, anti-academic. Around San Francisco State College, around Wayne State University, around the new University of Massachusetts in Boston, one can see developing small cadres of activist students who are academically highly capable, but who find reasons to reject the academic as irrelevant, conservative, or biased. In general, such students tend to be clustered in metropolitan institutions with superior faculty. So, too, in many of the great state universities, one can find both the new activist and the old collegiate students. What is astonishing is that they have not fought it out more among themselves for control of the campus. And one can find Negro colleges, too, where, as happens generally in the South, athletic and collegiate values are strong, and fraternity and sorority life glorious and full-blown, and where, at the same time, a small cadre of black militants rejects both the collegiate and the academic, insisting, sometimes with the aid of white faculty radicals and sometimes in a mood of hostility to all whites, that the college become black, rejecting the goals of conventional success, whether in terms of Woodrow Wilson Fellowships or of entrepreneurial achievement.

However, I am inclined to think that there are more black militants on white campuses than on Negro college campuses. When there are enough black students on a white campus—and it does not take very many—to form an Afro-American group or Black Students Union, there may develop a competition in militancy between white and black activists, as illustrated in a most dramatic way at Columbia and as one also might find in some of the New York State or California State Colleges. But, as administrators also may be discovering, the black students are ordinarily in search of concrete goals, such as living or meeting facilities, or special programs or courses in African or Afro-American history, whereas what the white students want is more indeterminate and therefore more difficult for institutions to cope with. The white student radical in America tends to be well-off; he comes from a college-educated family and, as Kenneth Keniston observes in his book, *The Young Radicals*, the student often is carrying out a mandate which he thinks his parents fudged or compromised—a mandate to make America more equal, more just, less warlike, and, in some vague way, more humane. But the tactics tend to be those borrowed from the civil rights movement, and they can escalate faster than the goals can, leading to a leap-frog between goals and tactics that baffle adults and many moderate students.

In the criticism of the university by the activist students, whether white or black, there are some themes strangely reminiscent of earlier American anti-academic attitudes. If the businessmen of an earlier epoch attacked the professors as impractical and unworldly men, student radicals today, and many professors, attack them for being irrelevant and uncommitted. The elder Henry Ford, in a famous remark, said that history is bunk. Many student radicals would agree, seeing history mainly as a source of cautionary tales warning them against provoking reaction. (I myself have written such tales.) Americans put up more readily with unserious student pranks and collegiate fun and games than with the present combination of the ribald and the solemn, the provocative and the righteous, the manipulative and the idealistic forms of behavior.

There is one group of student activists who have had relatively little attention of late, and that is the members of right-wing organizations such as the Young Americans for Freedom. I do not know how many campus chapters of the YAF are in existence, but I have seen figures indicating that the membership is on the order of 20,000, considerably larger than the Students for a Democratic Society were until quite recently. These chapters played a not inconsiderable role in arousing enthusiasm for Barry Goldwater within the Republican Party in 1964, but I have not seen any indication that they are part of the entourage of George Wallace, whose great support from young men in their twenties comes principally from blue-collar workers and farmers without college education. The rise of the Young Americans for Freedom is a curious, backhanded tribute to the rise of academic influence. For, while these students sometimes refer to themselves as "conservatives," they are not conservative in the American grain, which means being rather unpolitical and not ideologically flamboyant. In an earlier collegiate era, a student from a conservative family could arrive on a college campus and expect to emerge uninfluenced by cosmopolitan currents of liberalism and radicalism. Ideas did not touch him all that much. There are still, of course, many campuses where this is so, but there are many others where parents think it is so, and it is not. (I have visited, for example, Southern Baptist colleges where young people have been sent by their parents, rather than having gone on their own steam, and have found, when they got there, the winds of radical theology and radical pacifism and radical equality blowing strong.) And I would think that on the state college and university campuses there is now a sufficiently heterogeneous faculty and student body to put pressure on political somnolence and cultural complacency. In a setting where the articulate campus spokesmen, both faculty and students, are liberal or radical, a minority of students is apt to decide that conventional conservatism is an inadequate carapace of protection. They may start reading William Buckley, Jr.'s *National Review*; they almost certainly will have read Ayn Rand in high school; they will develop a much more doctrinal position than that of their parents and turn into radicals of the right capable of matching forensic talents with the SDS or the elected Student Government liberals.

One can find universities today where nonconformist, radical student leaders have a large following among the more collegiate students. They are able to mobilize the latter because both cadres object to anything compulsory, whether it is dormitory hours for women or distribution requirements in the curriculum or physical education or ROTC. For, just as in the labor union movement of a generation or two ago, union leaders could espouse international or even Utopian values and yet appeal to a work force that wanted more money for less work, so also student radicals today can tap a constituency that does not share their harsh judgment of American society nor their vision—usually an inchoate and barely formed vision—of what might replace it.

One extramural constraint, namely the draft, binds these cadres together now and almost certainly will continue to do so with increasing intensity while the war in Vietnam lasts. That war and its consequences for personal choice and student ethical dilemmas make me sympathetic with the students' solemnity and moral fervor I have referred to. It is dreadfully hard on a young man to have to ask himself if he is a coward because he is not going to enlist and perhaps be sent to Vietnam; to ask himself if he is a coward because, as a Quaker, he has accepted a conscientious objector deferment rather than going to prison or to Canada. It is dreadfully hard on a young man to ask himself whether he is fond of a particular girl or thinks that an element in his decision to marry her and father a child may be a better chance for deferment. And if he is attending medical school, is he there because he wants to help the sick, or because he wants to do research on the sick and would have gone into a Ph.D. program if he had not feared for his deferment? The situation that the country is in puts college students into these ethical dilemmas if they are at all sensitive, harasses them with the feeling that they are unduly privileged in an era when privilege increasingly is being rejected, and forces the omnipresent American question of masculinity on them in forms of often nearly impossible ambiguity.

Naturally, in what I stated just now, I have been talking about young men. It is perhaps noticeable that most of the literature about students refers implicitly to young men—young women get less attention from researchers. However, the issues of the draft that unsettle young men plainly do not leave their girlfriends unscathed. And the more general issue of privilege certainly does not leave them unscathed. The very desire of some of the more affluent young people of both sexes to identify with the deprived is a kind of paradoxical luxury of being able to afford wearing blue jeans and looking sloppy—and, of course, it is this often-unintended offensiveness which so infuriates the hard-working and struggling working class and lower middle class when confronted by the privileged young who seem to scoff at their own privileges.

The most visible cadre of deprived Americans today for most college students who think about such matters are the blacks. However, the majority of poor in America are white. Many are old. Many are rural or live in run-out mining and mill towns. They are not ghettoized; they are not dramatically visible in the way that the Negroes and, perhaps increasingly, the Mexican-Americans are. Another group that tends to get lost from view is the steadily rising number of middle-class Negroes whose children are attending both the predominantly Negro and the predominantly integrated colleges.

In the new mythology of race, the Negro middle class—especially students, faculty members, and administrators—often is caught between black militants with their white student allies and the stubborn white reactionaries. In this situation, some middle-class Negroes tend to identify or overidentify with the Negro proletariat out of precisely the same emotions of wanting to shed privileges and to share oppression that we find among some of the more affluent white undergraduates. I think, for example, of one extremely able and reflective Negro student at Harvard who said to me in the spring of 1968 that the previous summer he had avoided riots and trouble by going to Europe, but in the summer of 1968 he felt he had to share the lot of his brothers in the ghetto of which he had had no personal experience, and he was going to be on hand for whatever disasters might befall. Of course, in such attitudes there is an element of self-dramatization, but there is also a feeling of generosity toward the oppressed and of a wish to share what is considered to be the greater reality of hardship as against the lesser reality of indulgence.

One of the troubling side effects of the racial crisis within America, both for white and black students and for educators, too, is that we have become so preoccupied with our domestic inventory of social attention (refugees from Czechoslovakia only now are beginning to arrive) that it is desperately important for young Americans to see something of students elsewhere in the world. Radical students often assume that, because the slogans are the same, the problems of students everywhere are the same. Most of us know how false that assumption is, how crowded and oppressed are the students in Italy, for example, or even in France, in Tokyo or Madras, in Mexico City or Manila.

Yet the state colleges and universities, many of whom are struggling to increase their recruitment of minority American students, are bound, nevertheless, pretty much to a narrow geographic catchbasin. The legislature is apt to fear the "foreigners" from New York State, or New Jersey, and seldom will provide funds to bring foreign students in numbers to the campus, let alone resources to keep them from being isolated in a foreign student colony. Some of the state colleges and universities have had better luck with overseas programs for their own American students, terms doing Chinese studies in Hong Kong, or Spanish studies in Madrid. We all know that such foreign terms can have a PX quality, without real involvement with the host culture in any serious way. We know the resistance to foreign language requirements which can unite some of the most self-indulgent students with some of the most vocal activists. What I am saying is that American self-awareness would be a mixed blessing if it led to a new insularity, and that it is hard for many of us to be polygamous about problems and to think about more than one at the same time. Therefore, it is just because there is now such an interest, although an uneven interest, in problems of the ghetto, that I want to emphasize the need for continuing attention to problems and possibilities, curiosities and discoveries, overseas.

As I write these lines, the Fulbright grants for travel and study, particularly in Western Europe, either have been cut entirely or severely curtailed, reflecting not only the deep budget cuts in so many programs, but also (it is said) the vindictive hostility in the State Department toward Sen. Fulbright himself. There are many state colleges and universities which I know have had Fulbright scholars at them. Indeed, I would suppose that there are none of these colleges whose intellectual life has not been influenced directly or indirectly by non-American scholarship or travel abroad by American scholars. I hope we do not enter another era when non-American will be termed "un-American," for indeed, throughout our history, there has been nothing more American than our generosity toward the importation of people, inventions, and ideas. The early mills of New England often were built by workmen who smuggled the plans out of Lancastershire factories, and what students sometimes like to call "the academic mills" have benefited similarly from the influx of non-American scholars.

At the present time, the U.S. is less provincial than it ever has been, *and* we almost are overwhelmed by the immensity of our domestic problems. However, I do not think we can understand these in the absence of comparative perspective. In this respect, a college has the same duty that an individual does: to recognize roots in a particular time and turf and, at the same time, to transcend both.

5

REFORM IN HIGHER EDUCATION—
DEMANDS OF THE LEFT AND RIGHT

RICHARD E. PETERSON

AMERICAN HIGHER EDUCATION is presently experiencing a period of turmoil and change unparalleled in its history. Rather than the consequence of deliberate design, the change we are witnessing in the late 1960's tends to be the result of accommodations struck among a host of competing power blocks. At one time, say before World War II, authority in the colleges and universities was in general firmly in the hands of administrators and trustees. After the war, especially in the prestigious universities, faculty power and entrepreneurship began to mount as the marketability and mobility of professors grew. Then came the great watershed, the 1964 rebellion at Berkeley, and activist students around the country saw that they could have an impact on the shape of the university.

Authority in higher education has been seriously eroded; control of the university is up for grabs; and everybody is jumping in for a piece of the action. While these overstatements do not contribute much to our analysis, they do suggest the kind of environment in which governance through trade-off of demands is taking place.

One wonders whether authority in higher education has not always been essentially arbitrary. From where I sit, as an educational researcher, I am impressed by how little we know with any certainty

From *Liberal Education*, March, 1969. Reprinted by permission of the author and the editor of the publication. Richard E. Peterson is Research Psychologist, Educational Testing Service, Berkeley, Calif.

about the outcomes of various educational treatments: for example, do we really know whether a liberal education makes people better human beings? But that is another matter. What we need is a theory of higher education, or better still, a theory grounded in facts, to serve as a basis for authority. Yet we cannot even pin down the purposes of higher education, and probably will not be able to for some time—not until the pace of social change in America slows down a bit.

Assuming, then, this notion of an "authority vacuum" or near-vacuum in American higher education, the purpose of this paper is to outline some of the demands on the colleges and universities being pressed by groups of people looking for a piece of the action. I will not be talking about all the people who are *not* making demands: the politically apathetic majority of students, all the faculty who have come to expect change as part of the natural order of things but who expect the process to be orderly, and all the administrators who just want to keep the ship moving ahead on a fairly even keel.

To come to grips with the great range of demands—from the most radical to the most reactionary—I have reduced the array to four general categories. In keeping with the title I was given, the four analytic types are labeled: the Anarchist Left, the Reformist Left, the Nostalgic Right, and the Upright Right. As will be seen, I have defined the words "Left" and "Right" very broadly, and the other words—"Nostalgic," "Upright" and so on—are not going to make for a breakthrough in scientific political analysis. At the end I will suggest an interim role for college administrators that seems almost inescapable, given the present condition of governance in the university.

The Anarchist Left

I have come to the view that the radical youth movement in the Western World (and Japan) is best understood in terms of loss of confidence in the traditional forms of authority. In America the movement is comprised mainly of college students, accounting for something on the order of five per cent of the total student population. Highly sophisticated intellectually, these students have managed to learn through the mass media and other teachers that the human condition leaves a great deal to be desired. They blame the older generation for either creating this condition or acquiescing in it. They have come to reject authority for being, as Paul Goodman has put it, "'not only immoral but functionally incompetent.'"[1]

In response to the realization of "no confidence," some students become activists in the New Left, others become passivists in the hippie culture, a few prefer the put-ons and mockeries of the Yippies, and there must be other ways of reacting as well. Despite these differences, as well as the absence of organization, the Movement *is* a movement in which many things are shared in common. One thing is a style, by which the middle-class niceties can be rebuked on a day-to-day basis. Another shared value can best be summed up in the words "participatory democracy"; and participatory democracy is the essence of the "Anarchist social order" (Goodman's phrase)[2] as it has been put forward in the twentieth century.

In the colleges and universities, the New Anarchists want an end to the customary patterns of authority, which they regard as illegitimate, and they want a voice in creating the new arrangements. The new institution these students envision is characterized not only by decentralized decision processes but also by very great freedom in their academic and personal lives for all the individuals in the college community. People in the Movement speak of "human liberation." But they do not expect it all at once; they do not expect a "revolution" in that sense.

Instead, issues of a more limited nature are raised, demands for changes are made, a sufficient number of students are temporarily activated, and some sort of change eventually results. Agitation of this sort toward eliminating institutional controls on the personal lives of students has been mounting steadily over the past five years or so. It has happened faster at some types of colleges than at others—specifically, faster at the independent and public institutions than at the church-related and career-oriented colleges. The general demand is for an end to *in loco parentis*, leaving the students free to live the way they want to—to dress, wear beards, have sexual relations, smoke pot, and the like according to their own dictates. Judging from a survey of organized student protest we carried out last summer, protests over various dormitory and living-group regulations occurred during the previous academic year at one third of all

[1] Goodman, P., "The Black Flag of Anarchism," *The New York Times Magazine,* June 14, 1968, p. 13.

[2] *Ibid.*, p. 16.

the accredited four-year colleges in the country; dress regulations were protested at one in five colleges.[3]

While relaxation of *in loco parentis* in the colleges must seem incredibly slow to the student activists, from a five- or six-year perspective the shift seems to me quite remarkable. But then so is the rate of change in American life generally. Just six months ago I wrote about the coming confrontation between students and administrators over the use of marijuana.[4] I now think that, if there is going to be a confrontation at all, it will be between the students and the civil authorities (and various "upright rightists"). The colleges, I think, can see the futility of trying to make rules about pot stick. It will not be as easy for the *public* institutions to stand aside, however.

What about demands from the student anarchists for changes in academic affairs? Serious interest in educational reform on the part of students in the radical Movement began to pick up only in the past two years or so. Their efforts to work within established structures, however, have seldom led to more than token gestures, for at least two reasons. First, the radicals have been less successful in mobilizing moderate students around educational issues; our survey data show this. Secondly, of course, the faculty can normally be counted on to resist almost all demands for reforming instructional practices, course offerings and so forth.

What the anarchist-inclined students have typically done, then, is to work outside the established structures to build so-called "parallel institutions"—the free universities and experimental colleges, which currently operate on the edges of upwards of 300 colleges and universities.[5] The Experimental College at San Francisco State is presently in its fourth year.

It is as important to understand that these students want to have a say in determining the nature of their academic experiences as it is to understand the specifics of what they want. Unless authority in academic planning is shared meaningfully with students, the anarchist five per cent are not going to be happy.

This said, what kind of learning experiences do they want? As regards course content, they mainly want courses in which they can

3 Peterson, R. E., *The Scope of Organized Student Protest in 1967-1968*, Princeton, N.J.: Educational Testing Service, 1968.

4 *Ibid.*, p. 13.

5 Black, B., & Hamilton, B., "The Spirit of the Free Universities," *Change*, January-February 1969.

consider radical analyses of the country's and the world's great social problems, and courses in which they can consider themselves—existential psychotherapy, varieties of sexual response, Zen, encounter groups of all sorts. When possible, they want opportunities for direct work in the real world—as in the ghetto. On campus they want intensely personalized classes that allow the students, through interacting with each other, always to learn about themselves as well as the content of the course. They want no ritualistic requirements such as required attendance, periodic examinations and other appeals to presumed competitive motives; and they would prefer not to study within the confines of specialized disciplines. As Kenneth Keniston has noted, the young radicals are anti-academic, not anti-intellectual.[6]

In sum, we have a small but growing segment of the national student body, comprised of both New Leftists and the nonpolitical hippies, which wants to replace the present university with something which makes for greater community, human freedom and personal growth. You may say that the anarchy these kids want will mean disorder, violence, the jungle. Yet, hasn't it generally been found that when controls are removed from students responsible self-regulation, not chaos ensues? Even if ethical behavior could be counted on, you are likely to dismiss the whole anarchist bag as totally unpractical, given the complexities of our time and place. And you may be right.

Nonetheless, there is currently something of a revival of interest in anarchist thought—which, by the way, does not emphasize insurrection and bomb-throwing. A collection of anarchist writings entitled *Patterns of Anarchy,* edited by Krimmerman and Perry, was published not long ago.[7] Paul Goodman's article that I have referred to was in the *The New York Times Magazine* this past summer [1968]. Finally, the autobiography of that classical anarchist-activist Prince Peter Kropotkin, entitled *Memoirs of a Revolutionist,* originally published in 1899, has just been republished.[8] I can see Kropotkin taking his place among the Movement's deities alongside Guevara and Marcuse. Kropotkin is thus described in my 1955 Britannica:

---

[6] Keniston, K., *Young Radicals,* New York: Harcourt, Brace & World, 1968.

[7] Krimmerman, L. I., & Perry, L. (eds.), *Patterns of Anarchy,* New York: Doubleday, 1966.

[8] Kropotkin, P., *Memoirs of a Revolutionist,* New York: Horizon Press, 1969 (originally published in 1899).

Kropotkin had a singularly gentle and attractive personality, and was much loved and respected in England. He desired the minimum of government, and the development of a system of human cooperation which should render government from above superfluous.

The Reformist Left

Under this heading I will touch rather briefly on a number of sources of pressure for more modest changes in the structure and function of American colleges and universities. Often these demanded changes represent further extensions in patterns of change that have been underway for a decade or longer, such as foundation interest in higher education, or the university's involvement in public service. Generally these reforms are not addressed to basic authority relationships on the campus, which was the chief burden in the previous section. The reformists on the Left—perhaps they can be called liberals—are usually satisfied with piecemeal changes; the New Anarchists, on the other hand, are not likely to be pacified until the bosses and the rules are gone.

The Foundations. The great non-profit foundations, with seemingly unlimited funds at their command, have now, as we all know, come to assume a position of very large influence on American higher education. The general thrust from the foundations has been increasingly progressive and activist, providing a variety of goads for colleges to break out of old molds and experiment with new ways of doing things. Ford gives money to the Columbia Students for a Reconstructed University and to the National Student Association for their educational reform programs. Kettering allots thousands for studying Institutional Vitality. The Hazen Foundation issues a call for the university to place the student at the center of its concerns.[9] Danforth sponsors seminars on The Identity Crisis of Higher Education. The Esso Foundation underwrites a new journal called *Change.* A foundation wants to give a large sum to San Francisco State's Black Studies Department.

Perhaps of greatest significance is the Carnegie Commission on Higher Education. Last month it issued its first report, calling on the federal government, not to dole out money to all the country's colleges and universities, but to put money into the pockets of poor youths and let them pick their colleges. The Kerr proposals appear

---

[9] *The Student in Higher Education,* New Haven, Conn.: The Hazen Foundation, 1968.

to have a decent chance of becoming law; support for earlier plans for direct aid to institutions (for "general support") seems to be waning, and Carnegie president Pifer has become Nixon's chief education priority-setter. (Or if the Kerr proposals are not enacted into law under Nixon, the chances ought to be excellent under Edward Kennedy and a more populist political climate.) At any rate, if the Carnegie recommendations become public policy, I for one would fear for the survival of colleges that fail to develop programs to meet the needs of this new kind of student. And we are only just beginning to hear from the Carnegie Commission, which has three more years to run.

One begins to appreciate the immense foundation influence, which tends to operate not so much in direct ways on individual colleges, in the way that student and faculty groups press demands, but through the sweet reason contained in research monographs, annual reports, presidential speeches to educational associations, and the like. The "foundation will," so to speak, slides almost unawares into the mind of the academic planner, greased in part by the latter's vision of all that money.

The Students. Right now it is chiefly the black and Third World students (with many white sympathizers) who are making demands—demands which seem rather limited in view of the total work of the institutions involved, but demands which are being pressed in a most abrasive, impolite way. The black militants, it seems to me, have got their colleges buffaloed. The problem is that they (the blacks) are not playing by the rules we (white administrators) are accustomed to. They make demands that are "non-negotiable" (or so it happened at San Francisco State, Swarthmore and Brandeis). What does one do in the face of such demands? Generally you fall back on *your* rules; you appoint a committee or call for a study, and hope that time will take care of things. But before long, playing by *their* rules, the blacks have got you locked in your office, or have burned a building, called a strike, or whatever. And a full-scale confrontation is on.

Black activism in behalf of programs of black studies and more black students and faculty, according to our survey this summer [1968], occurred at 18 per cent of all the institutions in the sample, and at 41 per cent of the independent universities and 38 per cent of the public universities in the sample. And there appears to be little let-up this year. It is ironic that it is on the college campus, the presumed home of rational people, that race relations in America presently seem most nearly bankrupt. While I can understand reasons for the black anger, it is not clear to me how militant black separatism on the campus is going to lead to a time of real racial harmony in the U.S.A.

Besides the black activists, almost every college today has a contingent of reform-minded white student activists. Often they are elected student leaders; frequently they work on the campus newspaper; generally they identify with NSA. They are articulate, polite and relatively disinclined to long hair and pot. They are popular and respected by their fellow students. We call them responsible and moderate because the kinds of demands they make usually do not seriously threaten our positions of authority and can usually be met in piecemeal fashion.

The demands of these student reformers, however, are both intensifying and expanding into areas hitherto the exclusive province of other constituent groups. They speak with increasing firmness about student power—meaning they intend to be taken seriously, seriously enough to be included in the total decision-making structure of the college, not just in decisions about student life outside the classroom, which students at most colleges by now at least think they control. Students are seeking some share of authority in such *academic* matters as creating and eliminating courses, grading practices, examination policies and practices, assessing faculty teaching competence toward pay increases and tenure, selecting new faculty, establishing degree standards, establishing admission standards, selecting a new president. According to our survey, during the academic year there were organized protests about poor quality of instruction on 13 per cent of the campuses; over systems of testing and grading at 12 per cent of the colleges, and about curriculum inflexibility at 15 per cent of the institutions in the sample. Protests aimed at a larger student role in campus governance were reported at 27 per cent of the colleges, contrasted with a 19 per cent figure from a comparable survey in 1965.

Depending on whether or not the country is at war in Vietnam or somewhere else in the coming months, we may expect a continuation of student demands, chiefly from the Students for a Democratic Society, that the university end its "complicity" with the war effort. There will be "exposés" of classified defense research on the campus and of university investment of monies in war-related and "imperialist" business activities. There will be harassment of military and war-related industrial recruiters. Last year there were demonstrations against military recruiters on one in four of all the campuses, with the figure rising to over 40 per cent at the independent and public universities. Harassment of recruiters from firms like Dow and the CIA were reported at one in five colleges over all, and at more than half of the independent and public universities.

The Faculty. What about the faculty? . . . Last spring [1968] we heard of the establishment of the New Universities Conference (NUC), a league of young radical professors—mainly alumni of SDS—which was to serve as a base from which radical faculty and graduate students could criticize the role of the university in American society, press for educational reforms and promote their own job security. Is NUC still alive, or has its once idealistic membership been lured into the kind of careerism that predisposes professors away from any real concern for the welfare of their institution as a whole?

What about AAUP [American Association of University Professors]? With its 1125 chapters and traditional concern for academic freedom, tenure and decent salaries—all of which are now pretty standard in all but the most backward colleges, much to the credit of AAUP—does the Association now exist mainly as a kind of benign presence within the higher education establishment? In fact, there are signs of new forms of life. Not unexpectedly, AAUP has become interested in extending faculty participation in campus governance. Over the past several years AAUP has funded a man to develop a system for rating colleges in terms of amount of faculty participation, the idea then being to publish these ratings in a way similar to the faculty salary ratings. Some of the implications of a move along these lines are rather obvious; there should be some lively confrontations when AAUP-spurred Faculty Power pits itself against SDS-, BSU-, and NSA-spurred Student Power. (Bear in mind that AAUP dogma has it that the faculty must have primary authority for basic academic decisions at the college.) AAUP now supports the principle of collective bargaining, and at its annual meeting last spring took the position that faculty strikes may be necessary, as a last resort. (The AAUP chapter at San Francisco State, however, announced itself against the teachers' strike there.) This brings us around to AFT.

The American Federation of Teachers (AFL-CIO) has chapters

at some 110 colleges around the country, about half of which are public junior colleges. AFT locals tend to be found in urban areas where they can be in touch with the broader AFL-CIO bureaucracy (which helped get the campus locals started in the first place). Also AFT manages to have networks of chapters working in fairly close coordination, most notably in New York City and in the state of California; thus AFT strike threats at a half dozen other California state colleges added to the pressure on Governor Reagan and the trustees to begin talks at San Francisco. Typically, college AFT locals have been chiefly interested in obtaining a position to bargain with college administrators and trustees—"to negotiate a binding agreement"—regarding salary and other working conditions. Such collective bargaining agreements have been negotiated at about a dozen two-year community colleges, several coming after strikes.

The goals of AFT at San Francisco State have been changing in interesting ways as the hostilities there have unfolded. At first it looked as though the chapter was engaging in rank opportunism in hitching its strike for bread-and-butter matters to the student strike. The union's "image" then improved when, largely through efforts of the AFL-CIO apparatus in San Francisco, a "renowned" mediator was brought in and the state college trustees agreed to "talks" with the various other parties to the dispute (Governor Reagan has forbidden "negotiations"). Soon after, however, the downtown union leaders publicly disassociated the goals of the teachers' strike from the goals of the striking Third World students. But as the confrontation wore on, many of the AFT professors began to be truly radicalized or "anarchized"; having in a sense learned from the students, campus AFT spokesmen, at the time this is being written, have reaffirmed their solidarity with the student militants and are talking about faculty self-determination and decentralization of authority in the California state college system.

Faculty radicalism, of course, gets expressed in other, less organized ways. There are almost always active faculty supporters of student protests; most of these faculty members are themselves recent graduate student activists.

Finally it should be noted that there are young Turk radicals, especially in the social sciences at the large universities, who are giving the older men in their departments and professional associations fits about what their discipline should be all about. The new men want to make their professional work—their teaching, researching, writing—relevant to the great problems of the day, instead of reworking the great theories of the past, the "permanent truths," or whatever it is the older generation of academics is occupied with.

The Trustees. Last but not least, here are the college and university trustees around the country about whom there are stereotypes aplenty but almost no "hard data," as they say. And does it make any difference: do trustees for the most part merely rubber-stamp their administrators? For the most part, that *is* what they do. I say this on the basis of a survey of over 5000 trustees conducted last spring [1968] by Rodney Hartnett, my colleague at ETS.[10] To what extent can we expect college trustees, if not to press for changes themselves, at least to support others in their demands for reforms? Let me give you some of Hartnett's data from which you can draw your own conclusions: 16 per cent of the trustees regard themselves as "Liberal" rather than "Moderate" or "Conservative"; 11 per cent said they are both "Liberal" and "Democrat" (rather than "Republican"); 16 per cent said their views are "very similar" to those of Nelson Rockefeller; 12 per cent reported themselves as "very similar" in their views to Eugene McCarthy; to the late Martin Luther King, 7 per cent; to both John Kenneth Galbraith and the late Robert Kennedy, 6 per cent; and to the late Norman Thomas, 2 per cent.

So much for demands from the Left, with that word defined broadly enough to include pleas for abolition of traditional patterns of authority in higher education as well as pressures for more modest changes in structures, functions and, yes, faculty salaries.

I will have less to say about the Right, mainly because, as I view the situation, sources on the Right are making relatively fewer demands, and the demands that are being heard from the Right are more in the nature of *counter-demands,* that is demands that the colleges stand firm against the pressures for change coming from liberals and radicals.

The Nostalgic Right

My meaning for the word "nostalgia" is in part the same as Webster's: "a yearning for return to some real or romanticized period or irrecoverable condition or setting in the past." I want,

---

[10] Hartnett, R. T., *College and University Trustees: Their Backgrounds, Roles, and Educational Attitudes,* Princeton, N.J.: Educational Testing Service, 1969.

however, to extend the meaning of the word to include not just satisfaction with a bygone era but also satisfaction with the college in its *present* form. The first, the yearning for an older order, is to be found at institutions that have undergone change in the last twenty years or so; the second brand of nostalgia, which is really *status quoism*, would reside at colleges that have *not* changed appreciably in recent years. Manifestations of these two forms of nostalgia are probably about the same, and I shall not have anything more to say about the distinction between them.

We are talking here principally about faculty members and a kind of collective sentiment which abides at almost every college (indeed, in almost any kind of enduring organization). It can be seen at most faculty or department meetings—in the faces of men in their fifties and sixties who have devoted a lifetime to work in their field or to serving their college. It is when the college is considering some *new* program or function, in other words an innovation, that the nostalgia surfaces, in whatever form—shock, outrage, disbelief, stupefaction.

Only occasionally, it seems to me, do conservative perspectives on higher education get expressed in public any more; they are just not fashionable these days, Jacques Barzun and George Kennan notwithstanding.

Let me, however, take a few moments to try to distill out the main themes of nostalgic rightism, of which I see three: (1) the functions of higher education (or of a given college) ought not to change, which usually means expand; (2) the process of higher education, that is, of teaching, ought not to change; and (3) student activists ought not to be taken seriously.

In response to demands from the liberals that the colleges and universities assume new functions, there is the counter-demand that the university restrict itself to the ivory tower—to teaching or perhaps teaching and "scholarship" or "scholarly research." Barzun, in his recent book *The American University*, no doubt speaks for many faculty in the traditional academic fields when he denounces the university's increasing involvement in public service activities, likening, as he does, the modern university to a "public utility" and "a firehouse on the corner answering all the alarms."[11] Barzun's judgment is that "The new functions it (the university) has taken

---

[11] Barzun, J., *The American University: How it Runs and Where it is Going*, New York: Harper & Row, 1968.

on and the new methods it has improvised in a decade-and-a-half have torn apart the fabric of the former single-minded, easily defined university." Certainly the words of a purist.

In addition to "ivory-towerism," most individual colleges have their own particular traditions, adherence to which on the part of faculty serves to counteract various demands for change. Harold Hodgkinson has pointed out how what he calls the "myth of uniqueness," the belief among faculty that the college is in some way truly distinctive, can be an especially strong factor working against institutional reform.

Regarding the second theme, that of instructional process or method in higher education, Barzun's nostalgia also rings loud and clear. He stoutly defends the lecture system—properly, formally executed—and the master-pupil authority relationship in general. Barzun would also resist reforms in traditional course examination and grading systems. In arguing for preservation of traditional instructional procedures, I would guess that Barzun speaks for a majority of faculty members in American colleges and universities; and here, it seems to me, lie the seeds for a real battle in the 1970's: reform-minded students standing against tradition-minded faculty —to settle on what shall be learned and in what ways the learning shall take place.

Finally, there is the nostalgic academic's longing for students who come to the college *to study,* not to get involved in radical politics. or to reform the campus, or to smoke pot, or whatever. Mature scholars tend to regard students as immature, certainly not mature enough to share authority with adults in determining academic policy and practice. Attendance at college is considered a privilege; troublemakers should have the privilege revoked. Rational men also fault the student activists for their enthusiasm and emotionalism, their "transports of passion," in George Kennan's words. In his book, *Democracy and the Student Left,* Kennan upholds such campus virtues as calm, detachment, order and "good form."[12] And last, proper academic men are affronted by the personal styles and manners of the student hippies and radicals—their beards, flowing hair, outlandish costumes, public impulsivity, poor hygiene habits, lack of proper respect for age, and so forth.

---

12 Kennan, G. F., *Democracy and the Student Left,* New York: Harcourt, Brace & World, 1968.

In talking about nostalgia, at least a few words must be said about the alumni, who came to love their college, *as they knew it.* How can they help but be dismayed on knowing the college plans to go coed, or abolish compulsory chapel, or join a consortium of colleges, thus enabling sharing of faculty—one or all of which steps may be necessary if the college is to survive into the 1980's? No doubt a few college presidents, nostalgic themselves, are trying to stake the future of their nostalgia on the generosity of some number of nostalgic alumni. We should certainly wish them every success. Nicholas Von Hoffman in the October [1968] *Atlantic* quotes a member of the Harvard class of 1943:

Youth! *Agito ergo sum!* That's what they believe. Activist youth, short-sleeved shirts, open collars and closed minds; hobnailed boots and we shall overcome. All over the world it's the same, the same exhilaration of riding the wave of the future. These nineteen-year-olds need a good reaming.[13]

Nostalgia, yes; but also hatred. Perhaps so strong as to preclude support for *any* enterprise intended for youth.

The Upright Right

The far-right critics of higher education are first and foremost distinguished by their essential uprightness, their sense of strong moral rectitude, their strict regard for the right and the resolute. In contrast to many people across the land who are either uncertain about what is right and wrong or who are simply oblivious to common moral conventions, there is no doubt in the mind of the upright rightist about what is right, wrong, good and bad. Among the "goods" are old-fashioned Christianity, patriotism, law and order, parental authority, free enterprise and low taxes. Among the "bads" are Communists and other similar people, black activists, permissive college presidents, high taxes, and sex.

But there is more to it than moral certitude. People on the far right seem also to be frightened by nearly every new idea and event on the socio-cultural scene, believing that the values that they know to be right are being corrupted. More so than most other people, their minds are closed; they are indisposed to even *considering* the validity of alternative beliefs and behaviors. In short, the upright right is also uptight.

---

[13] Von Hoffman, N., "The Class of '43 is Puzzled," *Atlantic,* October 1968, p. 76.

How and where is pressure from the upright right finding expression these days? It is coming, of course, mainly from people and groups of people off campus, especially from politicians, newspaper editors and writers, and patriotic organizations. Most college presidents, I am sure, will also attest to sizeable reservoirs of uprightness among the parents of their students as well as among their alumni. Trustees? Again data from Hartnett: 22 per cent regarded themselves as "Conservative," rather than "Moderate" or "Liberal"; 40 per cent believed the administration should control the contents of the student newspaper; 69 per cent believed all campus speakers should be screened; 53 per cent supported loyalty oaths for faculty, and some 13 per cent said their views are very similar to those of Ronald Reagan (less than 2 per cent reported views like those of either George Wallace or Robert Welch).

To my knowledge, the far-right has no systematic programs for reconstructing higher education. Their demands are invariably counter-demands.

One recalls the events at Berkeley in late 1964 and the pressure put on Clark Kerr by, among others, the governor of the state, various state legislators and the editor of *The Oakland Tribune*; two years later, on the heels of Ronald Reagan's election, Kerr was ousted.

More recently the Eldridge Cleaver affair has stirred many of the forces on the California far-right. The regents of the university have censured the members of the newly created Board of Educational Development, under whose auspices Social Analysis 139X was set up, and they have also required that all plans for outside speakers who will speak more than once be cleared through President Hitch. Governor Reagan has proposed stricter controls on the authority of faculty to create new courses. The state legislature has become interested in defining or redefining academic freedom and its limits, including tenure provisions. Max Rafferty threatened every public school superintendent in the state, which would include the junior colleges, with loss of state aid if Cleaver were ever allowed to speak on their campuses.

Elsewhere around the Golden State, Governor Reagan described the events at San Francisco State College as an "insurrection," going on to say that "organized society cannot back down without giving up our rights; as long as I am governor we will not give up our rights."[14] Reagan and the state college trustees have agreed only with great reluctance to share authority with faculty and students in working out solutions for that battle-scarred college. In his State of the State speech (in early January) Governor Reagan dwelt mainly on what to do about the "criminal anarchists and latter-day fascists" on the campuses.[15]

In San Diego, the American Legion and the two conservative local newspapers have been calling for the outster of New Left theorist Herbert Marcuse. Nameless others have threatened his life.

At California State College at Fullerton, a controlled attendance presentation of the anti-Puritan play called *The Beard* touched off a furor that culminated in a hearing conducted in Fullerton by a committee from the state senate. State College Chancellor Dumke has said "that a number of legislators have said flatly that they will not tolerate outrages to the public decency" and "we've had it freely said in California (that) if they're going to put on plays like 'The Beard' . . . we just won't teach drama in the public institutions any more."[16]

Los Angeles Mayor Sam Yorty publicly charged that student demonstrations everywhere in California are being led by Communists, and he called for an investigation of radical student organizations by the House Un-American Activities Committee. (Shortly thereafter, HUAC chairman Ichord announced that his "first order of business would be to investigate" SDS.[17])

Therewith a sampling of the working of the uptight-upright mind in one state. It is at work throughout the country. George Wallace, with his attacks on "pointy-headed professors," captured the deep South and ran shockingly well elsewhere. There is nothing particularly new in the thunder from the right. I imagine most college presidents accept it as one of the natural phenomena on the political landscape. It grows louder as the forces for change grow bolder.

One development that is new, however, and which must be of immediate concern to college administrators, is the legislation that will deny federal financial assistance to any student "who has been convicted by any court of general jurisdiction" of a crime involving forceful disruption of a higher education institution. At least two

---

14 *San Francisco Chronicle*, December 13, 1968, p. 1.
15 *San Francisco Chronicle*, December 8, 1968, p. 1.
16 *U.S. News & World Report*, September 23, 1968, p. 52.
17 *San Francisco Chronicle*, January 13, 1968, p. 8.

states, Michigan and Ohio, have also passed laws having a similar intent. Can this sort of "reprisal legislation" be a portent of something rather more serious ahead?

Summary and Conclusions

In attempting an overview of demands being made on American colleges and universities by the political Left and Right, I have sorted the spectrum of competing parties into four categories labeled the Anarchist Left, the Reformist Left, the Nostalgic Right and the Upright Right.

I used the word anarchist because I think it correctly describes the kind of socio-political order sought by the people in the radical movement, or in what Theodore Roszak calls the "counter culture."[18] These "New Anarchists," who include New Leftists, hippies and others alienated from established authority, seek a revamped university in which the students, acting communally, can determine the nature of their educational and personal experiences. The counter culture appears to be expanding rapidly—out from cosmopolitan centers, up to affluent style-conscious people in their thirties and forties, and down into the teens and subteens.

Under the heading of Reformist Left, a number of rather disparate power blocks were considered, not all of which would themselves choose to be identified with the Left. Certain of the factions such as the black student groups and the AFT locals are making demands of a quite limited and self-interested nature, frequently employing disruptive tactics and other methods to which most academic professionals are unaccustomed. Reform-oriented student activists of all races, on the other hand, are and will continue to be pushing for reforms across a wide range of campus affairs—academic, non-academic and governmental. We will have to wait to see whether AAUP's move to further extend faculty participation in campus governance proves to be creative and maybe even magnanimous, rather than an effort to counter the growing strength of students in academic affairs. The influence of the great foundations seems now to touch on almost all the work of the university, and it is felt at many levels, up to and including the federal government. The

---

[18] Roszak, T., "Youth and the Great Refusal," *The Nation*, March 25, 1968. This is the first of four articles by Roszak on the "Counter Culture" appearing in successive issues of *The Nation*.

"foundation will," made known in civilized and convincing ways, is most certainly on the side of democratization and renewal throughout the higher education system.

The Nostalgic Right was said to be composed mainly of older professors, whose demands tend to be heard whenever the college is planning for innovation. Their nostalgia for an earlier condition, often in the shape of an ivory tower, or their desire to maintain the *status quo*, typically takes the form of opposition (1) to new functions for the institution, (2) to reform the educational (teaching) process, and (3) to giving students a meaningful voice in campus governance.

Finally, I depicted the Upright Right as spirited citizens and groups from off the campus—strong in moral certitude yet frightened that their values are being threatened—who can be counted on to demand that the college use all available means to preserve law and order, put down the revolutionaries and conspirators from the far-left, guard the students from subversive ideas, and protect everybody from affronts to their "public decency."

Toward the beginning I spoke of the need for a working theory of higher education. I cannot really say what such a theory could consist of. Certainly no coherent body of knowledge about treatments and outcomes is on the horizon. Perhaps the best we might expect in the foreseeable future would be a set of common understandings about very general purposes for the total system (which will be changing) and about some of the processes by which institutions may set policies in order to move in the desired directions.

In coming to a close, I would suggest that a working-theory-of-higher-education-for-our-times be premised in part on the assumptions, first, that great change is taking place throughout the fabric of American society and, secondly, that because of the very rapid change, there is bound to be tension and conflict in institutions of higher education, just as there is in other social institutions—the family, the church and so forth. The forces for change will be doing battle with the forces intent on maintaining the *status quo*. We are seeing it all around us.

With these assumptions, one surmises, then, that a critical ongoing task of college administrators is to facilitate resolution of conflicting interests and demands, to help competing factions reach accommodations. As the only ones on campus who are concerned for the well-being of the total institution, administrators, in short, should accept the fact of conflict and become experts in conflict resolution. Though hardly an exalted form of stewardship, and certainly not a form that should permanently characterize academic organizations, the role of administrator as conflict resolution expert seems an unavoidable one, given a quasi-revolutionary period and a nation that has limits on the amount of internal disorder and destruction it will tolerate.

In the absence of a body of knowledge about the whats, whys and hows of higher education, it behooves the leader-planner-conflict-resolution-expert to arrange for hearing all the voices that seek to be heard. One and all just may have something useful to contribute. Although participatory democracy is highly inefficient, it is highly humane, and the latter is the higher good. People who are alive, regardless of generation, or whether they are on the Left or the Right, will welcome the opportunity to participate in making decisions that affect their life and work. (The militant anarchists, of course, will *insist* on participation.)

Accepting the fact of conflict, rather than denying it or trying to quash it, could actually have a pay-off for the students who pass through the college. It can at least be argued that students who have been actively engaged in the conflict-resolution process should leave college better equipped to live, even prosper, in a society where change and conflict are the order of the day. But more immediately, haunted by the spectre of a demoralized San Francisco State College—where only about half the students were attending classes in 1969—one fears for the very survival of institutions that are unable to peaceably reconcile conflicting demands.

6

THE UNIVERSITY AND THE UNSTUDENT

IT STARTED, perhaps, at Berkeley, then moved through Chicago, Ohio State, Howard, Columbia, and eventually may spread to the most remote and least notable Podunk State and Private University. It is misnamed the Battle for Student Power; it should be called more correctly the War of the Unstudent.

This War of the Unstudent is distinguished by forceable occupations of college buildings in the name of free speech and by demands in the name of academic freedom to dictate university policy, from course content to the hiring and firing of professors, to where and whether buildings shall be erected, and to the rules or absence of them in dormitories. The struggle for power is not to assert student power as much as it is to demolish the power of the establishment; the resolve is not to replace one program with another, but to destroy the existing program. The deficiencies of the old order are detailed simply for they surround one, but the new order is explained only in the broadest terms: love, equality, justice, and flower power.

The roots of conflict in the university are ancient and honorable; they are centered in the struggle between the have-nots (students) and the haves (faculty), between those who have made it and those who are seeking to make it, between those who control destiny and

From *School & Society*, Oct. 26, 1968. Reprinted by permission of the author and the publisher. John F. Ohles is Associate Professor of Secondary Education, Kent State University, Kent, Ohio.

those in search of it. The teacher has the knowledge which the student must wrest from him. The institution selects the student, exerts control over him, establishes the means by which he progresses through the ritual, and elects finally whether he should receive the symbol of success, the academic degree. Within this context is the arena where complaints about academic requirements, course content, and quality of instruction are relevant.

A second area of relevant contention between students and the academic establishment is in the *in loco parentis* role of the institution. The enforcement of extended adolescence upon maturing and resisting adults has been expressed traditionally in escape out of (and entry back through) windows, in smuggled bottles, in panty raids, water fights, and the rest. If the students are amateurs in academic affairs, they are experts in their own needs for maturity and self-realization, in resistance to strictures against their adult independence.

But the War of the Unstudent is not represented in the traditional conflicts in institutions of higher education. A new development, mass education, is bringing into the college classroom greater numbers of those who had been excluded from the past academic scene. Increasing technology and extended requirements for admission into many vocations have brought new hordes onto college campuses; many of these new collegians have substituted vocational aims for academic curiosity, but most of them readily or hesitantly accede to the demands of institutional conformity.

Burgeoning enrollments also have increased the number of faculty, with an extended range of purpose and competence. Many of the new breed of professors are as unsure as the students of their relation to the establishment, the reason for their being, the means to their own self-realization. Some college instructors are allied more commonly with rebellious students than with their own colleagues. Occasionally, the students are made use of by faculty in the pursuit of power and status in the academic world. There are times, too, when students become pawns of administrators who are in conflict with the faculty. And there are times when the student becomes the tool of the non-student, who finds the campus an ideal place to further his particular crusade.

There is, finally, a larger proportion among today's students who are unstudents, those who enter the university without a commitment and who continue to wander through the academic halls only because of parental expectations, or social pressures, or as means of avoiding the draft or work or the responsibility of meeting the demands of the independent adult. Most questions about the motivation or dreams or expectations or behavior of the unstudent are unanswered; the only question that has a ready answer is whether he will accept the institution, its program, classrooms, professors, and administrators. The answer is no. The size of his roar must not obscure the fact that he numbers far fewer than five per cent of the student body. Even his hundreds in the multiversity are but a pittance among the tens of thousands.

The unstudent is the lost soul, once along skid row, but now with a place to sleep and an assured eating schedule; he is the hobo who wanders between those classes he does attend; he is the stowaway sailor who journeys on student junkets or drug-elicited "trips." But of all the kicks he seeks, none is more inviting, more rewarding, or more convenient than to shake the institution that shelters him. Society may be his enemy, but the institution at hand is his target.

The charming thing about many unstudents is that they are intelligent, frequently among the more intelligent of the student body. But intelligence is part of the problem, for the unstudent may ignore the books and cut classes and still compete academically. And the time that others consume in fighting to stay in the academic community he spends in bemoaning his existence, plotting his revenge, organizing his few supporters, and warring against the establishment.

In times past, the unstudent was likely to leave the campus for skid row, the lumber camp or migrant farm trail, or the life of the hobo or seagoing wanderer, or in the non-warring armed forces; and he often came back to the campus as a more mature student. But, today, the unstudent has fewer outlets; he may join the hippie colony, but here he still is subject to the draft and under public censure. He knows that there are few real means of escape; his options are limited. Having once left the campus, he may have difficulty in returning. His surest shelter is the university, where he may gain status and even extend his tenure if the institution surrenders to his demands and agrees to operate with the rules that he first extracts and is then free to amend. If he can bend the university to his will, he may find at least a partial solution to his problems. At any rate, he may enjoy that temporary satisfaction that comes from even a minor victory against society.

The role of higher education in reacting to the unstudent is not a simple one. It is, however, the task of the university to reject the non-student and to seek to sort out the legitimate complaints of the students from the irrelevant gripes of the unstudent. An unpleasant and difficult task, the job of sorting requires that complaints shall be specific, supported by evidence, and relevant. Above all, the university must establish reasonable and responsible avenues through which the screening of criticism takes place. The institution should exercise patience and require of itself and its students the acceptance of deliberate processes uninhibited by emotional excess. The university should identify the demands of the unstudent and, in large part, choose to ignore them. It reluctantly should meet his crude force with its judicious use of power. It can not permit him to run or to ruin the university.

That universities have problems in curriculum, teaching, and administration should be obvious to any serious onlooker. But it should be equally clear that to pursue the non-problems of the unstudents can only interfere with the resolution of the real problems of the students.

Universities exist solely for their students. They seek to protect the student from non-students, unstudents, and, sometimes, himself. The academic freedom that is bandied about so lightly and conveniently is, after all, freedom to learn rather than to teach or to administer. So that the student may freely learn, the professor is free to teach. And this freedom to learn requires that colleges and universities come swiftly to terms with the newest by-product of mass higher education, the confused and confusing unstudent. He is a new problem that must be solved swiftly, readily, sympathetically, humanely, and efficiently.

7

STUDENT UNREST IN PERSPECTIVE

W. H. COWLEY

PARENTS, professors, and politicians troubled by today's student unrest can take heart from the knowledge that collegians have been
ever thus. Full of vitality as yet unharnessed to the work of the
world, students have frequently rebelled against authority; and
sometimes they have become violent. In fact, violence has been fairly
frequent during the long history of higher education which extends
back in identifiable institutions to the founding of Plato's Academy
in 387 B.C.

The fourth century A.D. can be cited illustratively. Students who
disapproved of their professors' politics invaded their lecture rooms
and started fights, threw mud in their faces on the streets, and
dragged them out of bed to dunk them in any available body of
water. Because of this kind of behavior Augustine left the higher
school in Carthage where he taught and set himself up as a private
teacher in Rome, but he found conditions no better there. Youthful
Romans behaved just as riotously in and out of class and, to boot,
cheated him out of his fees.

During the Middle Ages students acquired extensive privileges by
means of riot and rebellion. In 1228, for example, the protest of
Parisian students over the price of wine precipitated a town-gown
battle in which the royal bodyguard killed several academics. This

From CTA Journal, March, 1966. Reprinted by permission of the author and the editor of
the CTA Journal. Copyright, 1966, by the California Teachers Association. W. H. Cowley
is David Jacks Professor of Higher Education, Stanford University, Stanford, Calif.

led both the faculty and the students of the University of Paris to leave the city en masse and to remain away for almost three years. Their absence caused such economic havoc that the king and the pope pled with them to return. A century later a tavern brawl in Oxford grew into a three-day pitched battle between students and townsmen, the toll being some fifty killed or missing in action.

Students acquired so much power in Italian universities that they fined professors if they arrived late, circumvented the lecture schedule, or failed to dismiss class on time. Indeed, it became customary for a student to be the administrative head of Italian universities from the thirteenth century until Napoleon's invasion of Italy late in the eighteenth.

Unrest has also been a characteristic of American academia since its earliest days. In the colonial colleges students frequently protested against the food served in commons and also against the paternalism of their clerical professors. At Yale, for instance, "students were wont to express their displeasure with their tutors by stoning their windows or attacking them with clubs if they chanced out after dark."

Thomas Jefferson sought to avert disturbances at the University of Virginia by entrusting discipline to a committee of student "censors," but soon after the opening of the University a protracted rebellion rived the idyllic air of Charlottesville. Three former presidents of the United States (Jefferson, Madison, and Monroe) sat at that time on the Virginia governing board. They had steered the new American nation through many storms, but they found recalcitrant students too much for them.

One other of many examples: I recently asked the Princeton University archivist for copies of some records of this period; he replied, "I can't send them to you because Nassau Hall has been burned down twice by students."

The refinement of American manners in general had much to do with the gradual tapering off of student violence, but perhaps even more important were the emergence of intercollegiate athletics and coeducation. Yet visceral unrest has not entirely disappeared as witness the highly publicized panty raids of the recent past. One occurred at the University of Denver in the Spring of 1964 and another at staid old Harvard two or three years earlier. The latter reversed the usual pattern: Radcliffe girls raided the Harvard dormitories. People hear little about such affairs today because a relatively new type of phenomenon has taken the front of the stage, namely, cerebral unrest, to which topic I now turn.

The emergence of the organized extracurriculum constitutes one of the most significant educational developments of the nineteenth century. Today we take it for granted, but few people know that extracurricular activities began as a form of protest: because of their intense dissatisfaction with their instruction students disengaged themselves from the curriculum and organized the extracurriculum. It has taken an uncountable number of forms, intercollegiate athletics being the most publicized. The latter began with a Harvard-Yale boat race in 1852, the first football game (Princeton vs. Rutgers) following seventeen years later. Immediately thereafter other kinds of athletics rapidly mushroomed, and so also did non-athletic enterprises.

Today the commonplace extracurriculum noticeably wanes, the essential reason being greater student involvement in the intellectual life of their colleges. Vastly improved methods of teaching have helped accomplish the change. So also have the phenomenal advances made in secondary education and the disturbed state of the world. Thus today's students are in general infinitely more serious-minded than their predecessors.

Many students are also idealists, and their unrest has cerebral rather than visceral roots. Discontented with educational institutions and with much about society at large, they have become vigorous activists, their activism taking two forms. The first seeks to ameliorate existing procedures in either or both the educational and public arenas; the second seeks substantially to reconstruct educational, political, and other social institutions.

I particularly want to stress the point that cerebral student activism has a long history too. Although Americans have been reading for many years about its eruptions in other countries, most people believe that until now nothing comparable has happened in the United States. I shall show this to be an erroneous conception.

Consider, first, the educational arena. The boredom that bred student visceral unrest provoked some serious-minded and imaginative students into cerebral activism: they organized societies devoted to extracurricular intellectual development and camaraderie, and these in time facilitated changes in official practices and programs.

Student societies sponsored debating, the communal ownership of important books unheeded in their courses, the writing of papers for reading at their meetings, and the carrying on of modest scientific investigations. Well under way by the late eighteenth century, the ventures in self-education did a good deal more for many students than their formal studies. To illustrate, the Lyceum of Natural History, founded in 1835 by eight Williams students, cultivated the neglected sciences there; and at Dartmouth during the same period the two student literary brotherhoods owned more books (more than 16,000) than the College itself (fewer than 15,000).

The heyday of student literary and scientific groups ended about a century ago in part because fraternities, athletics, and other new-type extracurricular activities began to absorb the interests of the great majority of students and in part, to quote Professor Frederick Rudolph of Williams College:

The colleges themselves took over some of their old purposes; built up broader collections of books, opened the libraries more than once a week, introduced respectable study in English literature, discovered history as a field of study, expanded the sciences.

In short, student educational activism helped facilitate the modernization of American colleges which began about a century ago; and the same generalization can be made about the efforts of students during the 1920's to help make education equal to the demands of this century.

Barnard College students opened that chapter during the academic year of 1921-1922. The following from a report written by a group of them epitomizes its spirit:

Are college students persons, or are they pupils? Most colleges treat them as pupils. But in some places they seem to be demanding admission to the human race. Barnard College has a group of candidates for such a standing. The Student Curricular Committee has made public a curriculum worked out by the students which they have asked the faculty to consider as a possible substitute for the present course of study.

This initial student report had little effect at Barnard, but two years later it provided the senior editor [W. H. Cowley] of *The Daily Dartmouth* with the subject for a dynamic editorial campaign. Hammering away persistently at the defects of his alma mater, he badgered Dartmouth's president to appoint a committee of twelve seniors to make "a complete survey, review and examination of [the College's] educational processes." After several months of reading, visitation of other colleges, and serious reflection, the committee produced a printed document which had wide influence. As a result of it being quoted and commented upon by newspapers and journals of opinion, a score of other institutions within the next few years established similar student groups.

These committees also published reports which helped faculties and administrators to understand student opinion. Many of them, like the Dartmouth statement, bore immediate curricular and related fruit. The most important yield, however, ripened at Harvard: during the intervening forty years the Harvard Student Council has produced about a dozen printed reports, each on a specific educational issue. They have been a continuing channel of student-faculty communication. This helps explain, I believe, why Harvard disorders are generally milder than those at many other institutions.

The student educational activism of the past has been almost entirely ameliorative; but currently much of it, in contrast, is fervently reconstructive. Like some faculty members, they propose that educational institutions be rebuilt from the ground up. They urge— nay, demand—that boards of trustees be abandoned or manned only by faculty members and students and that administrators be limited to such functions as providing debating forums, abundant parking places, and janitorial service. The legal structure of American education together with the inescapable necessity of administrative leadership, however, preclude, I feel certain, the adoption of their basic reconstructive formulas.

More must be said later about the educational arena. Meanwhile student activism on public issues needs to be put in perspective.

American students began to take positions on public questions during the Revolution. The nine colonial colleges enrolled only about a thousand students, but most of them forthrightly expressed their nationalistic convictions. Alexander Hamilton, for example, began his prodigious career as a student orator; and he and his associates were involved in driving out of the country the Tory president of King's College (now Columbia).

In turn, for about forty years prior to the Civil War, students North and South agitated on the issue of slavery. Oberlin College in particular developed into a dedicated abolitionist center with its own underground railroad, and at least one of its students died in a Southern prison.

After Appomattox student interest in public affairs took milder forms. Yale undergraduates in 1887, for instance, established the Yale Assembly for the purpose of discussing political and social problems. One of its organizers, Gifford Pinchot, later became a pivotal leader of the conservation movement and governor of Pennsylvania.

Soon after the turn of the century outside organizers moved into the colleges to enlist in their causes the nation's youthful elite. The first such group, the Intercollegiate Socialist Society, had its inception in New York City in 1905 under the leadership of Upton Sinclair. His associates included Clarence Darrow and Jack London, the latter of whom had just become famous because of his novels and short stories. Large numbers of students admired him; and traveling across the country, he established chapters at virtually every major institution which attracted not a few gifted students. To name three: Walter Lippmann during 1910-1911 headed the Harvard chapter; Louis Mumford belonged to the CCNY chapter; and Norman Thomas began his socialist career as a Princeton undergraduate.

World War One curbed the American socialist movement, the extreme left creating the Socialist Labor Party (Communist), the great majority of the members of the ISS moving back to traditional American political positions. The League for Industrial Democracy, its new name since the early twenties, continues to function. Other organizations, however, have become more important.

The ISS appears to have been the first invasion of the campus by outside socio-political groups—but not the last. During the booming twenties students by and large had no more interest in the state of the world than did most of their elders. Then came the depression. I lived through its uproars as a faculty member and administrator at Ohio State University, and I observed the students there during the turmoils of the thirties. Beyond doubt, outsiders helped foment protest movements. In any case, on April 12, 1934, high school and college students across the country rebelled in a peace strike against war. They repeated it exactly a year later and again in 1936 when half a million students participated.

During this period students protested not only against war but also against the underprivileged status of unions, child labor, and in particular the sorry state of Negro civil rights. Then, as now, youthful idealists bridled against social injustice.

I do not want to overstress the importance of outside organizers. They have long been active on campuses; but many students have perennially been discontented with the state of the world and have organized themselves. It would be surprising, however, if external propagandists did not invade the campus in the present situation.

On non-military issues the student clamors of the thirties probably had some effect, but the Peace Movement did not hamper the war against the Fascist powers; and at its end the G.I. Bill of Rights deluged the colleges with several million veterans. Some of us expected that these much-matured students would be so critical of existing methods of instruction and the onrushing research emphasis of faculty members that they would rise in rebellion. We were very much mistaken. Everybody predicted a depression, and the veterans were out to acquire their degrees and find jobs before it struck. A period of apathy resulted—the so-called Silent Generation. Then in 1960 the lid blew off again.

Much more complex than in earlier periods, current student activism thrusts into both the academic and public domains. Many of its leaders, moreover, operate simultaneously in both. Their ameliorative as distinguished from their reconstructive criticisms have clearly been productive and, in my judgment, largely sound. Thus student fault-finders have made administrators and faculty members face up to the abounding impersonalism that has come to characterize higher education, the inadequacy of many teaching procedures, the devastations of the publish-or-perish syndrome, the urgent need of establishing better methods of student participation in institutional policy-making.

In these and other academic matters ameliorative activism has been a boon, and the same generalization can be made about ameliorative activities in the public arena. The students who have joined the Peace Corps or the Poverty Corps and who, while still enrolled in college, work with underprivileged children and youths get relatively little newspaper publicity; but their numbers and effectiveness probably surpass those of the reconstructionists. Both groups, however, have helped arouse the nation's conscience concerning a number of crucial social inequities.

What about the future? It seems to me that the events of the past make several predictions reasonable. First, student activism will continue to be a fact to reckon with. Second, visceral unrest will on occasion emerge but, in the United States at least, will seldom

express itself violently. Third, student criticism of educational practices will be increasingly recognized as a valuable resource and will
be facilitated by better channels of faculty-student communication.
Fourth, during troublous times student idealists will take stands on
public issues; and their ameliorative ideas which win popular support will be productive. Fifth, when these youthful Utopians join
the ranks of those past thirty whom they now disdain, they—like so
many of their predecessors—will either become important members
of progressive movements or pessimistic reactionaries.

8

CAMPUS ACTIVISM AND UNREST

JAMES E. ALLEN, JR.

THE COLLEGE COMMENCEMENTS of 1968 had taken place in the glare of a spotlight. They were the focus of the attention not only of graduates, parents, and others directly involved, but of a public mindful of the widespread turmoil and tension.

The excessive manifestations that had generated much of this attention are regrettable, not only in themselves, but because they obscure and distort the more constructive aspects of today's unrest. Most commencement speeches have been tempered by these times, whether the speaker sees harm or hope in the developing trends.

There have been strong reactions of disgust, pessimism, almost despair. But underlying the increasing activism on our college campuses is a lively stirring, a sense of change within the academic community that, in its potential for a revitalization of our higher educational institutions, justifies a hopeful feeling of expectancy about the future.

One reason for optimism can be be found in the very nature of a commencement speech appropriate for today's graduating classes. In the past, a speech loyal to tradition would rely heavily upon the two elements of commendation and exhortation. It has been felt that one of the main responsibilities of the commencement speaker was

From *School & Society*, Oct. 26, 1968, and based on a commencement address, Manhattan College, New York City, June 9, 1968. Reprinted by permission of the author and the publisher. James E. Allen, Jr., wrote this address when he was New York State Commissioner of Education. He now is U. S. Commissioner of Education and Assistant Secretary of Health, Education, and Welfare for Education.

to urge graduates to put behind them the carefree days of youth, to leave the happy halls of academe, and to go forth into the world to begin the serious business of life. To speak so today would be a gross misreading of the temper of the young, ridiculous, indeed almost insulting, in the fact of a generation whose members very early are acknowledging an obligation for participating in the real concerns of man's search for dignity and meaning in life. While such a setting does not alter my conviction substantially that the commencement speaker is the least essential ingredient of the occasion, it does provide the inspiration of trying to be worthy of the seriousness of purpose already shown by the graduates.

The seriousness of purpose of today's college students is already, and will be increasingly, a major factor in shaping change both within and without the college or university. As more and more students have become more and more impatient with policies and attitudes that they feel deny expression of both their aims and their abilities, they have begun to seek new ways of expressing themselves and of finding means for direct participation in affairs of their concern. Thus, we are witnessing a degree of student activism, relatively new in this country, which has generated a sense of "student power" that will make itself strongly felt not only on the campus, but in all aspects of society.

It is not my intention to deal with the more aggressive manifestations of student unrest, except to say that worthiness of purpose can not be used to justify or excuse violent, excessive, and destructive forms of protest. What is of more significance in the student activism now taking so many different forms is that it is a part of an awareness of the world and its place in that it characterizes the younger generation of today. This is, in my opinion, a great younger generation despite some of the far-out ways they choose for self-expression, and commendation in a commencement speech is a tradition that has even greater relevance than before.

In attempting objectively to evaluate and understand the new student activism and to anticipate its future development, it may be helpful to consider some of the reasons why this movement should be taking place now. Certainly, one of the basic reasons is the fact that this is a generation whose members have grown up with the knowledge that constantly hanging over their heads is the very real possibility of man's self-destruction. While this knowledge has generated a certain amount of cynicism, its stronger effect has been the creation of a sense of urgency.

Motivating young people also is the character of the times. Man's age-old problems of attempting to manage his environment and to humanize his relationships have attained in this age a magnitude and a complexity that no longer will allow delay and indecision. The much more difficult human problems now are rapidly superseding those of mere material advance. The imperative need to deal with such problems and the possibility of finding solutions that offer real hope for the betterment of mankind's lot have a strong appeal to the idealism of youth.

Another powerful factor in producing student activism at this juncture is an environment that has nourished earlier competence and independence. Social customs and educational and parental influences have made this a time when there is opportunity for achieving maturity at an earlier age. Never have young people had greater freedom to move about, to express themselves, to make their own personal decisions. Earlier exposure to adult problems and experiences has produced a degree of youthful sophistication not prevalent in past generations. Transportation and communications, bordering on the instant, have given youth broad horizons which qualify them as citizens of the world, both in experience and in knowledge.

It is not surprising, then, that the greater awareness of themselves and their world, and the better preparation for coping with the problems they identify, which mark this younger generation, should have produced also a deep disillusionment and a restless impatience which are among the most compelling reasons for activist behavior. Eager for revolutionary change and the immediate correction of long-standing social ills and injustices, concerned young people have little tolerance for what they consider to be the failure of our traditional institutions to "get with it" and to adapt to change. They also have a profound distrust of conventional values and a supreme disdain for the gap between the preaching and the practice, the saying and the doing, which they see all too often in the private and public lives of their elders.

Most of the reasons for student activism have sufficient validity and substance to make reasonable the forecast that the movement will gain rather than diminish in force. With increasing emphasis on its constructive aspects, this is a development which will result in renewed vitality and relevance for our colleges and universities. It also will help to revitalize our society and bring about more quickly the improvements and the new directions that are needed so desperately.

The picture of the graduating class as standing on the threshold of life is today an anachronism. The boundaries of the campus now, in reality, encompass the world, for the students there already are involved so much in the practical affairs and real concerns of life beyond the academic.

With so much of the business of America and the world still unfinished—and with so much barely started—it is heartening indeed to observe that perhaps the greatest awareness of this unfinished business exists in the young. Look at their activities, listen to their talk, read their writings and it will be very clear that their attention is focused on the areas where man's failures and shortcomings are most conspicuous. Peace, poverty, urban decay, segregation of races, the quality of our education system—these are the kinds of issues and problems that speak to the spirit of the young and that are bringing them forth into the fray.

With exhortation of youth then not needed as it once was, the commencement speaker is free to direct his words of exhortation elsewhere. The previous reference to unfinished business gives a clue as to the proper recipients—obviously the older generation. It is we who need to be stirred, and the stirring must take place in two simultaneous ways. The first is, of course, the arousal to a greater effort to deal with the business before us, to change attitudes, to throw off inhibiting traditions, and to be willing to experiment and explore new methods and directions. Old dogs can learn new tricks, especially when survival is at stake.

But of even greater importance is the need to concentrate on ways of helping the young to realize the potential of their new sense of purpose and spirit of activism. This involves intensive efforts—far greater than yet evidenced—to provide full opportunity for first-rate education. It also places upon our colleges and universities the obligation to examine their policies and practices and to make those adjustments necessary for the proper exercise of student participation.

Wisdom, understanding, and, above all, patience will be essential, for in force, character, and degree, the present student activism is a relatively new experience in our country. There is, however, much historical precedent that should help in assessing and understanding our current situation. In other nations, the power of students long has been a factor in both the inner life of the universities and in the effect of youth upon political and social development.

Bologna, the first of our western universities, was an institution of students, and the difficulty experienced there in the adjustment of citizens and students to each other still is reflected in the overtones of the phrase "town and gown." The University of Paris was a university of masters—and there are many other examples of a structuring of university life that has given much more say to both students and faculty, allowing them a more influential role in both policy and administration.

Student influence can be seen also as a major factor in political developments, such as the Revolutions of 1848 in Germany and Austria, in the fall of Tsarist Russia, in movements for national independence for developing areas. In nations where education has been limited to a small proportion of the population, students often have spearheaded progress with advocacy for modern ideas of liberty, socialism, industrialization, and equality of opportunity. Seen in this perspective, it is surprising that a widespread, determined drive for greater student power has been so long in coming in this country.

An attitude of flexibility and objectivity is essential in considering this new activism and its present and future effects. But such an attitude is made difficult because of the unfortunate excesses that have occurred in these first, probing efforts to find means of effective participation. It is, however, the special role of elders to maintain perspective, to look beyond the immediate crisis, and to chart a course that will lead to emphasis upon the constructive aspects of a movement that holds so much potential for good.

It will be a grievous failure on the part of the older generation if we allow support of constructive potential to be sidetracked because of our rightful disavowal of the violent and disruptive tactics which have been used. Reaction to these tactics already has produced a demand for repressive measures, and this demand likely will grow in strength and fervor. But we must not be stampeded into hasty, ill-considered action, framed in reference to the immediate, with too little consideration of the possible long-range detrimental effects upon all the inherent principles, values, and goals of education.

While the recent disruptions are most serious and can not be dismissed lightly, there is a certain wisdom in the words of Russell Lynes, who suggests that "the trouble with so many of the middle-aged is they are shocked by the wrong things, the superficial extravagances of youth with which youth intentionally baits them".

Despite their generally greater seriousness of purpose, the members of today's generation are not without their own kind of frivolity and caprice, and, as is most natural, find a certain wry pleasure and satisfaction in the tug-of-war across the generation gap. But the truly significant thing concerning them is that, while they may be extravagant, they are strikingly free of superficiality. As the older generation, our task, in faithfulness both to ourselves and to our hopes for the future, is to respect the seriousness of purpose of the younger generation and to do everything in our power to achieve a coming together of the drive of youth and the experience of age.

Jean Piaget, one of the world's foremost psychologists, states his ideas of the goals of education in the following terms:

> The principal goal of education is to create men who are capable of doing new things, not simply of repeating what other generations have done—men who are creative, inventive and discoverers. The second goal of education is to form minds which can be critical, can verify, and not accept everything they are offered. The great danger today is of slogans, collective opinions, ready-made trends of thought. We have to be able to resist individually, to criticize, to distinguish between what is proven and what is not. So we need pupils who are active, who learn early to find out by themselves, partly by their own spontaneous activity and partly through materials we set up for them; who learn early to tell what is verifiable and what is simply the first idea to come to them.

These are, I believe, valid goals, and, judged in such terms, the student unrest is not, as many people feel, a failure of our educational system, but rather an evidence of its success. Much of the difficulty of adjustment being encountered by the older generation stems from a contradiction between our willingness to endorse such goals for education and our unwillingness to accept the results of achieving them. So, rather than challenging youth, it is they who are challenging us, and it is a most heartening and hopeful situation when exhortation is more needed by age than by youth.

In a report of the Trustees of Manhattan College to the Regents of the University of the State of New York for the year 1867-68, when the college's enrollment was 57, it was stated that "the trustees have adopted no statutes or by-laws, but have relied on the President and his associates for the progress of the students and the maintenance of order." Even then, this was, in reality, no small task, but how simple it seems when measured against the magnitude, the scope, the diversity of the higher education enterprise today. Reliance for the orderly progress of both students and institution no longer can be so easily, or so narrowly, placed. The importance of higher education to society demands the understanding, attention, and the dedication of students, faculty, administration, and the public.

In ways that are fundamental and serious—despite the more evident, highly regrettable, excesses of expression—it is the students of today, who, in their understanding, their attention, and dedication, are leading the way. In their awareness of a responsibility to get on with the "unfinished business" of bettering mankind's lot, they are shaming the lethargy, the apathy, the blindness that so tragically has limited the efforts of my generation.

They envision a world that can be better not just for a favored few, but for the waiting many. They call for and deserve our support. I hope we shall not fail them.

9

SCRATCHING THE SURFACE:
CAMPUS UNREST IN 1968

EDWARD D. EDDY

IF ONE TALKS at any length with the chief executives of our nation's colleges and universities, he soon uncovers a mood of gloom and occasional despair. Indeed, the despair borders on outright fear in some cases. There is a disturbing tendency to think of one's self in the grip of forces about which one can do very little.

The American campus is presently a humorless place. This absence of humor, more than any other factor, led us to assemble recently a group of leading educators on the Chatham College campus. For two full days we talked about the situation in which we find ourselves and about the immediate future of higher education in this nation. The Chatham conference included seven presidents, the heads of the American Association of University Professors and the Association of American Colleges, several psychiatrists who work with students, an urban planner, three representative students, and four foundation officials, among others.

What I report here is a kind of consensus of that group, tempered by my own convictions. It is difficult to say exactly where the conference stops and I start. This is a fusion—and probably a confusion—of ideas.

From *School & Society*, January, 1969, and based on a commencement address, Keuka College, Keuka, N. Y., June, 1968. Reprinted by permission of the author and the publisher. Edward D. Eddy is President, Chatham College, Pittsburgh, Pa.

One can not and should not begin such a campus analysis without a clear statement of the firm faith and confidence which all of us hold in the great majority of American college students. It is unfortunate that this must be stated—but it is well to do so since there are a great many Americans today, including some of those who write and interpret the news, who do not share this confidence. Those of us who have the privilege of working with college students and who can claim some right to perspective do not question a common faith in the majority.

Obviously, there is a small minority of students clearly bent on the destruction of the university in America in order that a new type of institution may arise in its place. Their success at Columbia University in bringing about change has given them an awesome strength for which they are not prepared. We must listen to them, of course. The difficulty is that it is hardest to hear and to understand when the noise gets loudest. This destructive minority has no clear idea of the kind of new institution which must emerge from the rubble. It is content to tear down and only then to build anew.

Most students are not substantially different from what the majority of college students always have been—with some important exceptions. The students today are more concerned because the times demand concern. They are humorless because the times do not make one laugh. They are better students generally because the stakes are higher.

But the tendency among the majority to listen to, if not follow, the lead of the minority is clearly evident. The minority *must* be heard, of course. It must not be squelched or we cut out our own tongues, too. And, we must admit, without any sense of begrudging, it is exactly in keeping with the American tradition—from the American Revolution to the present day.

Students today are saying different things—and they are saying them differently. Like it or not, we are forced to adjust to their rapidly changing ways of coping with ambiguities. It matters little that we would not have chosen necessarily to say what they say—or in the manner they say it. We are not the ones who are growing up this year.

Some of the language which they use is rhetoric. The word "demand" sometimes sounds amazingly similar to the "please" of yesterday. If we merely bristle at its stridency, we also merely block communications.

On the one hand, they are saying "Leave us alone"; on the other hand, and perhaps no more than two minutes later, they cry out "Help us." It is the old ambivalence of adolescence, but it is more dramatic, more urgent than ever before. It contains within it an inconsistency with which we must be willing to live—and to which we must be willing to adapt our institutions. We do a disservice to the nation if we expect consistency from students when we ourselves do not have it in ourselves. The very hand that snatches and burns a book of regulations within 24 hours may be dialing the college dean to ask for immediate help.

As one president put it, "One day a student will come to me saying, 'We are not doing enough for the people in poverty areas. We must do more, whatever the cost.' And the next day the same student will come back to complain that the parking lot should be built nearer to the new dormitories." And a university professor spoke of the rational man's ability to live with irrationality, and the inconsistent man's ability to live with the inconsistencies of others and not be lost by it.

It is not enough, by any means, to say that the campus unrest in 1968 is a passing phase. Our conference agreed that the end of the period of deep student unrest is nowhere in sight. For a long time to come, since colleges and universities as social institutions are slow to change, the students are likely to be strident in their several demands.

They will seek personal identity because they need it in themselves and they need it as citizens of a mass called a nation. They will seek it in the giants of Columbia and Berkeley because it is not there. And they will seek it in tiny places such as Chatham and Haverford because it too often, too soon is taken for granted. They will seek it in a spirit of self-pity which will turn the elders against them, and they will seek it in honesty which the elders may not recognize always.

Their second demand will be couched in more angry tones, less sentimental because it is without self-pity. They will seek involvement in everything which touches their lives—in the university, the nation, the world. And they will meet with continuing frustration because the results will not be always what they wish.

Let me offer one illustration of a possible and very real source of frustration: the direction of the 1968 political campaign—with its terribly tragic and comic stumbling forward and backward. The heroes of the students have been shot down or cut out. And they tell us that they tried to affect change through the normal process of political participation—but it did not work.

As a third point, these students will continue to seek relevance. This is a strangely popular word which is difficult to define. On some campuses, the word "meaning" is substituted as easily. Both relevance and meaning are aimed at the kind of educational experience in both its academic and social aspects which fits the needs of these students in *their* time, not ours. They will continue to tell us that dormitory curfew hours are anachronistic and that many aspects of *in loco parentis* are from another age, if not another planet. But parietal rules and pot will not hold the student interest very long. This is "Mickey Mouse" compared to the emerging central issue.

The greatest student discomfort in terms of lack of relevance is with the curriculum and methods of teaching. Many students feel that their teachers are out of touch with the major issues of the second half of the 20th century.

They are angry at what we have done—the injustice to the black man and the hidden wells of intolerance, the murders of two Kennedys, the devouring conflict in Vietnam which prevents the nation from righting itself before it tries to right others. And they want their college experience to prepare them to do a better job of leadership. Anything, they say, will be better.

This leads me to the conclusion that the ultimate confrontation on the college campus will not be between administrators and students, but between faculty members and students. The students point to the sources of chief satisfactions of the majority of faculty members—and they note that student contact, the supposed raison d'etre of the American university, is not even in the upper half of the list.

One student at our conference was asked why the students continue to pick on administrators. He gave the delightful reply that you can count on their being in their offices from 9 a.m. to 5 p.m., whereas one never can find a faculty member. And the students are concerned that the faculty member who is first to protect the Students for a Democratic Society in its quest for power on the campus also is often the first to tell the students to stay away from a reexamination of the curriculum. His radical liberalism for the student world stands in sharp contrast to the protective preservation of the status quo within the curricular world. Thus, we conclude that the future portends a distinct possibility of a flow of responsibility *away* from the faculty and *to* the student in a number of academic matters.

But this is only one of many major changes in the structure of higher education which appear to be both necessary and inevitable. Two probabilities emerge from a host of projected changes. First of all, the American university may have to abandon the idea of a self-contained university community which is unified within and separated from the outside world. This encompasses those who teach and those who learn. The chances are that the distinctions will be less well-drawn. The student may become accepted as a "junior partner," rather than a recipient of the wisdom which overflows.

The changes will be radical in organization, in grading, in the length and type of the academic year, and in methods of teaching. The elm-shaded tranquility of the college campus is already a pleasant remembrance of the past. The militant student and the Dutch elm disease have combined to render it obsolete.

Thus, the second probability is the necessity in America to accept controversy as a part of the academic way of life. The acceptance of controversy does not mean the condoning of physical force. It means, instead, an understanding of the sometimes subtle difference between violence and violent argument. This will not be the kind of campus community which we loved for its quiet respect of ideas. It will be a strident, bursting forth of controversy in an eager, tumbling, knock-down quest for ultimate truth.

And such a quest in such a manner will be hardest of all for alumni, parents, and the public to accept and understand. The advice to "throw the bums out" only will succeed in multiplying the bums. This is neither a sensible answer to a deeply rooted problem nor any kind of permanent solution. In the first place, these are not "bums" and, in the second place, only armchair strategists could reach such conclusions.

Nevertheless, the going will not be easy. We will continue to be plagued by the tendency to personalize human differences. We will be plagued by those who would change a reasonable argument into a vindictive individual attack. It will behoove us to stress the effective separation of people from ideas. If we tolerate personal attack, we run the very real danger of putting all the emphasis on the particular event rather than on its history. We will have lost the opportunity to stand back and look at what we are doing.

Perhaps our best solution to many of the problems of students and of society is to come to grips with reality: Might it not be time to give full adulthood in our society at the age of 18? This would include not just voting and drinking and other so-called "privileges" of citizenship, but the authority to sign contracts, to make agreements, to act as one's own agent. If this could be effected, then students might be accepted as adult members of the academic community who would be subject to the full civil law. Colleges would be relieved of any function bordering on the concept of *in loco parentis*.

The student must be regarded as a person of ability and responsibility. To accomplish this in its most subtle aspects, one returns to the crucial factor in higher learning: the quality of the relationship between student and teacher. It is this factor which may succeed in preserving some of the better small colleges of our nation—because they are adaptable; because they stress individuality, both in its personal form and in its institutional form; because they offer participation to the student as a member of a community which has a chance at relevance and meaning. If the small college can not respond to the challenge of 1968, it has no business staying in business.

The goals of higher learning run parallel to those of the contemporary student—at least the goals of undergraduate education in its best form. There yet may be an ultimate coming together if we do not lose our faith in either young people or in the institutions which society has developed to insure human progress.

George Kennan recently said, "Ours is indeed a partially sick society, and I yield to none of these extremists in the sense of the need for immediate diagnosis and treatment. We have not even scratched the surface."

The students have begun to scratch the surface. We must not be guilty of the kind of pride and protectiveness which says that the scratching is not ours to heed.

10

HYPOTHESES OF STUDENT UNREST

S. L. HALLECK, M.D.

STUDENTS no longer can be taken for granted. It does not matter that a great majority of students remain largely content, conservative and apathetic. A determined minority of restless college students have forced us to examine and sometimes change institutions, rules, and values which were once considered inviolate.

The most significant aspects of student unrest can be described as follows:

1. Some students reject the political and economic status quo and are making vigorous attempts to change the structure of our society. These are the student activists.
2. Some students reject the values of their society as well as the values of their own past and are developing a style of life which is contradictory to the Western ethics of hard work, self denial, success and responsibility. These students sometimes participate in efforts to change the society but for the most part they are withdrawn and passive. They can be described as alienated.
3. Both activist and alienated students tend to come from affluent, middle or upper-class homes. They are sensitive and perceptive individuals. They are also highly intelligent.
4. Both activist and alienated students have difficulty in relating

Address presented to the 23rd National Conference on Higher Education, Chicago, Ill., March 4, 1968, sponsored by the American Association for Higher Education. Used by permission of the author and the executive secretary of the association. Copyright, 1968, by the American Association for Higher Education. S. L. Halleck, M.D., is Professor of Psychiatry, University of Wisconsin, Madison.

to the adult generation. They are articulate, irreverent, humorless and relentless in their contempt for what they view as adult hypocrisy. Such youth are highly peer-oriented. They turn to one another rather than their parents when shaping their belief systems or when seeking emotional support.

5. Alienated students and, to a lesser extent, activist students find it difficult to sustain goal-directed activity. Their capacity to organize for any kind of action is limited. They often fail at work or school. Even their political efforts seem highly disorganized.

6. Alienated students live at the edge of despair. Although they seem at times to be enjoying life, there is always a sense of foreboding about them. Often they become depressed and suicidal. Activist students are more emotionally stable but are also prone to deep feelings of hopelessness and self-pity.

There is no dearth of explanations of the above phenomena. Some explanations seem to be based on opinions which support the prejudices of differing political view points. Others are more scientific and are presented with analytic objectivity. No hypothesis thus far advanced can be considered a sufficient explanation of student unrest. At best, each is only a partial explanation which sheds only a small light upon a highly complex phenomena.

Certain propositions often made about students are not hypotheses but are value judgements. The unsupported statement that the behavior of our restless youth represents a healthy and sensible response to the corruptions of our world is exhortative rather than explanatory. Such a position is embraced by those who are discontent with the status quo and wish to emphasize and exploit student restlessness as a phenomena that justifies their own grievances. Similarly, unsupported statements that students are more emotionally disturbed than they used to be have no explanatory value. Implying that students act as they do because they are mentally ill serves to demean their behavior by casting doubts upon the validity of the messages which that behavior is designed to communicate.

A more interesting proposition concerning student unrest is that it is neither new nor exceptional. Precedents can be sighted which suggest that there were times in our history when students were even more restless than they are now. Periods of unrest do seem to run in cycles and it is conceivable that we happen to be in an active phase of a predictable cycle. This proposition is reassuring to those who look forward to a quiet future. Its weakness, however, is that it assumes that those forces which make for cyclical behavior will remain relatively constant. My own opinion is that the world is changing so rapidly that using historical precedents to predict future behavior is a risky business. We can deplore student unrest or we can welcome it, but we cannot ignore it nor simply wait for it to go away.

Critical Hypothesis

Those who are critical of student activism and alienation are most likely to seek its causes in factors which they believe have created a moral weakness in our youth. They believe students are restless because they lack discipline, values or purpose. These deficiencies are believed to originate within the disturbed family, particularly that family which has been influenced by affluence, liberal thinking and modern psychological notions of child rearing. While these hypotheses may also appeal to those who are sympathetic toward students they are primarily critical in the sense that they imply that something is wrong with those students who protest or withdraw.

The Permissiveness Hypothesis

Perhaps the commonest explanation of student unrest is that it is the result of too much permissiveness in rearing children. The proponents of this view argue that some parents have, through painstaking efforts to avoid creating neuroses in their children, abdicated their responsibility to teach and discipline their children. In so doing they have reared a generation of spoiled, greedy youth who are unable to tolerate the slightest frustration without showing an angry or infantile response.

Although the permissiveness hypothesis has been used in the most crude manner to berate and deplore the behavior of youth, it cannot be lightly dismissed. There is considerable evidence that activist and alienated students are members of well educated families, deeply committed to liberal doctrines. In such homes children are given unusual freedom to criticize, debate and question. Restless students also have frequently attended primary and secondary schools dedicated to the ideal of progressive education, schools which in their efforts to maximize freedom and creativity seek to minimize discipline and frustration.

It can, of course, be argued that children raised in permissive homes will be better citizens than those raised in stricter homes. Restless students do seem to be more open to ideas, more involved with social issues and more flexible than their peers. The critics, however, can point to other characteristics of restless students which seem to be related to their permissive upbringing, and which are not so salutory. The response of such students to discipline, for example, is in no useful sense, adaptive. Arbitrary regulations enrage them. Even rational forms of discipline, such as the need to master basic concepts before moving on to more abstract ideas bother them. Restless students also react inappropiately when their demands are not immediately accepted. They are prone at such moments to protest violently, to give up and withdraw or to wrap themselves in a cloak of despair. Much of their abrasiveness and much of their ineffectiveness can be explained by their uncompromising demands for immediate gratification. This inability to tolerate frustration or delay must be considered a weakness or defect.

The Responsibility Hypothesis

Many who are concerned about the dangers of permissiveness also believe that our culture has been "psychologized" to an extent where youth become unwilling to assume responsibility for their own behavior. The expansion of the social and psychological sciences has confronted the public with elaborate deterministic explanations of behavior. When a behavior is totally explained, there is a tendency for people to act as though they are no longer responsible for that behavior. They confuse the theoretical issue of scientific determinism with the society's practical needs to have its citizens remain accountable for their own actions.

When the sociologist documents the impact of poverty and discrimination upon Negro youth he is conducting a logical and scientific exercise. The subjects of his research, however, are tempted to utilize his findings to support an individual and collective feeling of responsibility. The Negro adolescent who participates in a riot for example might say, "How could I do otherwise? I am moved by forces over which I have no control." Psychological explanations are also utilized to avoid accountability. It is becoming more common to hear criminals say, "I should not be held responsible for what I have done because I am neurotic or mentally ill."

Psychiatry, particularly Freudian psychiatry, has been maligned as a critical agent in producing a climate of non-responsibility. While there is nothing in the theoretical doctrines of psychoanalysis which favors abdicating personal responsibility, it does seem that the psychiatrist's ability to expand and legitimize the mental illness role has had an impact on the manner in which people view the question of responsibility. Behavior once considered bad is now considered sick. Sickness implies that one cannot help himself or that one is not responsible for his actions. The proponents of the non-responsibility hypothesis would argue that, by expanding the sick role to include forms of behavior that were once considered in terms of good or bad, the healing professions have helped create a social climate in which more people manage to avoid accountability for their actions. Youth growing up in such a society are tempted to behave in a pleasure seeking, anti-social and irresponsible manner. Many feel that this is exactly what restless students are doing.

The evidence that activist and alienated youth are deeply influenced by a climate of irresponsibility is inconclusive. Some activist students are often impressively willing to hold themselves accountable for their actions. On the other hand, most alienated students are not. They tend to seek medical or psychiatric excuses from their obligations at the first sign of stress. They also have a discouraging tendency to break laws and to insist that their own personal needs and problems are such that they should not be held accountable for these actions.[1] It is almost as if they say, "Because the world is so bad and because it has treated me so badly I cannot be blamed for my actions. There is no point in holding me accountable for things which I cannot help doing anyway."

The Affluence Hypothesis

A third hypothesis which appeals to critics of student unrest is based on the alleged hazards of growing up in an affluent society. It is sometimes argued that affluence which is unearned, and which is

---

[1] This situation with regard to use of marijuana is a case in point. Thousands of students use this drug illegally, yet it is practically impossible to organize students to do anything to legalize the sale of marijuana. When students are occasionally arrested for smoking marijuana, they almost always avoid punishment by becoming informants and thus not only avoid legal accountability, but seem unable to adhere to their perceived obligations towards their deviant subcultures.

unaccompanied by a tradition of service and commitment creates a sense of restlessness, boredom and meaninglessness in our youth. The child raised in an affluent society has difficulty finding useful goals. He does not learn to use work or creativity as a means of mastering some aspect of the world. He, therefore, according to this argument, is trapped in a never ending search for new diversions and new freedoms which sooner or later begin to feel sterile and ungratifying.

It does seem likely that man is less apt to be troubled if he is distracted by some monumental task which dominates his life goals. In a relatively poor society, the very need for survival creates a structured and seemingly purposeful life. In an affluent society man has the time and freedom to contemplate the meaning of his existence. Many restless students do come from affluent homes and many have decided that their lives are devoid of meaning. Sometimes it seems that their provocative behavior is designed primarily to invent new struggles and even imaginary hardships which will free them from their lethargy and help them atone for their guilt over "having it so good."

The affluence hypothesis has certain undertones of criticism directed towards the parents of restless students. Affluence, after all, does not always produce protest or indolence. Traditionally, many of our most useful public servants have been products of wealthy homes. The critics of student unrest would reserve their harshest barbs for those newly affluent parents who have themselves become so caught up in materialistic pleasure seeking life that they have failed to meet their responsibility of teaching children the kinds of values which would lend meaning to a young person's existence.

Family Pathology Hypotheses

A number of explanations of student unrest focus upon the disturbed family. According to these hypotheses, activist and alienated students behave as they do because they are responding to an unresolved conflict within the family unit. It is usually suggested that the restless student has been subjected to too much pressure by his parents or is "acting out" a need of his parents. A more general approach to the problem focuses upon a family structure in which the father is a weak or shadowy figure. This approach emphasizes the breakdown in authority of the paternal figure, the confusion of sexual roles in our society and the break with tradition which such confusion produces.

The evidence for the existence of a high degree of pathology in the families of restless students is inconclusive. Sociological studies of students and their families do not support any family pathology hypothesis. In fact, such studies suggest that activist students, at least, come from rather stable families. Psychiatrists, on the other hand, find some evidence of serious familial conflict in most of the families of restless students they treat. It must be emphasized, however, that the psychiatrist deals with only a small proportion of such students.

If family disorganization is an important cause of student unrest, the manner in which it exerts its influence must be complex and subtle. Sociological techniques are simply too superficial to get at the complexities of the problem. The findings of psychiatrists are based on depth explorations which may be valid for some families but which cannot be generalized. Neither sociologists nor psychiatrists can provide valid answers. The most we can say is that some aspects of student restlessness may be directly related to family pathology. Certainly, it is conceivable that in today's highly charged social climate, even minimal family disturbance may be translated into highly provocative behavior.

Sympathetic Hypotheses

The next group of hypotheses put the student in a favorable light. They view him as a victim of man-made circumstances and maintain that student unrest is a legitimate and rational effort to change these circumstances. The student is viewed as either a helpless victim of a world he never created, or as a hero seeking to cleanse the world of the evils of previous generations. To be useful these hypotheses must not simply define what is wrong with the world, but must suggest how various factors have made students more capable of perceiving and acting upon the injustices and irrationalities of our world.

The Two Armed Camps Hypothesis

This generation of students has grown in an age when the world has been divided into two large camps which compete with each other ideologically, politically and sometimes militarily. Since the Russians launched their first satellite, the competition has also been educational. Students today are trained in a school system which emphasizes the competitive acquisition of knowledge as a source of power and stability. By the time they leave high school they are better educated than any previous generation of students but they are also more overworked.

All of this emphasis on education and competition is not easily sustained after the student arrives at the university. By this time, he is at least partially "burned out." The personal benefits of intensive studying and searching for a profitable career begin to appear less attractive in an affluent world and particularly in a world which seems to be making it increasingly difficult for a young person to become an integral part of the economic system. As the student comes to objectively view the implications of our competitiveness with communism as a never ending phenomena, he also begins to question the social value of his efforts. Even if he maintains his enthusiasm for academic work through the undergraduate years, by the time the student reaches graduate school, he increasingly asks himself whether the competitive search for knowledge is worth it. At this point he begins to view our competition with the communist world (and sometimes competitiveness itself) as a form of mass paranoia and he views the university as an agent of the government which contributes towards the perpetuation of the paranoid system. He reacts by protest or withdrawal.

The War in Vietnam Hypothesis

Although student unrest began long before the war in Vietnam ever escalated to massive proportions, there can be little doubt that in the past few years this conflict has been the major factor influencing the behavior of students. The war is particularly unpopular on our campuses. A large proportion of students, perhaps the majority, see it as a misguided effort. A significant minority see it as wholly immoral. Much of the restless behavior of students can be directly related to their efforts to do something to stop the war or to their sense of total frustration when they feel powerless to stop it.

The draft and the inequities engendered by the 2S deferment also contribute to unrest. The major issue here is fear. The average male student is plagued with fears that he will fail in school, will be drafted and will run the risks of being killed in a conflict he may not consider vital to our interests. A second issue is guilt. The university student knows that he is spared from military service only because he is richer or smarter than someone else. While he may believe that the war is immoral, he also knows that his privileged status is immoral. When he accepts the 2S status he suffers guilt. Much of the activism on our campuses is a means of atoning for that guilt. Much of the alienation on our campuses is a means of denying the relevance of the society that created such guilt.

Students also feel some shame in not participating in those aspects of military service that might make them feel more masculine. It is rare for anyone even in peacetime to eagerly embrace military service and a normal late adolescent has justifiable concern with interrupting his career to face the harshness of life in the service. The unpopularity of this war gives the student a cogent reason for avoiding military service but it does not resolve his nagging fears that he is somehow or other being cowardly or less masculine by being treated specially

It is also true that the anti-war climate on our campuses makes the student progressively more disinclined to serve in this war the longer he remains on campus. Education breeds a dislike of violence. Furthermore, whatever romantic thoughts a young man may have about the war at the age of 18 are somewhat attenuated with a year or two of maturation. Students spend many hours arguing about the war, the draft, and means of avoiding the draft. This preoccupation creates a highly tense situation in which the student feels supported only by his peer group. He begins to relate to subcultures which become progressively more separated from the rest of the nation and particularly from the adult generation.

The Deterioration in the Quality of Life Hypothesis

There are many who believe that student unrest is an appropriate response to the deterioration of the quality of life in America. Over-population which results in crowds, traffic jams and businesses run on the basis of mass production has taken much of the joy out of life in our towns and cities. Personal care or service is hard to find in any shop, restaurant, or hotel. People begin to feel faceless and insignificant.

Students, it can be argued, are among the first to sense the painful anonymity associated with bigness. This is a particularly serious problem on overcrowded campuses where students are painfully isolated from their teachers and other adults. A sense of student-faculty intimacy or a sense of scholarly community are sorely lacking on any of our large campuses. Students find it difficult to develop a sense of identification or loyalty towards a University that they perceive is monolithic and impersonal. In their complaints that they are treated like numbers or IBM cards they strike a poignant note for all of us.

Overcrowding is only a relative thing and would not be so destructive if it were not for the manner in which we have incredibly neglected the planning and development of town and country. Our cities grow with no respect for the land. Beauty and wilderness are easy prey for the builder and contractor. Clean air and clear streams are almost a thing of the past. An adolescent who grows up in a world in which he must sit back and watch beauty fade and pollution gain comes to despair of the future. One way of looking at student unrest is as a massive reaction to the destruction of that kind of world and way of life which their forebears enjoyed but which will be denied to them. It is not uncommon to hear a student say to an adult, "In your world, life had some hope and meaning, but in the world you have left for me, these qualities are gone."

The Political Hopelessness Hypothesis

Many individuals see our mass society as immutable to change. It has been argued that our society is so complex, our systems of checks and balances so intricate and our interplay of pressure groups so self equalizing that really effective change is no longer possible. Our business oriented economy has so indoctrinated us into the role of credit bound consumers that we are all beholden to a way of life which may not be in our best interests. An increasing number of radical students are convinced that the forces of government, industry and education are totally interdependent and allied to one another for the purpose of warding off any reasonable attempts to change the society. They believe that a system of life has developed in our country which simply absorbs legal efforts to change our society, even protest, in a manner which ultimately preserves the status quo.[2]

---

2 In this regard it is somewhat distressing to note the manner in which hippies and protestors have not only been institutionalized as part of our folklore and humor but have been exploited by the advertising industry, an institution which they initially intended to destroy.

Guided by the philosophy of Herbert Marcuse many students are convinced that constructive change within our society is not possible by working through the system. They do not have any sort of vision as to what will replace the old order, but they are convinced that our society is fundamentally irrational and must be destroyed. They do not reject illegal acts or even violence as agents of destruction.

The Civil Rights Hypotheses

The civil rights movement not only increased youth's awareness of an historical injustice which made it difficult for them to be proud of this country, but also served as a training ground for future radicals. The new campus protest began at Berkeley when students demanded the right to work freely on their own campuses on behalf of oppressed Negroes. Many campus radicals shaped their images of "the Establishment" and of unreasonable authority on the basis of their early work in the civil rights movement. Students throughout the country have developed an amazing empathy and identification with Negroes. Their commitment to the Negro cause has taught them the psychological meaning of oppression and has encouraged them to seek out and attack sources of oppression in their own lives.

Neutral Hypotheses

Some explanations of student unrest focus upon impersonal processes. The causes of unrest according to these hypotheses are not to be found in the actions or philosophies of other men, but are believed to reside in changes in our highly complex society which seem to create the need for new modes of psychological adaptation.

The Technology Hypothesis

Man always has lived with hope, particularly with the hope that his efforts in the present will be rewarded with gratification in the future. A certain degree of predictability in the future enables one to make commitments to goals and to other people. To the extent that we live in a society in which past, present and future lose their inter-relatedness, the power of hope to shape man's behavior is diminished. New means of adapting to the world must then be found and the manner in which people relate to one another must be profoundly altered.

Postwar America has been characterized by a massive and continuous growth of technology. Our society is one in which the conditions of every-day life are constantly changing. Moreover, the rate at which technology changes our lives is itself increasing. No one can predict what life will be like in 20 years, 10 years, or even 5 years. Today's knowledge, today's work skills and today's values may be totally irrelevant to tomorrow's world. Kenneth Keniston has described the manner in which some youth, who, when exposed to an ever-increasing rate of technological growth, come to perceive that the values of the past will be totally inappropriate for the world in which they will be adults. Moreover, they feel powerless to anticipate or direct the future. In this environment, hope no longer sustains. It is adaptive to be cool, to learn to live in the present.

What are the advantages and disadvantages of living in the present? The advantages are more or less obvious. One is more flexible and superficially at least more comfortable. It is not necessary to delay gratification nor need one allow himself to be tortured by the mistakes of the past nor be deluded by unrealistic hopes for the future. The disadvantages of life in the present are more subtle, yet more powerful. To live in the present one must narrow his commitments. He must travel lightly and be ready for anything. More intimate relationships are unlikely since they cannot be sustained by reference to past experience nor to promises of a better future. Passion and romantic longing must be avoided because they may breed pain or impair one's flexibility. In short, if carried to extremes, life in the present is a selfish life which is incompatible with the growth of that intimacy and passion which man has always found to be essential to a fulfilled life.

Distrust of the future and a determination to live in the present seem to be characteristic of both activist and alienated students. The student activist seeks immediate change and has difficulty in developing the patience or optimism for long-term planning. The alienated student adopts the philosophy of the "hippy." Believing that the only certainty in life is change, or uncertainty itself, he adapts by "doing his own thing" and behaves as though he is responsible only to himself.

The Media Hypotheses

There are several hypotheses that attempt to relate the growth of new media, particularly television, to the troubling behavior of students. It can be argued, for example, that simply by being available to publicize the activities of protesters and hippies the media exaggerate the importance of these groups. The television camera forces all of us to take seriously forms of behavior that might have been dismissed lightly in earlier decades. Conceivably the media may be creating a "climate of expectation" in which youth are subtly seduced into dissenting roles which may not represent their actual interests.

It is also true that many television commercials, radio ads and most modern music are directed towards the youth market. The self-consciousness of youth, is thereby heightened. They are made more aware of their potentialities and sometimes develop an exaggerated sense of their own power.

Another attempt to relate changing media to student unrest has been implied in the writings of Marshall McLuhan. McLuhan believes that electronic media are bringing us all closer together in a more truly communal and shared society than ever existed. Our youth who have grown up with the new media are ready for such a society. Elders who are committed to sustain the institutions of the past are not. Much of youthful rebellion can then be visualized as an effort to make older people see that the world has changed and that many of the values of the past are now irrelevant.

While McLuhan's hypothesis has some attractiveness, it does not seem as plausible as those which focus upon the psychological impact of the content of media. Fredric Wertham believes that the massive degree of violence which young people see on television makes them more violent and less responsible. Vance Packard, for example, has argued that chronic exposure to the values implied in T. V. commercials could create a generation of unrealistic, demanding and present oriented youth. I would like to propose my own hypothesis of student unrest based on the manner in which the media influence the character structure of youth by prematurely confronting them with the harsh truths and realities of life.

As an animal whose growth and development requires him to be dependent upon others for a long period of time, man learns to rely on others for an optimal amount of structure and order in his life. It is obvious that authority is not always benevolent nor just, and yet it is true that no man can be at ease if he does not commit a part of himself to some authority, whether it be his church, his family, his government or an ideology. Nor can some one come to develop a firm sense of who he is without making such commitments. It is at least partly through experiencing limitations which are imposed by others, by respecting others, and by emulating those who are respected that one finds his own identity. The process by which one comes to terms with authority is not always deliberate nor rational. Sometimes even benevolent authority relies on faith, mystique, or untruth to retain its control.

This is especially relevant to the situation of young people. The most well-meaning parents must on occasion deceive their children because they know that children would find many of the hard and cynical facts of life to be unbearable. Until recently it was possible for young people to begin to experience the world as adults know it only after they have reached adolescence. Most of the time the adolescent absorbed this new knowledge gradually and painlessly. Even when he did feel that his parents had been hypocritical or had deceived him, his awareness of their dishonesty came so gradually that his resentment and rebelliousness were restrained. Today it is different. One of the significant developments in post-war America has been the influence of mass-communication media particularly television which are capable of disseminating information to all age groups immediately.

Even before adolescence, television acquaints youth with the cynical facts of life at a time when such truths may be indigestible. Other media communicate knowledge so quickly now that there is little opportunity for anyone to live comfortably with myth or self delusion. Beliefs which were once casually accepted are vigorously scrutinized. The belief that there is equality for all Americans can hardly be sustained when one has a front-row seat from which he can observe the Negro's unsuccessful struggle to maintain a decent life in this country. Blind faith in the veracity of leaders in the nation is quickly lost when one can watch the proceedings of an organization such as the United Nations in his own living room. I have no doubt that diplomats have always lied to one another but what is new about this world is that children can now watch them lie in living color.

The hypocrisies of older generations have always been with us. What is new today is that it is ridiculously easy to expose them. The effect on our youth of premature emergence of truth has been to create a deep skepticism as to the validity of authority. Neither the family, the church, the law nor any institution demands the automatic respect it once did. There may be other factors contributing to this decline in respect for authority but in my opinion it is best understood in terms of the psychological impact of our new media.

The Reliance on Scientism Hypothesis

Today's restless youth have grown up in a world which has not been dominated by religious faith but which has sought many of the answers to the questions of life in science. Many of us believe that science can provide the answers to life. We ask that the speculations and opinions of the social sciences contain the same hard truths as more rigorous findings in the physical and biological sciences. In my work with students, I am often impressed to find how easily they believe or once believed in the perfectability of man. Hostility is not seen as an innate quality of man but rather as a response to frustration. The teachings of the social psychologist that aggression is a learned phenomenum have gained prominence over Freud's more ominous warnings that aggression is innate.

This generation of students seems to have grown up with the belief that original sin in the religious sense of Thanatos in the psychoanalytic sense does not exist. (Much of this belief has been reinforced by the mode of their existence. Many are affluent and have grown up in suburban communities where, except for what they see on television, they are shielded from the tragedies of life. The realities of their own lives convinces them that whatever calamities are imposed upon others are not inevitable.) Statements such as "life is a vale of tears," or "the masses of man lead lives of quiet despair" seem absurd to them. In their adherence to scientific rationality they also cannot accept guilt. They are convinced that in a perfectable world man should be joyful and guiltless.

When a person raised with such beliefs encounters the harsh realities of life, he has little to fall back upon. If he perceives his own aggressive tendencies, he is frightened by them and attempts to deny them. He may project his anger upon those whom he feels are frustrating him or he may simply deny that such anger exists. When he perceives the evil of others he is mortified. In his conviction that there are rational solutions to any problem, he cannot help but be intolerant of the irrationalities of those who prevent progress. In his belief that life and especially the sexual aspects of life can be enjoyed without guilt, he becomes highly disturbed when he discovers that he cannot escape his past and that a certain amount of guilt is inevitable. He even becomes plagued with additional guilt over the realization that he is guilty.

The restless student is one who has taken the message of science, rationality and perfection literally. He is more open to action and change than were earlier generations of students. At the same time, however, he is not equipped to understand or deal with the depth of that irrationality in man which resists change and which leads man to seek his own destruction. Too often such a student finds it necessary to construct "devil" theories of history in which the existence of evil is attributed to only a few who block the progress of the many. He has sacrificed the comfort and patience which comes with the idea of accepting "original" sin.[3]

Conclusions

Hopefully this review has been more than an exercise in cataloguing. By emphasizing the diversity of explanations of student unrest, I have attempted to demonstrate the intellectual futility of searching for simple explanations of a highly complex phenomena. As citizens we may wish to either support or attack the causes which restless students have dramatized. But as scholars concerned with educating and understanding and helping students we need a more objective approach. We must recognize that there is some truth to the most critical as well as the most sympathetic hypotheses.

Some of the hypotheses suggest guidelines for action. The critical hypotheses remind us that youth are not always as wise or powerful as we might suspect. Like adults, their actions are as much determined by personal weaknesses and selfishness as by sensitivity or idealism. While youth certainly do not need more paternalism and coddling they still need our understanding and guidance. They can still learn much from adults who are committed to the pursuit of ideals in a climate of tolerance, compassion and responsibility. The critical hypotheses need not be used only to berate students. If their validity is appreciated they can be helpful in freeing adults from that unreasonable guilt which impairs an honest confrontation with the issues which students have raised.

---

[3] Sometimes the student becomes totally overwhelmed with the irrational aspects of the world and reacts by totally abandoning his earlier beliefs. In their disillusionment, some alienated students seem to be turning away from the promises of scientism and searching for solace in the most dubious forms of mysticism, magic, and astrology.

The sympathetic hypotheses emphasize the unusual degree of stress this generation of students has experienced. Those hypotheses which invoke the war, over-population, and pollution as sources of stress forcefully remind us that student unrest is often an appropriate response to what sometimes seems to be a hopelessly troubled world. Other hypotheses raise many questions for those entrusted with the management of our universities. Does the emphasis on education as a means rather than an end have any meaning in an affluent society? Should youth be encouraged to remain in a passive role as students throughout the first third of their lives? Are there means of bringing young people into important roles in the power structure of our universities and our social system before they reach the age of 25 or 30? Is the 2S classification anything more than a bribe which weakens the moral position of dissenting students and creates havoc upon our campuses? Should it be abolished? To what extent can we continue to depersonalize and enlarge our campuses without creating a generation of alienated youth who feel no sense of identity, no sense that they have a voice in what is done to them and no sense of commitment to anything but their own interests?

It is my belief that the neutral hypotheses are the most intriguing and the most powerful valid explanations of student unrest. At the same time they are the most difficult to live with optimistically. If progress itself, in the form of technology, science or new media, is the most severe stress in the lives of our young people, then we are faced with a seemingly impossible task—namely, how to control progress and change rather than allowing these forces to control us.

Students have demonstrated to anyone who is willing to read their message that a complacent drifting into the future, an unchecked growth of technology, science and media cannot take place without profoundly altering the nature of human existence and the character of man. Some of the behaviors of youth, including many forms of student activism, are efforts to warn us of the existence of overwhelming danger. They are adaptive insofar as they seek to ward off social calamity. Other behaviors of our youth, such as profound alienation, are byproducts or symbols of a process of social decay that may well be irreversible. They are efforts to live with a calamity that already exists.

Faced with the grim realities of the postwar world, how will man continue to survive with dignity? Most of our counselors, scientists, and theologians have faith in man's infinite capacity to adjust. They seem convinced that man can mold his personality, can adopt new values and can learn to live in a flexible and uncommited manner. Some find cause for optimism in the possibility that man might learn new methods of child rearing so that he could overcome the psychological lag between his needs and the demands of the new world. I wish I could share this optimism, but I cannot. It is not likely that child-rearing methods can be changed quickly enough to keep up with the rate of technological change. It is also possible that some of man's psychological needs are immutable. I doubt that man can live without intimacy, without compassion, without ideology, without faith, without autonomy, without privacy, and without beauty and still be man.

The only effective solution would require a drastic revision of many of the traditions and structures of our society. Our first need is to study and to plan, to determine what kinds of technological progress is consistent with making man a better human being and what kinds are not. The latter must ultimately be rejected. We must find a way to communicate those values that are essential to man's survival to our children in an open and questioning but non-cynical manner. We must re-examine our time honored reverence for affluence, power, and bigness and face the possibility that affluence bores, that power corrupts, and that big institutions diminish the stature of man. In a nation struggling with an unpalatable war and an excruciating racial problem, these problems may seem premature, vague, and almost grandiose. Where can one begin?

If we do nothing else we must at least begin to study the impact of technological progress upon man's personality. Only a handful of scientists and philosophers are seriously concerned with the study of man's psychological future. No university or government agency has ever created a department or institute to study this problem. This is an immediate and critical need. Only man's intellect and reason can protect him from himself. If we deny the existence of the problem, if we equivocate or if we merely drift, man's tenure on earth will have been truly absurd and meaningless.

11

INTELLECTUAL SOURCES OF STUDENT MILITANCY

JOHN MARTIN RICH

RECENT DEMONSTRATIONS by students in the U.S., Europe, Latin America, Asia, and even behind the Iron Curtain constitute a world-wide phenomenon that assumes disparate forms and engenders increasing consternation and disquietude among those in positions of power and authority. Desiring, as many do, to maintain control and halt further outbreaks, few have looked beyond tactics to the forms of thinking that may influence the activities themselves. A clue to the thinking behind student militancy can be gained in the following report from Paris: "In the vast cobbled, litter-filled courtyard of the Sorbonne, it looked as though an avant-garde affair, not a revolution, was taking place. Only the lemonade was missing. Students set up stands, heaping tables with the tracts and books about the thoughts of Mao, Marx, Lenin, Che Guevera, Fidel Castro, Prince Peter Kropotkin, Trotsky and Rosa Luxemburg. Their voices rose and fell and never stopped."[1]

Who are these authors? What is their message and what do they have to do with student militancy in this country? It is known that the leaders of the New Left are from more affluent homes, did not taste of war or the depression, and constitute some of the leading

[1] *New York Times*, June 17, 1968.

John Martin Rich is Associate Professor of Social and Philosophical Studies in Education, University of Kentucky, Lexington.

intellectuals on our campuses. They not only are activists; many of them read, and they read well. And if they read the works of the authors listed above, they will find, rather than a rigid, official monolithic dogma, a diversity of positions on socialistic issues which, at times, become sharply critical of one another.

From the Marxist heritage and the theoretical deviations of Engels after his mentor's death, we find, in contrast to Marx's teachings, that Lenin elevated the Party to a supreme position. This turn of events was opposed by the German intellectual and socialist leader Rosa Luxemburg, whose verbal thrusts against the new regime were sharp and penetrating until her pen was stilled by assassins. Trotsky, defeated in the power struggle by Stalin, stung deeply with his strictures on the betrayal of the revolution. As the Party modified their position and publicly condemned the excesses of the Stalinist regime, Mao adopted an orthodox Leninism, introduced the communes, and deviated from Stalin by using thought control to make dissenters into loyal Communists rather than exterminating them.

As the revolution was exported into Latin America, students could read about experimentation and the development of new strategies and tactics appropriate to different types of political and economic systems. In spite of popular belief in the West, there has not been one official dogma. Those following Castro argued vociferously with the Trotskyites in Latin America. Although Guevera's abortive movement in Bolivia has as its analogue the counter-revolutionary Bay of Pigs fiasco, for some student militants Guevera is a romantic figure. They also read about the experimental approach to revolution in Latin America in Regis Debray's *Revolution in the Revolution?* Debray, a French intellectual, was imprisoned by the Bolivian government after the collapse of Guevera's guerrilla forces. Finally, Herbert Marcuse, one of the leading figures on the left today, has dissected totalitarian elements in Communistic and democratic states.[2] Marcuse, who has been influential both in the U.S. and western Europe, attempts to demonstrate that, since American democracy is today built upon a theoretical cultural foundation that supports one dimensional thinking by repudiating the Hegelian dialectical process, the U.S. government and the mass media thereby

---

2 See Herbert Marcuse, *One Dimensional Man* (Boston: Beacon Press, 1964), and "Repressive Tolerance" in Robert Paul Wolff, *et al.*, eds., *Critique of Pure Tolerance* (Boston: Beacon Press, 1965).

impose many coercive and restrictive totalitarian practices on its citizens.

"The New Radicalism," according to Newfield, "is authentically new in its vague weaving together of anarchistic, existential, transcendental, populist, socialist, and bohemian strands of thought."[3] We could add that it is diverse in interests, opposed to strong ideological affiliations, and dedicated to specific programs of action.

We stress Marxism and its major variations and offshoots because of its dominance in socialistic thinking today and its influence on student militants. Anarchism consists of a diverse group of reformers whose ideas proved more influential in the 19th century than in our own times. Although there are anarchistic socialists, some anarchists, such as Thoreau and Godwin, were non-socialists; others, like Tolstoy, were anti-socialists. Most of them believed man to be naturally good and in the absence of coercive institutions could live creatively in peace and harmony. By abolishing private property and unjust coercive powers of the state, cooperative associations of producers, distributors, and consumers would grow and eventually embrace all mankind. Only a few anarchists were violent, and still fewer were pacifists. Prince Kropotkin is the anarchist read more widely by students today. He not only differed sharply from the social Darwinists, but also from those anarchists who emphasized man's individualism over his natural solidarity. City and countryside, he thought, could be brought into harmonious working relationship by man's natural proclivity for mutual aid.

Existentialism, too, has influenced student thinking by its emphasis on the quest for authenticity, free will, and full responsibility for personal acts, the concept of alienation, and the belief in the treatment of others as genuine persons rather than as things to be manipulated. The concept of alienation is the primary point of contact between existentialism and Marxism, with the existentialist's concept probably the more inclusive one.

Some students read Emerson and his form of transcendentalism. Michael Harrington and other observers find parallels in student militancy with the populist sentiment, an indigenous reform movement composed of Western and Southern agrarians and representatives of several labor and reform groups, which participated from 1892 to 1908 in five national campaigns. Jack Newfield[4] holds that

---

3 Jack Newfield, *A Prophetic Minority* (New York: Signet Books, 1967), p. 132.
4 *Ibid.*

the Bohemianism among the militants relates to the Beat Generation of the 1950's who protested against the evils of society, but, unlike the militants decided to "drop-out" rather than take direct social action.[5]

The New Left in higher education has inherited a multitude of rich and diverse sources of influence. However, the New Left can best be understood in a political and ideological sense as a species of socialism. This can best be shown by delineating the nature of socialism.

First of all, there are a number of misconceptions about socialism. Some believe, for instance, that all socialists advocate the abolition of private property. However, this policy would not be supported by two of the leading socialists of the past: Claude Henri Saint-Simon and Charles Fourier. It also is generally thought that socialism would mean the establishment of state ownership and control over the means of production. But, once again, this is only one form of socialism: the type known as state socialism. Cooperative socialism distrusts the state and bases its system upon the organization of independent producers such as advocated in the historical movements of guild socialism and syndicalism. Anarchistic socialism contends that the state is the ultimate source of exploitation and must be replaced by some form of voluntary groupings usually of an egalitarian nature (as with Kropotkin). Most student militants are opposed to state socialism. Instead, they favor a form of cooperative socialism or anarchistic socialism.

Socialism holds that existing political and social systems are unjust, not because of human nature but as a result of corrupt institutions. Socialists advocate a new moral order[6] and propose a program to effect it and thereby reshape man and his institutions. A true socialist is not interested merely in economic reforms, but advocates educational, ethical, and aesthetic programs. Finally, socialism calls for a revolutionary spirit to carry out the programs.

A revolutionary spirit does not mean that all socialists advocate violent overthrow of the government, although, due to the enormous influence of Marxism, this is generally thought to be the case. The experimental socialists believe the new society will result from social

---

5 The Beat Generation is represented by such writers as Jack Kerouac and Allen Ginsberg.

6 Even anarchistic socialism is a form of "social order," one that is thoroughly decentralized.

inventions; evolutionary socialists assume that the new order will evolve out of capitalistic societies; and agrarian socialists argue that the new society will emerge with the elimination of land monopoly.

Our thesis is that, once popular misconceptions of socialism are dispelled, the connection becomes more evident between cooperative and anarchistic socialism and the New Left. Student militants also agree on a number of points about American society: opposition to the Establishment; concern over the growing dehumanization and bureaucratization of social institutions; hatred of hypocrisy among the older generation and those in positions of power; obsolescence of higher education and its lack of relevancy to the great issues of our time; empathy with the civil rights movement and the underprivileged; and need for vigorous and concerted activism to rectify injustices and transform our institutions. Historically, the civil rights movement, more than any other factor, did more to arouse the students from their apathy of the 1950's, while the Vietnam war has done more to intensify and exacerbate their conflict with society.

The students not only oppose conservatism, but the older liberalism as well. They find the pragmatic-progressive type of liberalism of the New Deal hypocritical, non-experimental, gradualistic, and legalistic in its approach to social reform. If we define revolution as change that affects fundamental laws and is illegal under the laws it abolishes, then some student militants favor total revolution due to their belief in the inherently unredeemable nature of society, while others espouse limited revolution, preferring to concentrate their energies on one or two institutions that need thorough reconstruction.

Student militants have been condemned for having no clear-cut social system for the one they hope to replace. This charge, in a number of cases, is true. What they are against is clearer than is the exact nature of the society they are for. This tendency stems from their skepticism of utopian pronouncements and their aversion to older ideologies that have become dogmatic and ossified in the hands of unimaginative followers or powerful tyrants. It may very well be misleading to claim that students do not know the type of society they are for. As we have seen, it would be a form of cooperative or anarchistic socialism. The ideals and guiding principles for such a society have been with us for a long time—namely, to exemplify the ideals of American democratic life which too frequently have been denied in practice.

The question of our time is whether democracy still has the resilience to meet the challenges of minority groups, youth, and the underprivileged, or whether government, instead, will listen to the growing chorus of voices urging the reliance on coercion to respond to the challenge. Student militants desire, above all, to provide the conditions where each of the oppressed can "be a man among men . . . to come lithe and young into a world that [is] ours and to help build it together."[7]

[7] Frantz Fanon, *Black Skin, White Masks* (New York: Grove Press, 1967), pp. 112-113.

12

ON THE REVOLUTIONARY POTENTIAL: SOME RANDOM OBSERVATIONS ABOUT THE POLITICS OF CONFRONTATION

JOHN WILKINSON

THE WORD revolution was first used in something approximating
the meaning we give it today to describe certain events of English
history that began about 1648 and ended in the Glorious Revolution
of 1688. The concept of revolution, however, is much older than
the word. The word was originally used to indicate cyclical changes.
Under the Christian Empire of Constantine it gradually had the
meaning of "conversion," a once-and-for-all event. Still later it took
on its present meaning. But what has been changing over the
centuries is not so much the historical fact of revolution as our
awareness of it.

The Greeks had a well-developed theory of radical social change,
but it was used to avoid political revolution, not to promote it. For,
according to the theory, in the long run revolution changed nothing.
The Romans took the same view; the fundamental impossibility of
genuine revolution was implied in their doctrine of the eternal
recurrence. The anecdote about both Greeks' and Romans' "going

From *The Center Magazine*, March, 1969. This publication of the Center for the Study of
Democratic Institutions is published and copyright, 1969, by The Fund for the Republic, Inc.
Reprinted by permission of the author and the executive editor of the magazine. John
Wilkinson is a Senior Fellow (Philosophy), Center for the Study of Democratic Institutions,
Santa Barbara, Calif.

into the theater in order to come out of it," which pointed up the doctrine of recurrence, had a deeper meaning for classical antiquity than is generally supposed. Rebellions, internal uprisings, and foreign invasions, to be sure, were as common as today, and it is clear to us now that the murderous feuds and civil wars of the Roman Republic represented a revolutionary potential that was finally realized by Caesar and Augustus in the Empire, but though they experienced revolution, the ancients did not think of it the way we do.

II

It may not be possible even now to define the idea of revolution clearly. The same, however, can be said for most philosophic and political concepts; they can only be understood contextually. Yet, we can establish some of the necessary conditions for the correct usage of the word. Thus, a revolution is the result of a planned or at least a partially planned sudden mutation in the political, economic, or cultural order.

Revolutionary changes, in other words, are never completely unanticipated. The chanciness associated in our minds with them is always inserted into some historical context which is more or less known, or at least is knowable. The spirit of political revolution, for example, historically has been presaged by a revolutionary elan in the schools, whether one thinks of Plato's Academy, Rabelais' Abbey of Thélème, or even of Clark Kerr's "multiversity." It is necessary, however, to reverse the propositions Mr. Kerr put forth in his famous treatise on the multiversity—a book profoundly counter-revolutionary in purpose—in order to turn it into a document with revolutionary potential. Mr. Kerr intended only to write a description of how things were—and still are. He was not the first to discover that in doing so, he had also written a compendium of how things ought not to be. Revolutions are partially blueprinted by such descriptions. That is why the Students for a Democratic Society may owe more to Mr. Kerr than to Marx.

III

Jean-Francois Revel, writing in the immediate wake of the French events of last May, said quite aptly: "It is nonsense to reproach the students and the professors with having politicized their problem. The reproach ought to be that they haven't politicized it enough.

Politics is the battleground of *all* problems . . . and when the rod governs the school, the saber reigns in the Capitol. Is it an accident that we speak in France of the Napoleonic university and of the barracks-college?"

Revel pointed out that the history of the Renaissance and all our subsequent experience show that the "liberation" of the university makes the problem of education not easier but harder to solve. Merely suppressing the lecture system or examinations (and, it could be added, setting up symbolic barricades in the streets) is like breaking the thermometer to change the weather. In a highly technologized society it is difficult even to find the barricades, supposing that they exist at all. Throwing up a mountain of paving blocks across a street to separate the tormented from their mounted tormenters may have been all very well in the nineteenth century. Today such tactics, like locking oneself inside a building, probably do more to seal off the would-be revolutionaries from their potential followers than to promote revolution.

Yet, it is difficult to judge the future import of single events, violent or not, once the revolutionary spirit takes over. That has always been true and probably holds for the politics of confrontation. So far, it has shown a final revolutionary result nowhere but in Istanbul and Ankara. Student-led agitations there in 1955-60 resulted in the overthrow of the government and execution of the dictatorial Menderes. Typically, that revolution began with relatively trivial complaints about food, lighting, and so on. But the Turkish students were quickly politicized, enough to connect their movement with radical and wide-ranging reforms. And as usual, the regime helped matters along by staging extensive rioting among the populace, which was ostensibly directed against the local Greeks over the matter of Cyprus. What the regime did not recognize was that the spirit of rebellion, once it was loosed, would inevitably be turned against the ruling establishment itself as soon as all the Greek shops had been plundered.

This is only one example of many that might be cited to show that while revolutions are hard to begin, it is even more difficult to stop them once they get going.

IV

Neither in the United States nor in Europe has the politics of confrontation yet found the neuralgic "nodal" points of the university—and, *eo ipso,* the body politic. At most, at least so far, all the turmoil has merely led to the usual application of "liberal" corn plasters to what the revolutionary students diagnose as a malignancy. At worst, from the revolutionaries' point of view, it has taught the authorities how to beat the students at their own game. This should not be surprising, for every "blueprint for revolution" is also a blueprint for counter-revolution; sensitive nodal points can be protected by fail-safe devices.

On the other hand, the revolutionaries are aided by the tendency of the authorities—like those in Turkey in the fifties—to install fail-sure mechanisms. Messrs. Kennedy and Johnson, to cite examples, put pennies in the revolutionary fuse box with their Vietnam war. But the revolutionaries may not be favored this way much longer. With peace in Vietnam a possibility now, the American S.D.S. may be losing its principal recruiting device, at least for the time being. I have the impression that, without the war to rally them, they will soon be fighting with each other more than with the adversary. I have an equally strong impression, however, that it will not be long before the Nixon Administration will provide them with a new *point d'appui,* perhaps by instituting harshly repressive measures at home. S.D.S. leaders themselves have predicted this. If the game is played out according to the historic rules, they will probably turn out to be right.

V

The *dramatis personae* of the present revolutionary situation, with the exception of older mentors like Herbert Marcuse and Ernst Fischer, are young people. This has been the case in every revolutionary period since the time of the Renaissance.

Since the fifteenth century, superior intelligence has been accredited to youth. Rabelais very typically writes that he sees that young brigands, adventurers, and hostlers will "from now on" be more learned than the teachers and preachers. In the Middle Ages, youth, even up to the age of twenty-five, were frequently beaten by their elders for any or no reason at all. If the beatings were just, well and good; if unjust, the virtue of patience was there to be learned. With the Renaissance that sort of treatment of youth finally ceased.

The young revolutionaries of today are not only young, they are made up principally of university and college students. Even though most of these students may never have heard of the Athenian agora, something of the past, before industrialization and technology took over, seems to reside in their collective unconscious. Alain Touraine, the sociologist of Nanterre (who with many other sociologists has been rejuvenated by being "where the action is"), argues, I think correctly, in his book *Le Mouvement de Mai*, that while French students show little tendency to reject the basic values of the culture of today, the events of May were dramatic testimony to the social conflicts inherent in a technologized and computerized society. Touraine also called attention to the incongruity of students of the humanities sitting about in a slum while reading about the glories of Athens and Renaissance Florence. In the United States, as in France, the conditions of life in a slum are so dramatically different from those found in a human or humane culture that the contrast alone might be reasonably regarded as a substantial contribution to the push that converts the potential rebellious energy of youth into the *vis viva* of revolution.

VI

The black students, since they do not share and do not wish to share in the European past, will find their own ancestral equivalent. ("We will find our own way or we will invent it," as the Roman saying ran.) When they do, their revolutionary potential will be much higher than that of the white rebels, since it is exceedingly doubtful that the doors of white society will open very widely to them, or that they will find any inclination to make common cause with the young white Jacobins, who can be counted on to pass via terror to Bonapartism. It seems improbable that the full-scale guerrilla activities to which the blacks will be driven will succeed. Ironically, though, the blacks can only be repressed by tactics that will totally change the face of white America as thoroughly (if not in the same direction) as the most ardent S.D.S. student could wish—and this too will result in revolution of a sort.

VII

If, as I have claimed elsewhere, the autonomous, technological society that subverts every human culture, without exception, is the real revolution of our time, the old arguments of class struggle, colonialism, and all the rest remain true but are becoming epiphenomena. Wherever technology rules, revolutionary ideologies are just so much background noise. This is possibly the reason why anarchism and nihilism are playing such an important role in current revolutionary thinking. The real, if subconscious, content of revolutionary thought in the technological society is based on a vague nostalgia for a mythical golden age to be uncovered like an ancient inscription when the baked mud of the centuries has been removed. It represents a desire to return to where one never was, like the Luddites' longing for the return of the premachine age. Breaking up the stocking-frames, although it may have been spiritually satisfying to the original Luddites, however, did not succeed then and more than likely it cannot succeed now. The Luddites did not find the place to strike. Those who practice the politics of confrontation now have the same problem—they cannot find the neuralgic points in the modern social network. Finding them is especially difficult when the rate of political and social change has become so exponential that hypotheses about what is wrong are usually out of date even before they can be examined.

What, then, can be done? Not much. The only sure way to stop an exponential process is not to let it begin at all, or, at least, not to let it get past the point where it becomes irreversible.

The Greeks of the period before Alexander, who were profoundly counter-revolutionary, knew this. They subscribed to a policy that forbade innovation; the end they had in view in doing this was to return to a Golden Age. What they did not realize was that to be counter-revolutionary may, in a deep sense, actually be revolutionary. It was not without significance that the men of the Renaissance, the French revolutionaries, and Thomas Jefferson, all had their heads stuffed full of Brutuses, Catos, tribunes, Platos, and the like. The fact suggests that restoration or reaction may indeed be revolutionary, provided only that it is markedly different from what immediately preceded it.

VIII

A new approach toward understanding revolutionary potential must be made in the light of historic experiences. Otherwise the dialectic of revolution will begin to go round in circles. Counter-revolution may appear more revolutionary than revolution; it will not be clear what distinctions ought to be made between conscious and unconscious revolution; what is new will seem very like what is so old as to appear new; the roles of ideology and theory will be blurred; it will not be clear what is random and what is purposeful; it will be difficult to define what confrontation or participation means; the revolutionary youth of today will appear to be an ever-renewed species of avant-gardists who say nothing new.

One way to deal with such multiple confusions is to construct a model of a revolutionized social structure. Understanding such a model offers hardly more difficulty to common sense than reading a road map. A road map consists of a set of points representing places connected by lines that stand for channels of communication. The necessary conditions for what we must do to get from here to there are indicated on it. But these directions do not guarantee that we will be able to make the trip exactly as the map indicates, for a bridge may be closed down, a road torn up, etc. For that reason, detours and alternative routes are shown.

A social map must, similarly, consist of a set of points representing the decision-makers—not only individual men but whole societies, hierarchies, and institutions. The lines that join them stand for communications channels through which may pass messages and, in general, every sort of transaction. Because so many and such unforeseeable relations are involved, there can be no mathematical certainty about them; behavior will not be predictable. Even so, a number of important theorems can be established for such a network of relationships. For example, it can be shown that all of them will in time tend to develop the same structure, in the sense that each will represent more or less clearly and distinctly the whole network. This is not hard to understand when we recall that the brain programs its neural network to resemble the social network—a theory indispensable for understanding how language mirrors and affects the world.

Now, it is known in ordinary electrical network theory that to test the *stability* of the network it is useful to introduce small and random electrical impulses into the system, in order to analyze what takes place when it happens. Some shocks will blow the fuse, others will have stabilizing effects. The similarity of such a procedure to both shock therapy, in dealing with sick minds, and the politics of confrontation, in dealing with sick societies, is clear. In most cases cascading ("escalating") shocks throw the system into unstable and uncontrollable oscillations of increasing amplitude.

In this kind of theory "stability" is the crucial matter, for there is no revolutionary potential in a stable society, no matter how unjust it might be. The revolutionary tactic then becomes the testing of stability by probing the society with a series of random shocks. For that reason, the proponents of the established order can be counted on to attempt to protect the important nodal points of society from guerrilla activity by methods that do not produce a radical change of consciousness in the uncommitted. One can see that happening in the present scene. If it has to be said that the active revolutionaries have not yet found the neuralgic nodal points of American society, it can hardly be said that the counter-tactics of the police have been the reason for their failure.

The authorities are becoming accomplished counter-revolutionaries, in some instances by being made aware of the necessity for reform. Bringing about this awareness is the traditional role of the "liberals" based in the universities. Such persons are sometimes able to mitigate injustices in both communist and capitalist societies to the point where repression becomes tolerable. So successful are they at this that it is difficult for a revolutionary to find unprotected vital points in the domestic American or Russian structures, as long as these regimes continue to ward off depressions and avoid losing wars.

The situation is otherwise if the *foreign* empires of the U.S. and the U.S.S.R. are considered. American prosperity is founded on the fact that six per cent of the world's population uses up to seventy per cent of the world's resources. But the neocolonialism necessary to make that possible (which, instead of using occupying troops, relies on drawing governments, often military dictatorships, into the American economic network) is probably very fragile. A large-scale insurrection in Latin America could conceivably result in revolutionary changes in the U.S.

13

ANATOMY OF A REVOLT

ART BUCHWALD

THERE HAS BEEN a great deal of discussion about campus revolts spreading across the Nation. It is obvious the students are restless and it's making our educators very nervous.

The question is why, and I think I've got the answer. The reason the college students are doing so much demonstrating is that there is no one in class to teach them any more and the students have nothing else to do.

Almost every full professor is either writing a book, guest lecturing at another university, or taking a year off to write a report for [the] President.

Therefore, he has turned over his course to a graduate instructor who is either working on his Ph.D., traveling on a Fulbright Scholarship, or picketing in Montgomery, Ala. So he in turn has turned the class over to one of the brighter students who is never there because he works on the college newspaper, is a member of the student senate, or is a delegate to his national fraternity.

When the students arrive at class there is no one in front of the room, so usually a Socialist student takes over the class and tells the students it's about time they revolted against the system.

The students pour out on campus heading for the administration building to protest to the chancellor of the university who, unfortunately, is away trying to raise money for a new business administration building.

From the *Washington Post*, Washington, D.C., April 22, 1965. Reprinted by permission of the author and the publisher. Art Buchwald is a nationally syndicated columnist.

The vice chancellor is at the state capital testifying on a new education bill and the dean of men is at a convention in Phoenix, Ariz.

The dean of women is addressing a garden club in the next state, and the only one left in the administration building is the chief of campus police who isn't quite sure what the students are yelling about.

So he arrests the ringleaders of the group (those standing in front) and this plays right into the students' hands because now with the arrests they have something to demonstrate about.

In the meantime the chancellor flies home to see if he can settle the matter. The students present him with a petition demanding the release of the arrested demonstrators. He is about to do this when the Board of Regents holds an emergency meeting and votes to back the chancellor in meting out punishment to the "ringleaders."

The faculty, made up of visiting professors from other schools, votes to support the students and the chancellor finds himself in an impossible position.

He therefore resigns and accepts a grant from the Ford Foundation to make a study of higher education.

The state politicians call for an investigation of the student demonstrations to discover if they were Communist-inspired.

Finally, the Governor makes a statement pledging full support for law and order, whatever that means.

By this time the demonstrations start petering out.

The students begin wandering back to class hoping there will be someone to teach them something. But even the Socialist student who started the demonstration is not there. He's been booked on a lecture tour to talk about free speech at other universities.

So everyone decides to go to Washington and picket the White House over its policy on Vietnam.

14

STUDENT ACTIVISM AT BERKELEY
AFTER 1964

G. LOUIS HEATH

IN 1964, Berkeley student activists brought the direct confrontation tactics and non-violent ideology of the civil rights movement onto the American campus under the guise of the Free Speech Movement. The FSM was a clever façade for the abandonment of discussion and due process in a situation where the First and Fourteenth Amendments were guaranteed. The strategy of the Mississippi freedom rides and lunch counter sit-ins was misplaced at Berkeley. To be sure, freedom of speech was secure on the Berkeley campus during the FSM, unlike other periods in the university's history. On a campus where Presidential candidate Adlai E. Stevenson could not speak in 1956 because the content of his speech would have been political, Communists, Nazis, and Birchers were free to speak in 1964. University Pres. Clark Kerr even was given the 1964 Alexander Meiklejohn award by the American Association of University Professors for having promoted and defended academic freedom on the Berkeley campus.[1]

The activists' aim in 1964 was to create a sociological climate in

---

1 The AAUP conferred the award "for action taken in 1963 to restore to the University of California student body full freedom to invite speakers of their own choice to the campus." *AAUP Bulletin*, 50: 185, June, 1964.

G. Louis Heath, former U. S. Office of Education Research Fellow, University of California, Berkeley, is Assistant Professor of Social Foundations of Education, The City University of New York.

which discussion and democratic participation became meaningless so that they might advance their own causes and obtain direct access to power. A militant minority was clearly seeking to impose its will upon the idealistic majority. The disruption by the 800 in Sproul Hall, vocally accompanied by Joan Baez, was designed to force the administration to accept the militants' view of the university as an instrument of all that is malevolent in the society or see the university cease to function at all. When Mario Savio articulated his militant constituency's desire to bring the University of California to a "grinding halt" in order to secure "free speech" and student participation in university decision-making, he effectively issued the ultimatum christening the American student movement.

There has been considerable change in the student political milieu at Berkeley since 1964. The style of politics is in transition between one of issue-orientation to one founded upon a well-developed ideological base. In 1964, the demonstrators did not question the legitimacy of the social structure, but directed their criticism toward university policy and procedures, believing then that reform was indeed possible within the framework of American society. This limited optimism virtually has been eroded completely during 1964-70. As the Berkeley activists addressed themselves in the years following FSM to the Vietnam War, the draft, problems of poverty and urban blight, university complicity in military research and recruitment, ethnic studies, and even the "credibility gap," they became increasingly convinced that the very fabric of the society was inadequate for devising solutions for the social ills. Particularly after the 1968 Democratic National Convention in Chicago, but even before, the students were questioning the legitimacy of the entire political process. They could see little difference between Humphrey and Nixon, and viewed George Wallace as a caricature of both. As the activists repeatedly witnessed the inadequacy of sit-ins, teach-ins, and marches for effecting or stimulating social change, and believing no institutionalized channels for basic reform to be available or workable, they became committed increasingly to a comprehensive review of the American social order.

Although the incipient radical ideology at Berkeley is rudimentary and ill-defined, three major features are discernible. First, capitalism is viewed as the source of social evil. Any society based upon it is inherently unfair and structurally unsound. The argument continues, stressing that exploitation is a functional requisite in such a

society. This is, of course, a Marxian criticism. Second, the oppressed—the minorities and wage earners—are regarded as the good
people of the society. Hannah Arendt noted that young revolutionaries tend to view the impoverished and deprived as incorruptible
and pure of motive when they observe the wealth, profligacy, and
luxurious life style of the socially powerful.[2] This is a spurious way
of looking at the world, but it has much appeal to the Berkeley
radical. Third, the radical student politicians are calling for a work-
er-student-minority alliance to completely transform American society in order to liberate the oppressed. The activists argue that they
must educate the "proletariat" and minorities to heighten "class
consciousness" so that they can organize a coalition for revolution.

The center of gravity of campus politics has shifted considerably
to the left since FSM, if that is, indeed, possible in the national
public eye. The ascendancy of Students for a Democratic Society as a
type of militant leadership for the radical left has been a very
significant development. The success of SDS, however limited, indicates that the student movement at Berkeley is becoming less amor-
phous and more structured, developing an elite upon which it can
depend during crises.[3] Although the radical left is still deeply splin-
tered, the SDS leadership establishes the tone and defines the broad
contour of action for all groups. Their hope is to unite the radical
left, broaden its base of student support, and link up politically with
the minorities and wage earners, especially the younger groups, so
as to develop a revolutionary movement for re-structuring society. If
and when this loose coalition appears, the movement may have by
then secured considerable political power in the status quo, and will
thus tend to function as a limited vested interest, seeking major
reform rather than total revolution. In such a case, it will have been
effectively co-opted.

The argument for a revolutionary program is strong among the
Berkeley radicals today. The SDS, Young Socialist Alliance, Independent Socialist Club, Radical Student Union, Revolutionary
Youth Movement, and Progressive Labor, with a total membership
of over 600, are all speaking in terms of revolution rather than
reform. The Berkeley SDS supported Lyndon Johnson over Barry

2 Hannah Arendt, *On Revolution* (New York: Viking Press, 1963), p. 76.
3 For a discussion of the historic instability of the Berkeley student political
milieu, see G. Louis Heath, "Political Extra-Curricula at Uppsala and California,"
School & Society, 97:223-227, April, 1969.

Goldwater in 1964, issuing buttons counseling "Part of the Way with LBJ." Today, the radical left has exceedingly little faith in the American two-party system. Their cynicism had become so great by 1966 that a bloc of Berkeley radicals even campaigned for Ronald Reagan, arguing that his election would "hasten the revolution." The Berkeley radicals' literature and speeches are becoming more uncompromising in their demand for revolution with every setback in the frequent police-student confrontations on campus, the continuation of the Vietnam and Cold Wars, the emergence of a militant black movement in the San Francisco Bay Area, and the nation's increasingly heavy commitment to the arms race. The type of strategy that is being developed is exemplified by a 1969 Radical Student Union pamphlet: "The development of the revolutionary youth movement is a strategy to move from a predominantly elite, student-based movement to the more oppressed and less privileged working class youth as a way to deepen, intensify, and expand the revolutionary youth movement. This does not mean that we stop developing a broad-based anti-imperialist movement on campus or that we devote all of our time to organizing working class youth. Rather, we continue to develop a broad-based anti-imperialist movement on campus while expanding into all areas where youth are concentrated—high schools, junior colleges, the army, and jobs."[4]

The hard-core radicals now regard as futile trying to stop troop trains, occupying university buildings, demonstrating against Dow Chemical and ROTC, burning draft cards, organizing marches, and supporting proposals for ethnic studies in college. Little remains of the idealism and romanticism of the FSM. The activists are now calculatingly attempting to establish bases of political support in order to develop a revolutionary movement (what they sometimes refer to as a "militant counter-community," meaning an organized negation of the larger society). The possibility of realizing this goal is enhanced by the influx of a considerable community of hippie and radical non-students into the Bay Area since 1964. In fact, so great is the involvement of radical non-students in "student politics" that only 13 of 412 arrests during the October, 1967, Oakland Induction Center demonstrations were of students and only 40% of the 752 arrests during the May, 1969, People's Park crisis were of students.

The commitment to non-violence still exists for most Berkeley

---

[4] Berkeley Radical Student Union, "The Revolutionary Youth Movement," mimeographed, 1969, p. 1.

radicals, despite some spectacular excesses and the contrary image generated by biased newspaper coverage and uninformed public opinion. A few activists are arguing for tactical violence, however, in order to radicalize the liberal Berkeley student body. The radical elite enjoys great prestige and broadened support among the moderates when the police appear on campus, particularly if confrontation succeeds in eliciting a few arrests and beatings. This was notably true of the police removal of students who had barricaded themselves into Moses Hall in the fall of 1968 and the police abuses during the People's Park controversy of May, 1969. A few radical leaders now concur with Herbert Marcuse that non-violent protest against the establishment is counter-productive.[5] The fact is that they are succeeding in promoting violence, independently of most students' eschewal of extremist methods. What was once the non-violent FSM reform movement of 1964 is now a relatively violent revolutionary struggle on the Berkeley campus.

The setbacks of several reform movements addressed to specific issues have contributed to the development of a revolutionary youth movement at Berkeley. An example of a defeat on a specific issue is the Eldridge Cleaver debacle in the fall of 1968, when the student-run Center for Participant Education sought accreditation for Social Analysis 139X, a 10-lecture course on racism taught by the Black Panther Minister of Information and author of *Soul on Ice*. The Board of Regents responded by ruling that no course could be accredited in which a person not holding an instructional title lectured more than once. Cleaver spoke seven times and the College of Letters and Science enforced the Regents' policy by denying credit to students taking 139X. A group of 120 students sat in at the Registrar's Office to demand credit, but to no avail, and another group seized and barricaded Moses Hall, only to be forcefully removed by the Alameda County Sheriff's deputies.

The present condition of post-1964 student activism at Berkeley is very similar to that of the May Fourth Chinese student movement of 1919,[6] which began in the new universities based upon the

---

[5] The Berkeley radicals have been reading and discussing, in encounter group fashion, Herbert Marcuse's *Critique of Pure Tolerance* and *One-Dimensional Man*.

[6] Prof. Franz Schurmann, eminent sinologist, provided the information on the May Fourth Chinese student movement in a guest lecture for the Center for Participant Education course, "Asian Student Movements," April 17, 1969, University of California, Berkeley.

western university pattern of emphasis on scholarly research and publication and located in the relatively warm south China climate. There was a great proliferation of student underground newspapers. Berkeley is a new, research-oriented institution, too (only 101 years old), and also in a warm climate. Over 30 Bay Area student underground papers are read eagerly at Berkeley.

The qualities of newness, research orientation, warmth of climate, and student publishing promote activism: newness, because a young university is still rather flexible, allowing for the facile linking up of thought and action; warmth, for the reason that student demonstrations and political activity can proceed easily throughout much of the year; faculty research and publication, because sensitive, intelligent students, such as the ones at Berkeley are, tend to experience an alienation which impels them toward activism when they observe they are secondary in the educational process; and, student newspapers, in that the radical ideology for change can be developed and promulgated through this medium. Some Berkeley student publications are examining, for example, classic Marxist-Leninist doctrine as a possible base or component for a radical ideology. The *Barb, Tribe, Movement, Good Times, Student Mobilizer, Militant, Black Panther, Dock of the Bay, Student, Challenge,* and *Uhuru* are some of the papers contributing to the radical dialogue.

In both the Chinese and Berkeley movements, the students attained an intellectual plateau where they felt able to "liberate" society. In China, the students linked up with the masses; in Berkeley, they hope to do so. (A dozen or so Berkeley radicals working in Bay Area factories during the summer of 1969 attempted to educate and organize young industrial workers on the job, but without success.) The students in both movements, at one point in their ideological development, despised the discrepancy between the values of the society and social reality (which is where the FSM was ideologically), but later even expressed disgust with the society's underlying assumptions (the new look at Berkeley since 1964). The Chinese May Fourth movement wanted an entirely new set of ethics and values and so do the Berkeley radicals. And for this, reform is insufficient; revolution is necessary.

The Berkeley radical is a curious amalgam of mysticism, nihilism, anarchism, socialism, existentialism, and libertarianism, tenuously moored to society's underpinnings by a measure of honesty, inner discipline, and serious intent. He has brought several issues and campaigns before the campus public since 1964: ROTC, Dow Chemical, military recruitment and research, the Vietnam War, the draft, the Third World or Ethnic Studies College,[7] People's Park, the proposal for community control of Telegraph Avenue (the main thoroughfare in the south campus area), student-initiated courses, and the Oakland Induction Center protest of October, 1967. Seldom have the results been satisfying. The idea of student participation in decision-making inevitably encounters the resistance of administrators and faculty who are protective of their institutional prerogatives and university regents, politicians, and the public who discern no merit in student politics, particularly if the activists insist on foraying off campus in pursuit of their causes, and more particularly yet if they break the law in so doing. This situation makes a definition of the legitimate role of students in the political process (expecially the radical minority) a difficult one.

The Berkeley activists emphatically reject the traditional *in loco parentis* argument which implies that they need to be nurtured carefully through higher education. Gone are the days of 1881 when an entire class at the University of California could be suspended for defacing school property (even if it was a prank). That class responded by dutifully marching off campus, "class pins inverted, some with crepe on their arms, and many with tasty button hole bouquets," and singing the "Jolly Sophomore."[8] Such a blissful acceptance of authority is no more. Its passing can be regretted, but nostalgia for a University of California where football and Greeks were king will not help solve the present crisis of a student movement challenging institutionalized authority.

California's student politicians have defied their fathers who command power because they believe that the older generations are morally bankrupt. They have on occasion intensely embraced absolute ideals as only youth bent upon a better world can embrace them. What good has come of their idealism has often been in degree negated by the excesses to which they have resorted in pursuit of their lofty goals. Where pursuit of a cause through established channels might have achieved some results, intemperate direct action for "peace and freedom now" often has evoked retribu-

---

[7] For an analysis of the development of the "Third World College" issue, see G. Louis Heath, "Berkeley's Ethnic Studies College," *Integrated Education,* 7: 17-23, July-August, 1969.

[8] *Berkeleyan,* Oct. 31, 1881, p. 1.

tion from the authorities, massively supported by public opinion. The result has been an increasing feeling of disenfranchisement, alienation, and extremism among the students, and the demise of idealism. The radicalized students have assumed the mentality of an oppressed minority. They have become willing to take to the streets for their causes, some of which are contrived.

The People's Park controversy, where several students and non-students were shot (one died), is an example of how sizable numbers of youth can be mobilized about a specific issue which has no real relation to a constructive program of social change. For a few students to camp out on a vacant university lot, worth over a million dollars, and then expect the university to deed them the property does not really raise effectively any issue other than the appropriateness of certain forms of behavior devoted to change. The activists had certainly undertaken illegal acts to mobilize support for their cause. They had not injected into the public dialogue specific issues as they had perhaps hoped, but rather had diffusely threatened the society's structure of authority. They had grievously failed to articulate clearly what they wanted to achieve. All the public can see, particularly as the mass media tends to report student dissent, is a mass of disenchanted youngsters running about destroying property (the cornerstone of the society) and needing a good dose of discipline. The national guard is called out, violence ensues, and the issues are lost in the polemics of charge and counter-charge between revolutionary and reactionary. The interests of the majority of students (although a smaller majority than the "silent generation" of the 1950's) suffer most in the exchange. The university becomes a battleground for the polarities of the social order. The ultimate loser is the society itself because the sanctity of free and rational inquiry is trammeled.

The Berkeley student movement promotes values the public finds abrasive, if not outright subsersive. Student advocacy of equality of opportunity for minorities, banning the bomb, ending war, student participation in university decision-making, and exploration and sensitization of the self, often through the use of drugs such as marijuana and LSD, upsets generations of elders accustomed to an ivory-tower university, where conventional wisdom predominated and the students were willing to learn it. Many Berkeley students today want to develop their own education, studying what they will, so that they more easily may link contemplation and action. Over

2,000 participate in courses where field work in ghettoes and service in nonprofit organizations are staples. One student even was doing an individual major in "Revolution" before he was suspended for violating campus rules. The stress is on immediate commitment. The urgency is felt to be too great for total immersion in personal development, which is viewed as a selfish, socially callous use of one's life. It is unconscionable to the Berkeley "now generation."

The activists have built a new image of education since 1964. Raised permissively and educated progressively, they want a do-your-own-thing type of education. Education for them is a profoundly subjective experience. Turning on with drugs, pre-marital sex, encounter groups, light shows, and political action are for them some of the ingredients of a successful educational experience. The activists would rather read Camus, Hesse, and Malcolm X than Plato, Homer, and Shakespeare. They are obsessed with the idea of studying "relevant" issues. Their rejection of the Great Books, classical approach to liberal education in favor of education-as-action is an intense form of commitment to relevance.

For example, one student activist expresses a characteristic, deprecatory view of university education in the underground press: "Reality is allowed to penetrate the inner sanctum of Academia only after it has been sufficiently sterilized by the wizardly techniques of statistics and translated into professional jargon. The job is so complete that even the most idealistic sophomore is bored stiff; the graduate student, his idealism dulled by multiple hours of the same, no longer looks for any meaningful connection between what he memorizes and the world with which he once wanted to connect.

"The university may be well enough insulated to maintain itself as an anachronism and follow the same path as the church into total obsolescence. So what? Waste is a luxury we can probably afford in the U.S. But the rest of the world is neither so affluent nor so tolerant and our sins of omission are beginning to come home to roost."[9]

The education the Berkeley activists demand is really an autonomous youth sub-culture. Such a community constitutes a virtually complete negation of the values esteemed by American society. The purist call is for the adults of the world to lay down their power so that the world might be made perfect.

---

[9] Tom Maddox, "Graduate Students as Waste Material," *Berkeley Barb,* Aug. 8, 1969, p. 2.

The hyperactivism of the Berkeley radicals is partially a function of their feelings of powerlessness. They strongly resent society's paternalistic stance towards them. This resentment becomes undirected rage for some, particularly when the authorities use force to stop students who seek access to power through militant protest. Nothing is more dysfunctional for the activist than rage. What the Berkeley politico needs most is a clear definition of political and economic objectives, and a strategy for achieving them. Without a coherent program, rage is turned inward, producing self-defeating forms of withdrawal or violence among students and fear or guilt among elders. The social consequences of such a process are reaction and disruption. Orderly and democratic change becomes very difficult.

The student activists feel alienated from a society they did not build. They reject many of the dominant cultural values. Professional status, high income, a family and children, possession of comfort and luxury items, and the rest of the paraphernalia of success evoke for them little or no enthusiasm. The middle-class Protestant work ethic is considered a cultural relic. The older generation has "sold out," according to them, and they want no part of their world.

A Berkeley activist reflects a frequent criticism of American society: "Youthful delinquency is a violent expression of the rejection of the sterile choices offered by society. The delinquent's revolt, however, gives no way of escaping the system. He either yields to the lure of commodity consumption and gets a job, or attacks the commodity system itself."[10]

The student activists, a small and influential radical minority at the University of California, have found a new faith in the radical student movement since 1964 to fill the vacuum created by their disaffection with U.S. social, cultural, and economic institutions. Theirs is a secular faith which rejects the traditional authority of church, state, and family. They feel that the sacred values of past generations serve only to obstruct the coming of a man-made millenium, which must come if vast, complex bureaucracies are not to oppress men totally and highly destructive weapons systems are not to annihilate civilization. They vociferously reject the doctrine of fatalism, calling for men everywhere to control their own events. Their acting out of what was once youthful idealism, but now more closely resembles power politics, results increasingly, however, in uncompromising confrontation and violent disruption.

---

10 David Super-Straight (pseud.), *Berkeley Barb*, Jan. 5, 1968, p. 2.

15

THE WIDER SIGNIFICANCE OF THE COLUMBIA UPHEAVAL

MARGARET MEAD

DURING THE DISCUSSIONS that went on non-stop for days during this spring's [1968] upheaval, I was shocked that very little of what was happening here was brought into relationship with what was happening elsewhere in the city, the nation, and the world. Listening to the many discussions, including those conducted on April 30 and May 1, one might have supposed that Columbia University was situated on Cloud Nine. Yet, actually, the Columbia disturbances are more symptomatic of what is happening in the world at large than responsive to specific grievances and injustices within the sprawling structure of Columbia University. And it is the coincidence of conflicts within the Morningside Heights community, themselves reflecting the upsurgence of demands for black political power, and the dissatisfaction with their student status of students everywhere in the country, which has made the Columbia situation so acutely relevant to the world today.

For Columbia University, as an institution, is neither despotic nor systematically exploitative, neither prevailingly out-of-date nor widely neglectful of its faculty and students. The system is simply archaic. The university has grown in so haphazard a fashion that it

From *Columbia Forum*, Fall, 1968. Reprinted by permission of the author and the publication. Copyright, 1968, by the Trustees of Columbia University in the City of New York. Margaret Mead is Curator of Ethnology, American Museum of Natural History, New York City, and Adjunct Professor of Anthropology, Columbia University.

has become a clutter of fragmented departments, schools and affiliated institutions, each of which goes its merry, or less merry, way.
The faculty is not a faculty in the usual sense of the word. Many
administrative officers barely understand how the many parts of the
university function. But the events at Columbia mark the end of a
very long epoch during which students have been treated as wards of
academic institutions, a position that joins special controls with
special privileges and immunities from the civil authorities. The
disturbances at Berkeley heralded the beginning of the end. But the
University of California is a state institution and its students are
taxpayers and voters, part of the very apparatus against which they
were in open rebellion. Columbia, as one of the older and more
prestigious privately endowed institutions in the United States and
an heir to the traditions of the great English universities, is the
appropriate spot for dramatizing the end of the system.

Under the traditional English and American system, students,
whether they belong to the privileged classes or are permitted, by
scholarship or menial work, to enter the cloistered halls designed for
the privileged, are treated as academic novices toward whom the
university acts *in loco parentis*, and the students have been subject
to the authority of their teachers, as they are also subject to the
authority of their parents. Every detail of their lives—where they
sleep, what they eat, what they wear—has been, and to some extent
still is, subject to college authority. Their less privileged age mates
who go out to work become almost full adult members of the
working world, but students remain in tutelage, socially privileged,
but politically and economically in the position of minors who are
supported by parents or given just enough to subsist on by grant-
giving authorities. In the past they were expected not to marry, and
if their wild oats were sown too publicly they were expelled. Going
to college was, and still is, regarded as a privilege, and those who do
not obey the rules can be "sent down" (in the English phrase) or
"kicked out" (in the American). The college was, and still is,
treated as if it were a little autonomous kingdom, situated on the
best high ground, paying no taxes, and often enough barely giving
aid and comfort to the theological and economic dissenters from the
majority views of the surrounding community. In return for the
continued protection and teaching offered by the college, students
were expected to surrender part of their freedom as young adults;
but they were also permitted considerable license, in the form of

pranks, destruction of college property, defamation of sacred symbols, such as Alma Mater, importation of live stock into the classroom, organized cruelty to one another in the form of hazing, interclass ritual battles (only brought to a halt in the cases of severe maiming or death), initiation rituals rivaling those of savage tribes, cheating on a grand scale, and occasional forays into the town, where traditional town and gown conflicts were reflected in conflicts with the police. The police were expected to treat students with the gentleness their high status and tender years merited. Above all, in return for their protected state and license for fun and games, they were expected to be apolitical, and not, like some European and most South American students, to get mixed up in active politics.

Meanwhile, the whole face of the United States has changed. Half of our student-age people are in some kind of higher education and many of them are entirely state supported. In public institutions, instead of the old boards of trustees, custodians of endowments, there are governing boards subject to local political pressures. Study goes on far beyond the undergraduate college, which was once the preparation for academia, for a profession, or for a privileged life. Higher education is no longer a privilege or even a right. It is an arduous requirement laid on young people by the standards of employment in the society. Hundreds of thousands of students are husbands and wives, fathers and mothers, and wage earners who are attempting to carry the double load of study, still conceived of as an ivory tower activity, and full economic participation. Yet all students, those who are wage earners and those who are being supported by parents and scholarships in a nominal prolongation of childhood, are still set apart by their student status from full participation as members of society. Furthermore, although there is a draft that treats young men of 18 as ready to fight, there are also voting laws that deny them the vote and laws in most states that forbid anyone under 21 years of age, even veterans, to buy a glass of beer. The moralists, who have lost out in regulating the private lives of mature adults, still attempt to regulate the private lives of young adults by treating the late teens as an extension of childhood.

It is against this anomalous status that students are demonstrating and rioting, although the causes of rioting are variously defined: demands for the admission of members of minority groups; against dismissal or for retention of a professor; against classes on Good Friday; against the presence of Dow Chemical; against recruiting for the Marines; or just "general discontent." In this state of discontent, disturbances are triggered by any slight episode or by the organized disruptive behavior of small groups of the left or right. And every institution in this country is ripe for some kind of disorder. In some, the administration may have enough leverage to keep ahead of trouble; in others the students themselves have had the wisdom to anticipate the necessary changes (as when Cornell students voluntarily asked that the university no longer interpose its paternalistic arms between them and civil authorities). As in any potentially revolutionary situation, there are sporadic outbreaks, panicky and belated reforms, fumbles for leadership and, within the English speaking world, minor changes that are treated up to the last minute as unbearably revolutionary and destructive to our entire system as well as tremendous changes that are called minor adjustments.

The event that led to the involvement of Columbia students—undergraduates, graduate students, Teachers College students, students in the professional schools and in General Studies—as well as the young faculty who identified with the students, *vis à vis* the heads of their departments, was the dramatic revocation of the university's traditional claim to protect and discipline its own students when the administration called in the police. This reversal was made more dramatic by the long period of waiting, the sense of a power vacuum, the formation of an interim and an *ad hoc* faculty group, and the appropriate and often heroic attempts of the faculty to protect students from one another, from the administration, and from the police. A compact as old as the university system was broken. Students were treated like ordinary disrupters of the peace, trespassers, vandals, despoilers of private property, breakers and enterers, and this at the initiation of the university authorities. This brought outraged accusations of incredible brutality, far exceeding the outcry raised when three Negro students were shot dead at South Carolina State University in Orangeburg. Although the students at Columbia suffered few serious injuries, the sense of the overwhelming brutal power of the police was due to this sense of outrage at a broken compact.

But the compact needs to be abrogated. It is no longer appropriate to treat students as a privileged and protected group who, in return for this special station, abstain from political activity of any sort, submit to the regulation of their private lives, and risk expulsion for every sort of minor infraction of a set of outmoded rules. It is time we have the 18-year-old vote and recognize that students are making a valuable contribution in the economic and social life of the country by learning some of its more demanding skills. Furthermore, we must increasingly take into account the many students at universities who are not young adults, but middle-aged men and women who are returning for refresher courses or for completely new careers. Thus it becomes totally unbearable to identify studentship with the prolongation of childhood.

Today's students should no longer be dependent on their parents—those whose parents have any funds—nor should they be dependent on scholarships grudgingly doled out after a means test. They should be given full economic status, the status of an adult who is expected to marry, who works and has a Social Security number and may become a member of a trade union; someone who may get a mortgage and a telephone, buy furniture on time, and can, if necessary, collect unemployment insurance. Under the guise of privilege and protection, we have been penalizing our student population, separating them from participation in the affairs of the real world and impairing their capacity to understand that world.

There is a bizarre inverse correspondence between student groups and that other locus of rioting and destruction of property in today's American, the ghetto. The inhabitants of the ghetto are underprivileged, where the students are overprivileged, hungry where the students are well fed, living among dirt and rats instead of in subsidized dormitories. But still there is a resemblance. As long as ghetto dwellers were docile, respectful, and accepted submissively their second-class political and economic status, they too were allowed license—within their black communities—which would not have been permitted outside. As long as they fought only among themselves, cheated or stole from one another, took out their frustrations on one another, the dominant white community interfered very little, except, sometimes, "to fix" a case for a Negro who did come in conflict with the law. This a kind of bitter caricature of the way in which colleges and universities have been able to intervene on behalf of students who got into trouble with the police. Black adults and student adults alike have been treated as less than responsible, have been permitted to indulge in violent behavior as long as it was circumscribed and confined to their own territory. Too often, during the ghetto riots of the last three years, I have heard the comment, "Well, if they want to burn down their part of town, let them."

Demonstrations, civil disobedience, and inappropriate public behavior have been the perennial recourse of those who, lacking political power, seek to enter the world of the politically and economically privileged. German peasants during the Reformation, Quakers quaking in the streets, Buddhist monks who have forsaken their posture of peaceful noninvolvement, nuns who have come out of their cloistered walls, or housewives storming the House of Commons, all these are instances of groups that have resorted to various forms of unusual public behavior to attract attention to wrongs newly seen as wrongs, wrongs often so new that they had not yet been named.

Two generations ago, when women were fighting for the right to vote, they resorted to similar kinds of behavior—marches, hunger strikes, chemicals in mail boxes, tying themselves to the pillars of the White House, and throwing themselves down in the path of mounted police. Whenever a group that has been required to be docile, segregated, submissive, undemanding, and unparticipating, glimpses the possibility of wider participation in the society, we may expect phenomena like these demonstrations to call attention to their plight. And especially when the wider society has permitted limited license, we may expect violent contrasts as combatants overflow the limits of violence and challenge the complacency and safety of the larger society.

The fumbling, hesitation, contradictions, and confusion at Columbia in the period between the Tuesday when an associate dean was taken hostage and the Tuesday morning a week later when the police were called in, were overdetermined by the presence of not one but two explosive groups, the students and the inhabitants of Harlem. Fear of one reinforced fear of the other. At the same time, the contrast between the two were reinforced by the greater self-discipline of the Black Power group who are in all this in deadly earnest and cannot afford the ebullience that still characterizes campus radicals, who have been protected by the university *in loco parentis*.

The issue of the gymnasium is a symbol of the town and gown difficulties of a great landowning institution like Columbia, situated on the heights like the castles of old, while the poor live down in the valley. Here, as in the relations between students, the university, and the larger society, there is need for a new set of relations between the boards that control these giant educational corporations and the deteriorating slum communities that surround them. The gymnasium had been intended as a good will gesture, but it was a gesture, like that made by the students who made honest attempts to tutor children in Harlem. A "gesture" is no long the answer. Just as boards of trustees must become more responsive to the will of the faculty and to the current student body within the institutions for which they hold responsibility, so also boards of trustees of tax-exempt private institutions must find ways of responding to the needs and wishes of the other institutions and the residents of the communities in which they are situated. One of the problems in the Columbia area is that there are too few ordinary, householding citizens who can voice such needs emphatically. Mammoth institutions too easily become slum landlords, and in so doing they lose both the confidence and the recognition of the people who live in the surrounding slums, against whom they close their high iron gates. The day is past for town and gown opposition, both the traditional opposition between students, the townsmen and the police and the headlined opposition between educational institutions and the ordinary residents of the town.

But the student body has not, I believe, quite realized the meaning of the changes that will come. They demand more participation in the institutions in which they are currently privileged or condemned to study in years of incarceration away from the real work of the world.

At present their demands are inchoate and, in many cases, either articulately destructive or simply unrealistic. For example, giving students the right to hire and fire professors is as inappropriate as if the passengers on a single voyage demanded the right to fire the captain in mid-ocean or midflight. They will want to think through carefully, and in consultation, just which are the university activities in which student control and student autonomy and initiative are important. Perhaps all responsibility for their nonacademic lives should be vested in the students. Do they want this? They will need to recognize just what it will mean to be treated like other citizens, subject to the same rules and the same penalties, unsupervised but also unprotected. They will need to decide on the kinds of university policies they think should be reported and explained to them; on the kinds of situations in which they can be observers and those in which they can be consultants, working with faculty, administration, and trustees. What should be their knowledge of and their voice in such matters as the policy of the university toward Selective Service, tax exemption, acquisition or sale of land, disciplining or encouragement of articulate dissent, payment of employees, treatment of unions, the management, building programs, and community relations? When they begin to make socially responsible demands, they will almost immediately acquire the education in real life which they complain the university denies them. In one good humored conference between members of the graduate faculty and graduate students in anthropology, the students expressed a desire to listen in at faculty meetings, to which the answer had to be: "Fine, but we can't even get all the faculty into the largest room we have." Trivial, perhaps, but it is a problem that must be met if we are to have better communication.

There has been a tendency to try to find a hero or a scapegoat, some person or organization that can be acclaimed or indicted for what has happened at Columbia. Retrospectively, successful revolutions have heroes and unsuccessful ones have only scapegoats, or tyrants, to bear the onus of failure. True, in the Columbia situation one can point to conspicuous errors made by those in power, by those who sought to fill the power vacuum, and by small articulate groups of nihilistically oriented students. But this is not what is most relevant to the future.

What is relevant is the form taken by reconstruction. The more we can realize that the events at Columbia are part of a larger pattern of political unrest, ferment, and hope in the world, the easier it will be for us to relate the recreation of the university structure to the wider world. What can be accomplished at Columbia matters to the whole country and, because of the interconnectedness of the modern world, to educational institutions in other countries and to our changing political institutions. The task ahead is one of evaluating and implementing change, both the internal changes within the university organization and those intrinsic to the university's wider relations. If this double task is carried out with a self-conscious and articulate assessment of the true roles of the community of scholars in the contemporary world, Columbia will gain a new position in leadership and will become an institution in which students are prepared in practice, as well as in knowledge of subject matter, to take responsible action.

16

THE GREAT REVOLT IN HIGHER EDUCATION

WM. CLARK TROW

THE WAR ON CONFORMITY had been won. Beginning with the conquest of Madison Avenue, the gray flannel suit disappeared and, somewhat later, all uniforms. Skirts and trousers on both sexes, after a period of rapid shrinkage, if worn at all, assumed any length or girth their wearers wished. For the insufficiently hirsute, wigs or false whiskers could be used to decorate either sex, as could jewelry and cosmetics.

Youth leaders had recognized early that nonconformity in dress and bathing was merely an outward symbol, and that the positive aspect of their revolt was freedom. Emancipation from all rules except those they made themselves gradually came to be achieved. Freedom of speech, including freedom from the restraints of grammatical rules and from what formerly had been matters of taste, not only in language, but also in behavior, was theirs. One could say and do what he wanted, whenever and wherever he wished. Such words as propriety, taste, good breeding, and the like, were the only filthy words left.

Such freedom was not attained without a struggle. Mass meetings, marches, placards, sit-downs, lie-downs, sit-ins, teach-ins, lie-ins, riots, and arrests continued for some time. On college campuses black power fought white power, and white power fought black power until the Black-and-Whites took over, and continued the

From *School & Society*, Oct. 26, 1968. Reprinted by permission of the author and the publisher. Wm. Clark Trow is Professor Emeritus of Education and of Psychology, University of Michigan, Ann Arbor.

struggle, with the help of the Young Action Peoples' Society (YAPS) and the Social Nationalist Activists for Revolutionary Labor Schools (SNARLS). Gradually all arrived at enough of a consensus (which they usually spelled "concensus") to do business. When freedom from financial obligations came up as the next step in the reform of higher education, the opposition (all persons over 30) began to bestir itself. To meet the growing opposition, the students in one of the smaller state universities, one that earlier had been a teachers' college, achieved a breakthrough by smashing all precedent and promulgating the rule that students should constitute a majority on the Board of Regents. This went a long way toward clarifying the meaning of the earlier contention that students should have a voice in the determination of policy in matters in which they were concerned.

As would be expected, the constitutionality of the measure was questioned, and the state attorney general was asked to render an opinion. Surprisingly enough, he found that, by some oversight, the law stated that the control of the university should be vested in a duly elected board of regents. But it failed to state how many should serve on the board or by whom they should be elected. Great was the jubilation on the campus when the opinion was announced. The students forthwith duly elected 15 student members to counterbalance the 10 old members.

It was some time before the results of this momentous action began to make themselves felt. But gradually, a number of regental rulings were passed, all by a majority of 15-10. Among the first rulings was one under which rent paid by a student permitted him to live anywhere on the campus. Several readjustments were made under this ruling. Then one student who had a room to himself refused to permit another to occupy his room. The intruder claimed, under the regents' ruling, that he had a right to it, since he had paid his rent where he had been living. Angry words were followed by blows, and the intruder, after a struggle, threw the other out the window. The intruder was taken into custody, and the next day it was reported that he had no recollection of the incident. It was ascertained that he had purchased drugs at the student-operated book store. At the trial he was charged with murder, but he won his freedom on the defense lawyer's plea of temporary insanity.

Other minor incidents occurred, but the faculty raised no great objection since a later ruling released them from all teaching responsibilities because the movement required that all students should be free from rules about class attendance. A meeting of the liberal arts faculty was called to oppose the ruling, but it failed to bring out a quorum, and so no action was taken. The reason for the lack of interest was said to be the fact that the new plan gave faculty members practically full time for their research.

Things began to change, however, when, with the leadership of a few staff members from the sociology and mathematics departments, the regents were pressured to break all contracts with professors who were doing research on anything having to do with national defense, or which might be of possible use to the armed services or the war effort, and to spend at least six hours a day in personal contacts with students either in dormitories, other college buildings, or in their homes.

These rulings tended to increase the general opposition which, until now, had been only in the form of mutterings and complaints. At a secret rump session of the regents, to which the members of the student majority were not invited, the various actions that might be taken were discussed. Those that were voted gradually became evident in the days which followed.

The first event occurred at a student meeting at which a number of motions, amendments, and amendments to amendments, coupled with points of order and motions to adjourn so confused the student chairman and his cohorts that nothing was accomplished. The next occurrence was at an open meeting at which the speaker was a representative of the Cuban government. Questions came from the floor so rapidly that the speaker was unable to reply to them; and, though the chairman tried to channel them, he was unable to handle the situation and the speaker finally gave up. At a similar meeting, the applause began simultaneously with the speaker. The chairman tried to quiet the clapping and the shouts of "Bravo," pleading as he did so for the rights of free speech, when an unidentified voice yelled, "That's what *we* used to ask for."

These and similar happenings attracted little attention, however, as compared with the sit-in at the regents' meeting. The room was so crowded that neither the adult nor student regents could get in, and all moved to a larger room. The gathering soon became unruly and the police were called in. They arrested a dozen or so persons, supposedly faculty members; but they turned out, on further inquiry, to be non-professors.

What finally put an end to the nightmare was a motion made by a non-professor impersonating a non-student at a later meeting of the board of regents. (Since, for some time, the public had been invited to attend these meetings, it was felt that it also should be free to take part.)

The motion stated the fact that three-fifths of the cost of educating each university student was paid by the state. Hence, students were actually kept men (and women), their keepers being the despised over-30 age group. The motion called for the elimination of the unbearable situation. In the violent discussion that followed, someone yelled: "Can a kept man be a free man?" and the answer was a loud and vigorous "NO!" A number of the student regents realized what was going on, but were unable to keep their followers in line, and the motion passed.

After the students had voted themselves virtually out of college, other actions were reported by off-campus forces. The legislature voted to withhold all funds until the situation was stabilized. The AAUP issued a 56-page report on the situation and removed the university from its approved list. The State Department of Education withdrew accreditation, which meant that no teachers graduating from it legally would be certified to teach. A number of industrial firms sued for breach of contract. The university had failed to pay for some $500,000 worth of building equipment, and the firms were unable to get any reply to their inquiries. In one such case, the student advisor to the university treasurer had taken the statement home and lost it; he since had left college and his successor had not been appointed.

Meanwhile, the soap and clothing manufacturers had put on a vigorous advertising drive to increase their sales. As a result, conformity with former nonconformity in styles no longer was acceptable. Lacking the outward symbols of freedom, the movement began to fade out, hastened by the recognition on the part of the leaders that graduation time was approaching, and they soon would need to get a job from an employer who was over 30.

17

ACTIVISM IN THE HIGH SCHOOLS

SCOTT D. THOMSON

STEPPING TO THE PODIUM of a high school assembly in Palo Alto in the fall of 1967, the student body president impatiently fingered a lock of long hair and urged the audience to demand a student bill of rights. Meanwhile in Chicago, a group of teen-age activists busily organized a "Free High School." In Great Neck, Long Island, student protestors gained control of the high school newspaper and began to deprecate the principal and "The Establishment." In Montgomery County, Maryland, the County Superintendent of Schools accepted a demand to review with students the entire curriculum. In Southern California, pictures of Che Guevera, essays from Regis Debray, and the thoughts of Ho Chi Minh appeared on school bulletin boards. And on April 26, 1968, a self-appointed day of protest, thousands of high school pupils across the land stayed away from their classes. Suddenly activism has become a part of high school life.

Copying college student reformers (the Berkeley protests were nearly five years ago), the high school activists began during the summer of 1967 to organize in earnest. Supported by the Students for a Democratic Society, their college-age mentors, and fueled by a strong, adult anti-war sentiment, small groups of youth, 15-18 years of age, began to plan conferences on student power. Their purpose

Scott D. Thomson is Superintendent, Evanston Township High School, Evanston, Ill. A shorter version of this article appeared in the *Catholic High School Quarterly*, October, 1968, published by the Secondary School Department of the National Catholic Educational Association.

was to discuss and to act on a wide range of social issues, including the draft, the war economy, poverty, and racial discrimination in America. They also intended to revolutionize high school life by changing everything from courses of study to compulsory attendance laws. The activists were determined to determine policy.

Acting as a mini-manifesto, the 14-page pamphlet, "High School Reform," was published in June, 1967. Authored by a Southern California dropout, Mark Kleiman, and distributed by the Students for a Democratic Society, the document is highly critical of American society and ambitious for reform. Some excerpts:

Those responsible for our education have done their utmost to create an artificial community on the high school campus, a community which will demonstrate to us that it is better to "adjust" to an unsuitable society than to change the society into something in which we can live with dignity (p. 1).

The courses, which are irrelevant to the point of being ludicrous are forced upon us. Scientific courses are compulsory for those who will have little to do with science. "Health" classes warn us about drugs proven to be physically harmless (p. 3).

Both student and teacher are a tool of administrative totalitarianism. The student comes out of high school a finished product to be consumed by either the agro-business, the university, or the war machine (p. 5).

One method of gaining support is to begin agitation around issues students are already concerned about. We should be in the forefront of any student protest against administrative action. Everyone connected with us should run for student council. . . . Where we win control of any offices, we force the administration to either give in on major points, or continually override our actions, which makes the administration look silly to the students, our parents, and our principal's bosses downtown (pp. 6, 8).

What freedom we achieve must come from our own struggle. In order to change the ways in which people relate to one another, we must build a community, a community of resistance (p. 14).

For perspective, it is well to differentiate among three divergent student groups: the activists, the advocates of black power, and the hippies. All make headlines but each is a unique group. They are similar only in their protest of contemporary America. The hippies are largely apolitical. They have dropped out, separating themselves from a society considered grossly competitive and hopelessly materialistic. Hippies are heavily involved with drugs, with mysticism, and with communal living.

Activists are deeply committed to political action. They want change, the more radical desire radical change. They organize protests and engage heavily in political education. They tolerate hippies but scorn them as whimsical, not to be counted on for the tough in-fighting. Activists plan to reshape society by gaining power. Hippies flee from power.

The third group, believers in black power, sometimes forms alliances with the activists. However, most black power leaders are extremely cautious about white influence. They avoid being used by the student activists for the activists' own ends. Therefore, the black power students of high school age concentrate on issues of racial prejudice, of economic oppression, and on the development of an Afro-American curriculum.

Adult reaction to student activism reaches across the spectrum from cautious support through skepticism, uneasiness, and undisguised alarm. The more supportive adults define activist youth in such glowing terms as responsible, compassionate, and involved. Critical citizens, however, describe the activists as egocentric, political radicals bound on anarchy, people playing with a fire that could burn down the whole city. Perhaps both definitions are correct. Because the student power devotees place so much emphasis on explosive confrontation rather than dispassionate discussion, it becomes difficult to analyze the happenings. The dust and clutter confuse the mind. However, after a year of involvement, perspectives are improving. Certain elements emerge from the work of student activists even as the movement takes form.

The more radical activists despise much in American society. They say the basic institutions have failed miserably to solve the gut issues. They blame their elders for accommodating problems rather than solving them. They see a tremendous gap between professed values and adult behavior. They are especially contemptuous of the "Liberal Establishment," a group that activists feel gives only lip-service to social justice. Radical activists consider schools to be an institution created by the establishment to perpetuate itself, a place where young people are processed for job-training and where individuality is destroyed. Radical activists want a revolution *now* to eliminate war, poverty, and prejudice. They propose to implement this revolution by gaining control of schools, by "liberating" the students there, and by teaching the new order.

Moderate student activists have more modest goals. They feel much in school is irrelevant and want a decisive voice in curriculum, in student discipline, in appearance, in student activities, and in administrative regulations. They also want to evaluate teachers and to publish this evaluation. However audacious their goals may sound to adults, the activists are dead serious; they are confident, bold, and committed.

Most Americans would agree that our society, to include the public schools, could stand some shoring up. Certain goals of the student activists are, at most, moderately controversial. And student participation in educational policies can claim a heritage extending to Aristotle's Lyceum, where older students formed the curriculum, elected officers, determined school policies, and encouraged practical experiences. But what has turned off most teachers attempting to work with activists is their insistence on the politics of confrontation and their tendency to obstruct and destroy rather than to build.

Confrontation politics are used by activists to gain support for various student power causes. The tactic is simple but effective: First, gain the initiative. Find a cause popular with students and which, if successful, would increase student power. Demand of the administration the acceptance of this cause. Agitate if the demand is denied; claim credit if the demand is met. Maintain this tactic over a series of causes, always proposing while the administration denies. This places the authorities in a negative position and portrays the student power leaders as psychologically positive and the champion of student rights. Assure the general student body that, by sticking together, power is assured by sheer numbers.

Keep the initiative. Ask and agitate, gradually becoming the spokesman for wider circles of students. Probe, continually seeking new gains. Then, when the time is ripe and student support assured, apply the coup de grâce. Make demands. Don't compromise. Be adamant. Threaten massive student action should demands be denied. Apply pressure. Depend upon the other side to be tolerant and yielding. Set a deadline. If the demands are denied, cause a fracas, inform the press, and watch the principal burn in the news media.

The more militant activists require a confrontation. To seek out limits of power and know the consequences of passing beyond those limits appear to have great significance. And the process of gaining student power is considered incomplete until actual conflict occurs. Thus, an administration which accepts the demands of activists in the hope of compromise or appeasement will solve the immediate crisis only. The ultimate goal is confrontation. To quote one activist, "It was our unrepressed intolerance and thorough anti-permissiveness which brought our actions to success." School authorities who delegate a significant amount of power to activist leaders may be in deep trouble when confrontation finally is achieved.

Another concept proposed by the activists is "participatory democracy." Stated theoretically, this is the right of people to participate in decisions which affect their lives. Practically, in a school setting, the concept becomes most interesting. Decisions would be made only by those people interested enough to attend meetings. But the decisions would be binding on the entire student body. Decisions ideally would be unanimous, with consensus arising from discussion. Votes would be taken only as a last resort. Student legislatures and other forms of representative government would be eliminated. The ability of a small, well-organized elite to exert control in this type of laissez-faire atmosphere is obvious.

Student power devotees chafe under rules and regulations. They dislike authority . . . rules . . . laws . . . even when made by students. They function in an immediate, communal way. Because of this abhorence of authority and impatience with structure, student activists do not manage their programs well, even when elected to office.

The most descriptive terms for American activists are these: utopian, radical, humanistic, communal, and militant. They are also righteous, impatient, and involved. They are neither democratic nor liberal in the traditional sense.

The radical activists act with a rigid, emotional groupism quite similar to the Red Guards. They are not, however, Soviet-style communists in any sense. American activists abhor the bureaucracy, the impersonalism, and the materialism of the traditional communist state. They are more "Now Generation" Populists than Stalinists.

What is the activist personality? Many are bright; some are brilliant. Few are Merit Scholars. Most are modest achievers. Their interests run strongly to the humanities and social sciences. Few are interested in science, mathematics, business, or athletics.

Activists are highly involved with community problems. Many have marched with adults in street demonstrations. They seldom attend ball games or dances, they spend little time on cars, and they dress indifferently. Their lives do not revolve around the traditional interests of teen-agers. Nothing could bore them more than a money-raising contest for the class gift.

Activists have a limited number of close friends. They are not popular in the traditional teen-age sense. Their gatherings usually involve a discussion of "The Movement"—its tactics, its heroes, and its future. Most activists are singularly serious, lacking flexibility and humor. They have the blueprint for revolution and dedication to implementing their plan. With ambitions like these, little time remains for frivolity.

What forces in society created this new breed? Some analysts feel the causes to be negative, while others consider them positive. Detractors of student power blame permissive parents or broken homes, causing poor adult-student communication and a distrust between generations. Professor Urie Bronfenbrenner of Cornell University calls attention to the "split-level family," noting that youngsters today are raised by other youngsters and by television rather than by parents. Each generation lives alone with its own activities and customs. Few meaningful relationships are established with older people. Parental values are unclear.

Other critics believe that student power is simply a symbol of a serious breakdown in society, causing a lack of discipline, of responsibility, and of commitment to the general welfare. Still other skeptics blame activism on a rising affluence and its concommittant self-gratification, causing youth to be demanding.

Observers sympathetic to student power see positive influences at work. The influence of television in presenting the world first-hand in an absorbing media is cited. An increased awareness through travel and higher standards of education also is thought beneficial. Interests are widened, causing a rejection of the cashmere sweater syndrome. Involvement in politics is considered natural as a result of these experiences and the natural idealism of youth.

While these "positive" and "negative" factors contribute to student unrest, other more discreet causes are as important, including unhappiness with the social consequences of technology. Activists feel that older generations unabashedly have worshipped the machine, ignoring consequence to man and nature. They feel technology must be tamed. Activists want planning for human relationships to come first, to be followed by inventions compatible with improving the human condition. They feel today's world is dehumanized and destructive. They feel it will not survive long unless the course is changed.

A corollary of this attitude is the alienation of many activists from their concept of the future. Most are disinterested and unsuccessful in quantitative subjects. They are aware that an ever-increasing prestige goes with success in science or mathematics; even the cigarette ads attest to this. So they tend to feel threatened by a future in which their own personal worth could be questioned. They fear being surplus, discredited, and obsolete.

A second cause of student unrest often overlooked is the increasing ability of students to identify and define problems. For 10 years the new curricula have taught experimental techniques—the identification, observation, and analysis of a problem. As a result, pupils have developed "super skills" for questioning the observable. They are brilliant analysts, aware of each flaw to be observed. What we have not done for students is to develop along with this brilliance a parallel commitment to solving problems. Every defect in the fabric of society is readily observable to students. But the dedication to finding solutions within democratic values is missing. Thus we have created a modern Sophist who can ridicule with brilliance society's awkwardness in dealing with severe problems, but who himself lacks a solution save one based on impatient force. Today's activist is obsessed with ends. He lacks commitment to the democratic process in achieving these ends. Since process is the life-blood of democracy, the implications are serious. A parallel problem is impatience. Today's youth, more than ever before, live in an instant world. Few desires are denied. Gratification is the rule. Consequently, many students have a low frustration level. They become impatient with committees and debate. They expect immediate solutions. They want action. And with grandiose abstractions and a sensational vocabulary they demand action.

A third cause of activism is the release of power to students by teachers and administrators, a movement caused by four circumstances: (1) a conscious effort to develop independent, mature learners; (2) an emphasis on process rather than content (problemsolving skills, often entitled "learning how to learn," are considered essential in a society which replaces new knowledge with old at an ever-accelerating rate); (3) even the most competent, veteran teachers are unsure today of the exact nature of content to be taught; (4) the current popularity of independent learning as a mode of instruction (many teachers want to "get on the bandwagon" but lack sufficient experience or materials to do the job properly, giving students a totally unstructured environment).

As a result of these forces, many students are being given a greater latitude and fewer specific directions than ever before by a less confident faculty. Sometimes the authority is delegated well with adequate guidelines and specific expectations. But frequently the job is sloppy, giving students an unreal picture of their prerogatives and a too hazy understanding of the stewardship of the teacher and of the legal parameters established by state law. The misperceiving, aggressive student who has been taught to be independent in school and to use his initiative can breach consciously the parameters set for him by teachers unless these parameters are clearly established and discussed and unless these limits are enforced.

A fourth cause of activism is plain faddishness. Demands and demonstrations are the "in" thing to do. Protests have caused a storm beyond original dreams. Young people thrive on excitement. Stirring up the pot a bit with student power is exciting. Smug smiles emerge when the action burns hot. However, the implications go beyond a little hell-raising. The indoctrination of students with radical politics and attacks against constituted authority are dangerous games.

Activism in the high schools can be disruptive. It can cause a breakdown in student government. It can feed distrust between students and teachers. It can interfere with classroom teaching. It can cause a suspicious, nervous atmosphere throughout the campus. It can cause a community to lose confidence in its schools. And it can be used as a wedge for political radicals to influence students.

Activism in the high schools also can be valuable. It may make students aware of a world greater than themselves. It can get young people involved in profound social issues. It can provide a forum for curriculum improvement. It ordinarily demands a re-evaluation of student government. And it can present a working exercise in the relationship between freedom and responsibility.

Unfortunately, activism was initiated and presently is led by student radicals with a political purpose. Stated nakedly, the purpose is revolution—the replacement of our present institutions. Schools are to be the beachhead for this assault.

What is most needed now is for students and teachers to wrest initiative from the radicals and to place the movement in the hands of responsible leaders committed to the democratic process as well as to the solution of burning inequities.

18

STUDENTS IN SEARCH OF "SOUL"

FRANKLIN H. LITTELL

WHEN I STARTED TO THINK of the question why students revolt, and what these signs of alienation and frustration might mean, I remembered immediately an earlier column written by one of the gatekeepers of our society, Art Buchwald. [EDITORS' NOTE: See chapter 13 of this book for the complete text of the column.] This column was written in 1965 and it referred to another demonstration—not the one most familiar to us—but, nevertheless, it seemed to me that some of the alienation and frustration which is sweeping the student generation today continues to derive from the same sort of haphazard bumbling to which Art Buchwald referred. Contrary to popular impression, administrations are more confused and student demonstrations more directly on target. A study of 81 major outbreaks since the fall of 1966 showed that, contrary to public supposition, most of them are fortuitous and haphazard. Seventy-eight out of 81 centered down on one of two issues—either the draft and Vietnam or racial injustice. This would suggest that the students' action is not as frivolous as commonly interpreted. On the other hand, since many senior academics are in principle of the same opinions on Vietnam and racial injustice, it shows that there is a distinct breakdown of communication between students and administrations and faculty.

Based on an article from the *Journal*, September, 1968, published by the Division of Higher Education, United Church Board for Homeland Ministries, New York City. Used by permission of the author and the publication. Franklin H. Littell wrote this article when he was President, Iowa Wesleyan College, Mount Pleasant, Iowa. He now is Professor of Religion, Temple University, Philadelphia, Pa.

Or is it possible that the universities as corporations have become so completely a part of the military and white establishment that the students have concluded that these are the two points where they can affect public policy at the points nearest home? In either case, we must realize that the alienation and frustration reaches back over many decades and is not primarily a result of the present crises in our society—important as they are to all concerned.

There are several reasons for saying the present confusion has been building up for decades and I would like to list a few of them for your consideration. The first point[1] is that another recent study has shown that students are older biologically, physiologically, and more mature in many other respects than students of thirty years ago, or certainly sixty years ago. The point of physiological maturity among American youths, due to better food, vitamins, and medical care, has been sinking at the rate of approximately six months per decade since 1880. That is a fundamental point, which means that the students who enter are consistently older in terms of experience and in terms of their sense of dignity as men and women—rather than "children"—than they were earlier. In fact, they are three and a half years older than, say, in 1900. When you remember that most of our higher education patterns were fixed in the period 1890 to 1910, then you can see that our built-in obsolescence in higher education may not be equal to that in the automobile industry, but, nevertheless, that it is a major factor in shaping present problems. The students are adults and not children, although one is startled to see how often the latter term is used in communications among educators. They're old enough to breed and establish families; they're old enough to kill or be killed in distant places of the world. Many of them are working. And they have begun to resent protective custody much more than students did thirty years or sixty years ago.

Another factor which is working is that democratic family structure—that sense of partnership within the family from which many of our students emerge, a partnership which is one of the most significant social forces of the time—provides a very distinct discrepancy between the style of life in the family and the style of life in the high school and later in the college and university campus. Students who come to me are very aware of this gulf. About 19 out

---

[1] I am indebted to Dr. Edward J. Shoben, Jr., of the American Council on Education for calling my attention to this point.

of 20 of them seem to have come from high schools run on authoritarian principles, frequently backed by demeaning procedures (including an administrative espionage system), which technically might be called police-state structures, and they are resentful of administration. It takes at least a year of good work with any of them to convince them that any administration is honest or even honestly attempting to do what it claims to do. At the college level we inherit hostilities accumulated during high school suppression.

The greater freedom of the college or university invites delayed explosions. It's always dangerous to give guns to the natives. If you maintain close control, or espionage systems, such as most of them have experienced in high school, then their chances of revolting successfully and demonstrating efficiently are considerably reduced. But on most of our campuses, even though the discussions between administrators and deans and the others in authority seem to me to be distressingly control-oriented, students do discover more liberty than they have experienced in the high schools. Since they are resentful and distrustful toward administrations in general, they lie in wait; and sometimes college administrations take blows which are really meant for high school administrations.

Another factor of great importance is the massing process, which is widespread. Due to a tremendous increase in the numbers of students and also due to lack of planning (except for buildings and budgets, sometimes), we are still dependent upon structures and styles that are sixty to seventy years out of date and totally inadequate. In most cases the university tends to function as an assembly line. There are no channels of communication in most cases—even with faculty, let alone students. Most student governments with which I'm familiar are patent frauds and the students know this. What seems to me the most dangerous aspect of the whole situation is this: They are learning that to get a hearing it is necessary to adopt extra-procedural measures. I believe that it is utter hypocrisy for an institution to claim to represent civic virtue and to claim to impart self-government and republican principles and then to practice police-state measures to keep the natives under control. (Let me say, if I sound as if I'm speaking from a single particular situation, that last year I visited 57 campuses, and the year before, 56, and I am generalizing from conversations with other administrators and not just from my own experience.) I think that we are proletarianizing the American students—making revolutionaries, which some may think to be a good thing, and we should be aware of what we are doing. It takes more than the reading of books in American government and American history to convince youths that the system can be made to work, that our constitutional traditions of due process are still viable. It takes a great deal more than that, particularly if they aren't experiencing due process, liberty, and self-government. If we are making revolutionaries—that is, persons who have learned that the only way to get a hearing is to adopt extra-procedural measures and then go on to develop the ideology and practical discipline implicit in that perception—we are building for a radically changed society.

Another point: We are, in this process of massing, forging a one-generation culture of students, teaching assistants, and non-students in many of our schools. I don't think I shall mention the names of the institutions used for illustrations, but these are real cases. I have recently been talking with a trustee of one of the ten wealthiest universities in the world. He had just spent a week on campus learning his lessons as a new appointee, and he said that the most interesting experience of all was to spend an afternoon with over 500 teaching assistants who are doing about 90 percent of the undergraduate instruction in that institution. I thought that it was quite revealing, almost symbolic, that in the last major demonstrations in Madison the organization and the leadership was in the hands of the "Union of Teaching Assistants." In other words, if the peasants revolt, the slaves are going to be with the peasants—they're not going to be with the landlords. A few weeks ago I received a telephone call from the dean of students at one of the major universities, asking if we would accept a transfer foreign student who came from a prominent family in another land, who was used to being treated as a human person, and was slowly gurgling to the bottom in the massing process. I said we'd be glad to, and then I discovered that she had had as her smallest class a session of 500 participants and that she was in one "class" of 3500 students! I think that—although this is perhaps not as important in the Columbia situation as in some others—the truth of the matter is that American higher education has created the best graduate instruction program in the world by cheating undergraduates, and it's beginning to get back at us in terms of alienation and frustration and resentment and the head of steam that makes for explosive demonstrations. The point is that you cannot build a culture of continuity, richness, and depth without at least a two-generation interaction. The original charter of the first modern university, the University of Paris, defines this new thing as *universitas magistrorum ac scholarium,* a "fellow-ship" or a "community of teachers and students." You have to have two generations if you are going to function in a genuine learning process aimed at the maturing of wise persons. Preferably, and this is true in the best and most creative cultural situation, you need three. You cannot do without two. And if you drive persons into a one-generational culture, as I think we're largely doing in many of our institutions, we are also proletarianizing each youth generation—not in the Marxist sense, necessarily, but in the classical sense of producing persons who are "in the society but not of it." Such proletarians cannot accept the language or the values or the standards, or even the sincerity, of those who claim to govern them. A society which alienates and frustrates its future leaders is building for disaster; certainly it is building for a radical break between our present way of doing things and our present traditions of orderly change and the shape of the future. Whether that is desirable or not is something to be debated, as I said before, but at least we should be sure of what we are doing.

I am not pleading the small college as the answer, although I personally feel that we should limit the size of institutions with undergraduates to much smaller numbers than most of them now are. We should also plainly differentiate between the technical insti-tutes and universities concerned for wisdom and maturity. Many of my colleagues in the small colleges seem to think they have the answer. I will try to show that's not necessarily the case. The real issue comes down to the question of what we are doing in our so-called educational institutions, whether large or small. If we believe that there is a potentiality—a maturing and affirming poten-tiality—on our campuses to develop persons who can enjoy and practice and believe in liberty and self-government, we must of necessity cultivate the trans-generational dialogue and also the dia-logue between various schools and disciplines, which is the course by which wisdom may be attained.

The two poles of learning which I would stress to dramatize this key issue are the technical (*Techne*) and the wisdom dimension (*Logos*). A few years ago, at a large state university in the South-west, the following incident occurred. There had been demonstra-tions to press for the admission of Negro students, according to the law of the land. The university administration was delaying. The university was in fact a technical institute and the demonstrations were led by an assistant professor of philosophy, with that rank already chairman of a (minor) department. When he refused to desist, the president of the institution was finally provoked to say, "Well, I really don't think philosophy has a place in our kind of university." I have thought of that incident many times, because it seems to me that what we are doing in American higher education is to train technicians on a mass-production basis, largely ignoring the wisdom dimension. That is, we are training persons who are capable of analysis, critique, and the comparative method (a fairly sophisticated invention), and such experts can in fact be trained in mass situations. They can even be trained in good part by teaching machines. Mass production is possible as far as the technical dimension is concerned.

But wisdom has to do with the oral tradition, with the thoughts that are wound from behind, with memory, recapitulation, and reenactment, with the transmission of culture and the appropriation of one's heritage, with the achievement of one's self-identity. This dimension of learning cannot be served on an assembly line. It can only be served in a creative way through the dialogue which transcends generations, the dialogue which was supposed to be the business of the classical academy, and is the basic charter of the modern university. But the university has, in large measure, simply given up. We're engaged in producing what the market requires, the individuals technically competent—persons who may, however, have had no genuine experience of creative unity in the process of being trained. Now this process has awesome implications. As Justice Jackson said at Nuremberg, the most awful figure of the 20th century is the technically competent barbarian. What we are doing in much of our so-called higher education at the present time is to produce technically competent barbarians, and to short-circuit, indeed cut out, the whole pursuit of wisdom and cultivation of the wisdom dimension.

When we function this way, we are turning out incapacitated specialists. I say "incapacitated" because of a conviction which is highlighted by an experience of a colleague of mine at the Chicago Ecumenical Institute. E. I. had been experimenting with "sector groups." That is, they had building groups which reached out into the suburbs and pulled together the whole metropolis of inner city, suburb, and outlying district. In this case, they had formed a group of young adults, most of them from the city streets—black and Puerto Rican, a few whites—and then merged with them from the North Shore young adults, most of them from the white community. They learned in the experiment that the most significant thing was not the difference of race at all. The most significant difference was in response to a life situation. When a challenge was thrown into the group—a really important issue, an *Existenzfrage*—those who had grown up on the city streets, who had learned survival tactics, acted. They did not always act the way you'd want them to, but at least there wasn't a chasm between the person and his capability to act. Those who came from the suburban schools, however—those beautiful, laboratory-equipped schools—jumped back and thought about it. They reflected and analyzed, and of course they were frequently left behind by events. And then my friend, who told me of this, went on to say he had reached the conviction that those who were so trained in the *Techne* dimension—who would go through these wonderful high schools, would then go through scientific training in college, and many of them go on to graduate school—when they got through with that whole process, they would not be any good for anything at all.

What I am saying is this: It is imperative that there should be, for the sake of our society (as well as for religious reasons not here discussed), persons who are technically competent specialists, but who also have retained the capacity to make the humane and wise response. In their learning they have had the opportunity to appropriate their heritage, to dialogue with persons of another generation, to experience the wisdom dimension of learning.

In my own state, we have this issue dramatically illustrated by the conflict between the Amish and the Department of Public Instruction. The Department of Public Instruction is wholeheartedly committed to the proposition that all American youth should be able to use computers and shoot the moon. The educational pattern which they are pushing as ruthlessly as they know how is a monolith based on the technological premise. The Amish, by contrast, are anti-technological. For 450 years (their own sector since 1791 and the movement from which they derived since 1523), their people have been committed to the proposition that this technological age is a warring world, a world committed to violence, to dehumanization. They don't want to have anything to do with it. They are not opposed to education, in spite of attacks made on them to that effect. They are simply opposed to the kind of education which produces technically competent barbarians. In this battle which has been going on, the Amish—by unfriendly description a social fossil—represent certain values which our people in public education seem to have forgotten, and which I think most higher education has forgotten as well.

To plumb an even more demonic potential in an educational system dedicated to training technically competent barbarians, read Werner Richter's *Re-educating Germany* (U. of Chicago Press, 1945). The book is his story of what happened in the 1920's and 30's as the Radical Right, the Nazis, took over Germany's educational system. They finally eliminated all of the humanistically trained persons from The Ministries of Education and replaced them with public education people. As Richter said of the situation in which they found themselves, and he was the most brilliant young man ever to hold the portfolio for higher education in one of the German state ministries, "a new type of student came into being—a smooth-tongued, plausible, shrewd, arrogant, and often licentious busybody and go-between—who was superior to many an impractical professor not only in power but also in adaptability and cunning."[2] And then he spoke of the situation in which the leaders of the educational ministry found themselves, as the humanists from the university were replaced by the technicians. This meant that "a type of teacher came into prominence which had previously played no part at all in German education."

I think that the crisis which we face in American higher education has much larger implications than simple loss of communication between the generations, as serious as I consider the frustration and alienation of generations of students to be. I'm quite sure that totalitarian society likes to hire all the technicians it can get. I am also quite sure that by training technicians and by short-circuiting the wisdom dimension, by emphasizing the assembly-line approach and playing down the dialogue, we are turning out persons who are not equipped to make the American constitutional experiment in liberty and self-government work.

---

[2] Richter, Werner, *Re-educating Germany* (Chicago: University of Chicago Press, 1945), p. 73. (Richter was at one time *Rektor* at the University of Bonn, Chairman of the *National RektorenKonferenz*, president of the *Deutscher Akademischer Austauschdienst*, president of the *Alexander von Humboldt Stiftung*, and chairman of the German Fulbright Commission.)

The thing which encourages me about the student demonstrations, therefore, is that they have got hold of something which the people who are planning these structures and running the institutions seem to have forgotten: that is, the importance of style of life, the importance of public commitment, the importance of what is called "soul" in some circles—a quality much ignored by trustees and administrations, and even by faculties. The students know the university is betraying its vocation. They also know that they are being cheated in their education.

The typical small college answer to this situation is to say that the university's bigness and secularity are wrong, and that we must stay small and tidy and "Christian." As Bill Coffin said one time, "Small Christian colleges make small Christians." I think the direction of his remark was right, even if it hurts. I'm opposed to the direction which most of our small colleges are going. They are increasingly mothering a wealthy or upper middle-class elite. They are being shoved to the margins, or themselves moving willingly to the margins, of higher education. They are pricing themselves out of the market. I'm also opposed to the rural romanticism that characterizes many of them. Of course they think they have to make the best of what they are, for 80 percent of the seminaries and small Christian colleges in this country were founded out on the land someplace. During the 19th century our fathers, in their anxiety toward the pagan philosophies of the universities and with their suspicion of rising cities, built their colleges out someplace safe, and now they find themselves having to make the best of it. Frequently those who inherit their isolated oases are driven into the kind of romanticism and nativism which I think is disastrous to education and to the country. The truth of the matter is that the American people are a metropolitan people. Two-fifths of them live in the twelve largest cities and 80 percent of the American people live within easy commuting distance of cities of at least 25,000. If the small colleges want to be marginal and enjoy it, then one way for them to do it is to continue to talk anti-urban.

If the solution in higher education is not the assembly line, neither is it the tribe. I am opposed to the homogeneity of the business, economic, cultural, and racial trend, and in favor of the pluralism in our society. I'm opposed to the *Gemeinschaft* level of operation, the notion that the answer to the large corporation is a patriarchal family, a committee-of-the-whole operation. And I have the feeling that many times the student demonstrators, in their resentment of assembly-line situation and lack of channels of communication, tend to throw back to a primitive typology and image of education.

I am opposed to the anti-technological note. We can be thankful for the latest technology—audio-visual, air conditioning, etc.—and there's no return from it. It is a fatal mistake when persons who see the way we are moving, and are worried by the massing process, speak as though we can recover some lost and primitive virtue, some former time of simple social relations. I am also opposed to religious primitivism. I resent the kind of apologetic which has been developed by many of the small colleges—including compulsory chapel, custodial education, *in loco parentis* off campus, and the rest of it. It is an active temptation to talk this way against the large universities, but it is a serious mistake in education. This is the truth which is in the Student Bill of Rights, even though I think there are some aspects of the educational philosophy there represented which we have to talk about more fully. Even the large universities are pressed toward the parental and custodial role. I was interested to see that in the column which *Barron's* printed and is distributing so widely about the Columbia situation, they used language such as "aggression" and "appeasement," which is the language of custodial education. Their assumption is that we who are in authority should keep the animals under control—whether by diplomacy or ruthlessness.

I am opposed to the whole process of imperialistic church education, the disastrous consequences of which have appeared in recent months in St. John's University in New York, and—even worse—in Drew University, a unit of my own denomination in Madison, New Jersey. These tragedies should make clear to all of us, I think, that this type of approach—the determination to maintain an old and possessive pattern of education—is self-defeating as well as immoral. Christian colonialism can finally destroy this creature, this precious entity, the university. The secularization process is now historical, and it is to be welcomed.

The historical process of secularization means that law and justice and the structures of maturity are important. We cannot retreat into the past. Neither certainly can we affirm the course of a runaway freight train, which is moving with very little sensitivity and apparently with very little understanding, to the liberty, dignity, and integrity of human persons. We must move away from government of education by "deals" toward constitutional procedures, toward structured, rational, planned, purposeful education. Now what does this mean, frankly?

The argument here presented implies that the administration must develop corporate procedures which have efficiency and modernity, which have goals, and which, above all, have competent staffing. The major blight of the small colleges is that we have so many fourth-rate appointments, both academic and administrative, who are not competent in the areas of their responsibility. Corporations which have fixed goals, and which know what they're doing, have staffing, rational structures, goals, self-analysis. For the educational corporations to attain modernity, we must establish standards of integrity vis-a-vis off-campus activity. This is one of the major points at stake in the Columbia situation. Many institutions have so accommodated themselves to some other institution's purposes, chiefly along the track of research and development, that they pass neither tests of integrity of purpose nor rationality of operation. In this dialogical situation—which should have wisdom as well as technical proficiency—a major goal is to function rationally in terms of set goals. It cannot then function as an appendix to some other more or less useful institution's purpose—such as state government, or national government, or the defense establishment. I am frankly amazed that professors and administrations, who long since pledged their loyalty and their full participation to off-campus activity, now criticize their students because they make "off-campus alliances." Such alliances had seemed to me predictable, and the students were the last, not the first, to abandon loyalty to the university.

In short, I am arguing that we need to recover the integrity and liberty and the dignity of this creature, the university; that it must be a major center of social change; that it must function as the conscience of society; that it must resist the totalitarian impulse—whether it comes from an ideological state or simply from a government which has forgotten its proper function. It must maintain at all costs the raging dialogue which is the life blood or—better still—the oxygen of the open society.

What does this mean, then, to the trustee? It means trustees must develop an integrity in the practice of their stewardship. I think there have been some shocking revelations of conflict of interest, of what any ethical society would call conflicts of interest, in these situations, and that the trustees have a responsibility in their stewardship to remember where their commitments are. We have, of course, a much larger question, and that is whether the structure of the corporation itself—which has been the structure of the American university and college since Harvard's founding in 1636 as a company of adventurers—may not provide a gravitational pull which inevitably leads trustees into conflict of interest whether they recognize it or not. Most trustees serve on eight, ten, twelve, or perhaps even twenty boards, and many of them speak of these relationships—transferring to the university or the college the style of thinking which they have as board members of other corporations—in a terribly wrong-headed way. That is, they have "employees" (the faculty), and they turn out a known product which is in demand (the students). That is the reason why the tendency of trustees, unless they remember who they are and what they're there for, is to think in a manipulative way of this creature, the university. I'm using blunt language, because I think the university should have a dignity and integrity of its own.

The trustees need to institute checks and balances characteristic of a *Rechtsstaat*, of a government of laws rather than the personal, patriarchal, and direct form of government. They need, in my conviction, to highlight the function of three estates—trustees, faculty, and the students—students including past students, that is, alumni. And although I don't want to seem chauvinistic or particularistic, I do want to say that we have made considerable progress at Iowa Wesleyan in doing just this. I say this because I'm not just peddling theory, but talking about something which is part of my life. We do have a new charter for our trustees, which eliminates false relations to the denomination. We do have a new constitution for our faculty, which gives the faculty an integrity which it did not have two years ago. When I came in, I found that every faculty committee—every member and every chairman—was appointed by the administration, and the chairman of the faculty meetings was always an administrative officer. Under the new constitution, all faculty committees are set up by the faculty, and we have a faculty chairman elected by the faculty. We in the administration fought our case for a body which has dignity, which has liberty, which has integrity—and the faculty now has it.

A system of laws means that the students have to be integrated into the process according to their time and their place and their learning. I've said what I think of typical student government. I'm not really interested in "student government" at all. I'm interested in student participation in the governance of the institution itself. Next year we will complete the process of integrating the students into the governance of Iowa Wesleyan, including membership on faculty committees and representation on the board of trustees. The students, in short, are everywhere opposed to being treated as IBM cards, to being treated as Volkswagens rolling off the *Fliessband* in Wolfsburg. They want to participate. They want to have a part in deciding how this city-state, this community of learning, shall function.

In many situations across the country even the faculty has very little voice. In almost all situations the students have very little or no voice. This seems to me the opposite of training them for citizenship in a society which maximizes republican principles; rather it trains persons either to accept orders in a docile fashion or, at least, to revolt. Both of these alternatives seem to me to be, at this point, unnecessary and undesirable. We had much rather change the basic structures of our institutions, structures which have outlived their usefulness.

The claim of liberty and self-government is an anxiety-producing word, I discover. I had the privilege of giving the annual luncheon lecture at a meeting of one denomination's college presidents a few months ago. The denomination had some sixty institutions. I was arguing that the students, young citizens, learn how to make self-government work by having an opportunity to do it, not by reading about it first. And in the discussion period which followed, for over an hour one president after another insisted we administrators can't trust the students. We can't trust the students! They told these hair-raising experiences that they'd been subjected to. "You can't trust students!" "You've only been a college president for a year and a half. Wait until you've been a college president as long as I have. You can't trust the students." I was absolutely dumbfounded. Believing that self-government and liberty are worthy experiments, I was paralyzed to see how anxious administrators in this day could become. And afterwards, one of the presidents came up to me, a president of an institution whose name is certainly known to most persons, and at the end of the table privately said, "The truth is, you can't trust the faculty either!" This, to me, represented the kind of anxiety which grows out of the experience of persons who are trying to run institutional structures which are no longer adequate to the situation. They can't face the faculty. They can't face the trustees. They can't look at their students. And I think the primary reason is that we administrators are simply out of touch with the realities of the situation, are out of joint with the structures we have to work with.

I say, for my own part, thank God the students don't accept the goals of the marketplace and desires of this society or any society to protect the competent barbarians; thank God they're determined to raise some of the questions of what life is all about. This society cheats the public by building obsolescences, by polluting the streams, by destroying the national forests before a lazy Congress gets around to act, by profiteering on war; and I'm happy that the students aren't content with it.

I hope that we will move as rapidly as possible, in such places as we can act, to develop new structures—structures in which students, faculty, and trustees have balanced participation—for what should be a common goal and a common stewardship to the republic of learning. In this kind of a situation, the administration then can act not as a policeman or a close control operator, but rather as what Mr. C. P. Snow calls the "civil servant"—those who keep the lines of communication open, so that all are brought in who are entitled to participate in decision-making; who, of course, have the weight, in line with their experience and wisdom, but who are not manipulators.

Why do the students revolt, then? I think they revolt because they're Americans, and not content to be subjects or serfs. What is to be done about it? We need basic reform, radical reform, of structures which were set up when students were much younger; when we were a society where 83 percent of the population was rural, in a situation which could perhaps function for a time at the family-substitute level in the school of learning. This can no longer be done. At the present rate of lack of change and radical adjustment, disaster is, in my judgment, both inevitable and well deserved.

19

TOWARD REMEDIES FOR RESTLESSNESS: ISSUES IN STUDENT UNREST

~~~~~~

EDWARD JOSEPH SHOBEN, JR.

THAT "CERTAIN RESTLESSNESS" to which President Johnson referred in his 1968 State of the Union message manifests itself most strikingly in two American minorities. One of these minorities is, of course, our Negro population; the other is our youth, especially college students. The temptation is strong to explore the insights that might be gained from considering this juxtaposition of our most disadvantaged and, from at least one legitimate angle of regard, our most favored social categories. That temptation must be momentarily resisted, however, in the interest of a more immediate effort—an attempt to set in some possibly useful perspective the expressions of student unrest as they presently affect our institutions of higher education and our society.

We must begin with some problems of scale. Justly proud of the quantitative growth in our student bodies and in the increasing access of Americans to educational opportunity beyond the high school, we may still overlook the possibility that sheer enlargement, when it is massive enough, makes for qualitative changes that can be both unexpected and difficult to accommodate within older frames of references. The meaning, for example, of the familiar fact that roughly half of all our citizens are under 25 years of age is not

~~~~~~

From *Liberal Education*, May, 1968. Reprinted by permission of the author and the editor of *Liberal Education*. Edward Joseph Shoben, Jr., is Director, Center for Higher Education, State University of New York at Buffalo.

entirely clear; but there may be considerable significance in the implication that 50 per cent of our people have no direct memory of the Second World War and do not have built into their emotionally undergirded values an appreciation of the reasons for which it was fought. Unless there are improbable alterations in our population trends, a slight majority of Americans may be under 21 in 1972, the next presidential election year; they will almost certainly exceed 45 per cent. In that year, assuming no change in the legal requirements for voting, the median age of those casting ballots will be about 26. On the basis of numbers alone, one can hardly escape the inference that youth is becoming (if it has not already become) an intensely significant force in American life.

When we turn to *college* youth, we are confronted by another familiar fact the full meaning of which we may not yet have assimilated. The enrolment of between 6.5 and 7 million youngsters in colleges and universities is not only historically unprecedented; it represents something even more without antecedents: the presence of almost half the nation's high school graduates on college campuses. Whatever else it implies, this statistic suggests that students are more heterogeneous than ever before, reflecting the diversity of the American populace in a novel fashion and permitting young people from quite different walks of life and backgrounds of experience to become acquainted with one another and to form new coalitions of friendship and social purpose.

In any case, as their numbers have grown, students have achieved something of a corporate identity that is recognized across the country. The Selective Service System deals with them on special grounds; Madison Avenue's advertising firms mark them as a centrally important and distinctive "target public"; they are courted politically, and their mores are acknowledged, sometimes with a tolerant and even positive acceptance and sometimes with an angry and offended sense of outrage, as sharply different from those of older generations. National student organizations have shown a high degree of viability, and student leaders have been able to establish and maintain loose networks of individuals and groups which support and reinforce one another in the mutual pursuit of a variety of goals.

When numbers of significant size begin to interact with a sense of group solidarity, the result is a potential for power and influence. It is hardly surprising, therefore, that students have begun to press for a greater share in the making of those political, social and educational decisions that they perceive as affecting their welfare and their destiny. It is even less surprising that the campus is the locus of their efforts: The campus is where they are in critically impressive numbers; and the campus is the primary source of the sense of commonality and corporate identity that feeds their feeling of strength and sufficient unity.

To the extent that these observations are at all cogent, it is well to set them against the background of enrolment trends during the twentieth century. In 1900, less than five percent of high school graduates went on to college. In the fall of 1967, virtually fifty per cent of them entered some sort of institution of higher learning. For such an alteration to take place during the life of a man just reaching retirement age is itself an index of the rate of social change to which we and our culture must adjust ourselves. More immediately, it suggests that it is largely college-going, strongly abetted by the mass media and the new technologies of communication, that has given young people in so potent a fashion their contacts with each other, their shared concerns and aspirations, their opportunity to organize themselves, and at least a good bit of the knowledge and ideals of the basis of which their activities are rationalized. In this sense, the emergence of students as an influential bloc, both in our colleges and universities and in society generally, is at least partially an outcome of (a) a national policy that has steadily and rapidly increased the accessibility of higher education and (b) the college experience itself.

It is at this point that we may be dealing with a highly complex interaction among social processes that can only be sketched here. We know that at least the leaders of dissenting student movements come from liberal and well-educated homes. It seems quite probable that the parents of these youngsters were themselves strongly influenced by college faculties who were highly skeptical of traditional values and often sharply critical of the Protestant ethos in the American culture. This kind of intellectual determinant has been contemporaneous, of course, with the growth of more permissive forms of child rearing. Indeed, the ideas of liberal intellectuals have been the primary sources of justification for these more comfortable and acceptant socialization practices. For many of those who are now activist student leaders, it seems quite likely—to argue the minimum case—that university officials and governmental representatives are among the first adults whom they have met who have not at least pretended to accord the concerns of youth a weight comparable to those of elders. In short, the critical disposition, the self-determination, and the tendency "to think otherwise" that characterize student leaders may well originate in precisely the democratic commitments and the traditions of intellectual skepticism that our colleges have most proudly stood for. From one point of view, we may have erred in the kind of educational experience we have provided over the past fifty years; from another, our errors may consist in the lag between our stimulation of youthful concerns and participatory impulses and our creation of the social forms that would make them most useful and contributory.

In any case, our attempts to grapple with such questions are profoundly complicated at the moment by the issues that animate students, that impinge most directly on them, shaping the character of their futures and frequently evoking apocalyptic responses from them. These issues, obviously, are those connected with the war in Vietnam and the military draft associated with it, and with the polarization of American race relations—the popular symbol for which is black power—which, in ominous and tragic part, reflects the degenerative elements in urbanization and the aspects of decay and primitivism in our major cities. Set against the somber backdrop of nuclear weaponry and the dangerous fouling by man of the natural environment, the urgency and appalling properties of these grave problems are by no means the monopoly of youth, but their frightening, frustrating, and infuriating immediacy is most intense for young people. It is young people who are called upon to fight in Vietnam, and it is young people, not yet possessed of either the patience or the spiritual callousness (depending on one's point of view), who are most outraged by the widely acknowledged and highly visible injustice that typifies America's dealings with its Negro population. It is no wonder that as youth has become, by virtue of numbers and a sensed corporate identity, a force in society, it has also become especially concerned with these deeply troubling matters that most vitally affect them and their hopes for the future.

On the campus, however, the problems of Vietnam and racial injustice entail two serious difficulties. In the first place, these issues are ones over which the academy exercises no control; in the second, they represent a class of questions toward which colleges and universities have historically assumed no *institutional* posture. As a consequence, the fabric of the academic community is rent by student demands that our institutions of higher education become involved in the resolving of societal tensions that are political rather than technical, and many of the energies of student dissent collide with that most cherished principle in the college tradition, that of academic freedom. Academic freedom, it must be recalled, has never applied to institutions; the doctrine of *Lehrfreiheit,* for example, confers no immunities upon the university except one: the right to clothe its faculty members in a special protective armor as they explore *any* trail that may lead to truth and wisdom. In contemporary terms, it is generally accurate to say that any tenured member of any faculty is entitled to espouse any position toward the war in Southeast Asia without fear of losing his job or suffering other reprisals from the college or university at which he teaches. Like most ideals, this one sometimes is dubiously honored in the breach rather than in the observance, but cases like that of Professor Genovese at Rutgers underscore the principle here. Our central point, however, is that the condition of the institution's making this essential gift of security to its professors is that it must itself remain neutral. In a very real sense, the only commitment to a *social* value—in contrast to the academic values that guide the internal processes of scholarship, instruction, and the nature of its intra-institutional community life—that a university makes *as a university* is its intransigent commitment to academic freedom. So long as it takes no corporate stands with respect to the major controversies that beset all dynamic cultures, it can insist on the peculiar freedom of individuals to investigate, to publish, and to debate which is the cornerstone of the academic enterprise. By this insistence, it maintains an open campus on which, at least in laudable theory, *all* ideas may compete for a hearing and minority points of view can be safely maintained.

The faith in academic freedom, recently associated closely with Constitutional guarantees under the First Amendment, rests on at least two assumptions. One is that, given world enough and time, the processes of investigation and of debate among reasonable men will identify the solutions, or adequate approximations to solutions, of serious human problems. The other is that the complexities of moral decisions are better unraveled through discovery and rational analysis than through the organization of passionate convictions however

widely they may be shared. It is quite possible that the most significant development of our time in higher education is a challenge to
those assumptions. One way to formulate that challenge is as a
confrontation between the essentialist tradition in the *Wel-
tanschauung* of the United States and of Western civilization and an
existentialist mode of thought and feeling that has emerged in
vigorous opposition to it. Although the existentialist view of man
and the world is hardly the sole property of youth, it seems to have a
particular attractiveness for young people, especially under today's
troubled conditions. If we are to cope effectively and humanely with
this sharp conflict between basic ideas and values, it would be well
to understand it.

The broad essentialist orientation, which has in many was been
the intellectual keystone of the West, is based on an emphasis on the
transcendence of time and space. Whether idealists, emphasizing
ideas and processes that outreach the particularities of human experience, or naturalists, concentrating on men and the affairs of
earth, essentialists are preoccupied with eternal verities, with what is
permanent, rational, formal, and universal. They conceive of human
nature as being fundamentally the same over time, clime, and culture, and they are interested in the diversity of conduct and societal
contours primarily as variations on unchanging themes or as instances of anomaly. Because they prize continuity, they regard history and tradition as basic sources of wisdom and insight; and for
the same reason, they put a premium on foresight among the human
virtues and regard highly the man who looks to the future, who is
mindful of the "rainy day," and who controls his impulses in the
light of their possible consequences. This pattern of values italicizes
the desirability of both predetermined goals and the development of
rational and, where possible, standardized techniques for reaching
them. In turn, these desiderata define the groundwork for the pro-
mulgation of systems, intellectual as well as technological, and reinforce the notion that feelings, emotions, and the irrationalities of
experience, although they can be enjoyed sparingly and through
such formal devices as art, must fundamentally be curbed and suppressed as inimical to the effectiveness and efficiency of systems.

The existentialists, on the other hand, argue that the formal,
systematic vision of the essentialists leads inevitably to depersonalization and anomie, to the denial of individuality, and to the establishment of social structures that are, finally, inescapably authoritarian.

For the existentialist, the quest for meanings is the source of vitality, and meanings can be found only in the *concreta* of personal experience. When Socrates played the gadfly, pressing his fellow Athenians to question their implicit assumptions, to examine their own experience as the valid basis for belief, and to prize the process of inquiry beyond the acquisition of knowledge, he embodied the existentialist style. In Buber, Camus, and Sartre, what we have is an elaboration of that style into an elevation of the irrational and affective side of a man to a plane equal in value to the rational one. In their view, continuity with the past is less important than the relevance of things—of ideas, artifacts, social forces, and other people— to present and personal needs. Indeed, both the past and the future are experientially compressed into present memories and present anticipations; whatever is, is *now*, and that *now* is an insistent demand that cannot be gainsaid or go unanswered. Thus, the existentialist advocates an education that centers around sensed problems, that affords room for the development of the affects as well as the intellect, and that enables the individual man to engage himself socially and politically with established systems without losing his identity to them. In human relations, existentialists accept the concept of responsibility but find its authority and necessity not in rules or imposed obligations, but in mutual concern and caring. Similarly, knowing the way in which manners and formalized interpersonal styles can deteriorate into lies and manipulations, they opt for authenticity, for "telling it like it is," and for spiritual and emotional directness in the dealings of men with men. Ethically, tolerance of ambiguity is a higher virtue than foresight, and participatory involvement is more valued than rational prudence.

In this too rapid contrasting of two philosophies in conflict, the aim is neither to suggest that they have no regions of congruence nor to present one as superior to the other. Rather, it is to indicate something of the profound differences in assumption and stance that mark the two sets of proponents and to measure in some rough fashion the width of the gulf across which they must talk. Effective negotiation usually entails some accommodation between the parties in both basic conceptions and eventual goals. To an existentialist, the logic of institutional neutrality as the fundament of academic freedom is at once irrelevant and hard to understand when his moral passion is fired by the nature of the Vietnamese war or the unjust plight of American Negroes. Nor are the traditions of civility persuasive to him when those traditions, politicized, have been bound up with colonialism, racism, the suppression of the emotions, and formalist sterility in art and education. On the other hand, essentialists, who are overwhelmingly the current masters of the House of Intellect, are anxiously aware of the way in which existentialist radicalism can sometimes couple ignorance with impatience, always a dangerous combination, just as they are threatened by the existentialist's disregard of conventional amenities and his lack of faith in order and evolution.

From the luxurious standpoint of an outsider, the circumstances examined so far—and several others could be added to them—define two opposing powers, divided along both ideological and stylistic lines of cleavage, whose incentives for negotiation and mutual accommodation are perilously low. Philosophical differences, not fully articulate but functionally determinative, make conversation as difficult for one side as the other. The passionate, existential style of student leaders, not infrequently encouraged and strengthened by professors of similar persuasions, provokes among administrative and faculty leaders a reaction of distaste and defensiveness. Under this kind of duress, the temptation becomes extremely strong to assume the role of adversary, to resist all pressures toward change on the ground that virtually any meaningful concession amounts to a kind of academic Munich, and to condemn the opposition as made up of irresponsibles, nihilists, or the servants of some evil conspiracy. When such temptations are yielded to (a state of affairs that can easily and sympathetically be understood) it is a short step to policies of deterrence through restrictive regulations, espionage systems, and strong punishments.

On the other side, this tendency toward the escalation of conflict can be expressed in a variety of ways, all justified on the ground that petitions have received no responsive hearing. (It must be emphasized that a responsive hearing is not necessarily a synonym for sheer acquiescence.) As a consequence, if the university takes no official stand against the war or conducts war-related research, then Dow Chemical Company recruiters can be captured and mill-ins organized to prevent military and CIA representatives from reaching those whom they would corrupt. If the university provides insufficient support, either morally or financially, for ghetto tutorial programs or involvements with Negro political groups concerned with fair housing laws or better administration of tenements, then student support and protection can be given to the campus advocates of Black Power even when some of their ventures flirt with criminality. If the university fails to supply the educational experiences that meet the canons of personal relevance in student perceptions, then counter-institutions like free universities can be founded, an institutionally embarrassing underground newspaper can be established, or demonstrations can be staged at which draft cards are burned while speakers extol the virtues of Fidel Castro, Mao Tse-tung, or Ho Chi Minh.

There are a number of disturbing elements in this state of affairs. One is the basic challenge to the morality of academic freedom and the more general ethic of civil liberties of which it is a part. Such a challenge raises questions about the extent to which the college, which seems to have shared significantly in producing the leaders of the campus-based youth movements, has effectively communicated, by both precept and example, the fundamental nature of these values. It appears at least possible that soul-searching on this issue and attempts to discuss its ramifications with representatives of student groups could be profitable items on the agenda of the immediate future.

Second, the dynamics of escalation in the confrontation between our institutions of higher learning and their most numerous constituency mirror in some suggestive ways a problem that may be national in its scope: a crisis in our attitudes toward authority. But to the extent that this concern is a valid one, is there not also something of a crisis in the leadership in which that authority is formally invested? And is it not necessary for that leadership, as a part of its leadership responsibilities, to accept the task of a creative and honest review of the situation in which the academic community now finds itself?

Among the barriers to the undertaking of such a review is a possible factor that is easy to overlook. Existentialist activism is irritating, upsetting, and threatening not only because it sometimes assumes ugly forms, represents a new source of political power on campus, and bases itself in philosophical concepts that make communication difficult; it also distracts busy and dedicated men from going about the business that they have defined, quite appropriately, as of the highest importance. The administrator, jerked by necessity from the job of managing an institution, and the scholar, similarly yanked from his laboratory or library, are subjected to a shaking of their very professional selfhood; campus riots and revolts draw them from the activities for which they were trained, with which they are familiar, and on which their self-esteem hangs, to problems for which they typically were not trained, which are both unfamiliar and fundamentally unexpected, and which are ordinarily damaging to self-esteem. No man enjoys this kind of stress, and it becomes easy under these conditions for academic leaders to identify themselves as the beleaguered garrison of an attacked collegial fortress. Unfortunately, if they strike this defensive posture, they risk abdicating to others the raising of the great questions of such immediate consequence to both the academic world and contemporary civilization: How can universities better serve the society of which they are a part, and what does "better" mean in such a context? How can the college or university continuously reconceive its mission and reexamine its procedures in order to keep pace with the rate of technological and social change? How can university personnel think constructively about the educational process as the groundwork of a humane culture in this special era of man's history?

If such critical questions lose their high priority or go by a kind of default to others, the academic weather is likely to turn still more stormy. Comprehensive criticism from inside an institution is usually more meaningful and acceptable than attacks from without; but if criticism from within is to be effectively launched, then some difficult implications of the present situation must be faced. First, one must raise the issue of whether, in spite of provocations to the contrary, administrative and faculty leaders must strategically eschew the role of adversary in coping with student unrest and seek unremittingly for methods of anticipating student concerns on grounds that both keep the civil peace and, more importantly, are genuinely educative. Second, does not this strategic consideration lead to a substantive one? Despite their incredibly rapid expansion in the past half century and particularly in the past decade, our institutions of higher learning operate for the most part with organizational structures, rules of procedure, and conceptual goals and guidelines that were in effect at about the turn of the century. Is it time that our institutional leadership, which has become more and more heavily burdened with managerial and public relations functions of the utmost importance, turn its attention more forcibly and inventively to academic matters and the ways in which the process of learning in college interweaves itself with the character of action in the larger society? Such a step would require that the awarenesses, the existential orientation, and the resources, both intellectual and political, of a significant segment of college youth be taken seriously into account.

To raise these issues is to ask questions about our conceptions of collegial staffing, our procedures for developing faculties, the ways in which that ancient and honorable term "the academic community" can be given genuine communitarian vitality in our time, and the nature of the experiences which are most likely to be educative in the light of the new qualities that are discernible in modern youth and its subculture. Whatever their many other obligations, the college and the university remain *teaching* institutions. To fulfill their instructional function, it is probable that they will have to think more seriously than ever before about learning as an active process, about the characteristics of learners as these attributes affect learning, and about the nature of significance in the material to be learned. Most of all, given the philosophical split within the academy, the academic mind must turn its talents to the development of more inclusive modes of thought, especially in the application of intellect to the affairs of the university itself, that will encompass and accommodate both the essentialist and existentialist positions. Then—and perhaps not until then—will higher education run with reassuring swiftness in the race with catastrophe that, as H. G. Wells once remarked, is the definition of civilization.

20

FACING THE ISSUES OF STUDENT UNREST

FRANK J. SPARZO

DURING THE PAST FEW YEARS, evidences of student unrest and effective protest have become increasingly common on college campuses. Although this student unrest has been exaggerated and misinterpreted by some journalists and educators, it does seem to be developing into a significant factor on college campuses throughout the nation.

A major fact has emerged since the Berkeley protests of 1964: the college student today is exerting more and more power and influence on administrative decisions.[1] This new power can be labeled conveniently the "fourth estate," and may take its place beside the three traditional estates of trustees, administration, and faculty.

We see evidence of this new student power all around us. For example, in some colleges and universities organized teacher evaluation by students now is occurring. Students always have evaluated their professors, of course, but recently they have systematized their evaluations and now are sharing the written results with college administrators and the teachers themselves. Obviously, some professors do not accept the new way in which their students are evaluat-

---

[1] Influence will be taken, as synonymous with power, to be "the capacity of one actor to do something affecting another actor, which changes the probable pattern of specified future events." See Nelson W. Polsby, *Community Power and Political Theory* (New Haven: Yale University Press, 1963), p. 3.

From *School & Society*, Oct. 26, 1968. Reprinted by permission of the author and the publisher. Frank J. Sparzo is Assistant Professor of Psychology, Ball State University, Muncie, Ind.

ing them, nor do the faculty, administrators, and students agree on just what should be done with the results.

Michigan State and a few other universities now have an Ombudsman, a full-time position similar to that found on a national level in Denmark, Sweden, Norway, and Finland. Protecting students from excesses of bureaucracy and helping them solve their problems informally and quickly are the major tasks of this official.

Reform also is taking place in student-faculty committee assignments. Many colleges are promoting student-faculty cooperation by instituting new student-faculty committees and increasing or adding student representation on faculty and administrative committees.

These are but three examples of many which indicate that a new concern for students and the power they can exert is developing on campuses across the country.

It is now clear that educators will make a grave error if they expect this current student bid for greater power and influence to wane. The trend is irreversible, and for good reason. Students are more conscious of their influence; they know that their efforts to gain power have paid off in many instances. They have learned that reforms are possible. Moreover, today's college student not only is more sophisticated in general, but also more sophisticated about the running of a college campus. He even may organize and plan courses on his own and, on a few campuses, for university-approved credit. He is making progress in solving what previously has been a major obstacle to student power—namely, his relatively short stay on the campus. As students develop more permanent structures, in much the same way as college fraternal organizations have developed, they will make their influence felt continuously, regardless of the changing membership of the student body.

The use of the word "power," student power in particular, is undoubtedly unsettling to some educators. One can get the distinct impression of the students on one side opposing the faculty and the administration on the other. And this impression is quite correct. Often, both faculty and students act as if they belonged to peer groups destined to oppose one another. This attitude is a major obstacle in coping with student unrest.

We see one result of this opposition when students bring legal action against a college *and win*.[2] Such action tends to reaffirm the

2 For one example, a state college in Alabama was instructed to reinstate a student editor who had been expelled for failure to follow a directive from the

attitude of opposition. And, unfortunately, it also tends to define college-student relations in legalistic terms. Some educators like Cornell University's Pres. James A. Perkins are rightly concerned about the danger of substituting judicial processes for academic processes. The point is that college officials must anticipate and recognize student rights before a situation ends up in court or before students resort to irresponsible acts. Clearly, the fact that students are turning to the courts to win their rights implies something significant about the dialogue, or lack of dialogue, between college or school officials and students. It implies that something is wrong on the campus. With each new freshman class, more and more high schools and colleges will have to reconsider the question, "What rights, influences, and privileges should our students have?" And we shall have to consider this question in much the same spirit as we ask, "What influences and responsibilities do our faculty and administrators have?"

If there are to be continued student demands for greater power or influence, educators will have to face at least five issues which are related distinctly to student unrest. First, educators must learn more about the student's academic and non-academic life. Too many faculty and administrators have no idea of or completely ignore the fact that when students are living in overcrowded residence halls, and many are, there is a lack of privacy which can lead to significant problems for some. Too many ignore, decry, or minimize student sexual tensions. Too many openly verbalize their lack of interest in student problems and tend to regard themselves as academicians who necessarily have no responsibility to their students beyond the classroom lecture.

College educators must follow the lead of those who teach at the elementary and secondary level and become more sensitive to both academic and non-academic student problems. Facing this issue need not make higher education paternalistic or like high school, as some may say; it well may make higher education more like it ought to be.

Second, a related issue is one which has been recognized for many years by educators, as well as non-educators like Aldous Huxley, who remind us that we have neglected almost completely the nonsymbolic aspects of the process of knowing. Educators persist in their

---

president of the college regarding an editorial in the college newspaper. The judge ruled that the student's right to free speech had been violated.

neglect of the noncognitive and nonverbal aspects of behavior. We seem frightened, insecure, and confused when we deal with student emotionality or interpersonal relationships. Instead, we try to avoid facing these nonrational aspects of behavior, for example, by hiring such "professionals" as guidance counselors and staff psychologists or by limiting education to the higher mental processes, "thinking," reasoning, and problem-solving or "cognitive" activities. Other dimensions of human-ness, such as emotion, feeling, interpersonal response—the so-called irrational—are neglected.

A distinct implication, then, is that we must see students as people first, not as organisms into which we put a "liberal education." Most educators surely know this; nevertheless, the issue is yet to be faced squarely, as it will have to be, if we are to break down this very significant barrier to education and to better student-faculty relationships.

Third, we must come to grips with the fact that the principle of *in loco parentis* has been withering for some time. Students are less willing to have their behavior controlled by colleges. Educators and psychiatrists also are calling for changes; *e.g.,* a recent study concluded that the private heterosexual and homosexual behavior of college students need not concern college administrators directly, although such behavior traditionally has been a concern of the college.[3] Students are saying more and more, "We have a right to be wrong, to make mistakes, and, if necessary, to suffer the consequences of our mistakes." The basic issue to be faced is one which has been mentioned already—namely, in what areas do students have a right to make decisions even though some of their decisions may be wrong?

Fourth, students are more aware than ever that college officials are concerned greatly with restricting the deviant student, a concern not difficult to understand. Unfortunately though, the majority of students, quite capable of acting responsibly, feel they are restricted unduly by rules and regulations developed for other students, but which essentially are hampering for them. Today's students are asking educators to treat them with more trust than they have in the past and not attempt to over-regulate their lives solely because of the actions of a few.

Fifth, the student relationship to the bureaucratic college struc-

---

[3] Group for the Advancement of Psychiatry, *Sex and the College Student* (New York: Antheneum, 1966).

ture must be re-examined. Students have become increasingly concerned with the difficulties involved in solving many of their legitimate problems. For example, college officials often seem completely helpless to react to a simple student request. On some issues, college officials would side with their students, but refrain from doing so because of pressures from parents and the public. When confronted with such situations or with a legitimate student problem, educators too often respond by informing students that they have no appreciation for the "complexity" of the situation or that they are immature and inexperienced. Students are finding it very difficult to accept this kind of treatment. They are demanding that educators face issues more honestly. The result is that college officials are increasingly likely to be charged with hypocrisy, particularly when the students have been told again and again that college exists for them.

If educators are to make the necessary realignments to meet the challenge of student unrest on the college campus, they must concern themselves fully with these five issues. Probably, the reader has noted that the question of whether students should have more to say about the running of a college was not raised. This is because the writer does not believe the basic issue is whether students should or should not have a greater part in decision-making. Rather, the real task is to discover and accept those areas of college life which students can and ought to handle either for themselves or handle conjointly with the faculty and administration, areas which, if students were allowed such participation, would contribute significantly to their educational and personal growth. Lest we commit an error known as the "fallacy of limited decisions," the writer should be quick to add that college officials need not necessarily abdicate their current rights, responsibilities, and influences.[4] Nevertheless, realignments seem necessary. The problem is that neither the college nor the students really know or agree upon whether the college or the students, or both, should make the decisions in many controver-

---

4 Some economists use the phrase "fallacy of limited decisions" to refer to the notion that during any particular period of time there is a fixed or limited number of decisions to be made in connection with operating the economy. If the government makes more decisions, the private sector necessarily will have fewer to make. Political scientists often refer to this kind of reasoning as the "fallacy of the zero sum game." We must guard against making a similar error when analyzing college-student relationships; *e.g.*, if students are allowed more choices and more decision-making power, it does not follow automatically that the faculty and administration thereby will have less power and influence.

sial areas. Solving this basic and very complex problem well may depend upon facing the above issues honestly and creatively.[5]

---

[5] For some similar views of student unrest expressed in terms of proposed realignments, see Joseph Katz and Nevitt Sanford, "The New Student Power and Needed Educational Reforms," *Phi Delta Kappan*, 47: 397-401, April, 1966.

21

STUDENT UNREST:
ROOTS AND SOLUTIONS

THOMAS J. CASEY, S.J.

WHILE IT IS DEBATABLE whether college and university students should be designated now as the "fourth estate" of the educational world, alongside faculty, administration and trustees, there is no doubt that they are exercising a class consciousness and a class power that were foreign to our campuses even a few years ago.[1] The attention which the current news media have given to this phenomenon has forced an awareness on most of us that we are faced with a new and serious social problem which has been called popularly either student unrest or student activism. To view this situation from a sociological perspective offers little likelihood that the problems associated with student unrest will be speedily resolved. But such an approach does give promise of some understanding of the what and the why of current campus disorders and the possibility of ameliorating if not eliminating them. With this modest objective in view, an analysis of the roots of student activism is presented and some suggestions are proffered as to what might be done to channel current student dissatisfaction with our institutions of higher learning into work of construction rather than destruction.

---

[1] Joseph Katz and Nevitt Sanford, "The New Student Power and Needed Educational Reform," *Phi Delta Kappan*, vol. 47, no. 8 (April 1966), pp. 397-401.

From *Liberal Education*, May, 1969. Reprinted by permission of the author and the editor of *Liberal Education*. Thomas J. Casey, S.J., is Associate Professor of Sociology, Regis College, Denver, Colo.

Why the Student Rebelliousness?

To one who is familiar with the rise of organized labor in this country the similarity of social conditions found on university campuses today, particularly on the large state campuses, with those which obtained when labor first started seriously to form unions is noteworthy. In treating the social backgrounds of unionism in the United States, Brown lists among the institutional elements which contributed to the rise of unionism the concentration of businesses into larger and larger units with corresponding depersonalization and impersonalization of the relations between the owner or manager and the employee.[2] The larger the enterprise the greater, generally, is the division of labor and the greater the rationalization of production. People increasingly become aware that they need the institution for their welfare but that the institution has little need for them as individuals, and that individuals within the institution are increasingly interchangeable and dispensable. Thus they seek to unite with their fellows in order to achieve some control over their situation.

If there is one reason which is given before all others for their activism by those who have participated in student protest movements, it is that they are fed up with the impersonality and bureaucracy of the large university.[3] Perhaps the city editor of the *Daily Californian* during the Free Speech Movement at Berkeley best summarized the attitude of the students when she reviewed four books written by social scientists about the movement. She claims that they fail to understand the movement since they do not empathize sufficiently with the students so as to realize that what the students are striving for are personal relationships among faculty and students on the university campus. Without this type of relationship the students feel alienated from the university enterprise.[4]

In a more formal attempt to list the principal causes for the emphasis which students are giving now to their rights, Kauffman lists two other factors which seem to be significant in explaining student activism. One is that the university students have been

---

[2] Leo C. Brown *et al., Social Orientations* (Chicago: Loyola Univ. Press. 1954), pp. 256-257.

[3] James Petras, "The Politics of Democracy: The Free Speech Movement," *Phi Delta Kappan,* vol. 46, no. 7 (March 1965), pp. 343-344.

[4] Peggy Kraus, "Berkeley Revisited: Where Social Scientists Fail," *Phi Delta Kappan,* vol. 47, no. 8 (April 1966), pp. 421-423.

influenced by the Negro civil rights movement. Some of them participated in the Berkeley demonstrations and practically all are aware of the results that can be obtained through nonviolent social action techniques. It is a natural step for youth to try the same tactics in other areas of concern and the campus is a prime area of their concern. In addition to the lessons learned from the political civil rights movement, Kauffman feels that, because present day students come from a family and social milieu which has exposed them to redefinitions of values and because they have few personal restraints, they are willing to get involved in protest movements. Moreover, the universities are not clear in spelling out their expectations for student behavior on campus. In the resulting normative vacuum, purposive and disciplined behavior gives way rather easily to the enthusiasms of the crowd.[5]

It would be a mistake, however, to think that the student activism which gets the headlines these days represents the views of the majority of students on our campuses. Studies still indicate that the protest movement represents at best a minority movement and one in which most students are not seriously involved nor likely to get so involved.[6] In a Ph.D. dissertation at Kent State University, Gennett found that the majority of students were not pushing vigorously for more freedom. They rejected the idea that the faculty and administration were inflexible and uncooperative. Nevertheless, he still felt that the dissident students are a serious problem for our universities and should be listened to.[7]

Increased size and the problems it creates for organizational procedures, with the consequence that the rights of individuals are not always respected, are not the only factors which contribute to student unrest on campus. There is a heterogeneity on college and university campuses today which is something over and above that which naturally arises from a division of labor and the subcultures which it engenders occupationally and vocationally. The social backgrounds which the students bring to college these days—arising from

---

[5] Joseph F. Kauffman, "The New Climate of Student Freedom and Rights," *Educational Record*, vol. 45, no. 4 (Fall 1964), pp. 360-363.

[6] Nevitt Sanford, "The Development of Social Responsibility through the College Experience," in Earl J. McGrath, ed., *The Liberal Arts College's Responsibility for the Individual Student* (New York: Teachers College Press, Teachers College, Columbia Univ. 1966), pp. 25ff.

[7] "Student Freedom," *School and Society*, vol. 94, no. 2281 (November 12, 1966), p. 372.

the extremely broad class, ethnic, and religious differences that characterize the products of a universal public educational system at the primary and secondary levels—are already heterogeneous and reflect quite diverse values, attitudes and interests. The social composition of the modern campus represents a much different culture from that which Clark and Trow identified as the collegiate subculture and which was common on campuses until the depression and the advent of World War II. There is little evidence that colleges and universities have become sufficiently aware of the implications of this change from a predominantly collegiate-oriented student body to what they call the vocational subculture characteristic of those from the less affluent social classes who are interested in college chiefly for its opportunities to advance occupationally and socially.[8]

The problems associated with this change in the social composition of the student body—making it more accurate to say that many communities exist within the university structure rather than just one—manifest themselves particularly in the areas that are the concern of deans of students. It is one thing to handle infractions of rules that, though frequently broken, are generally accepted and are backed up by informal social controls imposed by a social community that cooperates with the administration. It is quite another to handle socially disruptive behavior which no longer acknowledges the right of the university to prescribe behavioral norms for the students. Many student activists today deny that the university administration should be concerned with the behavior of students once they get beyond the more or less immediate confines of the classroom situation. They are ready to employ all the recourses the legal profession can supply in order to maintain their position.

Most universities are not ready to conduct their affairs with students according to the model of the democratic state dealing with its citizens. Such a concept is foreign to the authority the university has traditionally had *in loco parentis*. It also does violence to the cherished concept of the university as a community of scholars jointly pursuing the truth from the point of view of a common universe of values and purposes. But these concepts hardly fit the current social realities in our campuses which call for new procedural practices to cope adequately with reality if the rights of all are to be guaranteed. Until these procedures are worked out it is likely

---

8 Clark Kerr, *The Uses of the University* (Cambridge, Mass.: Harvard Univ. Press, 1964), pp. 41-42.

that we shall continue to see much student unrest. The will of the crowd is likely to prevail owing to an administrative leadership that is unable to control student behavior for constructive ends because it is as confused as are the students themselves as to what the situation calls for.[9]

If misery likes company, presumably the troubled administrators and faculties of American institutions of higher learning can find some small comfort in realizing that their Japanese and European confreres are experiencing the same student unrest. According to *Time* magazine, the one hundred and two post-high-school institutions in Tokyo, while not all erupting into the campus demonstrations which have enlivened the American scene, manifest a rather serious degeneration in faculty-student relationships which could harbinger rather serious trouble for Japan's educational institutions in the not too distant future. Impersonality marks the large campuses and the faculties do not feel that they are being successful in imparting a sense of human values to their students.[10] In Europe, on the other hand, the students already show a mastery of Berkeley-style demonstrations and the United States is blamed by some for inspiring the student unrest.[11] It is notable that this type of student unrest is breaking out where American influence is particularly strong and where American ideas and organizational structures in education have been introduced if not welcomed. This indicates that the problems of student activism today arise primarily from institutional changes which traditional normative structures are no longer capable of handling, and not from the personal characteristics of administrative leaders in higher education. Hence it is at the institutional and organizational level that we must devise means of handling the problem, rather than merely to seek for the "right men" to run things.

Solutions to Problems Related to Student Activism

As is the case with social movements that are the result of a complex combination of factors operating in a situation where tradi-

---

9 Martin Trow, "Some Lessons from Berkeley," in Lawrence E. Dennis and Joseph F. Kauffman, eds., *The College and the Student* (Washington, D.C.: American Council on Education, 1966), pp. 126-130.

10 "Mass Production in Tokyo," *Time*, November 17, 1967, pp. 81-82.

11 "Students Abroad: Rebellion in Europe," *Time*, December 22, 1967, pp. 39-40.

tional normative patterns are inadequate for guaranteeing the realization of human needs, the current student activism will be channelled into constructive achievements and pursuits only through the development of normative and organizational structures which provide the means of meeting the needs which gave rise to the initial social unrest. At the present time one of the difficulties is our failure to perceive adequately just what are the needs which are not being met in our educational institutions and why this is so. In the first part of this paper some of the contributing factors have been indicated. We are now becoming aware of what changes have taken place on American campuses in the last two decades and what the implications are for education. But since our comprehension of the causes of current student unrest remains partial at best, so too the solutions we can suggest for alleviating the situation must be considered tentative and partial. It would be unrealistic to believe that at this time we have the complete answer to student unrest.

Nevertheless, there appear to be some steps which we can take with the confident expectation that we are moving in the right direction. Our first need is to see that people understand the organizational changes which become necessary as soon as large numbers of people have to be served by the same institution. If this service is to be performed at all adequately, there must be considerable division of labor within the institution. This, in turn, demands that individuals within the institution play restricted and specialized social roles. Human interaction has to be more or less limited to the playing of social roles within the organization. While people always mix their personalities with their jobs, the opportunity for so doing is necessarily going to be much less in complex organizations than in the small, communal type of organization characteristic of familistic societies where the kinship group is the state, church, school and economy all in one. Increasing complexity has been the characteristic direction of change for all our major social institutions, whether political, economic, religious, or now educational, as any introductory sociology text will testify.[12] An awareness of this development in our colleges and universities will not eliminate the problems it creates within a changing institution, but it should enable individuals to understand what is going on and thus cope with the problems

---

[12] Leonard Broom and Philip Selznick, *Sociology* (3rd ed., New York: Harper and Row, 1963), pp. 45ff.

more rationally. At a minimum, it would enable students and faculty to recognize that increased impersonality is almost inevitable in a large university. It grows out of new institutional forms and in no sense is it something that individuals are consciously promoting, nor does it arise from the conscious indifference of faculty towards their students. But it is something we have to learn to live with if we want the advantages that only a large scale cooperative institution such as the university can give owing to its opportunity to specialize, increase productivity, and make available the benefits of such increased productivity.

In this connection, perhaps if educators had taken Hutchins more seriously when he said that a modern heresy in education is the idea that the school should take care of all education, we would have been saved from some of the problems we have now.[13] It is now evident that we are not taking care of all human problems within the university nor are we responsible for all the education men get today when during the first sixteen years of one's life the typical student spends as much time with television as in school.[14] But Hutchins would contend that we should never attempt this. The community as a whole, as was the Greek idea of education, has its part to play in the general process of education. This implies that all of man's potentialities for human activity are reduced through educative experiences to their fullest possible development. The schools as such should thus restrict their activities to the imparting of that intellectual training for which they are specifically set up to do and for which they are uniquely qualified. In modern society all major institutions have specialized the limited functions to perform for the total community. It is only by restricting themselves to their specific tasks that they will be able ultimately to render a real service to the community and the individuals who live there. The jack-of-all-trades usually ends up master of none and without real commitment to any.

In line with this type of reasoning another practical step which may help alleviate current student unrest is to upgrade the prestige and value placed upon the teaching function within the university.

---

13 Robert M. Hutchins, *The Higher Learning in America* (New Haven: Yale Univ. Press, paperbound, 1962), p. 68.

14 Wilbur Schramm, Jack Lyle and Edwin B. Parker, "Television in the Lives of Our Children," in Derek L. Phillips, ed., *Studies in American Society* (New York: Crowell, 1965), p. 55.

Along with many others, Clark Kerr has admitted that the emphasis on research and the servicing of other members of society than the students have led to a downgrading of teaching in the multiversity as he describes it, particularly the teaching of undergraduates.[15] The university may aspire to serve many different ends and purposes, but if it is to do so effectively there must be provision for an adequate division of labor among all its members. Since the university still exists to instruct the young, it must be prepared to provide teachers who are willing and able to give them their full time and attention. But it is hardly going to get such individuals and have them committed to this work if it insists on considering them second class citizens of the academic community.

For this reason the current agitation to get a proper degree for college teachers takes on added significance.[16] There is no intrinsic reason why a degree for college teachers cannot be equally evaluated with a research oriented degree. No one has proof positive that research is a more important function for the university than that of bringing to full maturity the intellectual potential of the next generation through first class teaching. With such equal evaluation of degrees and functions within the university the teaching function may be performed again as it should be to the obvious advantage of the student since teachers will be motivated to give full time and commitment to it. They are not constantly trying to overcome their sense of inferiority and the discrimination against them in favor of the more prestigeful research segment of the university. They might also come up occasionally with a significant bit of research data as a result of efforts to improve their teaching and communication to the students, just as presumably our researchers occasionally learn how to teach from immersing themselves in their research methodology and findings.

A third step which might also be taken to mollify student unrest is to encourage some of the experimentation with curricula which is going on in the hope of involving greater interaction and individualized attention among faculty and students. This is one of the problems that Kerr believes the multiversity must solve and the structuring of curriculum is part of the solution.[17] In 1964 the Berkeley

---

[15] Kerr, *op. cit.*, pp. 64-65.

[16] "Grad School Meet Debates Degrees," *Rocky Mountain News*, December 3, 1966, p. 20.

[17] Kerr, *op. cit.*, p. 120.

campus of the University of California authorized the Experimental Collegiate Program which is suggestive at least of what might and might not be achieved through this type of program. The program envisions a student body of about one hundred and fifty students who work with five faculty members from various departments on a problem-centered approach to understanding significant periods of civilization. This interdepartmental approach allows for a great deal of independent reading, research and discussion among the students and faculty. While a good number of students learned to do independent work in this environment and were intellectually alive and interested in the program, many made minimal use of the opportunity for faculty-student dialogue and a fifth of the students transferred at the end of the first year to the regular academic program of the university. They felt the program was too unstructured for them to work effectively within its provisions. They were not sufficiently mature or ready for this independent and seminar type of approach to learning. The conclusion thus appears to be that, while such an experimental program may help some students avoid development of a sense of alienation from the university and its concerns, it is not a program that is suitable for all or even the majority of college students.[18]

A fourth approach that is being experimented with at present to improve faculty-student relationships and thus to enable the student to identify with the university is the so-called cluster college concept. Basically this involves structuring the physical facilities of the campus so that faculty and students are brought into close and frequent contact. This occurs because relatively small units of residence and work are set up wherein both faculty and students operate for the whole day. Dressel, however, does not believe that this structuring of the physical plant is going to improve matters much until more attention is given to the curriculum that goes with it. In his opinion little or no attention is being given to curriculum change by those who are now promoting the cluster college concept. He does not believe, therefore, that it will help the students find meaning in their undergraduate work and become interested and involved in it because the quality of their instruction has been

---

18 "Experiment at Berkeley," *NEA Journal*, vol. 56, no. 1 (January 1967), pp. 21-22; 78.

improved.[19] Whether or not the cluster concept will give a more meaningful and satisfying educational experience to the undergraduate remains to be seen. But the effort to devise new structures in response to what are definitely new needs of undergraduates today is certainly commendable. New structures are needed and the only question is, What should they be if we are to promote again satisfactory and meaningful student-faculty relationships?

In stressing the need for an understanding of the special-purpose nature of our institutions of higher learning and the necessity of so structuring them to achieve the limited purposes of such an organization, there is no desire to play down the importance of a personalized relationship between instructor and student. The most effective socializing and exercise of educative influence goes on within the confines of what sociologists call a primary group where communication is deep and extensive, where one takes account of the whole person, and relationships are characterized by friendship rather than utility.[20] Hence the university should always promote such relationships within its environment. But its capacity for doing so at present is not what it used to be. This must be recognized if it is going to make the faculty-student relationship as satisfactory as it might be under present circumstances. Moreover, if the university is to be successful in promoting such groupings, this will have to be done with new structural forms since the older ones no longer work. What these forms might be we still must learn. Whatever they may be they should not conflict with the structures necessary for the university to do its basic work of intellectual training, research and servicing of the knowledge needs of the community.

Quite probably what is called for is what I would designate as para-institutions. By this I mean institutions which service religious, medical, counseling, recreational and general social needs of the students without being totally identified with the universities.[21] To so separate out functions which have been assumed directly by the university administration because the university falls more or less within the category of what Goffman calls total institutions must be

---

[19] Paul L. Dressel, "Curriculum and Instruction," *Journal of Higher Education,* vol. 38, no. 7 (October 1967), pp. 393-396.

[20] Broom and Selznick, *op. cit.,* p. 111.

[21] Hutchins, *op. cit.,* pp. 110ff. The proposal made by Hutchins for research institutes connected with the university but whose members were not of the university faculties seems to be a practical example of what I would call a para-institution.

done so that the university may accomplish best the tasks for which it is specifically designed.[22] Obviously such institutions would be closely allied with the university and be interdependent. Such an arrangement would allow for sufficient distinction of identity and function so that the students and faculty would not expect the university to do everything for them and to service all their human needs. This realistic appraisal of the purpose and function of our institutions of higher learning should in turn enable the students to know what they may expect legitimately from the university. Thus they should not feel cheated if their every human need is not met there.

No less important, such an appraisal should also cause the total community to establish whatever other institutions may be necessary to service the student population with a correspondingly clear assessment of institutional responsibilities. Parents would no longer feel that they are able to turn their youngsters over to the school, confident that it will service their needs as the family has been doing. They would have to provide for other institutions to care for their children's religious, health, recreational and general personal and social needs. This implies a philosophy which expects all of one's needs to be fulfilled and met within the total community and not through one institutional area, even one as broad and comprehensive as education.

But if the analysis made so far is valid, that is what our current level of social development demands. The sooner we recognize the fact and set about making the necessary adjustments and institutional changes in our community life, the sooner may we expect to find our students satisfied with the educational institutions society provides. Their expectations relative to the institutions will be realistic. They will not experience the frustration of expecting a limited and particularistic institution of society, such as formal education is, to meet needs that only the total society can meet through the proper ordering and structuring of all its social institutions. In its turn, the educational sector of our society will be in a position to meet better the legitimate educational needs of students and society. It no longer will be burdened with an attempt to be a surrogate for society itself and thus it can concentrate on doing the job it is set up to do.

---

[22] Erving Goffman, "The Characteristics of Total Institutions," in Amitai Etzioni, ed., *Complex Organizations: A Sociological Reader* (New York: Holt, Rinehart and Winston, 1961), pp. 312-340.

22

THE OBSOLETE NEUTRALITY OF
HIGHER EDUCATION

NOBUO SHIMAHARA

THE PROBLEM OF NEUTRALITY of education has been a thorny one
and also will be a vital one in the future. According to conservatism,
education is a force which maintains the perpetuating order of
society intact against the impact of new forces. Those subscribing to
a "radical" view, on the other hand, contend that the schools should
contribute to social construction by helping youth develop critical
attitudes and habits of action. Dewey, as one of the persuasive
proponents of the latter position, argued that the former view
generates a negative social effect with its acquiescence in the perpetuation of social and moral disorder created by the development of
cultural complexity. The clarity of the social emphasis of the school,
he further contended, is demanded urgently.[1] His view, nonetheless, points to abstinence and futility in a conservative perspective.

This discussion aims to provide an alternative to Richard
Hofstadter's renewed appeal for neutrality in higher education. By
no means is it limited to any single university in trouble, but rather
widely related to dilemmas, with different degrees of intensity, that a

---

[1] John Dewey, "Educational and Social Change," *Social Frontier*, May, 1936,
p. 238.

From *School & Society*, January, 1969. Reprinted by permission of the author and the
publisher. Nobuo Shimahara is Assistant Professor of Anthropology of Education, Graduate
School of Education, Rutgers, The State University, New Brunswick, N. J.

number of institutions of higher education have confronted where student unrest exists.

Columbia University is one of the campuses in this nation where explosive student power burst out. Hofstadter, a distinguished Columbia historian, delivered the commencement address at his university in the face of student unrest.

He called for neutrality on the part of the university: ". . . neutrality should continue to define our aim, and we should resist the demand that the university espouse the political commitments of any of its members."[2] He emphasized that the central function of the university is to develop "free inquiry," "free forum," and "free criticism." One of the major roles is "to examine, critically and without stint, the assumptions that prevail" in our society. Thus, "To realize its essential character, the university has to be dependent upon something less precarious than the momentary balance of forces in society."[3] But it is impressed now by its grave fragility; a major evil causing this fragility is "politicizing" attempts by students. The needed ethical mandate, thus, is self-restraints and self-criticisms. Hofstadter further argued that to assault academic centers of study and thought as a way of changing social order is to show a complete disregard for the intrinsic character of the university.

The appeal to neutrality as an attempt to resolve the dilemmas is futile and obsolete. First, our colleges and universities are politically influenced to a significant degree and occasionally adulterated by politicians. The research patterns of an advanced university, for example, are determined, more or less, by the structure of investments of private industries and the order of political priorities of the Federal government. Moreover, university trustees and alumni, who usually control either local or national political and economic power, strongly influence university direction and basic policies. The university inevitably reflects the national political and economic structures. This realism should not be concealed.

Free inquiry is meaningful and beneficial when it relates itself to social life, including political realms. Although Hofstadter emphasized the essential status of free inquiry, he did not provide a practical reference to its relevance for the wide horizon of human life involving man's struggles to improve his culture by the use of scientific and humanistic inquiry; nor did he give any reference to

---

2 *The New York Times,* June 5, 1968.
3 *Ibid.*

the use of examined assumptions of our society. Should inquiry of higher education be an isolated laboratory process? Ought it be a monologue entirely detached from a dialogue with social life?

Human life is characterized by the principle of continuum. It operates in all processes of evolution, including the psychocultural. Free inquiry and forum, which examine the basic assumptions of a society and which produce new concepts and methodology, on the one hand, and social action, on the other, are on the same evolutionary continuum of human enterprise to create man's culture; theory and action are not self-determinative entities. Instead, they constitute complementary relations. The foregoing view is supported further by Whyte's renunciation of the neutrality of science as a manifestation of the illusion of "dissociated man" and a separation of science from inner human conflicts.[4]

A widely prevailing notion on educational management has been that the administration of higher education is endowed with unilateral authority to determine the structure and course of the educational institution. Students are computed numbers existing outside the processes of decision-making. It is essential to admit honestly the rigidified and politicized structure of the administration of higher education which is responsible for forcing students to political action.

Intellectual youth now are awakened and more perceptive than ever. Sartre's dictum, "Existence precedes essence," now is being translated into sociological and political terms—Process precedes structure. The rise of the French unrest, the civil rights movement, and student activism are illustrative historic events. Political, economic, and educational institutions have failed to meet students' needs and aspirations, and subsequent individual frustrations have given a rise to a process directed against the status quo, as well as an impetus of their struggles to restructure the present social reality. What is often absent in the orientative framework of higher education is an appreciable recognition of deep concern of intellectual youth with critical problems of the nation and the international situation.

Can we resolve the disturbing academic upheavals by preaching educational neutrality and ethical self-restraints? Can we do this by accusing students of, and banning, their politicizing attempts when

---

[4] Lancelot Whyte, *The Next Development in Man* (New York: Holt, 1948), pp. 276-277.

the authorities of their universities rationalize their own politicizing? My answer is negative. Therefore, I submit that neutrality for the university is dangerous because it is a disguised form of unilateral monologue. It discourages students' sensitivity and commitments to their society. Student political action must be cared for, and canalized into a constructive form where free dialogue has the possibility of resolving frustrations, anxieties, and revolts against authority. Universities and colleges should establish "chairs for the future and human crises"[5] that will canalize students' energy into proper action-oriented inquiry.

The collaboration between action and theory is urgent in our contemporary crises. Whyte aptly suggests that "presidents of universities should require of their heads of departments a statement of the direct or indirect relevance of their subject to the human situation today."[6] Inquiry makes a great service to men and women when it inquires into alternatives of human life and possibilities of human promise by carrying the thoughts and research of the campus directly to the heart of the human community.

Professors should serve as an ethical center for student activities, whether they are academic or political. They should be a vital agent directing their students through the adequate understanding of students' needs, hopes, and frustrations, instead of creating a monolithic, authoritarian setup for various types of students.

A meaningful dialogue should be created between administration and students, and between professors and students. The unilateral monologue practiced by administrators and professors should be converted to bilateral participation and dialogue so that students may engage in meaningful interplay with them through the implementation of effective communication channels.

As Whyte, Bertrand Russell, and other thinkers asserted, it is a pressing task of sciences and human struggles to identify a "formative process" toward a unitary, global order of human community. The effort to achieve this goal anticipates the development of what Whyte called the concepts of "unitary man" and "global thought." Polarization is most dangerous to the fulfillment of these concepts. Thus, it also is dangerous to separate completely political from

---

5 This was suggested in Julian Huxley, *The Human Crisis* (Seattle: University of Washington Press, 1963).

6 Lancelot Whyte, "The End of the Age of Separatism," *Saturday Review*, May 18, 1968, p. 65.

academic commitments since they are internal ingredients of unitary man. To develop a formative process and a unitary order, men and women should foster social and political sensitivity and commitments. Here free inquiry and forum, if meaningful at all, must play a significant role to work out effective methodology for political participation in the community embracing academic microcommunities.

The university will become a creative force if explosive energy of intellectual youth is canalized into constructive, responsible, and democratic forms by encouraging it to find effective channels of communication and by authentic and enthusiastic responses of university authorities to it.

23

CAMPUS COMMUNICATION: THE STUDENT AND THE UNIVERSITY WORLD

∿∿

WILLIAM S. PALEY

THERE HAVE BEEN MANY CHANGES in the world during the years since I was a university student. They have been years, for the most part, of disruption and upheaval, of revolution and revision, and of rapid and dramatic progress in every quarter and aspect of life. And the universities have not been spared a large share in shaping, and in being shaped by, these changes. Once a simple fellowship of teachers and students, the university has become a vast and complicated mechanism, carrying out such additional functions as huge government-supported research projects only indirectly related to teaching but frequently vital to our society. This expansion of the uses of the university has put upon it severe strains and strong pressures. And the university has had to pay a price for this—not the least of which is the quality of intimacy, with regard both to its inner life and to its relationship with its outer community. While often developing utopian vision for the larger world of its time, it seems also to have developed chronic myopia for the situation within its own gates and at its own doorstep.

Universities on the farthest frontiers of sociological inquiry often

Based on commencement address, University of Pennsylvania, Philadelphia, May 20, 1968. Used by permission of the author. William S. Paley is Chairman, Columbia Broadcasting System, and a trustee of Columbia University.

have insufficient insight into the plight of their own cities. Universities with burgeoning urban affairs departments wander into chaotic misuses of their sites. Universities with schools of architecture impose upon themselves buildings both incongruous and tasteless. In many instances, the colleges, once the focal point of the universities, have been eclipsed by the rise of powerful graduate schools with their many non-teaching preoccupations. There also has been a gradual abdication by faculties of some of their key responsibilities as the basic component of the university.

In some recent perceptive words on faculties today, McGeorge Bundy makes a central point of great importance. He emphasizes that the new power conferred on professors as a group since World War II has been used by them to advance their own interest as individuals rather than that of the university as a whole. This has led faculties too many times to act as though the internal strength and health of their institutions are no direct responsibilities of theirs. It has been my own observation that faculties tend to assume the attitude that they are a detached arbitrating force between students on one side and administrators and trustees on the other, with no immediate responsibility for the university as a whole.

It is essential that faculties be brought back into the main flow of university life; that their basic position as the central component of the university be reasserted; and that where trustees or administrators have left any doubt in faculty minds as to their responsibilities and powers, that doubt be clearly dispelled. It seems to me highly probable that the vacuum left by overly detached faculties has been responsible to some degree for student agitators moving in and claiming a ruling power for themselves.

The violent uprisings of university undergraduates may be the work largely of organized extremists, exploiting soft spots in our society. They may be, in considerable measure, passing phenomena, related largely to outside factors such as the war in Vietnam, civil rights, or the problem of poverty. Or they may be symptoms of a growing and deep-rooted disenchantment with the university itself. They are probably a combination of all these. But we have to go beyond this and move on to considering why these uprisings can rally behind them a large body of students who do not share extremist ideologies. Some general conditions of life today help explain this, even if not to excuse it.

One is the inherent activism in any student with intellectual

curiosity. Such students resent, I suspect, the notion that they should
spend four years, amid highly controversial events, as sponges,
absorbing knowledge about the world they live in but abstaining
from participation in it. Activism is in their bones. Concerned with
civil rights, they march in the South. Concerned with peace, they
declare themselves on Vietnam. Concerned with politics, they labor
in Presidential primaries in which most of them cannot even vote.

Concern leads to protest; and protest, in some cases, unhappily, to
violence. One of the most tragic and alarming facts emerging is
that even responsible and moderate students in large numbers are
beginning to feel that violence pays. After all the unread petitions,
all the unmade decisions, and all the endless dialogue, violence
seems to them to get results far more promptly than orderly processes and to be worth the risks—particularly if acts of lawlessness are
allowed to go unpunished.

On no grounds does violence have any place in a community of
civilized men, particularly in a university—which is committed to
reason, to letting everyone have his say without harassment, and to
depriving no man of his rights (even the right to be wrong). He has
the right to protest and the right to work for change. But he has no
right to break the laws and to trample upon the rights of others,
and anyone who does so must be called to account.

The acceptance of violence as an instrument of progress indicates
that something is clearly wrong with the organization and with the
machinery of our universities.

Communications between students, on the one hand, and faculties, administrators and trustees, on the other, have obviously become deficient. Students do have legitimate complaints. Curricula
may not meet their needs, their interests and their concerns. The
university may seem like just one more example of the establishment's trying to run their lives without consulting them. Trustees,
administrators and faculties must move swiftly and realistically to
introduce mechanisms and methods to make it possible for students
to get a hearing and to get action on valid complaints and suggestions. It is essential that we make it possible for students to work for
the correction of such conditions legitimately and effectively rather
than compulsively and violently.

Pennsylvania already has taken steps to bring about close and
better communication among all segments of the University. I understand the machinery is working well and that important improve-

ments have been noted. I congratulate Dr. Harnwell and the trustees for their forward moving action.

Most boards of trustees keep in touch with the student life of the university through committees, reports and other devices—but they are often too fragmented and oblique. Methods must be found to give them, as well as faculty and administrators, much greater insight into the interests, goals and problems of the students.

Universities very often articulate policies by actions rather than by words. Frequently, the first that students hear of trustee actions are through the grapevine or through brief announcements, or when the action takes overt form. Legally the university is the board of trustees, but actually it is very largely the community of teachers and students. That a board of trustees should commit a university community to policies and actions without the components of that community participating in discussions leading to such commitments has become obsolete and unworkable. Students now take their universities far more seriously than in the past and regard them as both expressions and instruments of national policy.

Of course, it is infuriating when a minority on the campus seeks disruption for disruption's sake and, further, seeks destruction of the university itself and maybe even more. But again we should not lose sight of the more responsible students among the dissenters. They represent a widespread feeling of sincere discontent, not only about the university but about the entire world. They want their insistent search for a better world to be reflected institutionally by the university.

Trustees, administrators and faculties are not going to arrest this drive for participation—and they should not try. They should try to bring about changes, whether structural or operational, to turn this student unrest into channels that will result in stimulating the university's growth in effectiveness and in relevance.

To do this, I do not know how thoroughly the corporate character of the private university should be changed—or whether it needs to be changed at all. But I do question the soundness today of the old theory of trustees as a small, self-perpetuating group of interested laymen, many chosen for life, into whose custody the full character and conduct of the university are reposed. Some modification of its role seems to me essential if we are to get the interrelationships of students, faculty, administrators and trustees into satisfactory working arrangements.

I have been a university trustee for many years, and I have reason only to admire the devotion to their tasks of the colleagues with whom I have worked. Some years ago I presided over a task force to determine the proper functions of the trustees of a private university. At the time I considered its conclusions sound, workable and right. They were, broadly speaking, that the functions of the trustees are to choose the administrative leadership of the university, to assume responsibility for its financial and material needs, and to oversee its general educational program and standards.

When it comes to selecting presidents, I am not now sure that this function should be entrusted solely to trustees. Trustees are usually careful in most cases to consult with faculties on the naming of a new president, but this is not always so. Faculties should have an assured place in the procedures naming the individual who is going to lead them, speak for them, and chart their future course.

It may also be no longer adequate to place the enormous burden for the financial soundness and material needs of multi-million-dollar institutions entirely upon a small band of dedicated men willing to push doorbells year after year, reach down into their own pockets when necessary and labor endlessly to keep them afloat. There is much to be said for amortization plans enabling students to pay the real costs of their education, rather than only approximately a third of it, with the rest coming out of endowment or current gifts. At today's levels there is a difference of perhaps eight thousand dollars between what a college education costs and what the tuition covers. A system could be devised to make it possible for the student, in accordance with his financial ability, to repay this difference over future years. Other non-philanthropic solutions to the financial plights of the university should also be more thoroughly investigated. Many of us are looking forward, in this connection, to the reports of the Carnegie Commission on the Future of Higher Education. If a good part of the fund-raising problem can be solved, the fields from which trustees could be drawn would be broadened considerably. Also, more attention then could be given by the trustees to other responsibilities.

As to the function of the trustee in overseeing and approving the kind of education provided by the university, this is really a function that should be entrusted, certainly in the main, to the administration, deans, department heads and faculties.

The role of the administrator is of critical importance. Professor

Sidney Hook of New York University, speaking recently from the experience of almost fifty years, has observed that, "Without administrative leadership, every institution, especially universities whose faculties are notoriously reluctant to introduce curricular changes, runs down hill. The greatness of a university consists predominantly in the greatness of its faculty. But faculties . . . do not themselves build great faculties. To build great faculties, administrative leadership is essential."

Let me add that resolute administrative leadership is equally essential if there is to be order. Regardless of how extensively university practices need to be changed, order must prevail. In many of the uprisings on the campuses, we have heard pleas for more democracy in university procedures. I am not sure this is the real difficulty. Not all institutions that serve democratic societies must themselves be democratic in their procedures. Nor can they be. A hospital cannot be run by majority vote of its patients, nor a research laboratory by that of its technicians, nor a newspaper by that of its reporters. But these institutions must be actively considerate of their constituents. They must find ways of consulting them more fully, of bringing them into their counsels more effectively and of responding to their needs and aspirations more directly.

This is the crux of the problem facing our universities: a free, open, mature flow of two-way communications through all university levels. And this is the framework of orderly procedures. Only in this manner will the university discharge its responsibilities properly and reach its goals proudly.

Our universities are not custodians of the old order, perpetuators of the proven, or curators of the established. They are open-ended ventures, selective of the past, critical of the present and oriented to the future. Let us look at them afresh. There is nothing sacred about the structure of a university. We can adapt it to new realities. There is everything sacred about the purpose of a university. It must not be compromised. The task before us is to advance that high purpose of inquiry and discussion.

Certainly we must not fail in that task. More than the future of the university is involved. The quality and direction of our whole life as a people are at stake.

24

A STUDENT VOICE IN ACADEMIC POLICY

WILLIAM J. PARENTE

ALTHOUGH THE STRIFE will doubtless continue in isolated groves of academe, the first round in the contemporary confrontation between students and the academic establishment has been concluded—and youth is triumphant. From Belgrade to Morningside Heights, students have demanded a voice and a vote in those decisions that affect "student life"—an ambiguous area generally circumscribed by *in loco parentis.*

But this is only the beginning. In a second phase, our Savonarolas have already crossed the threshold of the offices of university presidents and the meetings of trustees in an attempt to purify the political entanglements of the institution. Corporate investments in racist regimes and services rendered to the intelligence apparatus of government are the modern whores to be driven from the campus.

A third and yet more tumultous phase may lie ahead. Student participation in the formation of the curriculum and in the concerns of academic disciplines looms as the next *casus belli.* In Paris the French government is preparing to wipe away the residue of the *trivium* under the impact of student demands for a technologically contemporary curriculum. Prague students have successfully terminated "general education" courses in Marxism. There is every reason to believe that students will now enter that holy of holies, the departmental meeting.

From *Antioch Notes,* September, 1968. Reprinted by permission of the author and the publisher. William J. Parente is Assistant Professor of Political Science, Antioch College, Yellow Springs, Ohio.

Political Readiness

It seems best to interpret these student interventions as a manifestation of what political scientists term "the participation explosion" common to most contemporary political systems. It is the logical and inevitable progression of the gradual enfranchisement of the masses characteristic of Western political systems since at least the nineteenth century.

If one would have the British Prime Minister and the Presidents of France and the United States designated, respectively, by Wakefield coal miners, Breton peasants, and tenant farmers in Arkansas, it is difficult to object to the enfranchisement of university undergraduates.

As the development of newspapers and associational interest groups made possible the successful enfranchisement of the British working classes in the nineteenth century, the contemporary revolution in the technology of communication and transportation has made possible according political responsibilities to those under twenty-one. (One education commission even argues that there is "persuasive evidence" that as a result of better diet and medical care, today's freshmen are three years older physiologically than those of 1900.)

The point was formerly made that callow youth had not experienced what their elders had and were, therefore, unable to inform their judgment of where their political interests lay. It would seem that in our era the vicarious acquisition of these experiences through the communication media has hastened their actual acquisition and transformed the old political realities. One must conclude that this generation of undergraduates is better equipped with information and experience to form rational judgments on political matters than the generations of students who preceded them.

Student Participation in Academic Decisions

One is struck by how little the universities themselves have moved along the path of gradual enfranchisement. While eager to inflict our standards and our students in new political roles upon the larger society, we have somewhat jealously maintained the old forms when it comes to student participation in our own affairs.

I think we must now examine whether students informed, at least vicariously, on matters of foreign and domestic policy—certainly as well as a majority of voters—and therefore qualified to influence political decisions, are not equally well informed to participate in the election of college presidents or deans or share in departmental policy decisions.

This is to say that I am doubtful that college administration and academic disciplines are any more esoteric than the political system itself. The politician has to persuade the electorate of the rationale and public interest behind his difficult policy decisions. College teachers and administrators would now seem to have an analogous responsibility to persuade their student constituencies of the efficacy of their policies rather than dictating them.

Let me turn to the specific question of student participation in academic departments. It is here that the next battles will be fought. Overt conflict over this question is most likely to break out in accordance with the demonstrated political rule that finds Russia as the unlikely site for a communist revolution, and a state university (rather than a "radical" liberal arts college) the unlikely site for a student rebellion: the weakest link in the system rather than the most revolutionary.

Informal departmental student-faculty co-operation will probably not suffice. Within a dozen years the department organization, in many institutions, is likely to be radically altered. How can we institutionalize our inadequate informal procedures into something both adequate and dynamic?

Preliminary to a definitive reorganization of departmental goals and structure, we might initiate a two- or three-day conference of departmental majors and faculty members, led by an able outside practitioner of the discipline. Likewise, other consultants familiar with the discipline or with its administrative problems could be used.

This workshop could be designed to discuss departmental and disciplinary goals and current success or failure in reaching these goals.

The experience of teamwork among faculty and students evinced in such a workshop, the clarification and sharpening of departmental goals, would provide an excellent springboard for implementing the suggestions that follow.

To help institutionalize this teamwork, a formal departmental meeting of faculty and majors could be held the first day of the term. Its purpose would be to discuss the courses being offered that term and changes in the future schedule; academic opportunities (fellowships, graduate schools, and so on); field-study or work opportunities; individual concerns of professors or majors; election of the departmental chairman; election of students to a departmental executive council (with an equal number of students appointed by the faculty in order to co-opt students who are strong in the discipline but not in the political skills of getting elected).

The executive council of the department could meet at the beginning of the term to plan the implementation of the policy decisions flowing from the general meeting.

Continuing subcommittees of faculty and students might be charged with specific tasks: curriculum development—in response to requests for Afro-American or urban courses, for example; selection of visiting scholars; screening candidates for faculty positions in the department.

The executive council could be composed of an equal number of faculty members and majors. It would vote on and forward the "departmental recommendation" on new faculty members to the dean.

These integrative proposals might go far in channeling student energies into academic endeavors.

25

STUDENT POWER—IN RESPONSE
TO THE QUESTIONS

EDWARD SCHWARTZ

DURING THE PAST YEAR, I have written a variety of tracts and articles outlining my sense of what student power in universities should mean, and what it should not mean. The most recent of these appeared in the September, 1968, issue of *Mademoiselle*. As in earlier statements, I tried to spell out the general propositions of the program—student control over student institutions and rules; student-faculty cooperation on matters relating to the curriculum; student involvement in matters basic to university life, such as admissions and investments—and then proceed to place the program in a context of educational theory. The effort has been to formulate a coherent rationale for our arguments and to communicate this rationale in terms which could be understood readily.

I admit, however, that this approach has raised as many questions as it has answered. Why do students want power (as distinguished from *why* should students *have* power)? What is the competence of students to exercise power? Over which areas of university life? In our view, what changes in the university will be necessary if students are to be accorded power? Each of these questions has been asked,

From *The Future Academic Community: Continuity and Change*, edited by John Caffrey (Washington, D.C.: American Council on Education, 1968). Copyright, 1968, by American Council on Education. Reprinted by permission of the author and the publisher. Edward Schwartz was President, U. S. National Student Association (1967-68).

explicitly or implicitly, at meetings of the educational establishment where the issue of student power has been raised.

Consequently, my intent here is to deal with several of these questions in a fairly precise manner. I have always contended that the discussion of student power is more a battle about educational theory than it is a debate between corporate and democratic theorists, as much a discussion of the kinds of decisions that are made in universities as it is an argument over who should make them, and as involved with trust between people as it is with the structures through which people move. Yet to understand the relationship between these general themes and the specific points of contention between the establishment and the students, one must deal with specifics.

Some Whys of Student Power

Why do students want power in universities? Some argue that they really do not. J. W. Anderson, writing in the June 30, 1968, issue of the *Washington Post*, observed that, "The slogan 'Student Power' is misleading. The students do not want power, in any conventional sense of the word. They are not demanding seats on boards of trustees, and they do not see themselves as future administrators. They wish the university to be run with more regard for them, but they do not wish to run it themselves."

College presidents who recently have read student manifestoes demanding seats on the board of trustees doubtless would dispute this claim, and Anderson partially contradicts himself elsewhere in his piece by describing a protest at Roosevelt University in which the administration capitulated on precisely this demand. Yet Anderson is correct in one important respect—the demand for student power begins only after students become dissatisfied with the university policy. If students are satisfied with their institutions, they are more than willing to let the establishment govern them.

The experience of the author's alma mater, Oberlin College, is indicative. For years, students petitioned the Oberlin administration and faculty for change in campus social rules, with little success. Ultimately, they lost confidence that either group would agree to student wishes. At that point, they demanded power to make those rules for themselves, on grounds that only they had to obey the rules and that the Oberlin rulers did not understand or share student sentiment. The desire for power sprang out of disenchantment with policy.

On the other hand, Oberlin students rarely suggested that undergraduates should be involved with curriculum planning. The reason was simple. When asked, "Do you feel that you are getting a good education at Oberlin?" most students replied, "Yes." It is only in the past two years, when student leaders began to question aspects of teaching and the curriculum, that the demand for joint participation in decision-making about curriculum has arisen. In 1967-68, two students sat on the faculty educational policy committee and many important changes were adopted.

Hence, just as the American colonists endorsed a Declaration of Independence only after they had thrown tea in the Boston harbor, the student community demands student power only after requests that involve policy matters are rejected, or ignored. Often, administrators counter undergraduate pleas for power with a counter-plea for "trust in the university community." What these presidents fail to recognize is that student power movements develop because trust has broken down—for whatever reason, the students no longer trust the establishment to make decisions on their behalf. Not surprisingly, administrators who use this argument meet with little success.

Further, the degree to which a movement for student power is militant depends largely upon the process by which administrators reject a specific set of student demands. If the president, or dean, or professor fails to give the student a hearing; or if he seems less than receptive to extensive discussion with students; if, in short, he rejects a proposal because students initiated it, then he will be subjected to a revolution in short order. He may be subjected to a similar response if, despite his best intentions, he is inaccessible to students—the problem in most multiversities. In both cases, students feel that, not simply their proposal, but also their identity has been insulted.

Even the president who tries to "understand" and "reason" with his students may face a student power movement. Tolerance does not mean agreement, and if the areas of disagreement between students and administrators are sufficiently broad, then the demands that the students will make on their institution will broaden as well. A dean at Oberlin tried to be understanding. His approach to social rules, however, dated to the Oberlin of 1930. No amount of "rational discussion" could bridge the chasm between institutional and undergraduate values. Demands for student control over the rules were the result.

If student disagreement with university policy leads to demands for student power, administrative opposition to a particular *set* of demands, more often than not, explains their resistance to student power in general. Of course, both sides can argue their case in the most elevated and theoretical terms. Yet specific points of conflict often lie in the background. The dynamics of university battles are suggestive—the dean and president ally with the students when they seek power over the curriculum, since neither one exercises much power over this area; and the faculty is more than willing to cede student power over social rules, finances, and even issues involving recruitment and investments. Everyone in the university argues for student power at some point, provided such power is granted over somebody else's turf. Students become "rash, immature, transient, inexperienced, and incompetent" to a university official only when they challenge an area of governance over which that official exercises special control.

Consequently, one cannot consider demands for student power over given areas of university life without also considering the context of the policy questions that the students have raised. I doubt that any administrator would resist the accordance of institutional authority to undergraduate students if the students proposed, "We agree with what you're trying to do, and we want to help." Administrators often urge students to say just that. Yet student power is not sought in so submissive a spirit. That is the crux of the matter, and institutions will have to deal with it as an active force. I must outline each area of the student power program and unravel the debate surrounding it.

"Control Over Their Own Affairs"

Should students maintain control over their own affairs— organizations, student governments, speaker programs, finances, dormitory rules, social life? Those of us who argue this case point both to the proposition of democratic theory which states that he who must obey a rule should make it, and to notions of personality development which encourage the accordance of responsibility to those who must learn to accept it. Administrators retort that students aren't "ready" to assume this kind of responsibility, that they need guidance and control in doing so, and that they fail to consider the "long-range interests of the institution."

Yet what lies at the heart of these administrative objections? When a college president or dean speaks of the "long-range interests of the institution," he inevitably has in mind some short-range student misdemeanor that will jeopardize them. It is essential, then, to consider forms of student activity that threaten administration policy. In earlier periods, I might have listed the invitation of controversial speakers to the campus, or the creation of radical political organizations, or the publication of illicit doctrine in the campus newspaper as being among central administration headaches. The growing acceptance of student rights among administrators has reduced friction surrounding these issues, however, and concomitantly reduced certain barriers to student power.

Yet despite substantial reforms on a few campuses, battles over parietal hours and intervisitation remain fierce. Here, appeals to the "long-range interests of the institution" reflect essentially political considerations. Proposals to grant students control over their own rules—in the knowledge that those rules will be liberalized—conjures up visions in administrative minds of angry alumni, aroused parents, and incensed legislators railing against promiscuity and decadence in a presumed citadel of reason. Professors worry about the relationship between their school's "image" and its status. Frequently, both administrators and faculty ask, "How can you say that only students are affected by social rules when other segments of the campus may also suffer consequences of student behavior?"

At base, such arguments are symptoms to students of the *inability* of the professor or the administrator to govern rather than evidence of his strength. Men who decide on questions of "image" in our society are not among the specimens most admired by the younger generation, particularly in institutions designed to retain a critical independence from the surrounding society. Fear of controversy has silenced too many people from fighting injustice—permitted too many social crimes to remain untended—for the young to embrace this fear in higher education. In this sense, "student power" as a slogan may be an indirect plea for university power—a demand, an expectation, that universities should make decisions about their internal affairs based on the preferences of the people who live in them, not on the whims of people who surround them. If the administrator admits that he agrees with public sentiment, after using it to justify his stand, then he worsens his position. He emerges as a man who would hide behind a pile of alumni letters rather than defend his own beliefs—again, a coward, who merits little respect from students.

Of course, none of this is meant to imply that administrators who bluntly announce their desire to regulate campus sexual behavior will meet widespread undergraduate approval. That presidents and deans cloud such announcements behind rhetoric or politics is, in part, a tribute to student intensity of preference in matters of their nonacademic life. Young people, simply, are fed up with our society's obsession with personal and private morals, particularly when the obsession obscures the nation's disregard for a number of social morals. Intimacy between male and female should be a matter between the two, not between them and the world. Those who delight in determining rules for human interaction of this sort fall into a general category of people in our country who construct barriers to honest relationships of all kinds. Here again, young people are trying to break down those barriers. The cultural premise from which they spring has wrought too much social havoc as to render insignificant by comparison the cases of premarital pregnancy which arise from misuse or nonuse of birth control devices. Indeed, many students suggest that the helpful approach to the "relationship" question is the provision of birth control devices to prevent pregnancy, not the enactment of rules to prevent intercourse. The one facilitates a relationship; the other inhibits it. Students believe in facilitation.

The issue of student power over social rules, then, is enmeshed in the over-all generational battle over personal morality. Most universities would reject the approach deemed most helpful by students—the distribution of contraceptive devices in the dormitories. Yet institutions create real trouble when they exercise their value preferences in the other direction. Why should administrators *care* about student sex life? They seem to care about so few other areas of student personal growth and development—too few, in fact—that their choice of this particular behavioral pattern seems ludicrous. Indeed, that prestigious universities are abandoning these rules leads many of us to believe that the schools which retain them merely expose deficiencies in other areas of their programs. If institutions spent as much time generating an exciting educational climate as they do imposing rules, they might find that public reaction to their rules would diminish. This is the kind of question which students are rising—the question of priorities—and universities have been slow to answer it intelligently. Hence, the demand for student power.

On Teaching and the Curriculum

The quest for student power over curricular areas stems from a similar concern. A desire to sit around tables with professors discussing departmental matters is only a partial motivation for the demand. Indeed, in the past, many students were afraid to participate in faculty meetings—they respect their professors in a way that they do not respect their deans. Yet the challenges to university teaching and curriculum content have become sufficiently widespread as to delegitimize professorial stature and to loosen student self-restraint. Now that students are "flexing their muscle" in this area, there is little question that their demands will grow in intensity.

Here, too, much of the debate is theoretical. Students insist that, as learners, they should have a say in what they learn, and in how they learn it. After all, the students argue, they pay to receive an education. To these charges, professors respond that students lack the academic training to make appropriate judgments on curricular matters, that they are moved more by questions of popular taste than they are by standards of intellectual excellence, and that their participation in curricular decisions would erode a basic tenet of professional academic freedom.

Yet, as with demands for control over rules, specific grievances concerning teaching and the curriculum lie at the heart of student demands for shared power over the classroom. Each of these must be delineated.

To start, it is important to recognize that much of the student criticism about the classroom reflects discontent with the style of teaching rather than the content of particular courses. Dull lectures, perfunctory examinations, papers graded without substantive comment, lack of classroom discussion, inaccessibility of the professor, all these rank much higher on a list of student gripes than complaints that an English professor chose to teach *Hamlet* rather than *King Lear* in a Shakespeare course, or that a political scientist was a behavioralist rather than a traditionalist. Student Course and Teacher Evaluations are more critiques for teaching than they are proposals for curricular revision. The medium outweighs the message.

In raising these kinds of criticisms, moreover, students are challenging the areas in which professors have the least claim to professional competence. College teachers are not trained to be teachers; they are trained to be political scientists, economists, biologists, and philosophers. If they were trained to teach, and encouraged to teach well, perhaps there would be fewer student complaints about the quality of teaching. That they were not, however, renders foolish their argument that "professional competence" should be the standard against which student participation should be weighed. Conversely, students are not competent political scientists, economists, biologists, and philosophers, but they are competent judges of good and bad lectures, adequate and inadequate discussions, helpful and deficient comments on papers. Hence the area in which student critics can be most acute is the area in which the professor's skill is least developed—a condition which leads to enormous friction.

Indeed, faculty resistance to student power in the area of curriculum may reflect less concern about student "incompetence" than resistance to the kinds of questions which students are asking—uncomfortable questions about teaching which many professors do not want to consider. The academic faces extreme pressures to establish himself as a scholar, and he will argue that this task is far more related to his advancement than is any special attention paid to his students. Some claim to be bitter about this state of affairs. Bitter or not, they see little they can do to change the situation and they resent those who would demand teaching of them, when teaching doesn't pay off.

Yet, if faculty response to criticism of teaching is negative, then student power over the curriculum should become not simply a desirable goal, but an essential goal, to those who wish to create higher standards of teaching in universities. To whom else is the question of teaching more important? Departmental chairmen are interested in attracting distinguished scholars. University presidents may be interested in hiring national celebrities. Publication is the route to achievement of both goals. Only the students are solely concerned about good teachers and good teaching and will judge professors almost exclusively on that standard. If interest in a subject is a prerequisite to developing competence, then students may well have the greatest competence on the campus to evaluate teaching.

The real source of tension between students and faculty becomes even clearer, moreover, when one realizes that other kinds of student curricular proposals have met with some success. Undergraduate complaints about emphasis on grades and pressures to compete led to quick and widespread acceptance of pass-fail. Student pleas for "relevance" are yielding quiet revolutions in the designing of courses in the social sciences and humanities. Requests for "learning by doing" are being met slowly through the development of community action curriculum projects, which should become commonplace within the next five years. Greater flexibility in requirements, new opportunities for independent study, interdivisional majors, even student-taught courses all have become "respectable" innovations for a university to consider. It is only when the nature of the *relationship* between student and professor is challenged—through questions about teaching, about the teacher's availability outside the class—that the student faces all the familiar arguments about his "incompetence." Yet such arguments merely verify what students suspect—that professors are reluctant to develop relationships with students, that they may have to be pressured to do so.

On the Quality of Institutional Life

Students should participate in decisions basic to university life—the third general principle of student power. College presidents cringe in horror at this notion. "Which areas?" they ask. "What are students competent to decide?" "Do students want a say in *everything?*"

This sort of gut reaction reflects as much general presidential insecurity as it does hostility to students as a pressure group. I doubt if there are many professional groups more self-pitying than college presidents, who spend their lives bemoaning the number and variety of constituencies to which they must respond. Frankly, having spent two years in the office of the National Student Association, during which time I had to react to such diverse groups as the Central Intelligence Agency and the Students for a Democratic Society, the Ford Foundation and the "Dump Johnson Movement," the Columbia student strike and the American Council on Education, I am somewhat less sympathetic to all this pouting. Yet I can see that a college president who fancies himself the harassed intersection of a myriad of opposing vectors might become reluctant to add yet another interest group to his list.

Nonetheless, the "Oh, how pressured we are!" argument becomes downright obnoxious when attached to a notion of bureaucratic efficiency. As one prominent educator recently put it, "Why, we've got a job to do—turning out doctors, and lawyers, and engineers. If we spent all our time in this dialogue business, we'd never get anything done." In that one brief comment was embodied every notion about higher education which students are determined to change: that young people are "objects" who have to be churned off an assembly line for society; that the success of the educational process should be measured in terms of the number of students who can be processed; that interaction, discussion, mutual decision-making are hindrances, rather than assets, to education. The future "doctors, lawyers, and engineers" are tired of being viewed only as such. The future poets and social activists are quite prepared to destroy a system that treats them in this manner. Yet the educator's sentiments, I am sure, are widely shared.

The matter is complicated further inasmuch as, here again, the student demand for a say in basic university decision-making reflects a concern that new factors be considered among the criteria in making decisions. The introduction of a new variable does not make an equation easier to solve. Students feel, however, that certain variables must be weighed if *just* decisions are to be made by university administrations. Justice is not a function of efficiency. Indeed, justice may depend upon *in*efficiency. Yet students demand that considerations of justice outweigh those of efficiency.

They demand the consideration of justice, particularly in areas of university policy that relate to political and social questions of the nation. Among the areas involved are research grants, investments, recruitments, relationships with government agencies, extramural housing projects in ghettos, admissions—in short, all the areas about which the Students for a Democratic Society has expressed the greatest concern. When some of us argue that students should be accorded an institutional voice in certain of these areas, we meet the familiar arguments about competence. As with professors and deans, however, the presidential reference to competence often clouds a more central objection to considering concerns which students might raise about certain decisions.

Take the area of university investments as an example. Whenever I suggest to a university president or educator that students should have a say in where the institution invests its money, I am met with the reply, "Oh nonsense, students don't understand how to invest money, and we don't have time to train them. Even I don't fully understand these things."

The argument is well-taken, but misses the point of the students' demand. Even if most undergraduates could not evaluate whether an investment were an appropriate financial risk, they most certainly could and would point out that Mississippi Power and Light Company (in which Harvard invests substantially) may not hire Negroes, that the Chase Manhattan Bank helps support the economy of South Africa, and that the Dow Chemical Company manufactures Napalm for the war in Vietnam. They might make similar points about acceptance of grants from the Defense Department, the Central Intelligence Agency, or the Institute for Defense Analysis. About the market, students know little; about social issues many students are extremely perceptive and sensitive.

The real issue surrounding the accordance of student power over many of these areas, then, is the policy question—whether administrators will agree that the political stance of universities should be an important consideration in institutional decision-making. Such concerns are, indeed, inefficient. Occasionally, they even involve economic costs. Yet students would contend—often through vigorous means—that failure to confront these issues yields even greater moral and social costs. They find it strange that a college president who lauds student efforts to combat racism in the South becomes furious when the same student points out that a university project or investment contributes to racism. They feel that if the president is a morally sensitive man, he will want his students to raise these kinds of considerations, since so few people in the university, and even fewer outside it, are raising them. When the president rejects responsible contentions of students, they can reach only one conclusion—and they act on it.

What Kind of Rule?

What I have tried to suggest throughout this piece is that the debate over student power involves more than just the question, "Who rules?" It also involves "What kind of rule?" and "What are the qualities of humane rule? The impact of social movements for civil rights at home, for peace in Vietnam, has led to a demand that all institutions, and particularly those whose presence is felt immediately by the young, act humanely. University intrusion in private love affairs is deemed inhumane; professional disdain for teaching is deemed inhumane; administrative obliviousness to the social concerns of students is deemed inhumane. In every case, students are trying to inject a new sense of political and social responsibility in a society that appears to have ceased to honor either.

When leaders of the society, and of the university, resist the kinds of changes which students propose, the students then demand institutional power so that they may enact the changes themselves. Bob Dylan's exhortation that fathers and mothers should "Get out of the way if you can't lend a hand" is as clear and vibrant an expression of this feeling as any which has been offered. The student demand for power further tests the university's humaneness. A university which is decent to its students will grant student power as an expression of trust and as an indication that it sympathizes with the student concerns. When the university administration or faculty rejects the student cries for power—often by using arguments which skirt the real issues and insult the students' integrity—the young's image of the corruption of the old order is reinforced.

Yet the young will no longer accept corruption without a fight. Those who miss this sense of urgency do so at their own risk. What young people lack in argumentative skill and political experience they make up for in growing tactical sophistication and a willingness to apply it. They are determined to win points, and, judging from the pace of events, they probably will. The question is no longer whether, but how; no longer how far, but how fast; and these depend, essentially, upon the ability of an old order to move, to change, and to grow.

26

THE BOARD OF TRUSTEES AND
STUDENT BEHAVIOR

〰〰〰〰〰〰〰〰〰〰〰〰〰〰〰〰〰〰〰〰〰〰〰〰〰〰〰〰〰〰〰〰〰〰〰〰〰〰

JAMES L. CHAPMAN

STUDENTS, especially those of the New Left, tend to challenge the method of governance of institutions of higher education. This attitude is expressed either subtly or openly, by the following: "In any democracy the government obtains its authority and power to govern from the majority. As such, the president of a university is answerable to us, the students." The validity of this type of reasoning breaks down at the point where the assumption is made that a college or university is considered to be a democratic institution similar in form and structure to a democratically organized government. A form of government so organized does exist in fact by the will of the governed, and obtains its authority to act on behalf of them only by their consent. A valid argument certainly could be made that this is the way colleges and universities should be operated. In fact, the "free university movement" which has developed in recent years comes close to operating in such a manner. However, the point is that, under the present form of governance of colleges and universities, the authority for their existence rests with the few and is passed on to the majority. The "few" refers to the governing board and the majority to those persons constituting the academic

Based on an address to the American Personnel and Guidance Association, Detroit, Mich., April 7-11, 1968. Used by permission of the author. James L. Chapman wrote this address when he was Associate Dean of Students, University of Iowa, Iowa City. He now is Senior Associate, Cresap, McCormick and Paget, Inc., New York City.

community of a given campus—the staff and students. This is in contradistinction to society at large, since a democratic form of government is so ordered that the majority, namely the populace, gives the few its authority and power to govern. These are historical and legal precedents for the present method of operating a university and, until these are altered drastically, it is a naive assumption to speak of institutions of higher education as places where participatory democracy is in evidence. Naiveté at this point may come as readily from a glowing statement from the president's office regarding student involvement in the decision-making process of a given institution as from growling students at a student senate meeting.

With such administrative and legal realities, I would like to develop three approaches to serve as models for a governing board in dealing with student behavior problems, more particularly those which produce internal and external stressful situations in the college campus: the sit-ins, the demonstrations, and the protest marches which have been rather common on the college campus in recent years. Once the campus climate has been enveloped by such an activity, the governing board could respond in one of the following ways.

The *confrontation* approach is one in which the governing board firmly and openly asserts its power under such circumstances. The idea is expressed that policies have been established to handle matters of this type and they will be upheld regardless of the circumstances. The chairman of the board or his spokesman may choose to indicate verbally such a position to all elements of the campus. A confrontation of this type matches the power of policy and reinforcement by a constitutional body, as opposed to the psychological force of a group of students who are reinforced by a commitment to a common goal of producing stress in the environment. The governing board has a low threshold of tolerance even for dissent and the idea of disruption never is entertained. To illustrate, let me cite an editorial which appeared following a major demonstration, Nov. 1, 1967, at the University of Iowa, when 108 persons were arrested for preventing free access to the Union building where Marine recruiters were interviewing. It reads in part:

Obviously hoping to win Brownie points for the 1968 election, a few legislators have seized on the anti-war demonstrations at the University of Iowa to get personal prejudices on education off their chests.

Take the letter State Senator Chester O. Hougen dispatched to President Howard Bowen at the University of Iowa the other day. After telling the president what "the people" want done with faculty members (fire 'em posthaste) and students (expel 'em forthwith) who participate in demonstrations, the senator congratulates Dr. Bowen for his public statement putting future demonstrators on notice, but says it doesn't go far enough.

Then the senator gets down to what he really wanted to say all along:

The public is incensed with the liberal teachings, biased political views imposed on the students in and out of the classrooms, and the advocation of civil disobedience, law-breaking and interference with the basic educational rights of the other students in the name of so-called "academic freedom."[1]

The psychological frame of reference from which a board would operate under such a model would be that of insecurity, distrust, rigidity, and coercion.

The *confused* approach would lead the governing board to act without a knowledge of what its role should be in such matters. It would attempt to appease all elements by setting up hearings with the administration, the faculty, and the students. The policies on matters of this type are uncertain or, possibly, new ones made during the period of stress, as well as immediately following the hearings. The board actually would think that some action has to be taken, but it would not see the long-range implication of its misplaced and confused activity. Another quotation from a different editorial illustrates this approach to some extent:

We suppose there will be investigations into the riots and the blame will be tossed here and there until the whole affair is forgotten. But we blame everyone at the school; we blame President Howard Bowen, the faculty and all the students, not only those who participated directly but the thousands who allowed a few hundred to jeopardize the educational opportunities of all.

We have an archaic suggestion to throw at this point. Why don't those who don't like our universities at Ames, Iowa City and Cedar Falls, both students and teachers, quit? And why don't those who are left join recognized political organizations whose avowed aims are to improve not destroy society and cut out the ridiculous demonstrations?[2]

The psychological climate under which a board would operate under such a model would be that of uncertainty, frustration, and need for activity.

---

1 *Cedar Rapids Gazette*, Jan. 4, 1968.
2 *Council Bluffs Nonpareil*, Nov. 5, 1967.

The board using the *confidence* approach would consider the problem in the light of reason and good judgment. It would feel secure with its policy and place its confidence in the president and his administrative staff to work out satisfactory solutions to such problems. The policies could be reviewed at a time removed from the actual stressful encounter. The board would resist pressure from all interested groups—administration, faculty, dissenting students, and the public—to act with haste or unfairness in dealing with the problem. The review which did follow the problem would be one of looking at the policies to determine whether or not they could be carried out adequately by the proper university officials, as well as to determine the meaning of the substance contained in each. The attitude expressed in a third editorial which followed the demonstration at the University of Iowa illustrates the confidence placed in the president:

We commend President Howard Bowen for his firm statement this week declaring the State University of Iowa must continue to fulfill its clear responsibility to protect the rights of individual students in seeking access to placement facilities. In relation to the current situation, this means the university will continue to assist students who wish to interview recruiters, including officers of the U.S. Marine Corps.

We would expect the president of the university to take such a stand; but Bowen's statement is worth emphasis in view of the temporizing attitude taken by some other university officials on the issues of illegal sit-ins or other activity involving civil disobedience.[3]

The psychological attitude of the board would be one of security, trust, openness, confidence, and a willingness to ascertain and appraise the problem before acting, if it did act.

I favor the confidence model as the one which a stable board of trustees would want to accept. I also accept this model as the emerging pattern of response due to three changes which have occurred in our society.

The character of higher education has changed. There was a time in our history when higher education was for the elite, with a curriculum designed for those who desired to study law, theology, and medicine. This has changed to the extent that we now are educating the masses with curricula which range in scope from cosmology to cosmetology.

The character of academic freedom has changed. The AAUP

---

[3] *Waterloo Courier*, Nov. 3, 1967.

statement of 1915 indicated that academic freedom was the freedom of the teacher to teach in his area of competency. The most recent statement, which was drafted in 1964, stipulates "the freedom to teach and the freedom to learn." The student is free to inquire, to study, and to evaluate all possible options.

The character of constitutional liberties has changed. The racial "separate but equal" law was upheld as valid in 1896. The Supreme Court declared this same law as unconstitutional in 1954. A New York State Court of Appeals (1917) upheld the dismissal of a student from a state college because the student did not conduct himself off-campus in a patriotic manner. The decision in *Dixon vs. the State of Alabama* (1963) was in favor of the students, since the college from which the students were dismissed did not follow the basic tenets of due process.

Only that board of trustees which accepts the opportunity of establishing trust, openness, security, confidence, and understanding in working with the president and the other chief administrators will be able to cope with stressful situations.

27

SOME WAYS TOWARD CAMPUS PEACE

VICTOR A. RAPPORT

WAS THE STUDENT REVOLT at the Berkeley campus, University of California, an isolated expression of student discontent at being hindered from recruiting "volunteers and money for assorted causes, especially civil rights"?[1] Was it only concerned with the University of California's Free Speech Movement, or was the insurrection a manifestation of a more deep-seated problem concerning all campuses?[2] Educators should pose the last question to themselves.

Administrators also should ask themselves: Are we going away from our *primary* concern—namely, our faculty and students? The lack of similar faculty riots should not lull administrators into a state of presumed beneficence. Too much movement of faculty to other campuses negates such placid thinking.

Besides worrying about his faculty and students, the college and university administrator must seek to create a "good public image" before his board of trustees, his legislature, his community, his church, and before all other areas where "influence"—both positive and negative—may repose. But, primarily, the administrator is concerned with keeping his college or university in the best possible financial position.

---

[1] To use the words of Gilbert A. Harrison, *New Republic,* 151:7, Dec. 19, 1964.

[2] James Cass, "What Happened at Berkeley," *Saturday Review,* 48:47-48, 66-69, Jan. 16, 1965.

From *School & Society,* Summer, 1965. Reprinted by permission of the author and the publisher. Victor A. Rapport wrote this article when he was Dean for International Studies, Wayne State University, Detroit, Mich. He now is Dean and Professor Emeritus.

Of course, an improved faculty helps to secure an improved financial position and a growing student body assists in pleas to legislatures for more money, but more impressive to donors, perhaps, is the good public image. In seeking to gain and to improve this image, have administrators widened the cleft between administration and faculty, between themselves and their students? Has the faculty contributed to this separation? Consulting is lucrative but takes time and energy, leaving possibly only the dregs for a professor's students. Community participation may build the ego and contribute to promotability—besides doing necessary tasks—but it, too, takes time and effort. Research, though needed and rewarding, also may be a factor in divorcing teacher from student, contributing to further administration-faculty-student isolation. However, these faculty activities aid materially in building an improved faculty, which attracts more students and creates a better public image.

The average administrator delegates to one man concern for the happiness and contentment of the faculty and to another the task of maintaining a state of student bliss. It is a rare administrator who does not hold one or several "Meet the President" sessions, thereby creating a better image and convincing himself that he "really knows his students." Students who attend these affairs are enthralled by the warmth of their president, inspired by his fine collection of books. What the president does is usually done well.

Meanwhile, students who cannot or do not attend are filled with frustrations common to the "rat race" of the campus: the requirements, the competition for grades, the inability to see their professors, the inflexible hours needed for graduation. They resent a president whom they may see only when they graduate and a dean whom they may see only if they get into severe trouble. (For lesser difficulty, they see an assistant dean.) Their professors are available only by appointment, and then for perhaps a mere 10 minutes. These faults and flaws, commonly attributed to large universities but also present in small, select colleges, fan the anger of students against the entire educational process.

Harold Taylor, speaking at Wayne State University, April 23, 1964, forecast some of these student difficulties. But, surely, Taylor would not claim unique prescience. Nearly every administrator has written articles or talked to his faculties deploring the drift away from teaching, the glorification of research, the growing impersonality of colleges and universities, the increased regimentation, following these pious words with the exhortation: "I call on you, the faculty, to correct this situation." But, never or rarely does the administrator tell how.

What *can* be done to modify these disaffections of both students and faculty? Certain specificities—rather than unctuosities—are demanded.

The prime needs are to bring the faculty into closer relation with the student and to convince the faculty member that there is no necessary enmity between him and administration. These two-pronged assaults should not be considered as evanescent forays but as commitments to everlasting principles. Certain students now believe they have easy access to certain faculty members. The fact that they use this access does not necessarily mean they will abuse it. Only a very small percentage ever do. The road to peace on the campus demands that every student have ready reception in all units of the university and receive authoritative and understanding answers. Such procedures will strike at the heart of primary causes for much campus frustration. They may require three modifications of current practice: a retraining of some faculty members so that they become receptive to student concerns; a change in the interviewing tactics of department chairmen (or other hiring members) to include questions regarding the feelings of the prospective members toward students and the employment of only those who are clearly solicitous; and the possible addition of some added faculty because of the small extra time required to fill these concerns.

The other prong of the proposal—to convince the faculty member that there is no necessary enmity between him and administration—is thornier. The first necessary step may be to improve communication so that no longer will the customary ways of learning campus things be either through rumor or the press. Another concern—perhaps a facet of the preceding—is for swifter action on faculty recommendations. No faculty member is enamored of the procedure by which a matter he has expended considerable thought remains buried on an administrator's desk for months—sometime years—occasionally without even a courteous acknowledgment. Yet, an added item: many administrators are wont to appoint committees (consuming faculty time that could be better spent working with students), then, either taking the entire time talking to a committee which was presumably assembled for deliberative purposes, or disregarding the thoughtful results achieved after many hours of committee work. The very least such an administrator can do is to assemble the committee for a last session where he explains why the committee's recommendations must be deviated from or rejected.

Many faculty members and students could come up with far longer lists of fundamental concern, but the foregoing proposals generally require no additional funds. They are primarily matters demanding changed thinking, structure, and practice. If universally adopted as committed principles, many of the menacing threats would be dispelled.

28

A STRATEGY FOR CAMPUS PEACE

∿∿∿

LEWIS F. POWELL, JR.

THERE ALWAYS HAS BEEN a sort of "open season" on college presidents. They have long been the target of the traditional pressures—from alumni, trustees, faculty, students, and politicians. The college president also has been a man of distinction—an educator, a respected citizen, and intellectual leader. This respected role in our society, together with the satisfactions of educating the young, have made these traditional pressures endurable. But, in recent years, new and disquieting pressures have arisen. The combination of the new and old have imposed unprecedented burdens upon the office of college president. It is, today, no less an honor to preside over an institution of higher learning, but it now has become an occupation hazardous to health of body and mind, as well as to reputation.

Resignations by college presidents are increasing, and the task of filling the vacancies is incomparably more difficult. I am told that more than 100 respected colleges across the land are seeking chief executives.

In interviews recently published, several nationally known presidents stated quite frankly that the satisfactions they had found in intellectual leadership were outweighed by the agonies of the office.

Based on an address to the American Association of State Colleges and Universities, Washington, D.C., Nov. 11, 1968. Lewis F. Powell, Jr., is a lawyer; President, Virginia State Board of Education; a trustee of Washington and Lee University; and past President, American Bar Association.

UCLA's Franklin Murphy commented that "you have to be sadistic to ask a man to stay on more than 10 years." Dr. Elvis Starr, upon resigning at Indiana, referred to the "bigots and the zealots" now seeking footholds on the campus. These are, he said, "The groups that are determined to destroy [you] and the university. They don't want solutions, just confrontations."[1]

Even the wives of college presidents, noted for their patience and long sufferance, are beginning to speak out. Mrs. Henry King Stanford, wife of Miami's president, commented that the only people who should be university presidents are the "friendless, the orphaned and bachelors."

Now, before anyone feels too sorry for college and university presidents, let me sound a more positive note. As one who has been close to education for many years, I still view it as perhaps the greatest professional calling. There is little hope for the future of this troubled world unless the educational process is in the hands of wise, dedicated, and responsible men.

Prior to the SDS-led assault on Columbia, and despite the clear warnings from Berkeley and other besieged campuses, there had been a tendency to underestimate the militancy of the New Left. It had been fashionable to be tolerant, to temporize with sit-ins and lawless demonstrations, and to grant amnesty even to the most disorderly. Much of the "liberal" establishment applauded the self-proclaimed idealism of New Leftist leaders and ridiculed those who voiced concern.

The shock of Columbia may have had a therapeutic effect. Not only was a great university brought to its knees, but the conduct of the radical students—the vandalizing of furniture, the rifling of Dr. Grayson Kirk's personal files, the burning of manuscripts, and the personal filth and obscenity of the rebels—profoundly shocked decent people across our country.

But the New Left neither was dismayed nor deterred by the public reaction to Columbia. As revolutionaries, the New Leftists are as contemptuous of public opinion as they are of what they call the Establishment. Mark Rudd, the SDS leader, has boasted publicly of the goal "to create many more Columbias"—following the strategy advocated by Che Guevera.[2]

A school was conducted in New York in the summer of 1968

---

1 *Time,* Sept. 27, 1968, pp. 55, 56.
2 *Richmond News-Leader,* June 22, 1968.

called the Liberation School for the training of young radicals in revolutionary strategy and tactics on the campus. A reporter who infiltrated the school wrote that the students, totaling perhaps 500 persons, were taught a curriculum ranging from karati to the thoughts of Mao Tse-tung.[3]

The goals of the New Left are, first, to disrupt and then to destroy our most cherished democratic institutions—our system of higher education and our representative form of government. As stated in an article in the *New Republic* "[the New Left's] purpose is to destroy the institutions of the American establishment."[4]

J. Edgar Hoover, whose FBI is responsible for the internal security of our country, has warned that "revolutionary terrorism" on the campus "is a serious threat both to the academic community and to a lawful and orderly society." Mr. Hoover stated that the New Left, led by SDS, "plans to launch a widespread attack on educational institutions," an attack which could bring "revolutionary terror" to the college campus.[5] The strategic plan of the New Left, according to FBI investigation, is "to smash first our educational structure, then our economic system, and finally our government itself."[6]

The *Washington Post,* not always in accord with Mr. Hoover and rarely alarmist in its editorial policy, also has warned that "the [New Leftists] . . . regard the universities as the soft spot in a society they are trying to bring down. . . . The rebels are out of touch with and do not understand the principles of democracy. . . . The language they talk is that of anarchy. . . . They are totally at war with everything this country has ever stood for."[7]

What is the New Left? There is no single, monolithic organization as such. The term is loosely used to include a conglomeration of organizations, groups and individuals. The most radical organizations include Students for a Democratic Society (SDS), W. E. B. DuBois Clubs, Young Socialist Alliance, Socialist Workers Party,

---

[3] *The National Observer,* July 22, 1968, article by John Peterson.

[4] *Washington Post* editorial, May 14, 1968, quoting article in *New Republic.*

[5] *New York Times,* Sept. 1, 1968.

[6] *FBI Law Enforcement Bulletin,* September, 1968; *New York Times,* Sept. 1, 1968.

[7] *Washington Post,* May 14, 1968. A student publication at the University of California, *The Berkeley Barb,* states the New Leftist view as follows: "The universities cannot be reformed; they must be abandoned or closed down. They should be used as bases for action against society, but never taken seriously." *New York Times Magazine,* May 18, 1968, p. 104.

Student Nonviolent Coordinating Committee (SNCC), and Progressive Labor Party.[8] Militant Negro groups, such as the Black Panthers, often participate. Although many of the organizations are Communist oriented or supported, the dominant philosophy of the New Left is nihilistic, proposing no coherent system of social, political or educational institutions to replace the system the New Left seeks to destroy.

The principal threat to campus peace comes from the defiant SDS organization. Founded in 1962, it now claims 250 chapters and a membership of 35,000. Its inner circle of hard-core revolutionaries may not exceed 1,000.

But the capabilities of SDS cannot be related to its numbers. It has been estimated that its activist leaders have a capacity "to mobilize between 100,000 and 300,000 students, depending on the issue."[9] SDS not only sets the pace for other New Left organizations; it often attracts thousands of nonrevolutionary students who, motivated by naive idealism and taken in by the slogans, could become—quite unwittingly—the shock troops of revolution. We have seen this at Columbia, where sympathizing students far outnumbered the New Leftists. We have seen it in the Chicago confrontation between the police and the thousands of young people who attempted to disrupt the Democratic convention in 1968.

The greatest care must be exercised to distinguish between the revolutionaries and the vast majority of students and faculty members who, like society in general, are really the victims of the New Leftists. It also would be folly not to recognize that students often do have legitimate grievances, especially on the larger campuses. The Cox Commission, reporting on the Columbia revolt, was as critical of the administration, trustees, and faculty as it was of the students and the police. The Commission found that conditions at Columbia were almost as bad as the students had claimed.[10]

It is this combination of valid grievances, plus the widespread disenchantment and alienation of the young,[11] that produces an environment quite hospitable to ferment. The problem, thus, is by

---

8 Gene E. Bradley, "What Businessmen Need to Know about the Student Left," *Harvard Business Review*, September-October, 1968, p. 54.

9 *Ibid.*, p. 54.

10 *New York Times*, Oct. 13, 1968 (*The Week in Review*, E3).

11 There can be no doubt that such disenchantment and alienation do exist among millions of fine young people. The identification and amelioration of the causes of these attitudes profoundly concern thoughtful college administrators.

no means confined to the New Left. Rather, it is what a few determined leftists can do to inflame and mislead other students, especially where responsible student opinion is ignored, communications are poor, ground rules are ill defined,[12] and policy is vacillating and irresolute.

I now will discuss briefly three areas of special sensitivity: participation in decision making, the role of faculties, and academic freedom. Each of these poses difficult questions to which there are no easy or unequivocal answers.

The demand for student participation in decision-making ranges all the way from membership on boards of trustees to selection of presidents and faculty and determination of curriculum. If the full sweep of this demand were met, the present structure of higher education in America would be dismantled and replaced by the type of student power found in many Latin-American universities. You may be aware that the history department at San Marcos, Peru's largest university, was simply closed down. Students, controlling one-third of the university's governing board, actually dominated decision-making by methods of raw coercion.[13]

No responsible college administrator or board of trustees can accede to this type of demand. The student body is necessarily transitory, changing from year to year. Nor does the wisdom of student leaders always match their own conviction of infallibility. For these obvious reasons, the role and responsibility of students never can equate that of faculty, administration, or trustees.

Yet, student views are entitled to be voiced and seriously considered; appropriate channels must be devised to accomplish this; and a far greater effort made to make these channels meaningful. The wise administrator will work these out, with faculty and student participation, in advance of campus trouble. All of this must have substance and reflect a genuine desire to reach accommodation with responsible student views.

---

[12] The importance of clearly defined rules and regulations, with the penalties for infraction, can hardly be overemphasized. This is especially true as to the difference between legitimate and wholesome exercise of free speech and peaceful assembly, as contrasted with unlawful conduct which will not be tolerated. For helpful guidelines in the drafting of regulations, see *Freedom and Order on Campus,* an unpublished memorandum of the American Council on Education, and Van Alstyre, *The Judicial Trend Toward Student Academic Freedom,* 20 U. Fla. L. Rev. 290, 298 (1968).

[13] Bowen Northrup, *Wall Street Journal,* " 'Campus Politics' at San Marcos," vol. 172, No. 67, October, 1968.

But it must be remembered that no such program—however reasonable—will mollify the radicals. Their objective is revolution, not reform. The experience at Columbia demonstrates that SDS simply escalates its demands as concessions are made.[14] The hope must be not to placate the radicals, but to build a broad base of support among students in the main stream of campus life.

Another frequently voiced grievance relates to the faculty—often a justified cause for dissatisfaction. In his recent essay, John Fischer suggests that the primary cause of student unrest is faculty failure rather than agitation by New Leftists, the malaise of the Vietnam war, or disillusionment with our "materialistic society."[15] The reader may be surprised—perhaps even pleased—to know that Mr. Fischer blames the faculties far more than the administrators. He cited Irving Kristol for the view that, in most universities, "liberal education is extinct," that many faculty members have become a new privileged class—more concerned with their own income, influence, and careers than with teaching and counseling their students.[16]

Mr. Fischer probably has overstated and over-simplified his case. Yet, there can be little doubt that he has identified one of the most intractable problem areas, especially in the large university.

Pres. John A. Logan, Jr., Hollins College, has voiced a somewhat similar view: "Few laymen and even fewer students fully appreciate the power exercised by faculties today in a great university. They are in effective control of the curriculum, of faculty appointments and promotions, the requirements for earned degrees, admission standards, grading systems and academic rules and regulations, all conditions affecting academic freedom and tenure, and much of the planning and design of academic buildings. Student resentment against trustees and administrations is often misdirected, since much of the unrest is a protest, conscious or unconscious, against unfulfilled expectations about college teaching. To the extent that the faculty has downgraded the teaching function in favor of research and has become overspecialized, they have neglected their essential

---

14 *New York Times*, Sept. 22, 1968 (article by John Kifner).

15 John Fischer, "The Case for the Rebellious Students and their Counterrevolution," *Harper's*, August, 1968.

16 In contrasting the relative shift of power from the university administration to its faculty, Mr. Fischer states: "Students are inclined to attack the administration because the ostensible authority seems to rest with the president and the trustees. Few undergraduates yet realize how much of the administration's former power has now shifted into the hands of the faculty."

function in undergraduate education, which is to illuminate the good life by precept and example, to communicate sympathetically to their students a sense of purpose, and their own values and intellectual discipline."[17]

On certain campuses, when discord has threatened to weaken if not destroy the institution, the mounting faculty power has not been accompanied by an equal sense of responsibility. Indeed, support of the New Left by faculty members has not been insignificant, with far too many condoning or encouraging student disorders and civil disobedience.

Erwin N. Griswold, Solicitor General of the United States and former dean of the Harvard Law School, spoke recently of the violence at Columbia and its toleration by so many faculty members. Dean Griswold expressed an appealing view when he said: "The only persons for whom I have more contempt than for the student groups (which created the discord) are the faculty members who lent support to them."[18]

The problem is to stimulate faculty responsibility commensurate with its now unprecedented power. This problem is complicated by two of the most "untouchable" concepts in American life—academic freedom and academic tenure. Because both concepts are sound in principle—and are defended blindly and ferociously—few are bold enough to raise even the most restrained voice of analysis or doubt. The time has come for persons concerned with American education to understand that neither concept is so sacrosanct as to be above rational criticism.

I will cite several examples to illustrate the extremism which often is cloaked as academic freedom. Yale belatedly mustered the courage not to re-employ Prof. Staughton Lynd after his unlawful trip to Hanoi and his heavy involvement with the New Left. More recently, New York University dismissed radical Prof. John F. Hatchett after he had attacked Jewish teachers and publicly characterized Vice President Humphrey and Mr. Nixon as "racist bastards."[19]

The Berkeley campus was in ferment over the case of Eldridge Cleaver, a convicted felon, a black racist, and a leader of the militant Black Panther Party. With approval of an irresponsible faculty committee, Cleaver was invited to give a series of 10 lectures

17 Commencement address, Medical College of Virginia, June 1, 1968.

18 Erwin N. Griswold, address, Virginia State Bar Association, July 6, 1968.

19 *New York Times*, Oct. 13, 1968; *Chicago Sun-Times*, Oct. 12, 1968.

on racism. The California Board of Regents, in a stormy session and by a divided vote, overruled the faculty committee, limiting Cleaver to one lecture for credit. The faculty, supinely bowing to student demands, then approved 10 Cleaver lectures without credit. This resulted in sit-ins, obscenities, and disorders.[20]

A somewhat similar situation developed at San Francisco State College. The issue at first was whether Murray, a Black Panther lecturer who advocated the carrying of guns by students, should be dismissed. This escalated into a bitter confrontation in which radical students, with significant faculty support, resorted to mindless violence and vandalism.

In these, and like cases, the cry of academic freedom is predictably always raised. Hatchett charged N.Y.U. with violating "every principle of academic freedom." Students and some faculty members at Berkeley have accused the Regents of making a decision in the Cleaver case "essentially racist in character and in violation of academic freedom."[21]

The question, in simplest terms, is whether responsible educators will continue to allow "academic freedom" to be used as a cover for extremism on the campus, however violent or irrational. In reality, what is called "academic freedom" in these situations often approaches license without limit. Where tenure exists, it is virtually impossible to exercise restraint of any kind on such license beyond that vaguely, and often ineffectually, imposed by the mores of a particular campus.

As a lawyer, I subscribe wholeheartedly to the basic freedoms embodied in the concept of academic freedom. No one devoted to the educational process could entertain a different view. But the very existence of this freedom—virtually unrestrainable—imposes a higher degree of responsibility than that often manifested on our campuses.

The quality of education depends upon the wise exercise of value judgments, especially in the selection, retention, and promotion of those who teach. One may doubt that a Black Panther leader, a convicted felon, is qualified to bring anything worth while to the campus. If it is said that he knows much about racial hatred, it also can be said that a Mafia leader knows much about vice and extor-

---

20 *New York Times,* Oct. 24, 1968.
21 *Washington Post,* Oct. 13, 1968

tion, and that the Grand Dragon of the Klan knows much about bigotry.

Should the faculties of our great universities, dedicated to ideals of high scholarship and the search for truth, be demeaned by conspiring extremists who would defile and destroy the very freedoms they invoke? Are our campuses to become Hyde Parks and Times Squares, where a soap box is provided for every huckster?[22]

The time has come for responsible educators to be far more discriminating in the selection of professors and lecturers, and especially in the granting of tenure. The important qualifications of a professor—possessed, I am sure, by a great majority of this privileged profession—are still the ancient ones of honor, integrity, scholarship, intellectual independence, responsibility, and a genuine desire to teach.[23] The extremist who scorns these qualifications, whether he be of the right or the left, has no proper place on the faculty or, indeed, in the student body of an institution of learning.

There is, among all of us genuinely concerned with education, a broad consensus as to traditional campus liberalism: Our colleges and universities must be preserved as citadels of free inquiry. They always must foster and encourage—and never suppress—the freedom of both faculty and students to express divergent views, to protest injustice, and to promote social change in which they believe. Yet, this high purpose of the university surely will be frustrated and subverted if current trends toward license, discord, and even anarchy on the campus are not checked. Reversing these trends will require the highest level of courage and statesmanship from college administrators, faculties, and trustees. There must be a revitalizing of discipline, honor, and intellectual integrity on the campus, just as such a need exists so urgently for society in general.

The line must be drawn—sharply and resolutely—between those willing to observe traditional methods of peaceful assembly, rational discussion, and orderly procedures, and those who inspire and lead the sit-ins, the lawless demonstrations, and other forms of coercion.

---

[22] A distinction should be drawn between faculty membership as a professor or lecturer, and the casual visiting speaker. A broad spectrum of dissident views can be brought to a campus without conferring on an extremist the accolade of "faculty member" or "lecturer." But some value judgments should be exercised even as to the casual campus speaker.

[23] As Pres. Robert E. R. Huntley, Washington and Lee University, put it in his inaugural address (Oct. 18, 1968), "There is no higher goal to which a scholar can aspire than to be a vital teacher of young men."

The latter are usually the New Leftists on the campus and their followers. Like their heroes, Che Guevera, Fidel Castro, and Ho Chi Minh, the only language they understand is force. Such student extremists, and the faculty members who support them in their lawlessness, have forfeited any right to remain as members of a university community. The sooner they are expelled from student bodies and dismissed from faculties, the sooner our campuses will resume their historic roles as centers of reason and intellectual pursuit.[24]

It is important to understand that there is a close relationship between the discord on the campus and lawlessness in the streets. There is abroad in this country an escalating unrest which has led to unprecedented civil disobedience and disrespect for law and due process. As others have noted, we also are witnessing a pervasive permissiveness—on the campus, in the churches, the homes, and in our political institutions. Ancient standards of morality, decency, and good taste have crumbled; concepts of duty, patriotism, and responsibility often are subordinated. Even some of the most respected values of western civilization are under virulent attack.

The causes of this disintegration and disarray are complex and deep-seated. Some are related to the pressing needs in this country and other parts of the world. No thoughtful person would minimize the seriousness of these needs—for improved job and educational opportunities for all, for equal justice, for more effective means of participation in the democratic process, and, perhaps above all, for assurance of peace in the nuclear age.

But it must be evident that none of the grave problems of our time can be solved unless we preserve an ordered society in which law again is respected and due process is observed. This is as true on the college campus as it is in society in general. This is a first and overriding duty of all of us privileged to share some responsibility for higher education in this country.

---

24 But it must be remembered that students, however obnoxious, cannot be suspended or expelled without cause. Accused students are also properly entitled to due process. See Van Alstyre, *op. cit.*, p. 295-96; see also Comment, *Private Government on the Campus—Judicial Review of University Expulsions,* 72 Yale L. J. 1362 (1963); *Esteban* v. *Central Missouri State College,* 277 F. Supp. 649 (1967); *Jones* v. *State Board of Education,* 279 F. Supp. 190 (1968); *Hammond* v. *So. Carolina State College,* 272 F. Supp. 947 (1967); *Goldberg* v. *Regents of U. of Calif.,* 57 Cal. Repts. 463 (1967).

29

AMNESTY VS. ORDER ON COLLEGE CAMPUSES

ORVILLE W. JOHNSTON

DURING THE ACADEMIC YEAR 1967-68, much unrest prevailed on college and university campuses, and 1968-69 brought more of the same. It is time moderates spoke a word on behalf of law and order.

No society can exist without order, and to insure this order some system of law is required. A system of law has a way of developing with inequities toward certain segments of that society, usually a minority group. Therefore, the system that endures must have built-in procedures to allow for rectifying the inequities and inconsistencies. Our system of law in America does allow for its own correction, though that process is sometimes slow and painful. This should be expected as a part of democratic process. Rapid and careless change destroys order and effects anarchy.

In the early stages of the civil rights movement, it clearly was understood by leaders such as the late Martin Luther King that inequities in the law could be altered only by a painful, slow process. The procedure was peaceful demonstration in disobedience to the law termed unjust, and then endurance of full prosecution procedures under the law in the hope that the inequity would be demonstrated clearly. When the inequity was laid bare, both con-

From School & Society, Oct. 26, 1968. Reprinted by permission of the author and the publisher. Orville W. Johnston is Assistant to the President, State University of New York, Agricultural and Technical College at Alfred.

science and a sense of justice would compel the society to change the law. To call for and be granted amnesty in such a demonstration would have nullified its purpose.

Now we have a phenomenon spreading across our society in the great urban centers and our universities which identifies itself with the civil rights movement. It is true that these demonstrations may call attention to great illnesses in these centers; however, the direction of the current demonstration is more riotous and destructive than constructive in nature. The forces at work in our urban centers and universities today seem more intent on destruction as a means of retaliation than upon correction of supposed inequities in the system. However, beyond an initial calling attention to the fact, retaliation seldom offers any constructive elements.

Constructive change always must take place within the system in order to rectify it, unless the system is irreparable. It would seem, then, that abandonment would be a better policy than destruction. On our campuses across the country a minority element seems more intent on destroying the system than on correcting it, and more intent on inhibiting the rights and opportunities of the majority than on gaining rights and opportunities for a neglected minority. These minority forces then step outside the system of procedures of the university, and usually outside all systems of order, to call attention to themselves and their demands.

Certain acts are punishable by law in our society, *e.g.*, defacing and destruction of property, arson or attempted arson, injury to person, and libel and slander. It is an error to assume that such acts, when carried out on a college or university campus, somehow will escape the law. Interestingly, those who object most violently to the institution often look to it for protection and security. If such movements and demonstrations are truly movements for civil rights, then the participants should note that amnesty nullifies its effect. Only if the institutional system is right is it in a position to grant amnesty, for amnesty means pardon for an offense against the institution. If the institutional system is wrong, then it is preferable to bear the inequities of the system after calling attention to them. Presumably, under the full gaze of the society, the inequities become apparently unjust and, thenceforth, will be changed.

One university president, who has experienced much dissent on campus this past year, points out that he welcomes dissent on campus, but that dissent and demonstrations must operate within guidelines that do not destroy the rights of the majority or become destructive of property.

The only logical course for a college or university administration to follow currently is a policy of complete openmindedness to honest demonstrators or dissenters who are willing to discuss problems within the university system. Most administrators know that the present system is far from perfect and are anxious for its improvement. At the same time, administrators are not inclined toward anarchy, because they have learned the value of systems and organization if order and direction is to prevail in a society. While openness to dialogue with dissenters is essential, an administrator has no alternative but to turn to the law for full and complete enforcement of the law when it is broken. This means enforcement of order and stability, protection for the rights of others who may not be among the dissenters, and fullest prosecution for offenses under the law. Ultimately, one must understand that anarchy is self-defeating, and that law and order will prevail. The majority of a society will tolerate a great amount of dissent and disorder at times, but, when it reaches a certain point, a major retaliation sets in and order is restored, even though that order be totalitarianism.

Dissent, debate, and dialogue are excellent means for working change and improvement. Destruction, disorder, and the disruption of others' rights are self-defeating to the cause which instigated them.

30

VIOLENCE AND RESPONSIBILITY
IN THE ACADEMY

SIDNEY HOOK

WHEREVER American educators meet today, there is one theme of overriding concern that shadows their deliberations even when it is not on the agenda of discussion. This is the mounting wave of lawlessness, often cresting into violence, that has swept so many campuses. Shortly after the riotous events at the University of California at Berkeley in 1964, I predicted that in consequence of the faculty's refusal to condemn the student seizure of Sproul Hall, the administration building, American higher education would never be the same again, that a turning point had been reached in the pattern of its development. I confess, however, to surprise at the rapidity of the change, if not its direction, and by the escalation of the violence accompanying it.

Equally significant in determining the changing intellectual climate of our universities are some of the secondary consequences of the accelerating disorders. Among them are infectious, sometimes paralyzing, fear in administrative ranks lest their campuses erupt; confusion, bewilderment, and divided loyalties among faculties, together with some *Schaden-freude* over the humiliation of their administrations at the hands of disrespectful student militants;

From *Saturday Review*, April 19, 1969. Reprinted by permission of the author and the publisher. Copyright, 1969, by Saturday Review, Inc. Sidney Hook is Professor of Philosophy, New York University, New York City.

outright encouragement of student violence by disaffected, younger members of teaching staffs; sustained apathy among the majority of students whose education has been interrupted by radical activists; and the mixture of rage and disgust among the general public whose political repercussions already have been damaging to the cause of higher education.

In California, the indignation of citizens over campus violence has brought Governor Reagan to the peak of his popularity. More alarming, proposed bonds for educational expansion have been voted down. Of approximately 186,000 communications received to date by the trustees and colleges in the state system more than 98 per cent were against campus disruption. More than seventy separate bills, some of dubious wisdom, have been introduced in the Senate and Assembly to deal with disruption of campus activities by students and faculty. Similar bills are in the hoppers of other state legislatures, twenty in Wisconsin alone.

The situation in the East, although not marked by the same degree of physical violence (arson, bombings, beatings), educationally is equally grave. Some recent incidents at New York University, and its sister institution in New York City, Columbia, mark the extent to which violence has invaded the university and rational disciplinary restraints have been eroded.

Last December, Nguyen Huu Chi, the Ambassador of South Vietnam, visited New York University as an invited guest speaker. At a given signal, members of the Students for a Democratic Society from NYU and Columbia invaded the hall, stormed the stage, physically assaulted the Ambassador, and completely disrupted the meeting. Thereupon, they proceeded to another floor, battered down the doors leading to the podium of a meeting-hall where James Reston, executive editor of *The New York Times,* was about to deliver the annual Homer Watts Lecture before an audience of 600 under the auspices of the Alumni Association. The rampaging students spurned an invitation from Mr. Reston to state their objections to what they thought he was going to say, and by threats of violence forced the cancellation of the meeting.

Two students were suspended pending action by the University Senate, and after a careful hearing, at which they refused to appear, were expelled in March. The leaders of the SDS publicly applauded the disruptions, declaring that they disapproved of the positions of the government of South Vietnam and *The New York Times* on the

Vietnam war. Most shocking of all, nine members of the faculty at Washington Square in a letter to the student paper endorsed the breaking up of the meeting of the South Vietnamese Ambassador. Although they called the disruption of Mr. Reston's meeting "unfortunate" (as if it were an accident!), they strongly condemned President James M. Hester on the ground that, "we do not believe that the disruption of the Reston speech warrants suspension of the students." They had not a single word of forthright or vigorous criticism of the SDS attack on Chi. The effect of their letter can only be to incite further student violence. It is noteworthy that many meetings and rallies *in support* of the Vietcong and North Vietnam have been held without incident.

At Columbia, Acting President Andrew W. Cordier had petitioned the courts through the Dean of the Law School to dismiss the criminal charges against the Columbia students arrested for serious offenses last spring. The court was assured that the University would apply appropriate disciplinary measures to those guilty. The cases were therefore dismissed. In December, a Columbia College disciplinary tribunal of two teachers—one of them an instructor serving as chairman—two students, and an administrator decided to impose no penalties on the students whatsoever, despite the fact that the students proudly admitted violating University regulations and, to boot, denied the authority of the tribunal to judge them. This incredible decision was taken in order "to re-establish student relationship to the university." These students had won complete amnesty for actions that had been deemed worthy of criminal prosecution when they had occurred. Twice hearings in the Law School were violently disrupted by invading SDS students, and the faculty members of the panel were insulted with gutter obscenities. No one even dared to suggest that disciplinary action be taken against this new wave of disruption. The administrators and many of the faculty of Columbia University for months were deeply distraught. It appeared to some observers as if the University petition to have the criminal charges dropped against the students was a ruse by the administration to ingratiate itself with the militant students, to prove its "good will" toward them and, in this way, buy some campus peace. If so, the strategy failed. It provoked only contempt, jeers, and a stream of foul, four-letter epithets from the militants who held out for complete amnesty from the outset.

Encouraged by the amnesty, the Columbia SDS, with aid from

outsiders, began to disrupt classes; a leaflet was distributed to justify such "classroom intervention." In some instances, students tore the notes out of their teachers' hands; in others, they shouted them down. By December, according to one source, as many as thirteen "interventions" had been perpetrated. No action was taken either by the faculty or by the administration. An inquiry from an education editor, who had gotten wind of the situation, went unanswered. No one on campus would talk for publication.

Their appetites whetted by the complaisance or timidity of their victims, the students of the SDS escalated the scale of their disruptions. *The Columbia Spectator* of February 27 reported that "Members of the SDS yesterday interrupted nearly forty classes in six University buildings."

Finally, on March 10, a public statement in response to these outrages was issued by a hundred, mostly senior, professors. In it they declared that the University had an obligation to defend itself against hooliganism. Referring to the policy of amnesty, they criticized the abandonment of disciplinary proceedings for previous serious infractions. President Cordier immediately rushed to endorse the statement taking care, at the same time, to minimize the number of class disruptions, but failing to explain why he had remained silent about the breaking up of classes in December, although he was aware of it, and why he had welcomed the abandonment of disciplinary proceedings.

Punitive legislation, either federal or state, would be undesirable in this situation for many reasons. It would tie the Government too closely to campus events and discipline at a time when a section of the academic community believes that governmental presence is already too obtrusive. Further, the effectiveness of such legislation would depend upon the cooperation of administration and faculty in enforcing it. Most important, existing statutes of the University, and the criminal law, already provide sufficient penalties (suspension, expulsion, fines, and jail for trespassing and assault) to meet disruption, if they were enforced.

Why have they not been enforced? Why has the defense of faculties against these brazen attempts to violate their academic freedom, not only by disruption, but by demands to control the content and personnel of instruction, been so feeble and long-delayed? Why, as one professor observed who had helped the Berkeley rebels triumph in 1964, have administrations and faculties behaved like buffalos being shot, "looking on with interest when another of their number goes down without seriously thinking, that they may be next"?

Although the major causes of student unrest are outside the universities (Vietnam, the urban crisis, the black revolution) and cannot be solved by them alone, the way in which unrest is expressed, whether creatively or violently, can be influenced by the ideas and attitudes brought to it. This is particularly true today. For although comparatively few institutions have been the scene of violent demonstrations as serious as those at Columbia, Berkeley, and San Francisco State, there is hardly a college or university in the country in which there is not some marked uneasiness, some movement among students toward direct action on the verge of exploding into sit-downs, sit-ins, and other forms of mass violations of rules and regulations suddenly discovered to be as silly, anachronistic, or authoritarian as some of them undoubtedly are. But what struck me about the mood of the students in scores of colleges I visited is that even when these rules and regulations were *not* being enforced, and student conduct was as free and uninhibited as on campuses not subject to these objectionable rules, there was an insistence on their abolition—despite evidence that the formal abolition was likely to stir up a hornet's nest among alumni or townsfolk or state legislatures. This testified partly to student impatience with the "hypocrisy" of tolerating laws that were not being enforced, but even more to the presence of a desire to precipitate a showdown with authority, to be where the action is, to have the nation's television cameras focused on the local scene and on the local leaders of dissent. One of the undoubted effects of the kind of coverage given campus disorders by the mass media in their alleged desire merely to report these occurrences is to encourage them by exaggerating their scope and glorifying the heroes of the moment.

Frenzy and excitement among student bodies have always been contagious. Last year, events on some campuses, even chants and slogans, broadcast at once, had a direct influence on happenings on other campuses. That is why the universities of this country are in this "all together," and why capitulation to extremism anywhere weakens resistance to extremism everywhere.

To an already volatile situation must be added the Students for a Democratic Society, an explosive element which claims tens of thousands of militant activists in hundreds of chapters. The SDS is an openly social revolutionary organization, dedicated not to education-

al reform wherever needed, but to a strategy of politicalization of a
university by the tactics of physically violent confrontation. Its operating maxim could well be, "the bloodier the confrontation, the
better for our cause, and the worse for the Establishment." Its
presence is sufficient to convert a situation in which problems exist
into a permanent educational crisis. The members of the SDS are
ideologically confused but they constitute a hard, fanatical core of
highly politicized individuals among student bodies, extremely
skillful in the arts of generating conflicts and disruption through
agitation and manipulation of mass organizations. They and their
congeners among the New Left, including their faculty allies, would
be hard to contain by wise and enlightened administrators and
faculties. Unfortunately, these traits have not been conspicuously in
evidence even in places where one would expect them. This is
suggested by the fact that the worst excesses on our campuses have
occurred at the most liberal institutions. The University of California, San Francisco State College, the University of Colorado, Roosevelt College, Columbia University, and New York University—these
read like the beginning of a roll call of the centers of intellectual
dissent, experiment, and even educational permissiveness in American life. Events on these campuses, as well as at Swarthmore and
Oberlin, reveal the absurdity of the claim that the student revolution has been the consequence of dissatisfaction with the educational
curriculum.

Educational changes are often desirable, but it was not a failure to
introduce them that provoked the recent outbreaks of student
violence, or encouraged continuance of these outbreaks. Much more
warranted, as an explanation of the failure to meet the initial
challenge of student disruption and to stem its growth, is a mistaken
theory of liberalism, a reliance upon what I call *ritualistic* rather
than realistic liberalism—a doctrinaire view which does not recognize
the difference between belief or doctrine and behavior, and which
refuses to grasp the fact, obvious in law and common sense, that
incitement to violence is a form of behavior. It is a view which does
not realize that although order is possible without justice, justice is
impossible without order.

The realistic liberal outlook in education cannot be strictly identified with the liberal outlook in politics because the academic
community cannot be equated with the political community. Although we may recognize the autonomy of the academic community,

such autonomy cannot be complete since the political community in many ways underwrites its operation. But what both communities have in common is the centrality of the notion of due process.

Due process in the political community is spelled out in terms of specific mechanisms through which, out of the clash of public opinions, public policy is forged. Where due process is violated, consent is coerced, and cannot be freely given. The unlimited spectrum of ideas remains unabridged in the political community up to the point of advocacy, but not to the point of violent action of the incitement of violence. The forces of the state, the whole apparatus of restraint and punishment, enter the scene where the freedom of choice of the citizenry is threatened by extralegal activity.

Due process in the academic community is reliant upon the process of rationality. It cannot be the same as due process in the political community as far as the *mechanisms* of determining the outcome of rational activity. For what controls the nature and direction of due process in the academic community is derived from its educational goal—the effective pursuit, discovery, publication, and teaching of the truth. In the political community all men are equal as citizens not only as participants in, and contributors to, the political process, but as voters and decision-makers on the primary level. Not so in the academic community. What qualifies a man to enjoy equal human or political rights does not qualify him to teach equally with others or even to study equally on every level. There is an authoritative, *not* authoritarian, aspect of the process of teaching and learning that depends not upon the person or power of the teacher, but upon the authority of his knowledge, the cogency of his method, the scope and depth of his experience. But whatever the differences in the power of making decisions flowing from legitimate differences in educational authority, there is an equality of learners, whether of teachers or students, in the rational processes by which knowledge is won, methods developed, and experience enriched.

In a liberal educational regimen, everything is subject to the rule of reason, and all are equals as questioners and participants. Whoever interferes with academic due process either by violence or threat of violence places himself outside the academic community, and incurs the sanctions appropriate to the gravity of his offense from censure to suspension to expulsion. The peculiar deficiency of the ritualistic liberal educational establishments is the failure to meet violations of rational due process with appropriate sanctions or to meet them in a timely and intelligent manner. There is a tendency to close an eye to expressions of lawless behavior on the part of students who, in the name of freedom, deprive their fellow students of the freedom to pursue their studies. It is as if the liberal administration sought to appease the challenge to its continued existence by treating such incidents as if they had never happened.

There is no panacea that can be applied to all situations. It is not a question of a hard line or a soft line, but of an intelligent line. It is easy to give advice from hindsight, to be wise and cocksure after the event. But it is always helpful for the faculty to promulgate in advance fair guidelines for action, so that students will know what to expect. In general, no negotiations should be conducted under threat of coercion, or when administrators or faculty are held captive. In general, no amnesty for lawlessness or violence should be offered. In general, organizations that refuse to accept disciplinary principles worked out by official representatives of the student body and faculty should be denied recognition and the use of university facilities.

As a rule, it is the first step which is *not* taken that costs so much. Both at Berkeley and Columbia, failure to act decisively at the first disruption of university functions undoubtedly contributed to the students' expectation that they could escalate their lawlessness with impunity. Sometimes the attempt to retrieve a failure to meet student disruption promptly and fairly results in a greater failure.

When student defiance of reasonable rules and regulations is pointedly and continuously ignored, and then subsequently disciplined, the consequence may be worse than if the first infraction had been totally amnestied. Unnecessary delay in initiating the disciplinary measures, however mild, incurred by the infraction of rules, can make it appear to large numbers of the uninformed that these students are the innocent victims of vindictive and gratuitous punishment.

The fourth and largest illegal trespass at Berkeley—the seizure of Sproul Hall—came as a consequence of the summons to four student leaders to appear before the Disciplinary Committee several weeks after they had committed the violations for which they were being called to account. There was a similar situation at Columbia. The first action which presaged the events of 1968 occurred in 1965 when students forcibly prevented the NROTC award ceremony. In 1967, "the administration canceled the ceremony citing insufficient time to prepare against violence" (*The Cox Report*). Violence seemed to pay off. A handful of students had forced their will on the University at the cost of seven letters of censure. After the ban on indoor demonstrations had been promulgated at Columbia—both because it interfered with the teaching of classes and because of the dangers of violence between opposing groups of demonstrating students—it was not enforced on three important occasions where it was clearly violated. When the ban was finally invoked, it seemed to many who were unaware of the past history of student provocation and university restraint that the disciplinary action, even if feeble, was arbitrary. It is widely believed, even by some of the SDS members, that if the Columbia University authorities had moved vigorously to enforce existing regulations against the lawless trespass and destruction of property by the small group that sparked the seizure of buildings on the first day, subsequent developments would have been avoided. For campus sentiment was overwhelmingly hostile to the student rebels at the outset.

The ironical aspect of the situation is that despite the liberal character of the institutions in question, a false view of what it means to be liberal seems to provoke or to exacerbate disturbances on the campus. In certain faculty quarters especially, it is believed that the very nature of a liberal educational community necessitates, independent of any student action, an absolute taboo against physical or police sanctions. At a large metropolitan university during a student strike called by a small and rabidly fanatical minority to protest the dismissal of an administrator guilty of vicious anti-semitic incitement, a faculty group tried to get a resolution adopted pledging the university "not to call upon the police *under any circumstances.*" Had such a resolution been adopted it would have given those who made a cult of violence assurances in advance that they could carry on as they pleased no matter what the cost to life, limb, and university property. It would have encouraged the very violence those who favored the resolution professed to deplore. "What's so tragic about the destruction of a little property?" one professor inquired. He only shrugged when a colleague sardonically added, "Or a little fire?" In the academy as elsewhere there is no substitute for common sense. As it was, fire hoses were cut, elevators jammed to a point where their operation was dangerous to life and limb and their operation temporarily suspended, and the auditorium in the student center set afire.

Some faculty members see truly, in the words of a perceptive member of the Columbia staff, that "the authority of a university is not a civil authority, but a moral one." But he mistakenly concludes that the disruptive activities of students "can only be contained by faculty and by other students, not by the police." This is a morality not of this world but of the hand-wringing, ineffectual spirit that leaves this world and its universities in possession of callow, ruthless fanatics prepared to threaten or use violence.

"Confrontation politics" in the moral academic community "is inadmissible," we are assured by those who love everybody and want to be loved by everybody. Excellent! But what if some students do what is inadmissable? What if they resort to pillage, vandalism, personal assault? What if the torch of learning in some hands becomes a torch of arson? To say that only other students can contain them, and not the police, is to forget that once we leave the world of the spirit, this is an invitation to civil war.

Wars of containment, as we know, can be quite bloody. The police may have to be called in to prevent students from containing (and maiming) each other. And like all sentimentalizing in this cruel world, the fear of relying on the police in *any* circumstances to resist the militant politics of confrontation, which brutally scorns the rationalities of academic due process, is to rely upon the politics of capitulation. It is administrative and/or faculty cowardice masquerading as educational statesmanship. It receives and deserves the contempt with which the storm troopers of the SDS greet it as they prepare for the next phase in the escalating cycle of disruption and violence.

In the light of recent events on campuses and the reactions they have inspired, it should be obvious that the SDS is *not* a Trojan horse in American higher education. It is today the "armed warrior" of anti-education. It makes no secret of its desire to destroy American democracy and the universities that it considers as a faithful replica of that iniquitous society. No, the Trojan horse in American higher education is the rickety structure of doctrinaire thought that shelters the SDS even when it takes official responsibility for violent actions, gives it a free field for operation, retreats before the politics of confrontation, and either shrinks from applying fairly and firmly the rules of reason that should bind the academic community, or interprets them as if they had no more restraining force in times of crisis than ropes of sand.

The facts about the SDS are well known. It has the virtues of openness as well as courage. It takes public responsibility for its action of violence, and promises more to come. For it, the campuses are the front-line barricades in total war against American society. Persistent refusal to recognize these facts has prevented administrators and faculties from preparing proper defensive measures to keep the universities free. This refusal is sometimes undergirded by the odd belief that disciplinary action against an organization that officially organizes violence on campus is incompatible with the conception of a university as a "free market place of ideas." The conjunction of attitude and belief is a forerunner of educational disaster. This is illustrated by the pattern of events within the last two years at the University of Colorado. It culminated early this March in the most violent outbreak in the history of the University, when a guest of the University, President S. I. Hayakawa of San Francisco State College, was almost mobbed by bottle-throwing members of the SDS and their Black Nationalist allies to prevent him from speaking. Despite its previous actions of violence and the absence of any pledge to forswear violence in the future, the SDS had been reinstated on the campus on the ground that the University must serve "as a free market of ideas." The SDS promptly showed that its purpose was precisely to destroy the University as a free market of ideas.

The detailed story is too long to relate here, but it can serve as a paradigm case of high-minded blunder, panicky ineptitude, and self-righteous obtuseness on the part of some regents, administrators, and faculty members who are convinced that true tolerance requires that we tolerate the actively intolerant.

In the last analysis, it is the faculties who are responsible for the present state of American universities—responsible because of their apathy for what has developed in the past, and for missed educational opportunities. Despite what is said by outsiders, the faculties of most universities possess great powers which they have so far been reluctant to use. No policy in education can succeed without their support. Theirs is the primary responsibility for upholding academic freedom. Now that American higher education is at bay, challenged as it has never been before by forces *within* the academic community, the faculties must marshal the courage to put freedom first, and to defend it accordingly.

At the same time, as they move to safeguard the integrity of the educational process, faculties should, wherever they are not already doing so, undertake a critical review of all aspects of the curriculum and university life. Provisions should be made for the airing and public discussion of all student grievances. Students should be invited to assess existing courses, methods of teaching, the effectiveness of their teachers, and to make proposals for new courses.

It is a libel on American educators to imply that they are hostile to educational change. Most past criticism has inveighed against them for making curricular revisions too readily at the first cries of "relevance" by pressure groups. Educational crackpots, including some headline-hunting administrators, are now rushing to claim that had their curricular panaceas been adopted, student violence would have been avoided. They assiduously ignore the fact that the extremist student groups are trying to bring down bigger game.

John Dewey was fond of saying that in the modern world there is no such thing as the "status quo." Change in education, as in society, is inescapable. The only questions are whether the direction and content of change are sound, and what the rate and magnitude of change should be. Men of good will may differ about the answers. But no matter how profound the differences, they do not justify the resort to violence and the threat of violence to impose solutions. In a secular society, the places where human beings assemble to inquire and to reason together should be regarded as sacred ground. Whoever desecrates it should feel the disapproval of the entire community.

31

FREEDOM, DISSENT, AND RESPONSIBILITY IN THE ACADEMIC COMMUNITY

CHARLES E. DWYER

THE USE AND THREAT of violence and force, and the deliberate disruption of the activities of the academic community are now features of higher education in the U.S. An analysis of this phenomenon will be attempted and a set of arguments will be presented to support the position that these activities are undesirable, unjustifiable, and extremely dangerous. A proposal also will be offered as to how we might proceed to remedy this situation.

Violence refers to those activities which are intended to result in physical harm to persons, seizure of property, or destruction of property; *force*, to those which are intended to restrain, intimidate, or coerce, to provoke anyone to violence, or to block or interfere with anyone's free movement; *disruption of activities* within the Academic Community includes, but is not limited to, any attempt to prevent, halt, interfere with, or detract from such activities as classes, use of libraries, research, commencements, scheduled speakers, and the administrative functions supporting these.

I do not suggest that all who justify disruption of academic activities would underwrite the use of force or violence, or that those supporting force would condone violence. But these three categories do have significant, common characteristics: all call for controversial actions of questionable propriety, all are generally regarded as

Charles E. Dwyer is Assistant Professor of Education, Graduate School of Education, University of Pennsylvania, Philadelphia.

regrettable, even by those who use them, and all replace reason with the tools of emotional and coercive persuasion, discussion and argument with the tools of power.

Even if there may be situations in which such tactics are justifiable, the question at stake here is: Are any of them justifiable within the context of American higher education? I shall argue that none of them are justifiable in that context.

My comments on the possible causes of this phenomenon claim to be neither definitive nor original. Nevertheless, they may promote a clearer understanding of the situation and, thereby, help those who wish to deal with it to do so more effectively. Certainly, violence, force, and disruption of normal activities by groups calling for social change is nothing new. It is a world-wide phenomenon with a long history. In the recent history of the U.S., the most striking example might be the conflict between organized labor, industry, and government during the initial stages of unionization. In other parts of the world, *e.g.*, Latin America, these techniques have been the common property of students, sometimes joined by faculty in the struggle for reform. Accordingly, both the techniques and their use in higher education are not unique. What is unique is the rather widespread use of these techniques by students and faculty in the U.S. to press for various reforms. Why, when they have been known publicly for years, have these methods just recently been pressed into service by students and faculty?

Since the end of World War II, a number of interesting variables have taken their place in Western culture. The consequent international conflicts have brought diverse value systems into close proximity, a condition which inevitably led to the questioning of cultural norms. The forces of mass media have brought value differences forcefully to everyone's attention. The level of education in the general population has risen markedly. There has been an increasing accent on youth which grows stronger as a greater portion of our total population falls into the youthful age ranges. The maladies of the globe are daily brought to focus in our lives as mass media and modes of transportation shrink the earth still further. Youth has been singled out as the hope of mankind to cure these maladies. They have been told that they can change the world and that they can make a difference; they are encouraged to inquire, to doubt, to reject. All of this has produced a unique conceptual revolution in the minds of many Western youths, and in the U.S. particularly.

But this conceptual change has a twofold frustration built into it. Even if one is confident that he has been selected as the change-agent of the world, he must decide first what it is that the world is to be changed into. He will find no universally agreed-upon answer in a relativistically-oriented culture where old values have been reject-ed. Thus, one is highly motivated to bring about change, but uncertain as to what that change is to look like. Secondly, even when one knows what he wants to bring about, he must have some confidence that he can do it, some reasonable hope of success in effecting the change he seeks.

All of this has been provided for abundantly by contemporary society. There are always social visionaries eager for disciples to transmit their concept of how the world ought to look. The present environment increases both their number and their zeal. Those seeking a cause, a description of what ought to be, can select from a plethora of ideas about the right and the good. Armed with a new strength, they are now not only the legitimate societal agents of change; they have the right and the good on their side. They know they are right and this provides not only increased motivation, but also the justification of whatever means they select.

Finally, we come to the question of means, which provide the anticipation of, and confidence in, eventual success. The lessons of the civil rights movement have not passed by students and faculty (particularly younger faculty). Indeed, many of them initiated and are engaged in the movement. To the surprise of many, disruption of activities, force, and even violence were not only excused, but frequently condoned and even legitimated in the civil rights strug-gle. Moreover, these techniques succeeded in many instances. First came success in popularizing the cause and the makers of the cause via mass media. Secondly, and of crucial import, the Establishment capitulated in many cases; behaviors, practices, and laws were changed to fit the ideal. Nothing reinforces like success. Here stands the anointed change-agent armed with the shield of righteousness and the sword of proven, and even partially legitimated, means embarking on a holy war.

Of course, I mean only the serious-minded students and faculty who seek change through the means indicated above, not those who seek change in more peaceful ways or those who look for any opportunity and means to harass authority or any who disagree with them. Nor am I speaking just of those at Berkeley or Columbia, but rather of widespread attempts, by students and faculty, to effect institutional change by threats, intimidation, coercion, extortion, and general disruption of the activities of the academic community. Far more common than the spectacular sort of episodes typified by Berkeley and Columbia are threats by students and faculty to embarrass a university publicly or to bring its functions to a halt unless their demands are met.

Finally, unless very powerful countervailing forces are set in motion, a dependence upon violence, force, and disruption of activities will grow in use within academic communities. Despite the fact that such techniques may result in the exodus from an academic community of outstanding administrators, teachers, scholars, and students, and, even if the techniques rarely seem to achieve fully the objectives which led to their implementation (although those objectives are often diverse and unclear), there are far more powerful forces reinforcing the use of these techniques. Any controversial action which results in some change is likely to be looked upon as good by the change-agent so as to legitimate his activities. No one wants to feel that he is wrong and that his actions are unwarranted. The conviction that one is right will sustain one through a number of failures. But still stronger are the direct effects on the individual of such action. Many psychologists and sociologists claim that the primary drives of contemporary Western man are for recognition and achievement. Direct, public, forceful action in the name of what is right, and resulting in any change, is a source of great gratification for these needs. Thus, such action will grow in use as more and more students and faculty experience these satisfactions.

This analysis is not intended as a condemnation of such techniques or of the individuals who use them. Rather, it is an attempt to explain why this phenomenon has taken this form at this time, to help all within the academic community understand its roots, and perhaps to give a clue as to how it might be acceptably diminished.

For the most part, those who subscribe to these activities are not fanatics, but intelligent, reasonable people trying to bring about what they see as desirable change, by means which they believe are justifiable. As rational individuals, they offer reasons and arguments to support the legitimacy of their techniques. There are four such arguments which seem to hang together. Three of them may be considered political analogies and the fourth an appeal to a set of self-evident moral obligations. Let us examine these arguments.

A common source of justification offered is the American Revolutionary War. It is stated that violence, force, and disruption of activities were justified in that struggle and that conditions are sufficiently similar today to warrant similar activities. This argument by analogy depends upon two assumptions: first, that the tactics used in the Revolutionary War were justifiable, and second, that the situation at present is sufficiently similar in relevant respects to justify the use of those tactics now.

The legitimacy of the Revolutionary War is not a settled question. Not everyone, certainly not all Englishmen, are convinced our forefathers had all the right on their side. But, even granting the legitimacy of the war and its tactics does not grant the legitimacy of the use of similar techniques today in higher education. There seem to be several relevant differences between the two situations which significantly weaken, if not destroy, the strength of this argument by analogy.

First, the colonists were interested in setting up an autonomous political entity, not in seeking changes in a private (or publicly supported) institution. Second, the range and character of alternatives open to the colonists was neither wide nor reasonable, *i.e.*, continuing under the disagreeable system, prison, or moving out of the colonies. The set of alternatives available to students and faculty seeking change is not nearly so narrow or unreasonable, *e.g.*, leaving the institution, cutting oneself off from higher education altogether, peaceful non-disruptive demonstrations and petition, absence from classes to call attention to one's grievances (open to students), call for state or federal legislation to regulate these institutions in ways they deem desirable, formation of groups to support a particular cause, etc. Third, it has been argued (perhaps with a limited degree of historical accuracy) that a majority of the colonists sanctioned some sort of concerted action against the British. No such majority mandate for the sorts of techniques herein described is evident within higher education today. Fourth, if one is going to use the Revolutionary War as a justification, he should do so consistently. I have never heard anyone suggest that the British had no right to shoot back, to execute spies, and to imprison captured colonists. But today, within higher education, it is frequently argued that those using forceful means of dissent are immune to prosecution because they have acted from conscience and their cause is just. Such an assertion, certainly, cannot rest on the Revolutionary War as a precedent.

A second argument frequently brought forward for forceful measures in higher education is that colleges and universities are not democratic and that forceful measures are needed to bring democracy to the workings of higher education. This assumes that the principles of a political democracy ought to be, and can be, applied to private and public non-political institutions within the democracy. That case has yet to be established. The differences between an autonomous political entity and an educational institution seem greater than the similarities and thus the analogy seems untenable as an argument.

First, business corporations, hospitals and other charitable institutions, military organizations, and religious groups do not appear to be conducted in a democratic fashion in this country and few would argue that they should. The case for higher education as a democratically conducted enterprise is not at all clear and is yet to be made. Next, higher education is a unique institution which is not closely paralleled by any other institution in our society, including political ones. Thus, analogies with them from either viewpoint, while persuasive, have no justificatory force.

Furthermore, just how one would apply democratic principles to higher education, even if one could justify doing so? Who are the citizens? Who votes? On what issues? Is every vote to count the same? Who will take legal responsibility for the institution if all involved take responsibility for major decisions? Do clerical, secretarial, maintenance, and custodial employees get a vote? Certainly, they have as much at stake in the functioning of the community as others, and I have good reason to believe that they, too, have opinions and consciences. And what of those who pay for the operations of the academic community, *e.g.*, parents, alumni, friends, corporations, government, and foundations? Do they have votes?

I have yet to see a detailed comprehensive plan of democratic participation by faculty, students, and others in the academic community. Until such is offered and analyzed, the suggestion is an empty slogan neither operationalized nor justified.

A third argument comes from the techniques of the civil rights struggle. Disruption of activities and civil disobedience, as was previously mentioned, were at least partially legitimated through this struggle. Even if one were to accept fully the legitimacy of these activities, which can be seriously questioned, the parallel to higher education is still lacking in this analogy. One is a social struggle with political ends—the changing of laws. The disruption of academic activities and academic disobedience is not within the context of a political democracy, but within a non-political, non-democratic institution, and a separate case must be made for the two quite different causes.

A serious misconception has been perpetuated in the discussion of law-breaking in general, whether political or academic. When one engages in disobedience, either to change a law or to dramatize a cause, the justification is given that one's conscience is above the law, as though the law were some sort of entity independent of men. But putting one's conscience above the law is at the same time putting one's conscience above the consciences of other men, namely those who fashion them and those who support them. The existence of such a role or law is a *prima facie* case for its legitimacy and constitutes that by which those who enter the system agree to abide. The law constitutes the safeguard for the system and ought not to be changed even in democratic theory, unless one can show that a majority of those affected by it wish to change it, a demonstration which has been lacking in recent forceful campus activity. The law is indeed above the conscience, not in telling what is right or wrong, but in what is expected of one who freely enters under it in an institution. Change of it is not to be effected by force, violence, or disruption of activities.

All of these arguments are based on the same general principle that certain ends are so important that they justify the use of distasteful means such as violence, force, and the disruption of activities. I have attempted to indicate that the situations alleged to be analogous to that in higher education are, in fact, different in relevant respects and, therefore, the arguments do not hold.

Why should disruption of activities, force, and violence have no place in higher education, whatever the cause? The principle proposed by the academically disobedient is that each man, if he believes his cause to be just, is free to violate the rules of the institution and the freedom of others in pursuing his cause. But, in such a situation, there is no final arbiter, and, if an individual can gather enough support around him, he will be very likely to free himself from any disciplinary measures. Moreover, the breaking of rules, threats of embarrassment to the university, or disruption of its activities constitutes a power struggle, not rational persuasion. In any event, the likely consequences of acting under such a principle are typified in the following examples:

A group of faculty members threatens to embarrass the university unless a certain defense contract is cancelled. Another group, supporting the defense contract, then threatens to embarrass the university if the contract is not maintained. The university cannot escape embarrassment.

A group of students decides to occupy a campus building to publicize a cause and to coerce the university into meeting their demands. Another group of students, unsympathetic to this cause, decides to block the entrances to the building so to prevent its occupation by the first group. A violent struggle ensues, disruptive of the functions of the university and resulting in extremely bad national publicity, thus affecting adversely yet another group of potential students and faculty and the availability of funding both public and private.

One group of alumni threatens to withhold any further financial support to a university unless those who have violated university regulations are disciplined. Another group of alumni threatens to withhold any further financial support unless those who violated university regulations are exempted from any disciplinary measures. The university inevitably loses income for its basic research and teaching functions.

Violence begets violence, while force begets force, coercion, coercion, intimidation, intimidation, and disruption, disruption. Thus, the difficulty in acting out of conscience in the university setting is that one inevitably will clash with someone else's conscience. If, when this occurs, rules are ignored and coercion, intimidation, and violence are resorted to by all involved (justified on grounds of the rightness of their cause), the inevitable victim must be the university to the detriment of all except those who seek its destruction. This is a pragmatic argument against operating under this principle.

On the ethical side of the issue, there are even more disturbing implications. One is saying, under this principle, that, "if the university is unwilling to capitulate on what I know to be the right, then I am justified in implementing ever more extreme measures to bring about that capitulation." Setting aside the infantile attitude represented by this position, it becomes obvious that the rules governing the university will be formulated by those willing to take the most extreme action, since, by the principle indicated, they will continue to press ever more strongly until the university adopts the requisite policies. It should be clear that no institution could exist under the rule of those who are most unconscionable, who will do anything to get their way. Accordingly, no institution can or should exist under the principle exemplified by those who feel justified in using force, violence, and the disruption of activities to gain their ends in higher education.

If we cannot, and should not, operate under such a principle, what should we operate under? I propose the following principles in support of freedom in the academic community:

The right of students and faculty to inquire and to transmit knowledge is the prerequisite of any academic community. The right of those within the academic community to speak freely within that community is basic to the purposes of any college or university, and it must extend to students, faculty, and administrators. At the same time, it is universally agreed that freedom of expression in any setting has limits and this applies to the academic community as well. The responsibility to protect the safety and welfare of students, faculty, and staff, and to sustain an educational institution's activities uninterrupted must determine the limits of free expression within the academic community. The freedom of students, faculty, administrators and staff to continue, without harassment, interference, or disruption, the activities required for the functioning of the academic community is to be preserved.

In support of responsibility of the academic community it seems clear that the protection, development, and extension of these freedoms is the first responsibility of all members of the academic community. Safeguards should be established, and enforced. Therefore, any attempt to interfere with these freedoms by any means including violence, force or the disruption of activities is to be condemned, and those engaging in such attempts are to be disciplined by students, faculty, and administration.

In support of dissent in the academic community, adequate facilities must be made available for peaceful, responsible dissent. This does not mean that dissidents must be opposed or appeased, but rather that they be given opportunity to express their views and peacefully to solicit support for them by dialogue and lawful, orderly, non-disruptive demonstration and assembly. Further, any interference with such expression of views, demonstration, or assembly is to be condemned, and any member of the community participating in such interference should be disciplined.

The above are intended to provide working principles to support the overriding objective of higher education—the advancement and extension of knowledge. They are intended to insure stability, not to maintain the *status quo*. Constructive change is possible within them. Outside of them lies anarchy, chaos, and the possible destruction of higher education. Outside of them comes the threat of tyranny—of students, or faculty, or administrators—of those willing to wield the greatest force. All such tyrannies are unacceptable.

Therefore, I propose the discussion of these principles and the adoption by the academic community of some set of principles and policies which will ensure the stability and integrity of the academic community, while at the same time making adequate arrangements for constructive change and orderly dissent.

32

THE RESPONSIBILITIES OF DISSENT

STANLEY J. WENBERG

THERE IS A SAYING on the University of Minnesota campus that the function of the faculty is "to think" and of the vice presidents "to do." We have deans to see that the faculty does not start doing and the vice presidents do not start thinking. It would seem that, in the area of student unrest, many of us have been doing more about the subject that we have been thinking about it.

Gertrude Stein once made some relevant comments about education. "Education is thought about, and as it is thought about, it is being done. It is being done in the way it is thought about, which is not true of almost anything. Almost anything is not done in the way it is thought about and that is the reason so much of it is done in New England. They do it so much in New England that they even do it more than it is thought about." In the past two years, those of us in higher education may have been doing more about student life than thinking about it. One is reminded of the classic comment by Walt Kelly's comic strip character, Pogo: "We have met the enemy and he is us."

The draft issue, Vietnam, Dow Chemical, to name only three subjects, have placed new demands on both public and campus understanding of academic freedom, particularly as it applies to students. Withdrawing from the current furor for a moment, we see

Based on a commencement address, Mankato State College, Mankato, Minn., March 15, 1968. Stanley J. Wenberg is Vice President for Educational Relationships and Development, University of Minnesota, Minneapolis.

the common ground of "town and gown" expanding. More than a decade ago, Riesman pointed out that, at a time when academic life in America was becoming increasingly commercial, nonacademic life was becoming increasingly intellectual.[1] The graduating class of 1969 found the difference between "town and gown" markedly less than did mine only a quarter-century ago.

What then has produced so much tension in some of the current discussion? The answer may lie in a theory which runs to both the misuse and the misunderstanding of dissent. The theory may be stated by paraphrasing Gertrude Stein: Dissent is thought about, and as it is thought about, it is being done. It is being done in the way it is thought about, which is not true of almost anything. Almost anything is not done in the way it is thought about, but dissent is. Dissent is everywhere; in America it is everywhere. They do so much in America that they even do it more than it is thought about.

Although we may do more about dissent than we think about it, this is probably as it should be in our society. Dissent is relative to a great many things. There is nothing absolute about the right to dissent; nor is there anything absolute in the content of dissent, even though an increasing number of dissenters seem to believe they represent absolutes.

Our current problem is that both the crucial importance of "permitting and encouraging dissent" and the necessity of "its use and form being relevant and appropriate" are factors that continue either to be ignored or forgotten by most sides in the heat of current arguments. Users of dissent need to recognize that they are not working with absolutes; dissent is a viable concept only if the participants recognize this. The draft, institutional policies on recruitment, Vietnam, and other current issues have "pro" and "con" considerations. Dissenters must allow this if they are to lend credibility to their positions.

Also, we must recognize a very real phenomenon of our times that bears powerfully on the use and understanding of dissent: the intense rivalry among communications media. Too often, the sensational and attention-getting aspects raise an event to the status of "news." Too often this results in focusing on "deviation" as if the deviation in itself is the total event.

Vivid pictures and dramatic descriptions of physical forms of the

---

[1] David Riesman, *Constraint and Variety in American Education* (New York: Doubleday, 1958).

dissent virtually destroy the general public's capacity to comprehend the issues. What is more, all too often in such instances the protesters themselves are encouraged to perform for the media, further clouding the issues which underlie the dissent. Exploitation of the forms of dissent by news media creates new questions about the real objectives of certain dissent: Is it dissent for a cause? Is it dissent for the sake of dissent? Is it dissent for publicity?

We also should question if exercising the right of free speech is one of the criteria for identifying newsworthy events. Further, what is the significance of this factor for "responsible dissent?" Henry Steele Commager reminds us: "It cannot be too often repeated that the justification and the purpose of freedom of speech is not to indulge those who want to speak their minds. It is to prevent error and discover truth."[2]

Sheer "mind speaking"—unadulterated, assertive, emotional dissent—unconcerned with context or audience, but positively directed to attracting news media, long since has asserted its great potential, both for making news and for confusing large segments of the public on the basic issues. Increasingly, these dissenters are including physical forms of destruction, obstruction, and interference with the rights of others. It is paradoxical that many articulate exploiters of this form of dissent, as alleged contributors to building freedom, ignore the whiplash effect of their actions on the freedoms of others.

We have seen the violent dissenter seriously impinge on the rights of the responsible dissenter, creating tensions that yield the incredible notion that adherence to an opposing point of view requires punishment. The extreme exploitation of dissent yields extreme solutions: a draft protester is drafted; an ROTC student is ejected from a pacifist professor's mathematics class; a peace marcher is clubbed. Action punishment seems increasingly to emerge as a consequence of assuming differences in position. Such conduct should prompt the question of whether the extremists are committed genuinely to that which they claim to defend. The public consequence of their actions increasingly threatens strictures on free, open, and responsible dissent.

These points relate principally to the academic community's responsibility to recognize the absence of absolutes, the responsibility

---

2 Henry Steele Commager, "The Problems of Dissent," *Saturday Review*, 48:23, Dec. 18, 1965.

to recognize one's audience for what it is, and the obligation to fill the role of dissent responsibly. Some of the dissent on American university campuses has been exercised responsibly. The "teach-ins" are a remarkable demonstration of the students' understanding of a university's mission. They probed and awakened the conscience of America. They reflected the students' recognition of the university as a center for learning rather than an arena for irresponsible dissent.

Faculties and administrations must recognize the place of dissent on our campuses. Dissent is the business of colleges and universities but too often takes an unacceptable form because of the institution's failure to act responsibly. Excessively restrictive policies lead not only to irrational dissent; they often produce consequences that encourage a faulty public conception of dissent. However, it is not sufficient to make our campuses the homes for responsible dissent; we must do everything possible to develop sound public understanding of what our mission is in this respect.

Progress in the world of science has outdistanced progress in the world of our human relationships, in part because of our fear to examine the social, economic, and political environment with equal candor and vigor. Unafraid, we study cancer in the body, but too many tremble and scream "disloyal" if we examine and study a cancer in our society. Commager says the purpose of freedom of speech is not to indulge those who want to speak their minds, but to prevent error and discover truth. The public needs to understand that Commager is talking about a free marketplace for all ideas, not just discoveries empirically derived in the world of science or those concepts with which we happen to agree. A university that cannot tolerate rational, responsible dissent is a university that cannot tolerate ideas. Indeed, such an institution ought not be identified as a university. The corollary of this statement is that, if man has created the university as a forum for rational dissent, then irrational, irresponsible dissent is completely contrary to the mission of a university. The crucial point is that responsible dissent is not disloyalty; it is an imperative of our democratic system. The capacity to understand and foster this concept is one of the prime missions of a university. Indeed, one of the reasons for the system of faculty tenure is to ensure and secure the presence of divergent views and different opinions on our campuses.

There is a faculty and administration responsibility for dissent, not for its own sake, but for the honest, intellectual vigor it gives to a community of scholars. We vigorously must maintain the unending process through which educated men seek to find their way to a peaceful and full realization of their purpose in life: the vigilant and honest sorting of error from truth.

33

FREEDOM, POWER, AND RESPONSIBILITY
IN HIGHER EDUCATION

LINCOLN GORDON

VIEWED FROM ABROAD, the American scene in secondary and higher education—with all its defects—looks surprisingly good. We are the only nation in the world approximating the goal of high school education for all and moving rapidly toward higher education of varying periods for all able to take advantage of it. Along with the extraordinary expansion in numbers in recent decades, the last decade alone has seen a notable upgrading of the general quality of high school education and a steady upward pressure on quality standards in the colleges. There is dynamism and experimentation at all levels, higher, secondary, and primary. There is a thrust toward the conversion of teaching and learning away from the transmission and inculcation of received wisdom and toward the active participation of the student in a quest for knowledge in cooperation with the teacher. There are exciting experiments in educational methods, in ways of letting a student progress at his own pace, in new approaches to mathematics and science, in curriculum reform, and in postdoctoral training.

In proportion to population, the United States is an extraordinarily large contributor to the knowledge explosion of our times. Amer-

From *Teaching and Learning*, 1969. Reprinted by permission of the author and the publisher. Copyright, 1969, by The Ethical Culture Schools of New York City. Lincoln Gordon is President, The Johns Hopkins University, Baltimore, Md.

ican universities have also pioneered in relating higher education organically and fruitfully to the urgent policy problems of the day. Wherever there are movements for university reform—and that means almost everywhere in the world—it is to one or another of the many American educational patterns that the reformers mainly look for guidance.

Values vs. practice

However, we have no reason for complacency. We live in a time of deep malaise and dissatisfaction, both in society at large and in the educational institutions. There is a new awareness of the existence of poverty and apathy and *de facto* racial discrimination at odds with our professed values of equal opportunity for all. I believe that we must and will bring the practice constantly closer to the values. But I see no reason to permit the fact of the gap to condemn us as either a stultified or a static society. The merest acquaintance with history shows this charge to be false. The domestic malaise is compounded by the novel kind of large scale war in which we are engaged in far-off Vietnam. Its purposes and standards of victory or defeat are complex and obscure, while its tactical miseries of blood and fire and anguish have been brought by television into millions of quiet living rooms every evening.

Student malaise

In all societies at all times, high school and especially college students tend to manifest any kind of social malaise in amplified degree and often in aberrant forms. The reasons are obvious. These are the years of abundant physical energy, and of personal transition intermixed with the new involvement in a larger society. Boys and girls are moving from the shelter of the family into some sort of place for themselves in a complex world. They are seeking to find themselves as individuals; to find one another as partners in adventure, love, or marriage; to determine some sort of values, whether expressed or implied, by which to live. Unless they are unusually well endowed with historical sense or historical learning, they are inclined to believe that every experience and discovery is being made for the very first time.

This student search for *freedom* cannot be divorced from the student search for *power*. The essence of the search for freedom lies in the legitimate and laudable desire for treatment as personalized human beings, but limits on freedom must also be defined in terms of the legitimate rights and freedom of others. The essence of the search for power can also be a legitimate and laudable desire for participation in the shaping of the educational enterprise and its impact on the student bodies, but its limitations lie in the clear need to protect education from those who seek power merely for its own sake or as an institutional base for imposing minority policies on society at large. This latter type of power grab is well known abroad and increasingly visible at home. The major feature of our current problem is how to define and resist the illegitimate without so over-reacting as to destroy legitimate quests for freedom and partici-pation, quests which should be not merely tolerated but positively encouraged.

Student freedom is not to be confused with the ancient concept of academic freedom. The essence of academic freedom is freedom to teach and to expand knowledge through research, contemplation, and creative intellectual endeavor without political interference. That kind of academic freedom—freedom for professors—is a hard-won conquest of liberal civilization, and its defense is fundamental to the maintenance and vitality of a free society.

Student freedom

Student freedom is another matter. It is sometimes thought of as "freedom to learn," and sometimes in terms of the moral standards of student life. Should the college act *in loco parentis,* or has parental authority itself diminished to the point where this concept has little meaning? Or should the constraints on students be only those on all citizens, to be enforced by the police and courts of the community at large?

My own view is that we should not seek to act *in loco parentis,* neither serving as agents to enforce the public law, nor as protectors of the students against its enforcement by the constituted authori-ties. At the same time, we must recognize that there are, especially in residential schools or colleges, community and educational interests at stake which may require their own code of rules and correspond-ing disciplinary sanctions.

Cheating on examinations, for example, may not violate the public law, but it obviously impairs the integrity of the academic enterprise. Drug peddling on campus does violate the public law, but it also threatens the college community in a way which may well justify suspension of student peddlers pending their formal trial and conviction by the often very slow processes of public justice. Where student newspapers are not separately incorporated, libelous articles may become a direct financial burden on the school concerned, as well as debasing its public image, so that notwithstanding the distastefulness of the very idea of censorship, some form of control may be in order.

As to other aspects of student life, there is, in the leading institutions, really very little freedom left to conquer. Compulsory dress, compulsory attendance at chapel, dormitory hours and the like are all but obsolete on today's campus.

Freedom to learn

On the intellectual side, the concept of "freedom to learn" is much more fuzzy than that of academic freedom. There has been a long-cycle pendular movement in higher education from the set required curriculum to the totally free elective system, then to the selective general requirement and high specialization, back to the greater proportion of free electives, and so on. There has also been endless debate on whether the essential purpose of higher education is vocational training in professional skills (including the profession of scholarship itself) or whether it is the creation of humane and liberally educated free human beings.

Whatever freedom to learn may mean, it certainly does not include freedom *not* to learn, so long as one is attending an educational institution. The totally disaffected and alienated antilearner has no proper place absorbing the resources society has assembled in its institutions of higher learning.

Student power

But for the most part I find it a healthy thing that an increasing number of students should be interested in basic questions of educational policy and should seek some sort of representation in devising the response at any given time. This brings me to the question of student power, an even more difficult area than student freedom.

Despite the uproar in the mass media about student rebellion, all the evidence seems to point toward the search for power as a minority phenomenon among students—and probably a quite small minority. Most students are in college to study. They are also caught up in the personal joys of youth and in many cases in the intellectual fascination of the knowledge explosion which also characterizes our times.

By and large, the pre-medical students and those in the natural and engineering sciences face no difficulties in catching the excitement of the accelerated unlocking of nature's secrets. They are in a hurry to participate themselves in the scientific and technological revolution, and they are disposed to work hard to prepare themselves for it. And this is true of many, although a smaller proportion, in the social sciences and humanities as well. It is the young people in these fields, however, who are most prone to sense the inadequacy of objective science in the face of what seems to them monstrous social injustice. War where there should be peace; poverty in the midst of affluence; discrimination where there should be brotherhood. In their own jargon, they want to "remake society"; they want to do it tomorrow, and they want to do it by direct action.

The direct actionists are confused in many ways, but in none more than their assumption that objectivity is incompatible with strong motivation. I observed to freshmen at Johns Hopkins last year that medical researchers seeking a cure for cancer are as highly motivated as human beings can be. But they know it would be futile to release their emotions by parading around hospitals with picket signs proclaiming, "Down with cancer!" The remedying of the ills of our urban chaos is at least as complex a problem as the cure of cancer, and it will require no less highly motivated application of trained intelligence.

Role of demonstrations

This is not to say that demonstrations have no positive role in affecting the political workings of a free society. Abolitionists in their time; suffragettes in theirs; and political campaigners every year remind us of that. But demonstrations alone will not achieve solutions to complex problems, and the problems of our society are indeed complex.

In the literature of the new student left, the watchwords are "revolution," "action," "power"; all words which stimulate the adrenal glands but leave unstated the objective. Their authors are not like Henry Thoreau, ready to return to the hand loom and the horse-drawn plow. They want the benefits of technology and industry but reject the organization without which there could be no technology and no industry.

Heroes of the Left

Nor are they orthodox Communists. They view with horror the bureaucratic organization and the new elites of the Soviet Union as it passes its fiftieth anniversary. Their hero is, characteristically, the late Che Guevera, who is a good symbol for them. He was happiest when fighting for power in the Sierra Maestre in Cuba. When he and his associates acquired power, he was given the task of organizing the Cuban economy and made a total hash of it. He had no constructive goal, not even sharing Karl Marx's vision of society as one huge family in which each would contribute according to his capacities and receive according to his needs. His satisfaction was only in the process of revolution, not in its possible fruits.

His student admirers in this country have been the most vocal in laying claims to power within the university, including power to hire or fire professors and administrators. They begin with a pretension to power alongside the faculty, but in the longer run they have no more respect for faculty rights than they have for administrators or trustees. In their unguarded moments, they even admit explicitly that power in the university is intended only as a first step to power in society at large.

This group is not really interested in learning, because they believe they know the answers through direct feeling. Although many call themselves social scientists, they sneer at efforts for objectivity in social science, again oblivious of what has been done in economics, in social psychology, in education and in political science—developments which have contributed to a dynamic process of continuous change that makes the very term "status quo" hardly applicable to the United States.

Earlier student activists

In my own experience, I have twice seen the counterpart to this type of student activist. As a young man in 1933 to 1936, I spent much of my vacation time from Oxford in Germany during those critical years when that country was being taken over by young Nazi swashbucklers. Those young boys and girls also preached a "higher morality," which justified freedom only for themselves to further their own notions of what they called "remaking society."

I have also seen Latin American universities in country after country where minority groups of activist students have sought and won power. They began by capitalizing on eminently legitimate grievances of student bodies with the promise of constructive reform. They have proven to be very skillful politicians. They are often aided by permanent "professional students"—men in their late 30's or 40's who remain registered only for the purpose of student organization and who are subsidized by the local Communist parties or other extremist groups.

They use every trick in the handbook of agitation and propaganda, including terrorism against opponents, meetings called late at night in obscure locations to pass resolutions to preserve a veneer of legality, student strikes, and destruction of university property. They make great use of the Latin tradition of university autonomy, which in many countries includes physical asylum of the university premises from police intrusion similar to the medieval churches.

Once the power base is established through substantial representation on governing boards of the institutions, it is used systematically to prevent the recruitment or promotion of professors who are politically obnoxious to the student activists, and even to harry out of their chairs some who theoretically have rights of tenure. If one of their comrades fails an examination, this is ample reason for "disciplinary action" against the guilty professors. The mass of students who want to get on with their professional studies and who are often studying at great personal sacrifice (most Latin American university students today come from the middle and lower middle classes, and many are working their way through) soon come to find the atmosphere intolerable.

Breakdown of the university

At the University of San Marcos, in Lima, Peru, conditions of this type became so acute that most of the faculty and students of medicine broke away in despair a few years ago to establish a new private university. At Caracas, the university was converted into an arsenal and refuge for terrorist groups bent on the violent overthrow of Venezuelan hard-won democracy.

If I have stressed the dangers at the end of the road of the search for power by nihilist student activists, it is because the end of the road is an observed fact, not an imaginary figment. The best way to avoid ending there is not to begin.

Our dilemma is how to oppose firmly the nihilistic pretensions to power for its own sake while not only tolerating but indeed encouraging the social sensibilities of students, their interests and involvement in the great public issues of the day, and their actual and potential interest in helping to shape the academic enterprise to meet these issues more effectively than we do now. We should neither over-react against the nihilists activists nor accede to their demands because of their pressures. We should rather, as President Kennedy once said of aid to underdeveloped countries, do what is right because it is right.

By avoiding over-reaction and by responding positively to the legitimate concerns of the positive activists—in contrast to the nihilists—we should be able to promote two useful objectives. One is the enlistment of constructive student thinking in the improvement of our institutions, and all certainly have room for improvement. The other is the separation of the positively inclined from the nihilist leadership, which many now accept reluctantly only because they find no other channels for expressing their concerns with any hope of remedial action.

Representatives must represent all

To do this clearly requires systematic means for dialogue with student representatives. It also means assuring that such representatives are really voicing the broad spectrum of student opinion and not merely the views of an articulate minority. The constitutional arrangements for student representation should obviously provide an appropriate voice for all segments of the student body, graduate and professional as well as undergraduate.

Stress student individuality

Secondly, it means a heroic and sustained effort constantly to explore ways and means, despite the large scale of so many of our institutions, to treat students as human individuals, each with his distinctive personality, talents, and interests. More flexible methods of teaching, opportunities for service to the community, extra-curricular organizations, and living conditions on or off campus are all relevant to this effort.

Recognizing the constructive motivation of most students, we should help to arrange opportunities through which they can apply their energies directly to pressing social problems. Many more could well follow the lead of those who have pioneered in such programs as recreation for the disadvantaged, "Head Start" for Negro children from the ghettoes, rehabilitation of slum housing, assistance to the blind and elderly, and pre-professional legal and medical services. The Peace Corps has demonstrated all over the world the interest and capacity of our young people to perform such service. There is no reason why similar activities should not become, on a part-time basis alongside of formal studies, a normal feature of the American educational community.

Thirdly, it requires sharing by student organizations in the control of matters pertaining to student affairs, and some form of student participation in the development of the academic program. This might be done through advisory committees on the curriculum, bringing together administration, faculty and student representatives. The precise arrangements for any particular institution depend on its individual circumstances, but I would like to see every one, including my own, develop an explicit set of policy guidelines on these matters.

Although I cannot speak with authority on the question of student rights and responsibilities at the high school level, it seems to me that the same spirit and many of the specific measures may well be applicable there as well as in the colleges and universities.

I said at the beginning that, when viewed from abroad, the picture of American secondary and higher education looks remarkably good. The truth is that our defects loom much larger to those of us who struggle daily to remove them than they do to more distant observers. I believe this also to be true of the problem of adjustment to student non-conformity, a phenomenon which creates productive as well as destructive tensions. The radical activists are correct in one respect; that is when they identify the schools and universities as the greatest engines of change in contemporary America. That is why they want to capture us, but it is also an index of our responsibilities and opportunities.

Partners in challenge

We are in the midst of the most dramatic educational revolution in human history. We have no reason to despair of our liberal and humanistic values. They have served us well. We should not permit the alienation of a few to divert us from the main task of applying those values, to the best of our abilities, to the formation of the new generations who are our partners in this challenging enterprise.

PART II

Foreign Student
Activism

34

STUDENT UNREST IN U. S. AND
LATIN-AMERICAN UNIVERSITIES

RICHARD R. RENNER

DEMONSTRATIONS were reported in December, 1964, on 30 campuses in support of the so-called Free Speech Movement at the University of California (Berkeley), and the U. S. National Student Association promptly added its blessing. Since then, a more persistent militancy has developed in many of our universities manifesting a new awareness on the part of the student that his subordinate position in the university hierarchy might be improved by such activist techniques as those used in the civil rights movement.

This growing militancy is reminiscent of the numerous strikes and demonstrations which have characterized much of Latin-American higher education since 1918 when the *Reforma Universitaria,* as it was called, culminated in the "political university" with students on its principal governing board. An extreme case is that of the University of San Andrés in Bolivia with 50% student delegates. Besides organizing to promote educational reforms, students also felt it a duty "to sally forth," as Pres. Clark Kerr has so aptly put it, to defend or reform society as political conditions warranted. According to Luis Alberto Sánchez, former rector of the University of San Marcos in Lima, Peru, the Latin student sees himself not as a

From *School & Society,* Summer, 1965. Reprinted by permission of the author and the publisher. Richard R. Renner wrote this article when he was Assistant Professor of Political Science, Pennsylvania State University, University Park. He now is Associate Professor, College of Education, University of Florida, Gainesville.

"technical, scientific or humanist apprentice, but as a belligerent soldier in the social struggle." The Berkeley demonstrations and milder incidents in the East cause one to wonder whether this pattern is finding a home in the U.S.

Although the Latin phenomenon has taken many forms, there are some generalizations which permit comparison with circumstances in the U.S. Germán Arciniegas, a prominent Colombian scholar who knows U.S. higher education at first hand, once pointed out that the purpose of the U.S. university is directly opposed to that of its Latin counterpart. In Latin America, he observed, the definition of societal and governmental problems comes from the university; the North American university performs whatever tasks society assigns to it. This is not to say that faculty-student coalitions control Latin-American governments, but they do function as political forces which must be seriously reckoned with. And, since highly centralized governments usually provide only niggardly support to the "autonomous" public university, an effective method of university self-improvement and self-protection is the involvement of its students in national politics.

A further stimulus to off-campus student activity is the part-time nature of the faculty. At the University of Buenos Aires, for example, only about 150 of its 6,000 instructors were on full-time salary in 1960, while at the University of San Marcos only 11% were full-time. The result is a teaching body immersed in off-campus affairs, independent of administrators' pressures, and inclined to be outspoken. Students naturally emulate their professors' concern with real-life problems, and they also are occupied often with outside jobs of their own.

While U.S. students are mostly unaware of the political forces which shape their lives, politics are a vital feature of the Latin-American style of life. Latin secondary students may strike to oust a political hack named by the Ministry of Education as their new director, while their North American counterparts uncritically accept their teacher's assessment that voting is the ultimate in political responsibility. The Latin-American student believes that his future depends to a considerable extent upon his being well-connected, and, if he is not, learning how to exert political pressure is very useful. The judicious high school teacher, on the other hand, learns to eschew real controversy. He advances on his merits, rather than his connections, particularly if he suppresses his feelings on controversial topics in order to become an acceptable principal or superintendent. As a result, our students are reared in a climate which encourages diligence and adaptability rather than politics and activism. When they reach the university their perspective often remains unchanged.

Then, too, the Latin-American secondary school, the *colegio* or *liceo*, strives to produce an intellectual with a vision of the world as it ought to be. Because of this emphasis, its graduates have a high regard for liberal ideals by the time they matriculate at a university to begin professional study, whereas most technically oriented students in our state universities remain untroubled by questions of social justice, the "good," the "true," and the "beautiful."

Besides this, the Latin university student is tied to a rigid curriculum, with few if any electives. Pass or fail rather than letter grades evaluate his performance. The able U.S. student is more fully occupied in the competition for grades and his future opportunities relate more closely to the quality of his scholarship. Thus, our potential leaders are winnowed off by the nature of the system, while in Latin America they enjoy more free time to devote to political activities. Then, too, if a Latin student expends enough energy supporting successful causes, he may develop a following, or at least political contacts sufficient to get him a better-than-average position. But if he graduates in law, the social sciences, or the humanities, yet neglects his politics, he may remain unemployed, or at best an elementary teacher or clerk at a subsistence salary. In the U.S., student political agitation is not so rewarded and grades remain a dominant incentive.

A lack of clear battle lines is still another difference. Despite police involvement at the University of California, repression of students has been insignificant because they have not been regarded as a serious threat. In Latin countries, drastic police measures have nurtured equally malicious student retaliation. "Kill a student for the good of the country" heralded the revocation of the Reform Movement under Juan Perón. And jailed student strikers at the University of San Marcos in 1961 "suffered indignities" as the result of contacts with depraved criminals. Bitterness based on differences in social class further contributes to friction between students and police.

The history of U.S. higher education reveals another contrast. Our private institutions enjoy greater independence in dealing with unrest because their students have not claimed the right to intervene in university affairs as their democratic prerogative; in our state universities the same tradition has been observed. But in Latin America, nearly all universities are public and more subject to student pressures in the name of democracy. And, since rectors are elective, too, university politics often produce administrators who are relatively transient and consequently have less control over university affairs then their North American counterparts.

Despite these substantial differences, there is an even more compelling reason why our students are unlikely to match their Latin brothers' activism. This is a personality characteristic endemic in Latin America but rarely found in the U.S. It manifests itself as a combination of masculine daring and personal pride known as *machismo*. A Venezuelan vice-rector once told me, "I have to pose a sharply defiant challenge whenever students make demands. Otherwise they'll run all over me because they won't respect me as a man." Student leaders reacting to such an attitude, be it from a rector, a bureaucrat, or a dictator, are forced to take a more aggressive stance than the controversy itself warrants, because they, too, must demonstrate *machismo* in order to maintain their supporters' respect.

Such activities are of little significance in the U.S. Our multiversity administrators share a management ideology and pride themselves in their ability to adjust to circumstances. Embarrassing discontent brings forth concessions sufficient to forestall the growth of effective student power. Campus bookstore facilities, relaxed dormitory restrictions, and the airing of student discontent in official university publications are but a few of the concessions at our campuses since Berkeley which have weakened student inclinations to develop independent organizations. Yet, it is possible that these successes may stimulate further demands. Like Clark Kerr, the U.S. university president sees himself as a mediator, a practical man who wants to keep his institution orderly and financially strong, achievements which are notably absent in many Latin-American institutions.

So our mass higher education with its attendant alienation continues. North Americans of every persuasion, students or administrators, faculty or trustees, still place pragmatic self-preservation and operational efficiency high on their list of priorities, while among Latin-American intellectuals the medievally inspired, Thomistic sense of absolute values and commitment to principle generates a keener sensitivity to social injustice and a stronger reaction against it.

35

UNIVERSITY STUDENTS AND
POLITICS IN LATIN AMERICA

JAIME SUCHLICKI

LATIN AMERICA has had a lasting tradition of student political activity. In the past decade alone, university students of Colombia, Venezuela, and Cuba were important elements in organizing and supporting the revolutionary movements that overthrew several Latin American dictators. Student demonstrations greeted Vice-Pres. Richard Nixon during his 1958 tour of Latin America; student riots helped topple Bolivia's government in 1964; and student protests prompted the resignation of the University of Mexico's rector in 1966.

Even the U.S., which has had a past of little student unrest, is experiencing this hitherto prominent phenomenon of developing nations. The Berkeley riots and the continuous political meetings and teach-ins at the colleges are focusing attention on, and giving new impetus to, the study of student behavior. Many observers quickly found similarities in the actions of students on both sides of the Rio Grande. Certain differences, however, are noticeable. While the Berkeley riots were an attempt to bring the larger issues affecting this nation into the campus, Latin American demonstrations aim at projecting the universities outwardly. The function of the Spanish American university is considered to be political and social as much

From *School & Society*, March 2, 1968. Reprinted by permission of the author and the publisher. Jaime Suchlicki is Assistant Professor of History, Center for Advanced International Studies, University of Miami, Coral Gables, Fla.

as academic. It has assumed the responsibility of alerting the masses and guiding the country's political life. Furthermore, the violence, state of siege, and police intervention characteristic of Latin American student demonstrations were absent from the Berkeley affair.

The Latin American tradition of student riots can be traced back to the 15th and 16th centuries' European town vs. gown squabbles. In Spain during this period, the university enjoyed a privileged position in society. University of Salamanca students and professors recognized only the rector's authority and flaunted their exemption from civil arrest. Protected by this exemption from civil jurisdiction, students rioted frequently. Hostility between students of different "nations" and between students and townspeople led to numerous disorders. Spain transplanted this peculiar arrangement to Spanish America. In the three centuries of Spanish domination in America, the university's privileged position persisted, and the students' propensity to riot continued unabated. The most common problems then were the selection of new professors, grievances against townspeople, etc. The frequency and fury of student clashes over the appointment of new professors forced the University of San Marcos, Lima, Peru, to suspend its *oposiciónes* (professorial competitions) in 1631.[1]

The political cleavage between university and state characteristic today throughout Latin America did not exist in the colonial era. On the contrary, monarchy and university objectives coincided in most cases. The crown aimed at assimilating and integrating Indians and mixed bloods into the Spanish culture, and the universities provided trained clergymen for that task. Dominicans and Jesuits were the most active in founding and directing higher educational institutions. The crown, however, controlled the university's purse and influenced its internal affairs. In the 18th century, for instance, the Bishop of Puebla complained to the Spanish monarch that the Viceroy was instructing the University of Mexico to issue degrees to his favorites without their having completed the stipulated requirements.[2]

In the first quarter of the 19th century, the struggles for independ-

---

[1] John Tate Lanning, *Old World Background of Latin American Culture* (Tucson: University of Arizona Press, 1960), p. 22.

[2] Cristóbal B. de la Plaza y Jaen, *Crónica de la Real y Pontificia Universidad de México escrita en el siglo XVII* (México: Talleres gráficos del museo nacional de arqueologia, 1931), Vol. I, p. 8.

ence severed state and gown's harmonious relationship. In 1815, the Spanish monarch, Ferdinand VII, ordered his colonial officials to suppress the agitation for independence at the University of San Marcos and in all Spanish American universities.[3] In the chaos that followed the emergence of the new republics, *caudillos* attempted to control the universities and constantly intervened in their internal affairs. Faculty and students' growing liberalism or remaining royalism served as excuses for curtailing university autonomy and for incorporating many of them into the state. "The universities," explained Aguirre Beltrán, former rector of the Universidad Veracruzana, "became government agencies and the faculties public officials."[4]

Student unrest, although in existence throughout the 19th century, became crucial in the first two decades of the 20th century. Spanish translations of the writings of Rousseau, Locke, Darwin, and Marx were circulated widely throughout Latin America, paving the way for the students' intellectual revolution of the 1920's. The new influx of ideas, together with the events of World War I and the Russian and Mexican Revolutions, inspired Latin American youths with a desire to change their static societies. The first institution that came under attack was the archaic university.

The University Reform Movement started in Córdoba, Argentina, in 1918, and later spread to the rest of Spanish America. Students demanded and obtained a large voice in university management, and the autonomy was secured as a sheltering device from the encroachments of the political power. Yet, the movement's objective was not so much the reformation of the university as the creation of an institution capable of transforming and directing a Latin American culture. Students viewed the university as the embodiment of the national mind. "The basic concern of the movement," emphasized Harrison, "has never been with the university as an institution, but rather with the orientation of the national and ultimately continental conscience."[5]

This historical approach, however, only partially explains the

---

[3] See Daniel Valcárcel, *Reformas Virreinales en San Marcos* (Lima: Imprenta de la Universidad, 1960), pp. 67-68.

[4] Gonzalo Aguirre Beltrán, *La Universidad Latino-americana* (México: Universidad Veracruzana, 1961), p. 5.

[5] John P. Harrison, "The Confrontation with the Political University," in John D. Martz, ed., *The Dynamics of Change in Latin American Politics* (Englewood Cliffs, N.J.: Prentice-Hall, 1965), p. 229.

reasons for student political involvement. Basic to an understanding of student behavior is an appreciation of the Latin American attitude toward law and order. Civil disobedience and lack of respect for authority is a predominant characteristic of our neighbors to the south. While constitutions and laws are incorporated into the statutes with swift rapidity, there is a gulf between enaction and application. Latin Americans' dislike for rules, regulations, and discipline naturally is more evident among the non-conformist and idealistic youngsters.

Another factor is the educational system's lack of stress on competition and achievement. The emphasis on personal advancement, merit, grades, and scholarship so prevalent in the Anglo-American universities almost is non-existent in Latin America. High school students, upon graduation and after paying a nominal tuition, are admitted automatically into the universities. Then, the problem is passing courses—a feat which requires a minimum of effort. Failing courses is no ground for expulsion or even for probation. After finishing college, the graduate is admitted immediately into his profession. There are no boards as we know them in the U.S., and, therefore, very little need for "good behavior." Almost everywhere, advancement in a professional field usually is based not on personal merit and hard work, but on financial position, political influence, family name, etc. The Protestant-Anglo-Saxon stress on competition and success has considerably less importance in Catholic Latin America.

Certain features of the universities contribute further to student activism. First, the university usually is located in the very center of the capital city, directly exposed to the shock waves of Latin American political turmoil. Also, the large enrollments give the student bodies concentration and strength. Then the autonomy, originally a sheltering device, converted the university into a sort of sanctuary. The fact that police are not allowed to enter the campus has given the students and subversive elements, cloaked with student privileges, a safe emplacement from which to carry on anti-government activities. The universities are battlegrounds for contending national parties and communist elements. In many instances, student groups follow the orientations of these outside political movements. In Peru, early in 1966, while searching for a pro-Peking student leader accused of supporting the guerrilla movement, police raided the Student Federation headquarters of the Catholic University in Lima.

In retaliation, the pro-Peking communist students seized the University of San Marcos, keeping professors out and holding several university employees as hostages. When a clash between government and students seemed imminent, the rival pro-Moscow faction, aided by Christian Democrats and independent students, ejected the pro-Peking strikers and turned the university over to the faculty and administrative officials.[6] Also, the lack of U.S.-type student unions or library facilities is instrumental in keeping the Latin American student away from the campus. Finally, throughout Latin America, students have a voice in running the university to a degree unknown in the U.S. One of the reasons is that most faculty members are professional men who teach only part-time and remain on campus only for lecturing. They do not have, therefore, the feeling of responsibility characteristic of the North American full-time faculties. In most autonomous universities, control is shared in some respect among administration, faculty, and students. This, together with the power wielded by student organizations, has contributed to the breakdown of discipline so prevalent in the universities today.

The importance of the Latin American students' role in politics can not be overemphasized. The social, political, and economic conditions of their countries; the tradition of student involvement in politics; the Latin American attitude toward law, order, and politics; the lack of stress on competition; and the peculiar characteristics of the university coincide to produce the political student. The universities, together with the military, have been in the past and probably will continue to be the two main sources for political leadership. The issues debated and the tactics used on the campus by political groups reflect national issues. The universities are miniature laboratories for the study of these groups' struggle to gain power in the Latin American countries.

---

6 See "Embattled San Marcos," *Youth & Freedom*, Vol. VIII, No. 1-2, 1966, p. 29.

36

MEXICO'S STUDENT PROTESTS AND THEIR SOCIOPOLITICAL BACKGROUNDS

JAMES VAN PATTEN

THE STUDENT IN MEXICO occupies a unique position. Mexico's history and culture unite in giving him a certain recognized and accepted power to keep a vigilant eye on the role and place of authority and the individual in the social order. Since there are no simple answers to complex issues which created the conditions for violence in the fall of 1968, it is possible, nevertheless, to draw some tentative conclusions regarding possible causes based on an analysis of Mexico's history.

In a certain sense, Mexico's students are the expression, extension, and fulfillment of the Revolution of 1910. This was the force that lessened vested interests of élite church, state, business, and foreign groups that had wielded limitless power in Mexico. During the nearly six decades since, the route to democracy in Mexico has not been an easy one, since the factions that had held power relinquished it only after bloody violence wrested it from their hands.

After the Revolution was won for and by the peasant, it began to be regarded as a mandate to create a social democracy wherein all Mexicans would be able to share the fruits of the nation's production and wealth. Since 1910, the Revolution has become a live,

James Van Patten is Professor of Education and Philosophy, Central Missouri State College, Warrensburg.

dynamic, moving force which lives in the hearts and minds of Mexicans.

In 1917, after the worst violence had dissipated, a constitution was drawn up modeled after the Reform Constitution of 1857, which was developed during the Benito Juarez administration. Both documents reflect the will of the Mexican people in calling for massive social engineering to eliminate vestiges and symbols of, and opportunities for, oppression of peasants and workers. The constitutions provided for the full and equal participation of all citizens in the selection of their government and safeguards to prevent any single group from being disenfranchised by power groups. The intent was to provide for the political structure to found an operating social democracy and the social institutions with which to raise the standard of living of the nation's peasants and workers. Thus, Article 3 of the Constitution of 1917 emphasized the kind of education designed to be a weapon for social change, progress, and creativity.

The Constitution of 1917 has been amended periodically to reflect the changing social needs and will of the people of Mexico. In the 20 years immediately after its adoption, education served as a decisive instrument for social change through which the government educated illiterates for life in a democracy. During this period, education was a leveling influence by which the teeming millions of peasants gained knowledge enabling them to take the first steps toward cultural improvement and betterment. Education for the few was entirely replaced by education for all—education through church indoctrination was replaced by education for a rational, scientific approach to man and his universe. Education served as a network of communication providing the means by which the government communicated with the people, explaining its attempts to distribute the land more equitably, to improve the quality of every man's life, and to nationalize foreign controlled industries to provide more employment and control by Mexicans.

From 1910 to the present, presidents and other governmental officials have been elected by democratic process, peacefully for the most part. Each president has run and won under the banner of the Institutional Revolutionary Party—the major political party of Mexico. In the first 20 years after the Revolution, Mexico's presidents were dynamic leaders of institutional and social change. Lázaro Cárdenas was such a leader. Under his administration, education served as a dynamic weapon for national reformation; and students, government, and labor, both rural and urban, united to build a new society. The outmoded anarchic and feudal vestiges of traditional power cliques were exposed and eliminated peacefully when possible. Mexico gained new life, vigor, promise, and hope; and cadres of youth (*misioneros*) went everywhere helping the poor, illiterate, and isolated groups learn how to lift themselves from poverty through utilizing the avenues of social progress established by the government.

After Cárdenas, a series of conservative presidents began to speak and act, perhaps unintentionally, in terms of a static social establishment. They overemphasized order and stability, which many Mexicans remembered as the symbol of the dreaded Porfirio Díaz administration prior to 1910. Each of the conservative administrations was careful, however, to expand social reform programs. Under the Lopez Mateos administration (1958-1964), for example, great strides were made in social security, land distribution, and educational programs. New schools were raised everywhere in rural Mexico where they were needed most. New education programs were inaugurated to provide incentive for rural citizens to develop their own schools, which became known as "The House of the People," because they served as meeting places for adults to learn in the evening and children to learn in the daytime. These schools, as community recreation centers, reflected a major attempt for rural citizens to improve their culture. Industry, modern transportation systems, communications systems, and technological improvement dotted the landscape. These symbols of Mexico's prosperity and progress are everywhere visible in 1968.

However, since the early 1940's and especially under Pres. Gustavo Díaz Ordaz, there has been a subtle philosophical shift more to the right. The emphasis is coming to be on a stable, static, and ordered society, in which social welfare programs, though considered important, are beginning to take a second place to an atmosphere that encourages increased investment for profit.

Perhaps nowhere is this more evident than in the Institutional Revolutionary Party, which seems to have lost its connection with the purpose and goals of the Revolution. This major party seems to have become complacent and contented, and is for keeping things as they are. Presidents of recent years, and Díaz Ordaz in particular, seem to have been unduly influenced by business interests and a rising middle class now numbering over 10 million. These groups have begun to exert a powerful influence on the national party. This influence could have serious consequences for Mexico, if not carefully balanced with an awareness of the need for adequate representation for all Mexicans. The Institutional Revolutionary Party has been successful in Mexico through the years because it represented fairly and adequately all citizens and balanced all interests carefully. This the party must continue to do and not be encumbered with old party professionals who have become apathetic to the needs of all Mexicans. The party needs to be renovated and brought up to date in its structure and mission. It could stand some vigorous new leadership which understands and is able to communicate with the students, workers, and peasants.

Along with the subtle philosophical movement to the right in Mexico has come a degree of apathy in regard to the need for continued efforts to distribute the wealth more equitably. This, too, was a mandate of the 1910 Revolution. Today, with all the progress taking place, the majority of Mexicans have a standard of living little better than that which existed prior to the Revolution. True, they have better schools, more social security, and greater opportunities to enter new fields of work, but, in terms of real purchasing power, the Mexican peasant has not notably improved his position. Although there is a rising middle class, the number of peasants, rural or urban, living in destitute conditions also has grown accordingly. A series of Mexican governments have sought to improve tax collections and increase the tax base, but resistance has been so great little progress has been made. Some progress is being made in developing a new income tax program, but it is inadequate to meet the nation's need for funds.

The population explosion* has served Mexico ill, making it almost impossible for the gross national product to be effectively distributed for all citizens without extremely careful attention to expanding and implementing new programs to train the peasant for new positions. Existing programs are simply not adequate to keep up with the population growth.

Mexican students, as inheritors of a revolutionary creed, have been quick to note the subtle change of governmental policy.

---

* Mexico's population is over 45,000,000 today, and is nearly doubling every 20 years.

Through their rebellion, students have sought to reawaken the national consciousness to the fact that social justice and progress are due in no small measure to institutions that remain viable, willing, and able to change to meet new social demands and conditions. Student rebellion further indicates that the Mexican government cannot serve the needs of a growing population if it reflects the conservatism of one particular group, no matter how economically powerful that group is. Thus, student demands for curbing the use of police power, and for more representation in the decision-making processes, reflect an awareness that careful balance between authority and the individual is vital for fulfilling the mandates of the Revolution of 1910.

Another factor in Mexico's student rebellion is dissatisfaction with the educational philosophy exhibited by the organization of curriculum and the administration of Mexico's schools. This is particularly true of the secondary and higher educational levels. Students in Mexico, therefore, are seeking educational reform not unlike their peers in France.

Secondary and higher education, for the most part, have continued to resist modifications necessary to update the educational effort. The present secondary school in general is frequently isolated from the social order within which it operates. For those who wish to enter institutions of higher education, curriculum is generally geared to college preparatory work as it has been from pre-revolutionary Mexico's emphasis on a traditional core of subjects. Rote methods of teaching subjects add to student discontent. Rigorous examinations conducted throughout the course of study in college preparatory schools have led to a high rate of dropouts and failures. Such failures represent a serious loss to Mexico, since these pupils could provide much needed technical and professional service for the country if they were enabled to enter the university level. Serious efforts are being made to change the curriculum and teaching methods in secondary schools to more efficiently serve the pupils and the country. These efforts, however, are still inadequate to resolve the difficulties facing the secondary educational effort and attempts are being made to reform outmoded curriculums and examinations which in many cases were carried over from the days of foreign rule in Mexico and thus have proven inadequate to meet the unique and particular needs of the nation.

Students are particularly disturbed over the inequities existing in enrollments in university preparatory schools. Students who have been trained in secondary schools not connected with major universities often are discriminated against in favor of pupils who have been trained in university secondary schools. Since the *bachillerato* is required for entrance into the advanced cycle of secondary school and since this is offered only in certain institutions, resulting discrimination in student admissions has become a matter of serious concern to the directors of secondary schools. The Bureau of Secondary Education is rapidly moving to resolve the dilemma and is continuing to seek a broader admission policy to universities, particularly to the University of Mexico. One of the things the Bureau of Secondary Education and its parent organization, the Secretariat of Public Education, is continuing to emphasize is the creation of technical schools, such as the National Polytechnic Institute, which awards university-level degrees in the sciences and other technical and professional areas. These schools have a broader admission policy than the University of Mexico and admit pupils freely from all secondary schools in the country.

Students frequently feel the effort is not enough and are demanding a serious effort at massive educational reform. The Secretariat of Public Education is aware of the needed changes and is continuing to develop a more viable secondary educational program designed to meet the needs of Mexico. Student rebellion, however, is not only aimed at outmoded traditionalism in teaching and curriculum and toward discrimination in university preparatory school admissions, but also against excessive class sizes, particularly in urban areas, and teacher assignments which do not serve schools needs. Teachers frequently work in several schools and, consequently, are unable to know and counsel pupils in any given school. The Secretariat is working toward having teachers do most of their work in one school.

Student rebellion also has been aroused by Federal government measures which have encroached on the traditional autonomy of universities. When troops marched onto the University of Mexico campus in 1968, they infringed on the freedom of the school to govern itself, a sacred and honored freedom in the nation. Although the University of Mexico and other universities throughout the country receive Federal funds for their support and operation, these funds never have brought with them the spectre of Federal control. Students have long aided in the administration of the University of Mexico and other universities, and any encroachment on the self governance doctrine invokes immediate protest on the behalf of academic freedom and autonomy of administration.

These are some of the possible causes of student unrest in Mexico in the fall of 1968. A number of other factors may have contributed to student discontent, but students essentially are seeking to develop more social relevance in their educational programs and their social institutions. In this desire for social relevance one should not overlook student power as a possible force for social justice and cultural improvement. Student demands for changes in Mexican penal codes which might be used by authoritarian leaders to quell legitimate dissent indicate their awareness of the need to improve the democratic processes in the country.

The greatness, progress, and prosperity of Mexico in the 20th century reflects in part the willingness and ability of her students to encourage every public servant to remain imaginative, creative, and alert to the experimental nature of Mexico's continuing efforts to build a democratic society. The calls for law and order are important, but they should not receive priority over social justice and progress. For, when law and order receive such a priority, no matter how subtle or slight the change may be, there is a move toward the conditions which prevailed in pre-revolutionary Mexico. However slight the change may be, it never fails to invoke student attention, for they are the inheritors of the mandates of the revolution. If public servants are to remain flexible and capable of new and experimental alternatives on the road to social justice, they cannot let themselves even unwittingly slip into the staticism of a stagnate social order.

When all the reasons are analyzed in terms of history, however, indications are that students today, as in yesteryear, are speaking as the articulate voice of Mexico's millions of peasants and of a wide variety of ethnic groups. These people stand in the background, as they have throughout the history of Mexico, silently watching and waiting. Persecuted by the Spaniard for 300 years, oppressed by a powerful church-state elite for another century, they remain the mind and will of the Mexican Revolution—for in the final analysis it was their revolution. These millions of Mexicans wait and watch, hoping and expecting the results of social progress in a better life now. They stand inarticulate, but, in their quietness, they are still a force that must be reckoned with by every government in Mexico.

In a sense, the Mexican student is the only voice they have, for he originates in their midst, and will return, bringing new hope and expectation or new anger and despair. In their watching and waiting—Mestizos or Indians, or both, in isolated pockets of rural Mexico or in poverty pockets of urban Mexico—they exhibit understanding and encouragement of the students in their protest. They know the students will not allow social institutions, no matter how entrenched, to develop complacency, contentment, or rigidity. These institutions were molded by Mexicans for Mexico, and they are subject to remolding whenever they are allowed to weaken the embryonic thread that tied them to the goals of a dynamic, live, and viable revolution.

In the degree to which student rebellion serves to remind public servants of their need to be willing and able to change, and to see their social institutions change to meet the needs of a new era, the students are performing a vital service to Mexico. They keep alive in the hearts and minds of all Mexicans the vision and dream of the Mexican Revolution—*Educar es Redimir* ("To Educate is to Redeem").

37

STUDENT POLITICAL BEHAVIOR IN ITALY

MICHAEL ANELLO

THERE IS SUFFICIENT EVIDENCE around the world that student activity
in the institutions of higher education has become more militant,
and that students are more concerned with their political roles. In
many nations, student activism has had a notable influence in political and social reform. Student movements in South America, India,
South Korea, Bolivia, and Indonesia have produced governmental
change and reform. In more extreme cases, *i.e.,* Turkey and Japan,
massive student agitation has been responsible for the decline of
governments.[1] Student action also has had its effects on the educational process. Worthy of note are developments in Italy, where
militant student groups are critical of the pitifully slow progress
recent legislation has made in improving conditions at the university
level.

The Italian parliament has been slow in passing the extension of
Italy's school development bill for the successive five-year period,
1965-70. The new bill is an attempt to modernize Italy's university

[1] Seymour Martin Lipset commented on this point in an editorial in a special
issue of *Comparative Education Review*, 10: 129, June, 1966. The issue also
includes a number of well-documented articles analyzing student roles in politics
and higher education in some of the emerging nations.

From *School & Society*, Nov. 9, 1968. Reprinted by permission of the author and the
publisher. Michael Anello is Associate Professor of Higher Education and Director, Program
in Higher Education, Boston College, Chestnut Hill, Mass.

system.[2] There are signs of pressure from many quarters in Italy for meaningful university reforms, for a move away from purely liberal and humanitarian studies and toward the training required of university graduates in a modern scientific and industrial society.[3] Although university enrollments indicate a 50% increase by 1970, more must be accomplished in assisting students to complete secondary schooling and enter the university. Historically, Italy has resisted equality of educational opportunity, and has maintained a rigid educational elite. The inadequacies of the universities include a shortage of instructors, crowded classrooms, outmoded lecture halls and buildings, inadequate financing, outdated curriculum, and a lack of teaching facilities.

Among the students, we note a tendency to form meaningful political groups to improve the content and conditions of higher education in Italy. The Italian university student always has been involved in political affairs, and the universities have a rich history of student participation, which can be documented from the medieval period, to the time of Garibaldi's victory for unification, to the social reforms of Mazzini, to World Wars I and II.[4] In general, however, student activity in Italy has been confined to a very small percentage of students, whose demands usually were manifested by such visible forms of activity as street demonstrations, strikes, riots, picket signs, and the like. The evidence in recent months points to a revival of student political interest and participation whereby student groups would have a legitimate and powerful voice in the affairs of the university. Student leaders are seeking a more active

2 See "Linnee directive del piano di sviluppo pluriennale della scuola per il periodo successivo al 30 Giugno, 1965," No. 1073, September, 1964, Ministero della Pubblica Istruzione, Roma, and Michael Anello, "Trends in Italian Higher Education," SCHOOL & SOCIETY, 94: 272-74. Summer, 1966.

3 A few of the recent writings critical of university studies are: Giovanni Calò, "L'università in rapporto alle nuovo strutture ed esigenze della società contemporanea," *Annali della Pubblica Istruzione*, January-February, 1964. G. M. Bertin, "La scuola e la società Italiana in transformazione," *Scuola e Città*, September, 1964. Alberto Sensini is critical of the proposed reforms, stating that they lack shape and content and ignore scientific and technological development in Italy: *La riforma università* (Florence: Sansoni, 1966).

4 See Helen Zimmern and Antonio Agresti, *New Italy* (New York: Chautauqua, 1920), p. 91. For interesting accounts of undergraduate activities in the medieval university, see R. S. Rait, *Life in the Medieval University* (Cambridge: University Press, 1937), and Pearl Kibre, *Scholarly Privileges during the Middle Ages* (Cambridge: Medieval Academy of America, 1962).

role, using the political process to stimulate improved university conditions.

In 1966, the fact clearly emerged that students have become more conscious of their own political power. Recent student disturbances at the University of Rome, where 60,000 students are enrolled, resulted in the resignation of the rector.[5] The growth in enrollment in Italy's universities will provide a good base of strength in numbers for student groups.[6]

The nature of student political organizations must be explained in the light of Italy's political structure and the general attitude of Italians toward politics. Since student organizations tend to associate with the branches of the various political parties and reflect their political philosophy, the following is relevant to a comprehension of student political behavior.

Italy has a multiparty system composed of nine active political parties. The three major parties, which gain over 80% of the national vote, are the Christian Democratic party, the Italian Communist party, and the Italian Socialist party.[7] Political progress is complex since no party has a substantial majority and each party views governmental policy from a different perspective. If one examines election results in Italy, one can understand the inability of the Italian parliament to form a majority vote on specific issues. Moreover, one can understand why governments in Italy come and go with such confusing regularity, and why political parties in Italy are so fragmented. The political system has been referred to as one of "unstabilized stability."[8]

---

[5] Italian newspapers made interesting news of the forced resignation of Prof. Giuseppe Papi, rector of the University of Rome, after he had become involved in student demonstrations between Fascist and anti-Fascist student groups. An excellent English translation of the story can be seen in *Minerva*, 4: 586, Summer, 1966.

[6] Consider the potential student political power at the universities of Rome, Milan, and Naples, where the combined student population is over 100,000.

[7] A recent survey shows the following voter strength: Christian Democrats, 41.2%; Italian Communists, 26%; Italian Socialists, 13.8%. At this writing, the Communist party seems to be in a state of ambivalence suffering from a lack of leadership. In 1966, out of 306 communes voting for mayor, only 239 mayors were voted back into office. See E. A. Bayne, "Non-Crisis in Italy," *Foreign Affairs*, 45: 354-55, January, 1967.

[8] J. P. C. Carey and A. G. Carey, "The Italian Elections of 1958—Unstable Stability in an Unstable World," *Political Science Quarterly*, 73:566-89, December, 1958, and P. A. Allum, "The Italian Elections of 1963-64," *Political Studies*, 13:324-45, October, 1965. Both articles deal with the complexity of elections in Italy.

The intricacies of Italian party politics are the result of long-standing and complex factors, but most recently they stem from a rapidly changing Italian society. Italy has been undergoing swift technological and industrial development. Economic improvement[9] has given hope for the good life to many. There are signs of prosperity at all levels: in the second half of 1966, steel and automobile production was at a new high; tourism was up some 15%; telephone and television sets sold had nearly doubled; employment was at a respectable level; exports had risen some 20%, and trade with countries within the Common Market and with other countries in Europe was at a high.

Industrial development normally brings with it rapid urbanization. This is true in Italy, as evidenced by the movement of workers to the North to seek employment and better living conditions. Although some industrial development has been going on in the South, a visit to this area quickly confirms the notable gap between North and South. In many instances, the appearance is of two distinct social and cultural entities, each section looking at the other with disdain, mistrust, and hostility.[10]

Cultural and class divisions, as characterized in the North and South, do not tend to support a stable political system. Scholars who have studied this problem know that social diversity as exemplified in Italy produces inadequate political communication, fragmentation, and isolation.[11] Many Italians are isolated from the news, unconcerned with developments in their society, and without opinions on contemporary issues. This political isolation is not a problem of the entire society, to be sure, yet the contention does have support from a variety of studies.

The data of one study draws the picture of Italian political culture as one of alienation and of social isolation and distrust. It points out that Italians are lacking in national pride and are not

[9] There is evidence that the Italian economy is strengthening its recovery from the recession. My personal interview with Miss Jean M. Wilkowski, economic advisor at the American Embassy in Rome, confirms this evidence. Data is available from her office. See *Annual Statistical Bulletin*, American Embassy, Rome, June, 1966; also *The Italian Economy in the Spring of 1966*, unpublished, American Embassy, Rome, June 3, 1966.

[10] Writings concerning the South are voluminous. A concise treatment of these problems can be located in *Il Veltro*, Vol. VI, December, 1962.

[11] See Joseph LaPalombara, *Interest Groups in Italian Politics* (Princeton: Princeton University Press, 1964), p. 55.

likely to participate in political affairs.[12] On a questionnaire, 72%
of respondents, aged 18-25, indicated little or no interest in national
and international affairs.[13] In another study completed in France,
volved them. Only 23% had any awareness of the Common Market.
An overwhelming 67% had little interest in political matters.[14]

Among university students today, political attitudes do not vary
significantly from those of the general public. Although they tend to
be more interested and knowledgeable about political matters, students regard the political system with mistrust and disdain. Talks
with students at a number of Italian universities verify their disillusionment with the bureaucracy.[15] Therefore, student political participation is limited.

Those who do participate in student political activity tend to
support the radical groups, left and right. Although there has been a
large degree of support for the center party, the Christian Democrats, this party has not been successful in pushing university reforms. Hence, voting among Italian youth now seems to favor the
Communists and Socialists, on the left; the Monarchists and the
Italian Social Movement on the right. Italian youth are fairly confused about their political values. Their voting behavior is tied
strongly to gratification; support of a political party depends upon
the degree of satisfaction youth have with present conditions.[16]

In each of Italy's 40 universities or institutes of university rank,
there is an elected group of students which represents the entire
student body. In most cases, the student organization is a member of
the national student organization called Unione Nazionale Universitaria Rappresentativa Italiana, or U.N.U.R.I. According to its con-

---

[12] Gabriel Almond and Sidney Verba, *The Civic Culture, Political Attitudes
and Democracy in Five Nations* (Boston: Little, Brown, 1965), p. 308.

[13] Joseph LaPalombara, "L'Orientamento politico dello gioventù," in Alberto
Spreafico and Joseph LaPalombara, eds., *Elezioni e comporamento politico in
Italia* (Milan: Edizioni di Communità, 1962), pp. 495-516.

[14] Conducted by the l'Institut Francais d'Opinion Publique for Gallup International (Paris, 1962), and quoted in Bayne, *op. cit.*, p. 361.

[15] I spoke with students for the universities of Rome, Bologna, and Perugia,
asking them of their political associations. The general impression was that they
were not concerned in politics, but rather with a degree, employment, financial
security, and better standards of living.

[16] Joseph LaPalombara and Jerry Waters, "Values, Expectations, and Political
Predispositions of Italian Youth," *Midwest Journal of Political Science,* 5: 57,
February, 1961.

stitution, one of the primary functions of U.N.U.R.I. is to represent student interests to policy-making bodies who are responsible for improvement of the university.[17] The intention is to involve students in university policy making. U.N.U.R.I. unavoidably becomes involved in political activity since the university is under government control. Unfortunately, the impact of U.N.U.R.I. has been less than desirable, since it has not been able to unite students in a common cause for university reform. Although U.N.U.R.I. purposes to cut across party lines, its effectiveness has been weakened because it, too, runs up against ideological fragmentation.

There are four affiliates of U.N.U.R.I., each representing a different political persuasion. The two major affiliates are the Unione Goliardica Italiana (U.G.I.), composed of student activists from the Socialist, Republican, Communist, and Radical parties and the Intesa, consisting of Catholic students who support the Christian Democrats and the Church. Two other groups represent the extreme liberal student groups and the neo-Fascists on the right. They are Associazione Goliardica Independenti (A.G.I.) and Fronte Universitario di Azione Nazionale (F.U.A.N.), respectively. At a recent congress in Viareggio, Italy, these student groups attempted to come to some consensus as to the role of the Italian university in a modern and changing society.[18]

Out of the student debates has come a movement called *sindacalismo studentesco*.[19] The movement is an attempt to organize the students within the various affiliates of U.N.U.R.I. to exert political pressure on the legislature.

Students want change, a change away from the medieval characteristics which still pervade the system; from regimentation; from an irrelevant curriculum; from the universities' alienation from con-

---

17 "Unione Nazionale Universitaria Rappresentativa Italiana," *Statuto* (Rome, 1957), Art. 1-6.

18 Reputable Italian newspapers provide readable accounts of the debates. The accounts portray the student as more active and concerned with social problems. See for example, "Gli universitari vogliono dar vita a degli organisimi piu rappresentativi," *Il Messaggero*, March 23, 1966; and "Associazioni universitarie in polemica," *Il Corriere della Sera*, Jan. 4, 1967.

19 Syndicalism is the French word for trade-unionism, and was implemented where unions were weak—for example, in France, Spain, and Italy. For similarities between French and Italian student movements, see Jean-Pierre Worms, "The French Student Movement," *Comparative Education Review, op. cit.*, p. 359; "Sindacalismo giovanile; gli interessi degli studenti," *Il Corriere della Sera*, Oct. 5, 1966; and "Nuovo corso del movimento studentesco," *Il Corriere della Sera*, Dec. 28, 1966.

temporary society. The student syndicalistic movement is an attempt
to make known specific problems in a unified way through the
political process. It does not claim to be a revolutionary movement
to overthrow democratic procedures or to establish a corporate
society to control university policy. It is, more dramatically, a movement by students, designed to transmit in orderly fashion scholastic
demands to the Italian parliament.

Student leaders are hopeful that the movement will not be reduced to a critical defense of petty political interests and that
significant problems can be solved to the benefit of the university
and the Italian community. As one leader has stated, "The only
objective of student syndicalism is a modern and efficient school
system, where, in a spirit of collaboration, students, faculty, and
governmental agencies can prescribe the role of the university in
modern society."[20]

---

[20] This statement was made by Dr. Carrado Aforza Fogliani, vice-president of
the Liberal Italian Youth, "Il ruolo dello studente nella società moderna," *Il
Corriere della Sera,* Oct. 12, 1966.

38

GERMANY'S STUDENT REVOLT

~~~~~~

GERMAN UNIVERSITIES and their student bodies are undergoing important changes. While reform gradually is altering the curriculum and the lecture hall, student dissent sometimes challenges the basic premises of German society itself.

Student activism resembles in tactics and ideology its "New Left" counterparts in the Netherlands, Italy, England, and the U.S. It began in Germany in the early 1960's as an expression of discontent over crowded classrooms and limitations on "academic freedom," but it has reached a stage of open "revolt against the quality of life and values of a materialistic society," as *The New York Times* said in a recent editorial.

The extremists among the students—organized in the "Socialist German Students Association" (SDS)*—have declared themselves to be the revolutionary vanguard of a future and better society. Once allied with the Social Democratic Party, the SDS was expelled in 1960, when it refused to go along with the political decisions of its parent organization. The SDS has resuscitated Marxist theories, adding Freudian tenets and certain ideas of Trotzky and Mao Tse-Tung, but sympathizing at the same time with 19th-century German humanists and Utopian thinkers.

---

* Of the total student population of 405,000, U.S. correspondents in Bonn estimate 2,500 SDS members and 11,000 "hard-core radicals," while *Der Spiegel* counted 22,300 demonstrators in eight German cities during the most violent of student-inspired riots; these estimates by independent observers amount to three-five per cent of the total student body.

~~~~~~

From *School & Society*, Oct. 26, 1968. Used through the courtesy of the German Information Center, New York City, and reprinted by permission of the publisher.

The student revolt has many links to Germany's radical humanist tradition that grew out of early 19th-century Hegelian idealism. The struggle of German liberals in 1819 against Metternich was led by German students, as were the mass democratic appeals launched by the Goettinger Manifest and the Hambacher Fest in the 1830's. These movements later erupted into the ill-fated Revolution of 1848. In the ensuing decades, many German students were among the followers of the principal figures of socialism and humanist philosophy. Feuerbach, Marx, Engels, Lassalle, Bebel, and Liebknecht, to name a few. The same liberal tradition of dissent inspired the "White Rose" group, led by students Hans and Sophie Scholl, to agitate against Hitler at the University of Munich in 1943 in the middle of the war—for which they paid with their lives.

Today, student ideology is influenced noticeably by an additional source—the writings of Herbert Marcuse (an American professor of philosophy at the University of California, San Diego), whose nonconformist ideas and terminology recur frequently in the pamphlets, speeches, and discussions of the SDS. The socialism of the SDS has little in common with Soviet-style communism—not to speak of the East German Stalinist version—which the students feel is just as "repressive" as the democratic "establishment." The students declare that they are waging a struggle against an "overdeveloped and overrepressive" society, in which man is more alienated than Marx ever dreamed—largely because of an "uncontrollable bureaucracy," political party "machines," and labor unions that have made an "accommodation" with business and government. It is a society that has failed to check war, poverty, and injustice, in spite of 20th-century technology.

These ideas, along with the original protest against inadequate university conditions, have stimulated thousands of students to follow the SDS demand for mass direct action. They consider "extra-parliamentary opposition" to be the only effective means of influencing the establishment. To most student rebels, the riots and other disturbances that they instigate are not violence but happenings—publicity devices to focus attention on them and their demands. They feel that they are in the mainstream of an international movement participating in the civil rights and anti-war crusade, a party to student protest wherever it occurs—Berkeley, London, Paris, Rome, Tokyo, Czechoslovakia, or Poland.

The re-direction of the original student appeal for university reform into a battle cry for social revolution has meant a head-on confrontation with social and government—at home and abroad— over such issues as the Shah of Iran's visit to Germany, the Greek military regime, the Vietnam war, emergency legislation, the attempt on the life of the student leader, Rudi Dutschke, and the charges of reactionary journalism against the Axel Springer Press, a German newspaper combine, the owner of which has become a chief target of student protest.

Most Germans take student unrest seriously. The Federal government and all the political parties represented in the Bundestag sympathize with the student majority that directs its efforts at the reform of the universities, but condemn the use of violence.

Chancellor Kurt Kiesinger has conceded that "a large number of institutions and traditions in our educational system are too deeply rooted in the epoch of pre-industrial society to be able to meet the requirements of our completely transformed world." The Chancellor agrees that "the demand for a speedy reform is perfectly understandable and justified."

The Federal government, however, has no jurisdiction over the universities. The individual states are in charge, and coordination between them is assured through the Standing Conference of the State Ministers of Cultural Affairs and the Conference of Rectors of the Universities. They and special committees of the political parties, together with other organizations, are dealing with urgent problems, such as modernization of research, reorganization of the curriculum, curtailment and tightening-up of courses, reform of university rules and regulations, coordination of specialized colleges, and cooperation between lecturers and students.

Although many of the students' original reform goals have been reached, much still remains to be done. To some of the student radicals, nevertheless, these goals are not being reached fast enough, and they have added over-all political aims to their protest movement. The militant among the students well may try to carry on their future activity with new political issues in an even bolder manner.

If their violence increases, the militant student minority probably will lose the bulk of their student followers and end up in isolation. This is particularly likely as more and more improvements in the universities make themselves felt for staff and students. The statutes of many universities already are being reviewed to allow greater participation of students and junior staff members, and annual expenditures of state governments for universities are now more than double than in 1960. Staff appointments have increased by more than 100%, while the number of students has risen only 29%.

It can not be denied that student dissent—even if only a fraction of the student body as a whole is involved actively—is helping to accelerate a change in the nature of education in Germany. It can add—if it abstains from resorting to violence—a lively and constructive element to the discussion of new basic principles and their adaptation to the new challenges upon which a modern democracy thrives.

39

STUDENT PROTEST IN FRANCE

GEORGE A. MALE

IN MAY, 1968, French university students took to the streets in protest. Pitched battles occurred between police and students and a whole section of Paris was occupied by the protesters. As the movement spread to other universities in France, and to workers in factories who went out on strike, the French government tottered. Observer after observer has been struck by the parallel with the French Revolution, and it has been suggested that, in some mysterious way, the spirit of the original French Revolution has re-emerged.

The temptation is strong to explain the current student activism in psychological terms. Thus, one notes the jarring contrast between the freedoms of university student life and the tight family control so typical of the French. Add to this the preceding seven years of tightly controlled life in the academic secondary school and one can imagine the pendulum swinging toward aggressive activism.

Lewis Feuer has analyzed university student protest on a world-wide basis and characterizes it as a mixture of selfless idealism on a very lofty plane and aggression against the older generation, with the young student trying to reject the paternalism of the father and all similar authority figures. In this case the university serves as a convenient father figure. Many will object to this line of reasoning as an unwarranted revival of Freudianism.

Another explanation, also psychological, is that the other kind of

George A. Male is Professor of Comparative Education and Director, Comparative Education Center, University of Maryland, College Park.

student protest, namely copping out as a hippy, was tried on a wide scale by French university students long before America discovered hippydom and was found to be basically unsatisfying and self-defeating. Consequently, the French students are trying a different approach, *i.e.,* lashing out at the nation's values more openly and aggressively.

One such deep-seated value is reverence for the past.[1] At its worst, this leads French education, and France itself, to ignore the current needs of society. Thus, relevance becomes a key word in the speeches of the student protesters, but it was a key word in the writings of French educational reformers after World War I and again after World War II. This backward looking stance of France discourages change, but paradoxically keeps the French Revolution of 1789, with all of its heady activism, alive in the hearts of all Frenchmen, including the young students.

The roots of the current protest go back at least to the 1950's and to the problems readily apparent at that time. Among these were overcrowded classes and other physical inadequacies, a teaching method characterized by aloofness and lack of contact between professor and student, a brutal examination system which took the top 20% of an age group and on three separate occasions cut the group in half and labeled the lower half as failures, and above all a tendency to glorify verbalism without a counterbalance of applying and testing ideas. The result was a tendency toward lofty statements and ideologies and, under the right circumstances, rash actions.

According to the student protesters, all these problems remain and have been joined by a host of others. A popular phrase is the "malfunctioning university." As evidence the students cite the failure of universities to educate—70% of those who enter do not finish. Moreover, with rising enrollments and a growing number of university graduates, many do not get suitable jobs in the economy. Within the university, disciplines are compartmentalized and aloof from each other and exist in a hierarchy of prestige which goes back centuries and has little meaning in current life. Most discouraging of all, in terms of immediate problems, is the failure of physical facilities to improve and the likelihood that they will get worse as enrollment increases outstrip the capacity or will of the French national government to appropriate the needed funds.

---

[1] Francois Nourissier, *The French* (New York: Knopf, 1968), chap. 2.

There was an awareness of lack of university facilities and staff in the late 1940's and 1950's as such French journals as *Esprit* and *Le Figaro Littéraire* spotlighted the problem and gave notoriety to such cases as seven teachers of English for 1500 students, a chemistry laboratory with one thermometer for 800 students, a library at the Sorbonne with 300 seats in the 1950's which was exactly the same as in the 1890's except that enrollments had increased ten-fold by the 1950's. All of this has been exacerbated by dramatic enrollment increases in the 1960's. Approximately 200,000 students were enrolled in French universities in 1961, and seven years later the figure was over 500,000.

The predictable results of such an expansion has been unbelievably overcrowded lecture halls and even less contact with professors, already noted for their aloofness. Among the steps taken by the national government to meet this crisis in the 1960's has been the opening of seven new universities since 1963. This points up the failure, however, to open any new universities between the end of World War II and 1963, in contrast with England where seven new universities were established by 1963 and seven more after 1963. France did take steps in the 1960's to meet the staffing problems by creating a new post below the assistant professor level. In addition, education budgets of the 1960's allocated as much as one-quarter of the funds to new buildings, laboratories and other facilities, but it was a case of too little too late.

In 1968, at the time of the student outbreak, stories still circulated of cases of eight students to a microscope, 32,000 students using a library designed for 500, and similar instances of inadequate facilities. Moreover, moderate reformers were fearful that the national government lacked the will to fully support a further expansion of French higher education.

More important than lack of physical facilities is the defect in spirit and atmosphere of French universities. Again this was clearly noted by French critics of the 1950's and early 1960's. The stereotype of French university teaching, then and now, includes rigidity, dull lectures, copies of lectures circulated and memorized for examinations, professors pouring out a stream of knowledge and not appearing to care whether it was understood or not, professors unconcerned about the relationship of their subject to other subjects, few seminars, and generally poor contacts between professors and students. Professors, on the other hand, often blame the students and accuse them of using such secondary school methods as "servilely copying the lectures dictated."

One can imagine the French university students becoming discouraged after noting the several decades since World War I that French reformers have sought to change the methods and general atmosphere of higher education. Equally discouraging is the defensive tone taken by professors, even by such a responsible social critic as Raymond Aron who ends up in 1968 justifying the traditional lecture method.[2]

Yet, government officials have spoken out in favor of change. The director-general of higher education in France stated at the end of 1958 that the aim of French higher education should be to develop creativity and that the university must keep in close touch with life.[3] Two years later a high level national commission issued the Rueff-Armand Report which declared that higher education in France should be oriented toward the current needs of society.[4]

In response to such urging, the higher education curriculum broadened, a new degree was offered in applied science, and new emphasis was given to such fields as technology, business administration, sociology, journalism, population study, and demography. Some of these officially announced changes were implemented rather slowly, and charges of outmoded and backward oriented curriculum still are made by critics. Here we have a typically French problem, *i.e.*, the wide gulf between words and action. On the other hand, student protesters may lack the perspective to recognize the progress that has been made. Perhaps, as is the case with Negro militants in the U.S., *some progress* is no longer acceptable.

It is also well to wonder whether rationality is the prevailing mood among student protesters so that progress when made would be acknowledged. Feuer asserts that irrationality has characterized student protest movements throughout history.[5] In the case of France, there is the paradox of a nation with a reputation for rationality and logical thinking celebrating irrationality through French humor and vignettes and even glorifying it under the guise

---

2 Raymond Aron, "After the Barricades," *Encounter*, Aug. 26, 1968.

3 *Education in France*, 4: 6, December, 1958.

4 The Rueff-Armand Report is summarized in *France Actuelle*, 10: 1-7, Jan. 15, 1961.

5 Lewis S. Feuer, *The Conflict of Generations: The Character and Significance of Student Movements* (New York: Basic Books, 1969), p. 8.

of individualism. Witness the familiar stories of Frenchmen refusing to obey traffic signals. The phenomenon escalates into farmers blockading rural roads to prevent produce from going to market and millions of Frenchmen refusing to obey the law in regard to paying taxes. It should cause no eyebrows to lift when French university students decide to make their own laws to fit their mood of the moment.

One of the first acts of legislation of the student protesters during their brief occupation of the French universities was to outlaw the examination system. For a traditional Frenchman education without examinations and a massive rejection of candidates is unthinkable. Thus, only 35% of an age group enter an academic secondary school and half of these fail to finish. The 18% of an age group which goes on to a university meet the examination system again and less than half finish and get a degree. Here again the reformers were at work in the 1950's and early 1960's in largely ineffective attempts to modify the tendency of the examinations to encourage cramming and memorization at the expense of real thinking.

The examinations have such a massive impact precisely because they are run by the national government with deadly efficiency and a remarkable lack of personal touch. The examinations symbolize to the student protesters all the evils of centralized control, which is a basic feature of French government and French life generally. The student militants dream of a decentralized socialist society run by committees. More immediately, they demand autonomous universities free from control by the Paris governmental bureaucracy. The lack of freedom of each university to develop in its own way and to hire its own staff has long been resented by the faculty.

National government control of the universities is a tradition dating back 160 years to Napoleon's decree of 1808. As a result, professors, and more especially deans and rectors, of universities have been regarded as civil servants, and, according to the critics of the 1960's, have acquired the limited mentalities of bureaucrats. In the 1960's, a growing tendency of the national government to regulate the universities was justified in terms of securing adequate personnel for the nation's economy and fitting all institutions into the 5-year economic plans which were being used by the national government to coordinate the economic development of France.

After the May, 1968, student protest, the national government promised more autonomy to individual universities and to individual departments within each university. Each department, whether it be law, medicine, or whatever, is to be governed by an elected council made up of faculty, students and even representatives from nearby communities. What is not promised is a change in spirit away from the French system of doing things, and yet this is what the students demand.

When the students speak of destroying the system they say they mean capitalism and its chief agent the "bourgeois university," which they characterize as "a culture of exploitation and dehumanization."[6] This singling out of the university reflects the growing importance in France of a university education and the close relationship which has developed between the economy and the universities.

The students are disturbed by the failure of the university to include in its student body a fair representation from all the socio-economic groups. The record here of the French universities is like that of the rest of Western Europe where typically less than 10% of the university students come from families where the father is a farmer or factory worker. In sociological terms the vast majority of university students are upper middle class. This conflicts with a major aim of the student activists—namely, an alliance of students and workers. The students demand healthy subsidies for all university students, presumably to enable lower class children to enter the universities. Suspicious critics of the student protest movement note that factory workers through their taxes already are subsidizing upper middle class students and would be asked to increase this support. Moreover, those immediately benefiting would be the upper middle class students already at the universities.

The workers show little inclination to make common cause with the student protesters. The issue of lack of democracy in higher education remains alive, however, thanks to the open reluctance of the professors to welcome newcomers to the university scene. Rather than warming to the thought of tapping new wells of talent, the tendency is to speak of the new crop of university students as less well prepared than ever before, even though the expanded enrollments still include less than 20% of an age group.

Also under attack are the traditional forms of political democracy, including political parties. In their place the student protesters

---

[6] Peter Brooks, "French Student Power," *New Republic*, 158: 13-14, June 1, 1968.

would have "participatory democracy," where students and faculty run the universities, factory workers run the factories, and so on. In the case of universities, committees of faculty and students would decide everything, with unlimited freedom to discuss and to disseminate ideas and unlimited access to printing presses and other media of communication. These demands have become so extreme as to cause liberal faculty members to call for restoration of law and order, which the students interpret as a return to the French tradition of honoring the custodians of knowledge, *i.e.*, the professors.

Many of the liberal professors have been alienated by the tendency of the student activists, and the radical university instructors who support them, to redefine democracy to mean participation by all those who believe as they do. Those who disagree are ignored or even silenced by force if necessary. Freedom-loving activists see no inconsistency in shouting down someone from the other side who wishes to speak. The leader of the union representing mainly young radical instructors in the universities made this clear in describing the role of a group of student activists. "It represents the students in movement, not the inert ones, which in my opinion, gives it total representativity. The latter do not exist in a revolutionary period, only the former count."[7]

The call for participatory democracy reflects a deep lack in French life of genuine interaction of persons and groups.[8] The pattern has been strong rule from above and grudging acceptance of control from below, with little ability, or willingness, to share, to bargain, to cooperate. This lack of open participation is true of politics, of social life, and of life within schools and universities. Lacking in practical experience the student protesters call for an idealized state of participatory democracy which has little chance of succeeding. This all or nothing style of protest is typically French and inhibits social change.

The way to induce rapid social change, according to the student activists, is to have the universities assume the role of chief critic of society, not in the sense of traditional scholarly criticism but in some not clearly defined activist sense. Here the realities are a university system which prefers the 16th century over the 20th for purposes of

---

7 Hervé Bourges, ed., *The French Student Revolt: The Leaders Speak* (New York: Hill and Wang, 1968), p. 36.

8 For an analysis of this facet of French life, see Stanley Hoffman, "The French Psychodrama," *New Republic*, 158: 20-21, Aug. 31, 1968.

research, teaching, and examinations. Moreover, the verbalism of French education may cause the students to settle for heady slogans and ideologies.

The slogans are much in evidence as the students express deep misgivings about the present-day world with its computers, impersonalization, neglect of the hungry, and dehumanizing effects of technology. If students have acquired a deep understanding of these sophisticated developments, it suggests that they have been taught well in secondary schools and universities. This, in turn, calls into question the allegations of bad teaching and outmoded curriculum. It may be that the teaching has been better than students admit but far less than what their rising expectations tell them is desirable.

Most students, and young people generally, exhibit a lack of capacity to wait. A university education which prepares for life later is judged wanting, especially by liberal arts students. This seems to be less true of students of engineering and applied sciences, who use their newly acquired knowledge almost immediately. Since French universities give relatively little emphasis to applied subjects and fields the incapacity to wait syndrome is that much more powerful.

The waiting ended for French students soon after the recent outbreaks of student protest at Berkeley and Columbia in the U.S., and one is tempted to find a simplistic answer to the origin of French student protest by citing the foreign influence. The head of the National Union of French Students (UNEF), Jacques Sauvageot, has stated that the French student movement was aware of developments in other countries and influenced by them. Moreover, according to Sauvageot, student protest is inevitably international in character. He adds his opinion that the French movement had its own rather unique features namely, the existence of a group of university students "highly politicized," *i.e.,* more dedicated to political action than studies, and a student organization (UNEF) highly politicized.[9] This radicalization of the students is a reaction to the strict policy of French universities prohibiting any political activities or meetings on the campus. The ending of this ban was one of the major demands of the May, 1968, protesters, and the national government now has modified the rule to allow political meetings on university property.

The political tone of several of the leaders of the student protest

---

[9] Bourges, *op. cit.,* p. 14.

movement is so far to the left as to make Communism look conservative. This quite small group of French students is indulging in an orgy of mouthing revolutionary doctrine taken from Red China, Cuba, and the like. Raymond Aron, former head of an institute of sociology at the Sorbonne, has characterized these student activists as "anarchists, nihilists, ex-Communists . . . and a whole variety of aesthetes of destruction."[10]

The political tone of the organizations supporting the protest movement has turned radical also. This is especially true of the National Union of French Students, which enrolls approximately 14% of all university students and The National Union of Higher Education (SNE Sup), which claims to represent one-third of the teachers in the universities, especially the younger, more radical men below the rank of professor. The National Union of Higher Education ordered these university teachers into the streets in May, 1968, to man the barricades alongside the students. This union sees the older professors as part of the enemy camp, with privileges and powers far beyond what is desirable. In part, the SNE Sup's support of student protest is a tactic to redistribute power within the university structure—in effect taking power from the old and giving it to the young. This is a special kind of generation gap among adults and reflects the larger problem of generation gap between youth and adults.

France, like all other advanced, industrial nations, has the problem of generation gap. As the educational levels of the sons outstrip those of the fathers the two generations increasingly come to live in different worlds. The differences are accentuated as the young tend to think and act as a distinctive group and to assert their solidarity and their dislike of the adult world.[11] Add to this the fact that in France the tightly-knit family with the parents in control persisted through the 1950's. It could be that in the French student protest of the 1960's the French equivalent of the Victorian father has met his come-uppance.

Clearly the sons expect something different from the universities than did the previous generation. Bruno Bettelheim suggests that many of the new crop of university students are not interested in the

---

10 Aron, *op. cit.*, p. 23.

11 John Barron Mays, "Teen-Age Culture in Contemporary Britain and Europe," in Don Adams, ed., *Introduction to Education: A Comparative Analysis* (Belmont, Calif.: Wadsworth Publishing Co., 1966), p. 220.

knowledge offered, but rather want a group therapeutic activity to meet and satisfy their emotional needs. Since universities are not equipped to provide such experiences, the students are deeply dissatisfied and seek other outlets.[12] It is significant that several observors of the French student uprising, including the students themselves, report that it was an exhilarating experience. Robert Nisbit, in a different context, makes the same point by seeing boredom as an accompaniment of the loss of respect for authority in a social order, and boredom, in turn, links up with brute violence.[13] In the case of France, boredom, violence, and the need for therapy may be related to teaching methods which rob learning of any freshness, of joy, of any unpredictable qualities.

The poet, Stephen Spender, strolled among the students in the midst of the May, 1968, upheaval and characterized the scene as a breaking out of forces long suppressed, an outpouring of spontaneity, of participation, of communication, of imagination, of love.[14] Few educators in France would argue that schools have provided adequately for spontaneity, for participation, for communication (in spite of rampant verbalism), or for imagination, though imaginative literature is dissected to death. In short, the emotional side has been neglected presumably to develop the intellectual side. Here it is fitting to repeat Feuer's point that "student movements . . . are forms of vague, undefined emotions which seek for some issue, some cause, to which to attach themselves."[15]

---

12 Bruno Bettelheim, "The College Student Rebellion: Explanations and Answers," *Phi Delta Kappan*, 50: 512, May, 1969.

13 Robert A. Nisbit, "When Authority Falters Raw Power Moves In," *Washington Post*, Outlook Section, May 19, 1969.

14 Stephen Spender, "Paris in the Spring," *New York Review of Books*, 11: 18-20, July 11, 1968.

15 Feuer, *op. cit.*, p. 10.

40

CONFUSION AND HOPE:
STUDENT UNREST IN JAPAN

^^

VICTOR KOBAYASHI

EXCEPT DURING WORLD WAR II, when dissent was effectively suppressed, Japan has had an active and continuous history of student movements for more than 50 years. The first student strike took place at Keio University in 1879, but the student movement did not establish strong roots until the 1920's, the very time that Japan had established herself as the major Asian power in the Pacific. From its very outset, and to this day, the movement has been heavily influenced by Marxist ideology and has been oriented towards political and social reconstruction.

Today, student activists claim space in the nation's newspapers nearly daily. In the first half of 1969, almost a fourth of the nation's over 300 universities endured some form of student interruption of its activities. As many as 82 universities were suffering either class boycotts or barricaded buildings on a single day—April 9, 1969. Some of the disruptions have lasted continuously for several months. Sophia University was closed for over a hundred days in early 1969. After 253 days of occupancy by radicals of several structures, including the Administration Building and the offices of nine colleges, the authorities of Nihon University, Japan's largest university, regained control of its campus. The College of General Education of Japan's prestigious University of Tokyo opened classes, with still some inci-

---

Victor Kobayashi is Associate Professor of Education, University of Hawaii, Honolulu.

dents occurring, late in March, 1969, after being closed since the summer of 1968 due to a student strike. Another state university, the Tokyo University of Education ended an eight-month long student seizure late in March, 1969, when its acting president called in the police to aid in quelling the take-over. Its administration had to cancel entrance examinations for the next school year.[1]

These are only a few examples illustrating the seriousness of the Japanese "University Problem," as it often is called. Incidents involving students have taken place at every kind of university—private, national, prefectural, municipal, church-related, "name" universities, and even small, relatively unknown universities. Street fights, riot police, mass arrests, tear gas, helmets, water hoses, sticks and stones, heckling, lock-ups of professors and deans in barricaded buildings, injuries and occasional deaths, resignations of administrators, have become as much a part of Japanese campus life as Gingko trees and coffee houses. Commencements, entrance examinations, and enrollment ceremonies have become the occasions for intrusions by student radicals.

The turmoil recently has spread into the high schools, which have pupils affiliated with university student groups. Several graduation ceremonies in 1969 were interrupted by such incidents as the barricading of the commencement auditorium or the valedictorian departing from his traditional speech to condemn his schooling and the authoritarianism of the teachers. The National Police Agency estimates that 2,800 high school students belong to radical organizations, while about 20,000 are sympathizers.[2]

The immediate issues triggering the various confrontations range from international controversies (such as the Vietnam War) to national issues (such as the passage of the law establishing a national efficiency rating of school teachers by their superiors) to numerous intramural controversies about such matters as student control of dormitories, the enrollment of Self-Defense Force personnel in colleges. Private universities, which enroll about 70% of all college students, have been especially hit by protests originating out of

---

[1] Much space in Japanese popular journals have been devoted to the activities of student protesters. Some of the pictorial spreads even glamourize the life of a radical. See, for example, *Sande Mainichi*, Feb. 20, 1969. The entire issue, complete with color photographs of barricades and police clashes and a map of Japan showing afflicted campuses, is devoted to student unrest.

[2] *Japan Times*, March 1, 1969.

tuition increase decisions. The climbing costs of higher education have created a crisis for many private schools, which depend on student fees and tuition for their major source of income since they neither have major endowments as a rule, nor have significant grants from the state. The perennial financial problems of private universities have also led to a pupil-teacher ratio that is over three times that of national universities, and to the common practice of professors moonlighting at other colleges in order to increase their income.[3]

In 1966, Waseda University endured a six-month dispute with students sparked by a decision to raise tuition. After the long strike, the university, with a new president and board of trustees, was able to reopen the campus, after some concessions were made to the students. A strike over fee and tuition increases also took place the previous year at Keio University, which, with Waseda, is among the nation's most famous private universities.[4]

U.S.-Japan relations figure prominently in the issues taken up by student protestors. An estimated half of the university students took part in the strike expressing disapproval of the renewal of the *"Ampo"* (The Japan-U.S. Security Treaty) in 1960. Student demonstrations prevented President Eisenhower's visit to Japan, and helped to force Prime Minister Kishi's resignation, who nevertheless was successful in pushing through the treaty in the Diet. An estimated 100,000 students stormed into the Diet building in the 1960 *"Ampo"* riots, where a Tokyo University coed was trampled to death.[5] Anxiety is mounting because the treaty is up for renewal in 1970, and similar riots, perhaps more violent, seem to be in store.[6] The "Okinawa Day" riots, when thousands of students demonstrated throughout the nation, calling for the return of Okinawa to Japan,

---

[3] The average monthly salary in 1965 for a university teacher, age 55, was $276.60 in national universities, and $237.80 in private colleges. See Appendix X, "Salaries of Teaching Staff at Japanese Universities," *Journal of Social and Political Ideas in Japan*, 5: 302-304, December, 1967.

[4] For an excellent discussion of the Waseda strike, see Michiya Shimbori, "The Sociology of a Student Movement—A Japanese Case Study," *Daedalus*, 97: 204-228, Winter, 1968.

[5] A lengthy and useful analysis of the student movement in the 1960 anti-Security Treaty campaign is provided in Kazuko Tsurumi, "The Japanese Student Movement," *Japan Quarterly*, 15: 430-455, October-December, 1968; January-March, 1969 (in two parts).

[6] A government public opinion survey in January, 1969, had revealed that 19.6% of respondents said they were very concerned about the Treaty renewal, 41.9% said they felt a bit uneasy, and 13.6 reported no misgivings. *Japan Times*, April 16, 1969.

portend for many Japanese the impending crisis that will flare when the treaty is considered. Students stormed railway stations and put a halt to several major rail services. The riots took place on April 28, 1969, the 17th anniversary of the San Francisco Peace Treaty and of the occupation of the Ryūkyū Islands by the U.S.

The immediate and specific issues that trigger student outbursts comprise only one piece of a complex puzzle. As the controversy develops, other tensions emerge that transform the incident into a more complicated social problem. The Waseda University strike, for example, started as a protest against tuition hikes, but, as it progressed, various hidden emotional tones surfaced: the suspicion among authorities that the tuition issue was being exploited for larger, revolutionary political ends by professional radicals, students' concerns about their right to operate the Student Hall, faculty fear of government and police intervention into university affairs, and the feeling among students that much of university education was impersonal and meaningless.

Another part of the puzzle has been the nature of the student activists. Besides those who sporadically participate in demonstrations, there are a minority of hard-core members of the Zengakuren (National Federation of Student Self-Governing Associations) who, due to its variety in ideologic hues, comprise a complicated sub-puzzle in itself. The nature of the Zengakuren associations vary not only from school to school, but within each campus are competing factions. Student movements everywhere tend to be plagued by internal dissension among their organizations, perhaps because youth are so vigorous in debates about their ideology. But in Japan, hard-core Zengakuren factions are so hostile to each other that they have violent public clashes, sometimes in the midst of a student confrontation with a university administration. A major clash occurred, for example in February, 1969, when one faction attempted to disrupt a meeting of the other on the Kyoto University campus. In the ensuing melee that involved Molotov cocktails, staves, and water cannons, about 150 students were injured and university property was damaged.

In general, there are two main categories of the Zengakuren and both are leftist in ideology. The Minsei (Democratic Youth League), often referred to by the press as the "moderate faction," is affiliated with the Japan Communist Party and seeks to change Japanese society through non-violent means. This policy is in agreement with that of the Japan Communist Party, which over ten years ago renounced the use of violence in promoting a Communist society. However, Minsei members accept the use of violence in fighting their rival student groups on the principle of self-defense, claiming that their rival, which they label "Trotskyite," has been the aggressor in these clashes.

The more radical category of the Zengakuren groups is the so-called "anti-Yoyogi" camp (because the Japan Communist Party has its headquarters in the Yoyogi district of Tokyo). It is itself split into several factions, all ideologically unique, but all in agreement that the Japan Communist Party has "sold out" on the "Revolution." The major "anti-Yoyogi" group is the Sampa Rengo (Three Faction Alliance), since it itself is a coalition of three sub-factions, which considers the established Communist parties in Japan, China, and the U.S.S.R. corrupt. Although the *Sampa* is more committed to violence in their dealings with the establishment, authorities seem to dread the pro-Communist Party faction more, since it is stronger in numbers and has the greater potential for growth. It is believed that the Minsei faction can muster about 35,000 students for a demonstration, while the anti-Yoyogi group about 30,000.[7]

Right-winged student groups, characterized by their emphasis upon patriotism and anti-Marxism, have always sprung up in the history of student movements in Japan. So far, none has played a major role in acting as a counterforce in student demonstrations, although there is the possibility of a strong reaction forming with radical groups becoming more vociferous. One of the recently formed national organizations is the National Liaison Council for Student Self-Government Organizations (Zenkokugakukyo) which met early in May, 1969, in a conference attended by an estimated 1,500 students. Besides working for the recovery of lands lost to the Soviet Union after World War II, members hope to gain control of the student self-governing associations of the various universities and thus take over the Zengakuren.

The lack of trust that pervades the relationships between groups within the student movement is also characteristic of the national political milieu within which the students operate. Opposition political parties are suspicious of the moves made by the conservative Liberal Democratic Party in its attempts to solve the university

[7] Kiyoaki Murata, "'Moderates' Start Resorting to Force," *Japan Times,* Feb. 23, 1969.

crisis. Faculty disagree with each other as well as with administrators as to which course the university should take in order to alleviate the problem of student unrest. University administrators are fearful of losing their autonomy and academic freedom of their universities, and have, as one official pointed out, an "allergy" to police—they are most reluctant to call in the police to help quell even the most severe disturbances. Academicians often suspect that the government is attempting to exert a stronger hold over universities; they remember the dark days of the thirties and early forties, when educational institutions were made pawns of chauvinistic and militaristic interests. The government has repeatedly urged universities to call in the police whenever violence occurs on their campuses. The National Public Safety Commission has insisted that the university take a tough stance in its approach to dissident students, and has blamed college administrators for escalating the conflict by failing to take quick action against illegal acts on campus. The Commission chairman has even charged some of the university presidents for siding with the student radicals. The Ministry of Education also has consistently requested that universities cooperate with the police, but its requests have been publicly criticized by liberal faculty and college presidents. On April 21, 1969, the Ministry issued a more explicit directive that not only called for greater contact between the university and law enforcement officers, but also allowed the police to intervene whenever there are incidents that threaten lives. The understanding up to this time has been that police could not enter the campus unless specifically authorized by the university. Furthermore, the Central Education Council, an advisory body to the Ministry of Education, has also recommended that the Ministry be given greater power to intervene in settling campus disorders.

The Council, in its proposals of April 30, 1969, also disapproved of universities permitting student representatives to participate in decision-making. Several universities, including the University of Tokyo, had recently been adopting measures to increase student participation in the decision-making structure, including a say in the selection of presidents. Various groups, such as the major opposition parties, the Japan Teachers Union, and liberal professors have spoken out publicly against the government's proposals and recommendations. Several university presidents, including that of the University of Tokyo and of Osaka University, have sharply criticized the government moves. To add to the tense, polarized atmosphere, student groups have included the government's attempts to intervene in university affairs in their long list of occasions when snake dances and street fights are called for to express disapproval of authority. The Ministry Directive of April 21, for example, was met with nation-wide rallies and clashes with the police.

The political atmosphere is thus charged with paranoia and a lack of faith in the credibility of extant forms of legal procedures to bring about social order. What is happening is a general questioning of various forms of formal authority, and a frantic, often confusing, search by intellectuals, student radicals, and other alienated groups to reconstruct Japanese society in the name of peace, democratic participation, and freedom. Despite their economic affluence, they are frankly woried about the rebirth of fascism and a return to the militarism that led Japan to a disastrous war. And then, of course, there is the specter of the Bomb. Whether they are hard-core activists or not, many students seem alienated from the existing social structure, and are groping for new meanings in their relationship to the society. They can neither return to the relationships defined by the feudal past with all its cultural glories, nor remain within existing political, economic, and social forms which seem to breed war and inhumanity.[8]

With the United States and other advanced nations now having their share of student alienation that seems to be expressed in more violent forms, and with student unrest so widespread throughout the world, the Japanese case requires an interpretation that takes into account the whole problem of the modern world. No longer can student turmoil be explained only in terms of local conditions, like Japan's notorious university entrance examination system, or the economic conditions of Japanese students; it also must be understood as part of the social strains that the entire world is presently undergoing in the general process called "modernization." The student attempts at making a breakthrough may often appear confusing, misdirected, and threatening, but the gestures express the effort to arrive at hope in the future.

". . . Loneliness is the price we have to pay for being born in this modern age, so full of freedom, independence, and our own egotisti-

---

8 A thoughtful discussion of the psychological problems of Japanese youth is Robert Jay Lifton's, "Youth and History: Individual Change in Postwar Japan," in Erik H. Erikson, ed., *The Challenge of Youth* (Garden City, N.Y.: Anchor Books, Doubleday, 1965), pp. 260-290.

cal selves," said the old teacher in *Kokoro*, a book by Natsume Soseki, the great novelist of the Meiji Period (1868-1912), when Japan first entered the modern world.[9] If youth is the time when the loneliness is most intense, then it also may provide the greatest energies, and hope, in the search for home.

---

[9] Natsume Soseki, *Kokoro*, Gateway Edition, translated by Edwin McClellan (Chicago: Henry Regnery, c. 1957), p. 30.

PART III

~~~~~~

Documents on
Student Unrest:
A National Dialogue

COMPILED BY STANLEY LEHRER

The collection of official statements, letters, and addresses on the following pages represents most of the serious responses to student unrest in the United States between mid-1967 and mid-1969. Introductory notes were prepared for every selection. William W. Brickman provided some of the documents.

S. L.

JOINT STATEMENT ON RIGHTS
AND FREEDOMS OF STUDENTS

In June, 1967, a joint committee, comprised of representatives from the American Association of University Professors, U.S. National Student Association, Association of American Colleges, National Association of Student Personnel Administrators, and National Association of Women Deans and Counselors, met in Washington, D. C., and drafted the "Joint Statement on Rights and Freedoms of Students," the text of which is published below.

The multilateral approach which produced this document also was applied to the complicated matter of interpretation, implementation, and enforcement, with the drafting committee recommending (a) joint efforts to promote acceptance of the new standards on the institutional level, (b) the establishment of machinery to facilitate continuing joint interpretation, (c) joint consultation before setting up any machinery for mediating disputes or investigating complaints, and (d) joint approaches to regional accrediting agencies to seek embodiment of the new principles in standards for accreditation.

Since its formulation, the joint statement has been endorsed by each of its five national sponsors as well as by a number of other professional bodies. The endorsers are: U.S. National Student Association; Association of American Colleges; American Association of University Professors; National Association of Student Personnel Administrators; National Association of Women Deans and Counselors; American Association for Higher Education; Jesuit Education Association; American College Personnel Association; Executive Committee, College and University Department, National Catholic Education Association; and Commission on Student Personnel, American Association of Junior Colleges.

From *AAUP Bulletin*, Summer, 1968, published by the American Association of University Professors. Reprinted by permission of the managing editor. Copyright, 1968, by *AAUP Bulletin*.

Preamble

Academic institutions exist for the transmission of knowledge, the pursuit of truth, the development of students, and the general well-being of society. Free inquiry and free expression are indispensable to the attainment of these goals. As members of the academic community, students should be encouraged to develop the capacity for critical judgment and to engage in a sustained and independent search for truth. Institutional procedures for achieving these purposes may vary from campus to campus, but the minimal standards of academic freedom of students outlined below are essential to any community of scholars.

Freedom to teach and freedom to learn are inseparable facets of academic freedom. The freedom to learn depends upon appropriate opportunities and conditions in the classroom, on the campus, and in the larger community. Students should exercise their freedom with responsibility.

The responsibility to secure and to respect general conditions conducive to the freedom to learn is shared by all members of the academic community. Each college and university has a duty to develop policies and procedures which provide and safeguard this freedom. Such policies and procedures should be developed at each institution within the framework of general standards and with the broadest possible participation of the members of the academic community. The purpose of this statement is to enumerate the essential provisions for student freedom to learn.

I. Freedom of Access to Higher Education

The admissions policies of each college and university are a matter of institutional choice provided that each college and university makes clear the characteristics and expectations of students which it considers relevant to success in the institution's program. While church-related institutions may give admission preference to students of their own persuasion, such a preference should be clearly and publicly stated. Under no circumstances should a student be barred from admission to a particular institution on the basis of race. Thus, within the limits of its facilities, each college and university should be open to all students who are qualified according to its admission standards. The facilities and services of a college should be open to all of its enrolled students, and institutions should use their influence to secure equal access for all students to public facilities in the local community.

II. In the Classroom

The professor in the classroom and in conference should encourage free discussion, inquiry, and expression. Student performance should be evaluated solely on an academic basis, not on opinions or conduct in matters unrelated to academic standards.

A. *Protection of Freedom of Expression*

Students should be free to take reasoned exception to the data or views offered in any course of study and to reserve judgment about matters of opinion, but they are responsible for learning the content of any course of study for which they are enrolled.

B. *Protection against Improper Academic Evaluation*

Students should have protection through orderly procedures against prejudiced or capricious academic evaluation. At the same time, they are responsible for maintaining standards of academic performance established for each course in which they are enrolled.

C. *Protection against Improper Disclosure*

Information about student views, beliefs, and political associations which professors acquire in the course of their work as instructors, advisers, and counselors should be considered confidential. Protection against improper disclosure is a serious professional obligation. Judgments of ability and character may be provided under appropriate circumstances, normally with the knowledge or consent of the student.

III. Student Records

Institutions should have a carefully considered policy as to the information which should be part of a student's permanent educational record and as to the conditions of its disclosure. To minimize the risk of improper disclosure, academic and disciplinary records should be separate, and the conditions of access to each should be set forth in an explicit policy statement. Transcripts of academic records should contain only information about academic status. Information from disciplinary or counseling files should not be available to unauthorized persons on campus, or to any persons off campus without the express consent of the student involved except under legal compulsion or in cases where the safety of persons or property is involved. No records should be kept which reflect the political activities or beliefs of students. Provisions should also be made for periodic routine destruction of noncurrent disciplinary records. Administrative staff and faculty members should respect confidential information about students which they acquire in the course of their work.

IV. Student Affairs

In student affairs, certain standards must be maintained if the freedom of students is to be preserved.

A. *Freedom of Association*

Students bring to the campus a variety of interests previously acquired and develop many new interests as members of the academic community. They should be free to organize and join associations to promote their common interests.

1. The membership, policies, and actions of a student organization usually will be determined by vote of only those persons who hold bona fide membership in the college or university community.

2. Affiliation with an extramural organization should not of itself disqualify a student organization from institutional recognition.

3. If campus advisers are required, each organization should be free to choose its own adviser, and institutional recognition should not be withheld or withdrawn solely because of the inability of a student organization to secure an adviser. Campus advisers may advise organizations in the exercise of responsibility, but they should not have the authority to control the policy of such organizations.

4. Student organizations may be required to submit a statement of purpose, criteria for membership, rules of procedures, and a current list of officers. They should not be required to submit a membership list as a condition of institutional recognition.

5. Campus organizations, including those affiliated with an extramural organization, should be open to all students without respect to race, creed, or national origin, except for religious qualifications which may be required by organizations whose aims are primarily sectarian.

B. *Freedom of Inquiry and Expression*

1. Students and student organizations should be free to examine and discuss all questions of interest to them, and to express opinions publicly and privately. They should always be free to support causes by orderly means which do not disrupt the regular and essential operation of the institution. At the same time, it should be made clear to the academic and the larger community that in their public expressions or demonstrations students or student organizations speak only for themselves.

2. Students should be allowed to invite and to hear any person of their own choosing. Those routine procedures required by an institution before a guest speaker is invited to appear on campus should be designed only to insure that there is orderly scheduling of facilities and adequate preparation for the event, and that the occasion is conducted in a manner appropriate to an academic community. The institutional control of campus facilities should not be used as a device of censorship. It should be made clear to the academic and larger community that sponsorship of guest speakers does not necessarily imply approval or endorsement of the views expressed, either by the sponsoring group or the institution.

C. *Student Participation in Institutional Government*

As constituents of the academic community, students should be free, individually and collectively, to express their views on issues of institutional policy and on matters of general interest to the student body. The student body should have clearly defined means to participate in the formulation and application of institutional policy affecting academic and student affairs. The role of the student government and both its general and specific responsibilities should be made explicit, and the actions of the student government within the areas of its jurisdiction should be reviewed only through orderly and prescribed procedures.

D. *Student Publications*

Student publications and the student press are a valuable aid in establishing and maintaining an atmosphere of free and responsible discussion and of intellectual exploration on the campus. They are a means of bringing student concerns to the attention of the faculty and the institutional authorities and of formulating student opinion on various issues on the campus and in the world at large.

Whenever possible the student newspaper should be an independent corporation financially and legally separate from the university. Where financial and legal autonomy is not possible, the institution, as the publisher of student publications, may have to bear the legal responsibility for the contents of the publications. In the delegation of editorial responsibility to students the institution must provide sufficient editorial freedom and financial autonomy for the student publications to maintain their integrity of purpose as vehicles for free inquiry and free expression in an academic community.

Institutional authorities, in consultation with students and faculty, have a responsibility to provide written clarification of the role of the student publications, the standards to be used in their evaluation, and the limitations on external control of their operation. At the same time, the editorial freedom of student editors and managers entails corollary responsibilities to be governed by the canons of responsible journalism, such as the avoidance of libel, indecency, undocumented allegations, attacks on personal integrity, and the techniques of harrassment and innuendo. As safeguards for the editorial freedom of student publications the following provisions are necessary.

1. The student press should be free of censorship and advance approval of copy, and its editors and managers should be free to develop their own editorial policies and news coverage.

2. Editors and managers of student publications should be protected from arbitrary suspension and removal because of student, faculty, administrative, or public disapproval of editorial policy or content. Only for proper and stated causes should editors and managers be subject to removal and then by orderly and prescribed procedures. The agency responsible for the

appointment of editors and managers should be the agency responsible for their removal.

3. All university published and financed student publications should explicitly state on the editorial page that the opinions there expressed are not necessarily those of the college, university, or student body.

V. Off-Campus Freedom of Students

A. *Exercise of Rights of Citizenship*

College and university students are both citizens and members of the academic community. As citizens, students should enjoy the same freedom of speech, peaceful assembly, and right of petition that other citizens enjoy and, as members of the academic community, they are subject to the obligations which accrue to them by virtue of this membership. Faculty members and administrative officials should insure that institutional powers are not employed to inhibit such intellectual and personal development of students as is often promoted by their exercise of the rights of citizenship both on and off campus.

B. *Institutional Authority and Civil Penalties*

Activities of students may upon occasion result in violation of law. In such cases, institutional officials should be prepared to apprise students of sources of legal counsel and may offer other assistance. Students who violate the law may incur penalties prescribed by civil authorities, but institutional authority should never be used merely to duplicate the function of general laws. Only where the institution's interests as an academic community are distinct and clearly involved should the special authority of the institution be asserted. The student who incidentally violates institutional regulations in the course of his off-campus activity, such as those relating to class attendance, should be subject to no greater penalty than would normally be imposed. Institutional action should be independent of community pressure.

VI. Procedural Standards in Disciplinary Proceedings

In developing responsible student conduct, disciplinary proceedings play a role substantially secondary to example, counseling, guidance, and admonition. At the same time, educational institutions have a duty and the corollary disciplinary powers to protect their educational purpose through the setting of standards of scholarship and conduct for the students who attend them and through the regulation of the use of institutional facilities. In the exceptional circumstances when the preferred means fail to resolve problems of student conduct, proper procedural safeguards should be observed to protect the student from the unfair imposition of serious penalties.

The administration of discipline should guarantee procedural fairness to an accused student. Practices in disciplinary cases may vary in formality with the gravity of the offense and the sanctions which may be applied. They should also take into account the presence or absence of an honor code, and the degree to which the institutional officials have direct acquaintance with student life in general and with the involved student and the circumstances of the case in particular. The jurisdictions of faculty or student judicial bodies, the disciplinary responsibilities of institutional officials and the regular disciplinary procedures, including the student's right to appeal a decision, should be clearly formulated and communicated in advance. Minor penalties may be assessed informally under prescribed procedures.

In all situations, procedural fair play requires that the student be informed of the nature of the charges against him, that he be given a fair opportunity to refute them, that the institution not be arbitrary in its actions, and that there be provision for appeal of a decision. The following are recommended as proper safeguards in such proceedings when there are no honor codes offering comparable guarantees.

A. *Standards of Conduct Expected of Students*

The institution has an obligation to clarify those standards of behavior which it considers essential to its educational mission and its community life. These general behavioral expectations and the resultant specific regulations should represent a reasonable regulation of student conduct, but the student should be as free as possible from imposed limitations that have no direct relevance to his education. Offenses should be as clearly defined as possible and interpreted in a manner consistent with the aforementioned principles of relevancy and reasonableness. Disciplinary proceedings should be instituted only for violations of standards of conduct formulated with significant student participation and published in advance through such means as a student handbook or a generally available body of institutional regulations.

B. *Investigation of Student Conduct*

1. Except under extreme emergency circumstances, premises occupied by students and the personal possessions of students should not be searched unless appropriate authorization has been obtained. For premises such as residence halls controlled by the institution, an appropriate and responsible authority should be designated to whom application should be made before a search is conducted. The application should specify the reasons for the search and the objects or information sought. The student should be present, if possible, during the search. For premises not controlled by the institution, the ordinary requirements for lawful search should be followed.

2. Students detected or arrested in the course of serious violations of institutional regulations, or infractions of ordinary law, should be informed of their rights. No form of harassment should be used by institutional representatives to coerce admissions of guilt or information about conduct of other suspected persons.

C. *Status of Student Pending Final Action*

Pending action on the charges, the status of a student should not be altered, or his right to be present on the campus and to attend classes suspended, except for reasons relating to his physical or emotional safety and well-being, or for reasons relating to the safety and well-being of students, faculty, or university property.

D. *Hearing Committee Procedures*

When the misconduct may result in serious penalties and if the student questions the fairness of disciplinary action taken against him, he should be granted, on request, the privilege of a hearing before a regularly constituted hearing committee. The following suggested hearing committee procedures satisfy the requirements of procedural due process in situations requiring a high degree of formality.

1. The hearing committee should include faculty members or students, or, if regularly included or requested by the accused, both faculty and student members. No member of the hearing committee who is otherwise interested in the particular case should sit in judgment during the proceeding.

2. The student should be informed, in writing, of the reasons for the proposed disciplinary action with sufficient particulars, and in sufficient time, to insure opportunity to prepare for the hearing.

3. The student appearing before the hearing committee should have the right to be assisted in his defense by an adviser of his choice.

4. The burden of proof should rest upon the officials bringing the charge.

5. The student should be given an opportunity to testify and to present evidence and witnesses. He should have an opportunity to hear and question adverse witnesses. In no case should the committee consider statements against him unless he has been advised of their content and of the names of those who made them, and unless he has been given an opportunity to rebut unfavorable inferences which might otherwise be drawn.

6. All matters upon which the decision may be based must be introduced into evidence at the proceeding before the hearing committee. The decision should be based solely upon such matters. Improperly acquired evidence should not be admitted.

7. In the absence of a transcript, there should be both a digest and a verbatim record, such as a tape recording, of the hearing.

8. The decision of the hearing committee should be final, subject only to the student's right of appeal to the president or ultimately to the governing board of the institution.

READMISSION OF STUDENTS REJECTING THE DRAFT

The American Civil Liberties Union has called upon universities to readmit qualified students who go to jail "rather than participate in a war they feel is morally indefensible." In a statement sent to 630 college presidents in the spring of 1968, the ACLU said that to refuse to readmit a student who prefers imprisonment to military service because his moral convictions against the war are so deeply rooted is to "punish him twice for the same offense and run[s] counter to the spirit of a basic principle of American justice embedded in the Fifth Amendment safeguard against double jeopardy."

The statement, prepared by the ACLU's Academic Freedom Committee, after a review of the civil liberties aspect of the problem, was sent to the college presidents with a letter signed by John de J. Pemberton, Executive Director, ACLU, and Samuel Hendel, Professor of Political Science, City College of New York, and chairman of the committee.

Although opposition to the war in Vietnam has been growing in intensity among all segments of the population, the strongest protest continues to come from college and university students. Many graduate and undergraduate students have been engaging in acts of resistance to Selective Service regulations and opposition to the war, often at the risk of incurring severe legal penalties.

The recent government ruling ending blanket deferments for graduate students raises the probability that students, in increasing numbers, will be moved to refuse induction into the armed forces and go to prison rather than participate in a war they feel is morally indefensible. The educational future of graduate and undergraduate students who choose this alternative is an issue of major concern to the academic community.

From *School & Society*, Oct. 12, 1968. Reprinted by permission of the publisher.

The Academic Freedom Committee of the American Civil Liberties Union believes that the student whose moral convictions against the war are so deeply rooted that he prefers imprisonment to military service is entitled to the opportunity to resume his education when he is free to do so. To refuse him this opportunity, after he has paid the penalty imposed by society, would be to punish him twice for the same offense and run counter to the spirit of a basic principle of American justice embedded in the Fifth Amendment safeguard against double jeopardy.

The Committee holds, therefore, that it is incumbent on colleges and universities to assure qualified students in these circumstances that their applications for readmission will be honored without prejudice to eligibility for financial aid.

The Committee notes that the graduate faculties at several leading universities, including Princeton, Harvard, Yale and Columbia, have already adopted policies providing for the readmission of students in good standing whose education has been interrupted as a consequence of the war. These policies have been framed broadly to include students who have served time in jail and, in some instances, have been made applicable on a university-wide basis. The Committee commends these institutions and urges the faculties at colleges and universities throughout the country to formulate policy along similar lines.

A policy of this nature does not embody political implications or judgments; nor does it encourage violation of law. As an expression of confidence in the integrity of those members of the student body who make a decision grounded in strong moral conviction, it will, however, foster a relationship of mutual trust and respect between teacher and student and contribute to an atmosphere of intellectual freedom on campus.

THE DISRUPTION OF THE EDUCATIONAL OPERATIONS OF ACADEMIC INSTITUTIONS IN THE COURSE OF DEMONSTRATIONS

On April 28, 1968, the Council of the American Association of University Professors authorized the immediate release of the following statement.

The outgoing and incoming Presidents of the American Association of University Professors today strongly endorsed and amplified a resolution passed by the Association's Fifty-fourth Annual Meeting condemning actions taken to disrupt the educational operations of academic institutions in the course of demonstrations.

Ralph S. Brown, Jr., of Yale University Law School, the new President of the Association, together with outgoing President Clark Byse of the Harvard Law School and Bertram H. Davis, the Association's General Secretary, made their remarks at the close of meetings in connection with the professors' gathering.

Brown said that he believed that it was particularly important for the leading faculty organization in the United States to recognize as disruptive the participation by individual faculty members in some demonstrations which have led to the occupation of campus buildings and the halting of ordinary academic pursuits, the detaining of faculty and administrative officers, and even threats of physical harm.

Byse and Davis emphasized the commitment of the AAUP to a campus structure in which faculty, students, and administrators can exercise their academic freedom. They pointed out that the Annual Meeting had just endorsed a *Joint Statement on Rights and Freedoms of Students* which is to serve as a charter for the recognition of a strong and proper student role on

From *AAUP Bulletin*, Summer, 1968, published by the American Association of University Professors. Reprinted by permission of the managing editor. Copyright, 1968, by *AAUP Bulletin*.

campus. The Statement called, they said, for the right of students to "be free to support causes by orderly means which do not disrupt the regular and essential operations of the institutions."

The Council of the Association asked the two Presidents and the General Secretary to make the public statement in view of the continued and widespread problem of disruption on American campuses. The Association had earlier released a statement condemning both efforts to prevent speakers from appearing on campus in the form of speaker ban laws and efforts to prevent invited speakers from giving their talks once they arrived.

A MESSAGE TO ALUMNI, PARENTS, AND OTHER FRIENDS OF COLUMBIA

~~~~~~

The following statement was distributed from the office of Pres. Grayson Kirk, Columbia University, on June 1, 1968.

As you know all too well, many serious events have occurred on the Columbia campus in recent weeks. Because it concerns you deeply, I know that you have been following closely the reporting by the press and the broadcast media of the events that have so disrupted the closing weeks of our academic year. This reporting has been extensive but, necessarily, it has been disjointed and fragmentary. As friends of Columbia University you should have some information about these happenings directly from the president's office.

Ever since the outbreak of violence that swept over our Morningside campus in the days following April twenty-third I have wanted to be in communication with you. I have wanted to give you a full and objective account of the events as they came upon us and to tell you why we moved when and as we did to cope with them. Unfortunately, my colleagues and I have been so caught up in the fast-moving sequence of developments that we have had no time until now to prepare such an account. Still less have we had sufficient time to analyze these events and to reflect upon their meaning, in policy terms, for the future life and growth of the University that means so much to all of us.

In time, of course, many detailed accounts will be written, but we cannot wait for them because you, more than the general public, have a special and proper concern over what has been taking place; others, in particular your non-Columbia friends, will expect you to have information from official sources. Hence, on the eve of Commencement I have decided to send you this interim message giving you my personal answers to some of the

~~~~~~

From *School & Society*, Oct. 26, 1968. Reprinted by permission of the publisher.

questions that are being asked by our friends and the concerned public.

I am sure I do not need to recount for you in detail the facts of the disruptions that have occurred.[1] On the afternoon of April twenty-third, a group of students consisting chiefly of members of the Students Afro-American Society (SAS) and the Columbia chapter of Students for a Democratic Society (SDS) occupied Hamilton Hall and held the Acting Dean of the College, Henry S. Coleman, hostage for nearly twenty-four hours. Shortly before six a.m. the following morning, the white students participating in the occupation left Hamilton and forced their way into Low Library, injuring one of our security guards in the process. These SDS students then broke into the suite of offices on the second floor occupied by Dr. Truman, myself and our secretarial staffs, and proceeded to barricade themselves inside. At about ten p.m. on the same day other students seized Avery and by the next morning they had barricaded all entrances to that building. At four a.m. on April twenty-fifth, Fayerweather Hall was seized and shortly after midnight on Friday, April twenty-sixth, the Mathematics Building (formerly the home of the School of Engineering) was broken into and occupied. In the melee at Mathematics a janitor was injured and hospitalized. Thus, by Friday morning, four of our principal buildings, plus my own offices in Low Library were in illegal occupancy.

After long and fruitless efforts at discussion and negotiation by officers of the administration, many devoted faculty members and helpful persons from outside the University, it became clear that the administration had only two possible courses of action. We could either grant the student demands, including full amnesty for all participants, or we could request the City police to remove the students by force. We were not willing under any circumstances to grant amnesty for these illegal acts, so we began to make the necessary arrangements for police action. In the early morning hours of Tuesday, April thirtieth, a force of more than 1,000 police removed the students from the occupied buildings. More than 700 arrests were made (including over 500 students), mostly for criminal trespass, though some persons resisted arrest and were so charged. About 100 persons were treated for injuries. Three persons were hospitalized, two of them policemen, and at the time of this writing the two policemen were still in the hospital.

Thereafter, the SDS, joined by others, called for a student strike. After a

---

[1] A full account of the events of April 23-30 was given by Dr. David B. Truman, vice president and provost of the university, in a television program three days after the buildings were cleared. The program, entitled "The Columbia Crisis," and broadcast "live" over the Educational Television Network, was arranged and conducted by students in the Columbia University Graduate School of Journalism. A transcript of the program, edited for brevity, is available on written request to Dr. Truman's office.

few days when feelings ran high on all sides as a consequence of the emotional shock produced by the police action, most of our classes, except for those in Columbia College, the School of Architecture and the School of General Studies, resumed normal operation. In those divisions of the University where disruption continued because of sympathy with the strike, many classes continued to be held off-campus, in the homes of professors, or in other buildings in the vicinity.

Other disruptions occurred later. On the evening of Friday, May seventeenth, the SDS, together with some people in the neighborhood who have opposed Columbia's physical expansion on Morningside Heights, held a rally and then forcibly occupied an old and partially empty apartment building owned by the University on 114th Street between Broadway and Riverside Drive. They announced that they proposed to remain in the building until the University changed its housing and expansion policy. The City police were called in at once and later in the night the building was cleared of its illegal occupants. More than 100 arrests were made—about one-half students—but the clearing operation was carried out without violence and no injuries occurred.

On the afternoon of May twenty-first, certain students, including the SDS leader, Mark Rudd, had been directed to appear before five p.m. in the office of the Associate Dean for Student Affairs of Columbia College for a disciplinary hearing relating to their part in the previous disturbances. These students challenged the legality of the hearing, announced that they would not appear, and about four p.m. convoked a study rally at the sun-dial which culminated in a march to Hamilton Hall and its reoccupation by the students.

The Joint Disciplinary Committee—to which reference will be made later—had recommended that a student who failed to appear before the Dean when summoned for a disciplinary hearing should be suspended. An announcement was made after five p.m. that the summoned students who had refused to appear had been suspended. With the authorization of my office the Acting Dean of the College then announced to the occupants of Hamilton Hall that since they had ignored his order to leave the building, the University would summon the police to evict them by force if necessary, and that any students arrested would be subject to suspension.

At about 2:30 a.m., May twenty-second, the police arrived on campus and cleared the building. Approximately 100 students and 30 outsiders were arrested. The evacuation of the building was handled in a rapid and orderly manner.

Almost immediately, however, further trouble developed. More than half of the students in Hamilton had left before the police arrived. Some of them and others who had not been in the building now began to attack other buildings. Paving bricks were thrown through nearly twenty plate-glass windows. Glass doors were broken and fires were set in both Hamilton and Fayerweather Halls. Irreplaceable notes in one professor's office were deliberately burned.

Hundreds of persons were roaming the campus in this orgy of destruction. The threat to the University was so great that, after consultation with my senior administrative associates, I requested the City police to return and clear the entire campus. An announcement of this decision was broadcast immediately over the student radio station and over bull-horns to the crowds. Warning was given that all persons who refused to leave the campus would be subject to arrest.

In this operation, carried out shortly before five a.m., numerous arrests were made and a substantial number of civilian and police casualties occurred. The University carried on its usual operations the next day, although access to the campus was controlled by the same inspection of Columbia identification cards that has been the practice on the days immediately following the first police action.

In a public statement made in the early morning hours, I concluded with these words:

> The essential activities that constitute the life of this and every other university—teaching, discussions among faculty and students, scholarly and scientific investigation—cannot be carried on in an atmosphere of actual or threatened violence.
>
> There may have been some disbelief on the part of some of the rebellious students that the University would ever discipline large numbers of students. I think it important for me to state that if disciplinary probation, suspension, or even permanent expulsion must be dealt to any number of students, this action will be taken. Columbia University must and will honor its commitment to educate those students who genuinely want what a great university can provide them.

Since that time the campus has been reasonably quiet, though filled with rumors of impending trouble. It is the earnest hope of the administration and the great majority of our faculty and students that calm will continue and reason prevail.

Let me now undertake to answer some of the questions which I am sure are in your minds about these disruptions.

On the occasion of the first occupation of buildings, why did you delay for several days the decision to call in the police to remove the trespassers?

There were three reasons for the delay. First, my colleagues and I were well aware of the strong feeling that permeates all American universities against the use of municipal police for any purpose on university property. The ancient and traditional view that a university should be a sanctuary where police are not supposed to intervene has influenced academic attitudes in this country. Moreover, the magnitude of the problem we faced, as evidenced by the number of arrests actually made, was such that any police action inevitably would be accompanied by physical injuries, and this, we knew, would leave emotional scars among faculty and students that would not easily or quickly disappear. Hence, we felt strongly that police action should be postponed until all other alternatives were exhausted. My concern on this point was borne out by the fact that many persons who had been previously unsympathetic to the aims of the SDS joined in the demonstrations against the University administration on May first and second after the police action.

Second, there was a natural and serious concern at City Hall, which we shared, about the possible reactions of our neighbors in Harlem to the use of police in Hamilton Hall. As indicated, Hamilton was entirely occupied by black students and, in view of what had happened in Harlem following the assassination of Dr. Martin Luther King, the possibility of actions directed against the University had to be weighed carefully.

Third, many of our senior faculty members honestly and sincerely believed that, given more time, they could negotiate a peaceful settlement. They devoted long hours of work toward this end, and we felt that the University should not move with force until it was clear that their efforts would not be successful.

It may well be, with hindsight, that we should have moved earlier, as we were naturally tempted to do, but I still believe that we followed the course best calculated to uphold the dignity and integrity of the University. At no time did timidity or indecision affect our conclusions.

Were many persons unconnected with the University involved in the occupancy of the buildings?

One reason, I am sure, why Columbia was considered to be a natural target for this assault was the obvious fact that the demonstrators could so easily swell their ranks by calling in reinforcements from other parts of the New York metropolitan area. When the buildings were cleared, approximately 26 percent of those arrested were not Columbia students. The arrest list included some radical agitators and many such leaders are known to have been in and out of our buildings during the occupation.

What were the demands of the students?

Although the precise wording varied from time to time and from one group to another, there were six basic demands frequently listed as preconditions that the University must meet before the students would consider evacuating the occupied buildings. They were:

1. Construction of the gymnasium in Morningside Park must be terminated.

2. The University must sever all ties with the Institute for Defense Analyses, including the withdrawal from the IDA Board of Trustees of both William A. M. Burden (a public member of the IDA Board and a Columbia Trustee) and the President of the University.

3. The establishment of a permanent student-faculty Commission, democratically elected, to hear and pass binding judgment on all future disciplinary matters.

4. All legal charges against student and nonstudent demonstrators to be dropped.

5. All University disciplinary action against student demonstrators to be dropped.

6. Existing University regulations prohibiting indoor demonstrations to be rescinded.

What did you do about these demands before calling in the police?

1. The Gymnasium

I will discuss later the background of the gymnasium problem. At this time, let me say merely that at the request of Mayor Lindsay, and in view of the strong sentiment expressed by some faculty groups, the Trustees, in an endeavor to calm the troubled situation, authorized me to say that they had agreed, without prejudice to continuation at a later time, to suspend construction of the gymnasium pending further discussions with community leaders and other interested parties. The announcement of this decision was made on Thursday night, April twenty-fifth.

2. The Institute for Defense Analyses

This organization was created in 1956 at the request of the Secretary of Defense who felt the need for a new mechanism that would enable the Defense Department to enlist scientific talent of the highest competence to carry out studies on matters relating to the defense and security of the United States. Twelve universities were invited to become institutional members of the organization. Each institution agreed to designate an officer of the University to serve on the IDA Board. In addition, these institutional members elected a number of public members who served in an individual capacity.

The sole purpose of institutional membership of this not-for-profit organization was to enable it more easily to recruit high-quality scientists. No member university exerted any pressure at any time on its faculty members to join IDA or to serve as consultants.

As was well known on the Columbia campus before the first demonstrations occurred, the Institute Board had voted in March to modify the status of its university members so that, in the future, the sole connection between a member university and the Institute would be the nomination by institutional members of a senior officer to sit on the Institute Board in an entirely independent and individual capacity. He would not serve as a representative of his institution. This new arrangement had been approved by the Columbia Trustees at their March meeting and publicity had been given to that action.

The IDA issue, therefore, was largely symbolic. It was distorted by the demonstration leaders in order to enlist the support of students and faculty members who, being opposed to the war in Vietnam, could be led to believe that the University through IDA was directly and officially involved in the war.

Some months before the disorders occurred, I had approved a request from the University Council to appoint a committee to examine all of Columbia's external relationships, including IDA. That Committee has not as yet submitted its report but expects to do so in the near future. Final decisions concerning its recommendations will, of course, rest with the Trustees of the University.

3. A Joint Disciplinary Committee

During the first period of trouble, and on the basis of faculty recommendations, I appointed a three-man faculty committee to propose the organization and scope of operation of an administration-faculty-student disciplinary committee. Following the submission of this report, and prior to the first police action, I appointed such a committee consisting of seven students, seven faculty members and three administrators. I asked the Committee to accept two tasks:

(a) to recommend the range of disciplinary penalties and the procedures to be applied for their use with respect to all students involved in the disturbances, and

(b) to recommend permanent organization and disciplinary procedures for the future.

This Committee is now in effective existence and proposes to exercise appellate jurisdiction over certain classes of disciplinary decisions reached in the first instance by the appropriate deans and then by faculty-student-administration tribunals in each school.

4. The demand that all legal charges be dropped

Once an arrest for criminal trespass has been made, the University, acting alone, cannot drop charges that have been lodged against any offender. It can recommend leniency, if it so desires, and this request may or may not be accepted by the court. Where charges more serious than those of criminal trespass are made, e.g., resisting arrest or assault, police officers are the complainants and the University has no part in the court proceedings.

The Trustees of the University have stated publicly that in individual cases, where there appear to be mitigating circumstances, they will recommend leniency.

5. The demand for amnesty with respect to University discipline

The Joint Disciplinary Committee has proposed that all students involved in the April disturbances be placed on disciplinary probation for a year, and that all students found guilty of more serious offenses be subject to more serious penalties. They have also recommended that students who refuse to appear before a Dean to hear charges against them be immediately suspended. At no time has the University indicated that it was prepared to grant blanket amnesty.

6. The demand that the existing prohibition of indoor demonstrations be rescinded

Existing University regulations permit outdoor picketing and demonstrations by recognized student organizations with the proviso that they must be carried on without disruption to normal University activities. It is virtually impossible for indoor demonstrations to occur without such disruption, and this, apparently, is the reason why those who wish to disrupt University activities have demanded that the ban be lifted.

What is the gymnasium problem?

I find it difficult to write calmly to our alumni and friends about the gymnasium. The whole project has been so distorted by its opponents that reason and objectivity no longer seem to apply to a plan that was devised as a benefit to the community as well as to the University.

The idea of the gymnasium in Morningside Park grew naturally out of our success with the Columbia-Community playing field which has existed in the park since 1957. When the playing field proposal for the southern end of the park first was launched, the park land in question was garbage-littered and virtually unused by anyone. On the basis of a permit from the Parks Department, Columbia spent $250,000 to reclaim the land, transform it into an athletic field, and to construct a small field house. The plan was that Columbia would use the field for our students during school days and would staff at University expense an athletic program for neighborhood teen-age boys during week-ends and on a full-time community use basis during the summer months. The program has been so outstandingly successful that more than 2,500 youngsters, divided into a hundred teams, now use the field each year. Were it not for this program—Columbia directed and Columbia financed—these boys would be on the streets of Harlem and not on the playing field during the hot summer months.

The plan for a joint-use gymnasium, adjacent to this field, was developed by the Parks Commissioner and myself, with the help of many University associates. In brief, we all agreed that the rocky escarpment in the park along Morningside Drive would be utilized to build a combination University-Community gymnasium that would be of benefit to both parties and would not in any significant way occupy usable park land. It was agreed by all that the building should be in reality two buildings, one superimposed on the other. Since most of the community users would not come from Morningside Heights, it was decided that the lower floors, with a ground-floor entrance opening to the East, would be set aside for the Community, while the upper floors, opening on to Morningside Drive, would be devoted to the needs of Columbia undergraduates.

Columbia agreed to find the funds to finance the entire building cost and to staff the athletic programs in the community gymnasium at its own expense. We drew plans to put into the community gymnasium all the floor-space and athletic facilities which the Parks Department indicated it wished to have available.

We went into this program hesitantly because we recognized the legal and political hurdles that would have to be overcome before such a project could be carried out. One by one these steps were taken, and they were taken with full publicity. The project was approved successively by the Mayor, the Board of Estimate, the City Council, the Municipal Art Commission, two successive Parks Commissioners, both houses of the State Legislature and the Governor. Open public hearings were held by the Board of Estimate before its approval was given.

When all these City and State officials and bodies had officially approved the proposal, a lease for the necessary land (2.1 acres) was signed and we began to draw our final plans and to try to raise the necessary funds for what we knew would be a costly building and program. To date, we have raised $5,900,000[2] of the $11,500,000 needed for construction.

The third Parks Commissioner, Mr. Hoving, unlike his two predecessors, was not sympathetic to the plan and he used his official position to encourage neighborhood groups to try to block its execution. Also, some citizens on the Heights, who had no interest in the gymnasium project *per se* but who were opposed to the physical expansion of the University on the Heights, seized upon the project as a means of causing trouble generally for Columbia.

After many meetings with City officials and neighborhood leaders, the University voluntarily proposed, and the Board of Estimate approved, an amendment to the lease to authorize the University at its own expense to add a swimming pool to the community facilities. The cost of this pool, plus costs of supervision, meant that the University was making a total

---

[2] $3,591,000 actually received, balance in pledges.

contribution to the community of nearly $3,000,000 to provide a facility nowhere else available for the teen-age boys of the community.

Much has been made of the fact that only 16 percent of the total floor space of the combined building will be in the community gymnasium, but I must reiterate that we placed in that part of the building exactly what the Parks Department desired. Far from being a "land grab" by the University, it is a sincere and costly attempt to give to the community a badly-needed facility whereby during the winter as well as summer months neighborhood boys will be engaged in healthful athletic competition under trained supervision and all at Columbia's cost.

If the present opposition should prevail, and if the University permanently abandons the project and builds its gymnasium elsewhere on the Heights, the neighborhood boys will be the sufferers. Columbia will have a gymnasium in some other location, though it will lose several million dollars in the shift, but the teen-age boys of the neighborhood then will have none.

What steps have been taken to re-examine the University's structure and procedures?

Reference has already been made to the establishment of the Joint Committee on Disciplinary Affairs. Such a Committee has not existed at Columbia in the past, not because there was any official reluctance to create one, but because a University such as Columbia has had few disciplinary problems that could not normally be handled by ordinary disciplinary procedures operating under the authority delegated from the office of the President to each Dean. We had not, hitherto, been faced with disciplinary problems arising from mass violence, and we had not believed that any Columbia students would be prepared to disregard the normal canons of civilized behavior and to resort to such tactics. We have now been obliged to set up such an appellate committee and disciplinary tribunals, though we hope they will have few cases to handle once these disturbances have come to an end.

Next, because in the atmosphere of the past few weeks there has been much discussion about the need to "restructure" the University, the Trustees have created a special Committee under the chairmanship of Alan Temple to study these problems. This Committee will elicit proposals from, and carry on discussions with, student, faculty and alumni representatives in the months ahead.

In an endeavor to secure student opinions that would be as representative as possible, the Temple Committee requested each division of the University to elect representatives for this special consultation. One representative was allocated for each 500 students and each segment of the

University with fewer than 500 students was authorized to choose one representative. Some of these student representatives have been chosen and meetings with the Temple Committee have started.

At a joint meeting of the voting members of the Morningside faculties held on April thirtieth, a resolution was passed creating an Executive Committee of these faculties to assist in bringing order to the campus. Subsequently, this Committee was invited to work with the Trustees Committee. Several joint meetings of the two committees have been held. The faculty committee, with the approval of the Trustees, plans to carry on a program of research this summer dealing with the structure and procedures of Columbia and other comparable universities.

The Executive Committee of the Morningside faculties with the support of the Trustees has also brought into being a Fact-Finding Commission, headed by Professor Archibald Cox of the Harvard Law School, to establish the underlying facts and circumstances that led to the disruptions of April twenty-third. This Commission has been taking testimony from students, faculty and administration. In addition, Mr. Harold McGuire, Vice Chairman of the Trustees, has testified before the Commission concerning the problem of the gymnasium. The findings of this Commission will be awaited with much interest by all parts of the University community.

What are the avowed, long-range goals of the SDS?

The SDS is a national organization with chapters in many colleges and universities. It is overtly dedicated to the destruction or radical transformation of all political, social and economic institutions. Tom Hayden, twenty-eight years old and a former student at the University of Michigan, is one of the national figures in the SDS movement. In our recent trouble he spent several days with the student trespassers in the Mathematics building. Two years ago he wrote:

The Movement is a community of insurgents sharing the same values and identity, seeking an independent base of power wherever they are. It aims at a transformation of society led by the most excluded and "unqualified" people. Primarily this means building institutions outside the established order which seek to become the genuine institutions of the total society. Ultimately this Movement might lead to a Continental Congress called by all the people who feel excluded from the higher circles of decision-making in the country.

"The Politics of the 'Movement'" in
The Radical Papers, edited by Irving
Howe, New York, 1966, p. 377.

More recently and specifically he wrote:

The Columbia students were . . . taking an internationalist and revolutionary view of themselves in opposition to the very institutions in which they have been groomed and educated. They did not want to be included in the decision-making circles of the military-industrial complex that runs Columbia; *they want to be included only if their inclusion is a step toward transforming the University* (author's italics)

T. Hayden, "Two, Three, Many Columbias,"
Ramparts, June 15, 1968.

Even more succinct, perhaps, was an open letter recently addressed to me by Mr. Rudd, the head of the Columbia SDS, who has now been suspended from the University. In it, he wrote:

If we win, we will take control of your world, your corporation, your university, and attempt to mold a world in which we and other people can live as human beings. Your power is directly threatened since we will have to destroy that power before we take over.

Such statements speak for themselves. They indicate that the leaders of the SDS—as distinct from an unknown number of their supporters—are concerned with local or parochial university issues only as they serve as a means to a larger end.

Why are American universities being chosen as targets by the SDS?

For this, there are two obvious reasons. First, a university is particularly vulnerable to violence. Universities are by nature and definition hospitable to the free interchange of all ideas and doctrines. They have assumed that the members of each group will have the same respect for contrary opinions that they demand for themselves. When a group asserts that the justice of its views legitimatizes recourse to violence, a university is ill-prepared by organization and temperament to cope with the threat.

Second, any substantive victory would offer large rewards because the University could then be transformed from a home of liberal learning into an instrumentality for social revolution. This has happened in many Latin American universities as a consequence of student power which by careful organization has become radical student power.

Why did the SDS leaders receive such wide support from other students after the police were called in?

In my opinion, the mere shock of seeing a large force of helmeted police on the campus, followed by the sight and the firsthand experience of violence, brought to a head the unease and emotions of many students. The tensions caused by the Vietnam war and the then-recent assassination of Dr. Martin Luther King, Jr. were obvious contributing factors.

Does the Columbia "affair" have significance for all higher education in the United States?

If any of our alumni have any doubt on this score, I wish they could read even a sampling of the thousands of telegrams and letters we have received from every part of the country. Hundreds of college and university professors, deans, presidents and trustees, have written to say to us that the outcome of our controversy will have a profound effect on their ability to preserve the future integrity of their own institutions.

Our struggle has a special relevance to the future of private institutions of higher education. The demonstrators conveniently overlook the fact that a private university is free, under the general guidance in our case of the State Board of Regents, and in accordance with the terms of its Charter, to establish its own rules. Its Trustees not only have the legal authority but the responsibility to direct the affairs of the University. In practice, they delegate general educational and curricular policy to the various faculties, but they cannot be expected to share decision-making power on any subject with a group of students if that group has the avowed policy of destroying the integrity of the University.

One final word: As men and women devoted to one of America's great universities, you may be fully confident that the Trustees, the administration, and the great majority of the faculty and students, will protect and preserve the kind of Columbia you have known. If there should be any turmoil in the months ahead, it will be dealt with firmly. We know from the immense quantity of mail received in recent weeks that the eyes of the nation have been fixed upon Columbia, and you may be sure that we shall not be unmindful of our responsibilities to you, to our University, and to all higher education. Throughout a long history Columbia has given much to our country. No minor troubles will be allowed to mar her opportunity to do even more in the bright future that lies ahead.

/s/ GRAYSON KIRK

ACLU ON STUDENT DEMONSTRATIONS

The following statement on campus demonstrations was released by the American Civil Liberties Union's Academic Freedom Committee, June 26, 1968, following an exhaustive survey of recent campus disruptions throughout the country.

Recent demonstrations, strikes, sit-ins and other outbreaks on college campuses in various parts of the United States are evidence of a serious malaise in American academic life as well as in the society at large. Their causes are complex and involve other groups in the university besides the students, so that they cannot simply be dismissed as due to immaturity, alienation, irresponsibility or conspiracy. On many campuses there have been grave violations of the principles of sound academic governance by administrations which have denied students reasonable participation in matters of university policy in which their interests have been clearly involved, by faculties which have been indifferent to the needs and aspirations of students, and by students who by various actions have interfered with the processes of teaching, learning and the right to free speech. The values of academic freedom associated with these processes are as relevant in moments of stress as in normal times, and cannot be suspended for however worthy a cause without doing serious or irreparable damage to them.

In some cases the police have been called in under circumstances reflecting a complete breakdown in the internal discipline of the university. The invitation of civil authorities onto the campus endangers the autonomy of the institution, and should be resorted to only when *all* other avenues have failed and then preferably under strict procedural rules laid down and agreed to by administration, faculty and students. In view of the brutality of some police actions the formulation of such rules appears to be a matter of urgent priority. While any group sufficiently bent on disruption can

From *School & Society*, Oct. 26, 1968. Reprinted by permission of the publisher.

presumably force an intervention of this kind, such groups generally represent a small minority among the students and would not be likely to succeed in large-scale actions on campuses where there was a manifest unity of interest among faculty, students and administration.

The manner in which demonstrations have been conducted, at least in some notorious cases, must be condemned as disproportionate to the grievances of the students and as categorically in violation of basic principles of academic freedom. The fact that significant reforms may be won by violent action does not justify the resort to violence, even if such action seems plausible to some in a society marked by violence both internally and in its external actions, and even if an apparent justification after the fact seems to be provided by a violent response, for example a police action. The so-called "politics of confrontation" invites, and is intended to invite, such a response, but in so far as it seeks its ends by means which infringe on the liberties of others it is out of keeping with the principles by which and the purposes for which the university exists.

It must be admitted that an examination of the conditions which have triggered demonstrations shows that in a majority of cases students have had a prima facie justification for their concern, if not for their manner of expressing it. They have protested against compulsory ROTC (Tuskegee), the suspension of politically active students (Stanford), the neglect of Negro students (Northwestern), alleged mistreatment of controversial faculty members (Roosevelt), the use of slum parkland for a university facility and the university's ties with defense-related research (Columbia). The list could be prolonged. These causes are of unequal weight and have sometimes been used, even by students without political or ideological commitments, as excuses for the expression of more fundamental hostilities, reflecting among other things a widespread frustration and disillusionment with the foreign and domestic policies of the present government. But the fact that local pretexts have been so easily come by is no more to be overlooked then the problems of war and race which have set the stage for so many of these episodes.

The internal condition pointed to by the frequency and intensity of these disturbances can best be represented as a progressive neglect of certain principles (full and open communication between all elements within the university—trustees, president, administration, faculty and students—and a rigorous priority of academic and human considerations over financial and organizational ones) together with a change in the nature of the student body and its relations with faculty and administration, a change of which the latter groups have hardly been aware. Three aspects of this change, familiar enough in isolation but rarely considered together, are the demographic shift to a younger population, the extension of the period of formal training and therefore of dependence, and the lowering of the age of social maturity. The passivity of many faculties has allowed most of the power in the university to pass into the hands of the administration, and the administration has been only too ready to accept this power and to exercise it in an essentially managerial way, with little regard for the characteristic intellectual and social realities of academic life. It is a significant fact that many university administrators are as much at home on the boards of large corporations and in the upper echelons of the bureaucracy as they are on their own campuses. Activist students have played a useful role in helping to draw attention to the imbalance of power within the university, as well as to the increasing identification of the university with a social order of which it should properly be the critic and conscience. At the same time it seems shortsighted, in the attempt to modify this social order, to seek to destroy the only institution capable of playing such a role effectively.

The American Civil Liberties Union, attaching great importance as it does to the preservation of a strong and viable university system as one of the underlying conditions for civil liberties in general, is concerned that the meaning of these events should not be lost sight of through concentration of attention on their more dramatic features. The Union's interest in the principles of academic governance and organization is of long standing. But the time is overdue for a review of the structure and internal relations of the university on every campus, in order to secure the full involvement and cooperation of all concerned groups in the formulation and execution of academic policy at all levels.

LETTER ON STUDENT CONFRONTATION

Rev. Theodore M. Hesburgh, C.S.C., President, University of Notre Dame, sent the following letter, Feb. 17, 1969, to his faculty and students.

Dear Notre Dame Faculty and Students:

This letter has been on my mind for weeks. It is both time and overtime that it be written. I have outlined the core of it to the Student Life Council, have discussed the text with the Chairman of the Board of Trustees, the Vice Presidents Council, all the Deans of the University, and the Chairmen of the Faculty Senate and the Student Life Council. This letter does not relate directly to what happened here last weekend, although those events made it seem even more necessary to get this letter written. I have tried to write calmly, in the wee hours of the morning when at last there is quiet and pause for reflection.

My hope is that these ideas will have deep personal resonances in our own community, although the central problem they address exists everywhere in the university world today and, by instant communication, feeds upon itself. It is not enough to label it the alienation of youth from our society. God knows there is enough and more than enough in our often non-glorious civilization to be alienated from, be you young, middle-aged, or old.

The central problem to me is what we do about it and in what manner, if we are interested in healing rather than destroying our world. Youth especially has much to offer—idealism, generosity, dedication, and service. The last thing a shaken society needs is more shaking. The last thing a noisy, turbulent, and disintegrating community needs is more noise, turbulence, and disintegration. Understanding and analysis of social ills cannot be conducted in a boiler factory. Compassion has a quiet way of service. Complicated social mechanisms, out-of-joint, are not adjusted with sledge hammers.

The university cannot cure all our ills today, but it can make a valiant beginning by bringing all its intellectual and moral powers to bear upon them: all the idealism and generosity of its young people, all the wisdom and intelligence of its oldsters, all the expertise and competence of those who are in their middle years. But it must do all this as a university does, within its proper style and capability, no longer an ivory tower, but not the Red Cross either.

Now to the heart of my message. You recall my letter of November 25, 1968. It was written after an incident, or happening if you will. It seemed best to me at the time not to waste time in personal recriminations or heavy-handed discipline, but to profit from the occasion to invite this whole University community, especially its central Councils of faculty, administration, and students, to declare themselves and to state their convictions regarding protests that were peaceful and those that threatened the life of the community by disrupting the normal operations of the University and infringing upon the rights of others.

I now have statements from the Academic Council, the Faculty Senate, the Student Life Council, some College Councils, the Alumni Board, and a whole spate of letters from individual faculty members and a few students. Some of these are enclosed in this letter. [EDITORS' NOTE: This book includes some of these statements at the end of Pres. Hesburgh's letter.] In general, the reaction was practically unanimous that this community recognizes the validity of protest in our day—sometimes even the necessity—regarding the current burning issues of our society: war and peace, especially Vietnam; civil rights, especially of minority groups; the stance of the University vis-a-vis moral issues of great public concern; the operation of the University as university. There was also practical unanimity that the University could not continue to exist as an open society, dedicated to the discussion of all issues of importance, if protests were of such a nature that the normal operations of the University were in any way impeded, or if the rights of any member of this community were abrogated, peacefully or non-peacefully. I believe that I now have a clear mandate from this University community to see that: 1) our lines of communication between all segments of the community are kept as open as possible, with all legitimate means of communicating dissent assured, expanded, and protected; 2) civility and rationality are maintained as the most reasonable means of dissent within the academic community; and 3) violation of others's rights or obstruction of the life of the University are outlawed as illegitimate means of dissent in this kind of open society. Violence was especially deplored as a violation of everything that the University community stands for.

Now comes my duty of stating, clearly and unequivocally, what happens if. I'll try to make it as simple as possible to avoid misunderstanding by anyone. May I begin by saying that all of this is hypothetical and I personally hope it never happens here at Notre Dame. But, if it does, anyone or any group that substitutes force for rational persuasion, be it violent or non-violent, will be given fifteen minutes of meditation to cease and desist. They will be told that they are, by their actions, going counter to the overwhelming conviction of this community as to what is proper here. If they do not within that time period cease and desist, they will be asked for their identity cards. Those who produce these will be suspended from this community as not understanding what this community is. Those who do not have or will not produce identity cards will be assumed not to be members of the community and will be charged with trespassing and disturbing the peace on private property and treated accordingly by the law. The judgment regarding the impeding of normal University operations or the violation of the rights of other members of the community will be made by the Dean of Students. Recourse for certification of this fact for students so accused is to the tri-partite Disciplinary Board established by the Student Life Council. Faculty members have recourse to the procedures outlined in the Faculty Manual. Judgment of the matter will be delivered within five days following the fact, for justice deferred is justice denied to all concerned.

After notification of suspension, or trespass in the case of non-community members, if there is not then within five minutes a movement to cease and desist, students will be notified of expulsion from this community and the law will deal with them as non-students.

Lest there be any possible misunderstanding, it should be noted that law enforcement in this procedure is not directed at students. They receive academic sanctions in the second instance of recalcitrance and, only after three clear opportunities to remain in student status, if they still insist on resisting the will of the community, are they then expelled and become non-students to be treated as other non-students, or outsiders.

There seems to be a current myth that university members are not responsible to the law, and that somehow the law is the enemy, particularly those who society has constituted to uphold and enforce the law. I would like to insist here that all of us are responsible to the duly constituted laws of this University community and to all of the laws of the land. There is no other guarantee of civilization versus the jungle or mob rule, here or elsewhere.

If someone invades your home, do you dialogue with him or call the law? Without the law, the university is a sitting duck for any small group from outside or inside that wishes to destroy it, to incapacitate it, to terrorize it at whim. The argument goes—or has gone—invoke the law and you lose the university community. My only response is that without the law you may well lose the university—and beyond that—the larger society that supports it and that is most deeply wounded when law is no longer respected, bringing an end of everyone's most cherished rights.

I have studied at some length the new politics of confrontation. The rhythm is simple: 1) find a cause, any cause, silly or not; 2) in the name of the cause, get a few determined people to abuse the rights and privileges of the community so as to force a confrontation at any cost of boorishness or incivility; 3) once this has occurred, justified or not, orderly or not, yell police brutality—if it does not happen, provoke it by foul language, physical abuse, whatever, and then count on a larger measure of sympathy from the up-to-now apathetic or passive members of the community. Then call for amnesty, the head of the president on a platter, the complete submission to any and all demands. One beleaguered president has said that these people want to be martyrs thrown to toothless lions. He added, "Who wants to dialogue when they are going for the jugular vein?"

So it has gone, and it is generally well orchestrated. Again, my only question: must it be so? Must universities be subjected, willy-nilly, to such intimidation and victimization whatever their good will in the the matter? Somewhere a stand must be made.

I only ask that when the stand is made necessary by those who would destroy the community and all its basic yearning for great and calm educational opportunity, let them carry the blame and the penalty. No one wants the forces of law on this or any other campus, but if some necessitate it, as a last and dismal alternative to anarchy and mob tyranny, let them shoulder the blame instead of receiving the sympathy of a community they would hold at bay. The only alternative I can imagine is turning the majority of the community loose on them, and then you have two mobs. I know of no one who would opt for this alternative—always lurking in the wings. We can have a thousand resolutions as to what kind of a society we want, but when lawlessness is afoot, and all authority is flouted, faculty, administration, and student, then we invoke the normal societal forces of law or we allow the university to die beneath our hapless and hopeless gaze. I have no intention of presiding over such a spectacle: too many people have given too much of themselves and their lives to this University to let this happen here. Without being melodramatic, if this conviction makes this my last will and testament to Notre Dame, so be it.

May I now say in all sincerity that I never want to see any student expelled from this community because, in many ways, this is always an educative failure. Even so, I must likewise be committed to the survival of the University community as one of man's best hopes in these troubled times. I know of no other way of insuring both ends than to say of every member of this community, faculty and students, that we are all ready and prepared and anxious to respond to every intellectual and moral concern in the world today, in every way proper to the University. At the same time, we cannot allow a small minority to impose their will on the majority who have spoken regarding the University's style of life; we cannot allow a few to substitute force of any kind for persuasion to accept their personal idea of what is right or proper. We only insist on the rights of all, minority and majority, the climate of civility and rationality, and a preponderant moral abhorence of violence or inhuman forms of persuasion that violate our style of life and the nature of the University. It is, unfortunately, possible to cut oneself off from this community, even though the vast majority of our members would regret seeing it happen. However, should this occur, the community as a whole has indicated that it will vote and stand for the maintenance of this community's deepest values, since this is the price we all pay for the survival of the University community in the face of anyone and everyone who would destroy or denature it today, for whatever purposes.

May I now confess that since last November I have been bombarded mightily by the hawks and the doves—almost equally. I have resisted both and continue to recognize the right to protest—through every legitimate channel—and to resist as well those who would unthinkingly trifle with the survival of the University as one of the few open societies left to mankind today. There is no divine assurance that the University will survive as we have known and cherished it—but we do commit ourselves to make the effort and count on this community, in this place, to uphold the efforts that you have inspired by your clear expression of community concern. Thanks to all who have declared themselves, even to those who have slightly disagreed, but are substantially concerned as well.

As long as the great majority of this community is concerned and involved in maintaining what it believes deeply to be its identity and commitment, no force within it, however determined or organized, can really destroy it. If any community as a whole does not believe this, or is not committed to it, it does not deserve to survive and it probably will not. I hope we will. To this, I commit myself with the presumption that the great majority of you are with me in this concern and commitment.

I truly believe that we are about to witness a revulsion on the part of legislatures, state and national, benefactors, parents, alumni, and the general public for much that is happening in higher education today. If I read the signs of the times correctly, this may well lead to a suppression of the liberty and autonomy that are the lifeblood of a university community. It may well lead to a rebirth of fascism, unless we ourselves are ready to take a stand for what is right for us. History is not consoling in this regard. We rule ourselves, or others rule us, in a way that destroys the university as we have known and loved it.

Devotedly yours in Notre Dame,

(Rev.) Theodore M. Hesburgh, C.S.C.
President

[EDITORS' NOTE: *The statements below were enclosed with Pres. Hesburgh's letter of Feb. 17, 1969, to faculty and students of the University of Notre Dame.*]

The Academic Council at its meeting of November 26, 1968, endorsed the following statement:

"Peaceful protest is legitimate and in the view of some at times necessary; protest that infringes on the rights of other members of the community or obstructs the normal function of the University is cause for separating from the community those who indulge in such action."

Note: This statement was not released following the meeting so as not to prejudice the discussions yet to take place by the Student Life Council and the Faculty Senate. The Academic Council reserves the right to discuss the matter further following the statements from the other bodies.

The Student Life Council at its meeting of December 2, 1968, endorsed the following statement:

"We hold that without the corollary of an 'open listeners' policy, i.e., without a guarantee that any member of the University community can exercise his right to hear or to consult with other members or authorized visitors to the campus, then the 'open speakers' policy of the University becomes a mockery. This realization means that when a portion of the community dissents with the views of other members, or authorized visitors, or dissents with the policies of the institutions which they represent, then this dissent must be expressed in a manner that does not abridge the freedom of those members or visitors to carry out their authorized activities on the campus. This principle demands in particular that dissenters refrain from sustained 'heckling' of a speaker, and that they refrain from actions which forcibly obstruct the authorized activity or render the conditions under which such activity can be carried out repugnant to common human sensibilities. To violate these limitations on the expression of dissent is to engage in totalitarian tactics which are alien to a university. We reiterate the provisions of the Notre Dame Student Manual which specify that such actions shall make the violator subject to disciplinary action as provided for in said Manual, and we urge other segments of the University community to be equally frank in their disavowal of these violations of the free nature of the University community."

The Faculty Senate at its meeting of December 3, 1968, endorsed the following statement:

"RESOLVED, that the position of this University in the mainstream of our time and society provides certain occasions for a wide variety of persons to be present on our campus for a multitude of purposes. It is entirely out of keeping with the position and purposes of the University for such persons to be impeded or forcibly interfered with in pursuing their lawful concerns.

To participate in such obstructive tactics is a serious disciplinary offense. We recognize that there are appropriate provisions of the Student Manual pertaining to this matter, and we urge the vigorous implementation of these provisions through normal judicial procedures."

The Engineering College Council at its meeting of December 5, 1968, endorsed the following statement:

"Recognizing the danger to the university community posed by disruptive activity, we pledge our full support to President Father Hesburgh in whatever action he deems necessary to prevent or to deal with such activity including action to discipline promptly any member of the university community who may be involved in such activity either directly or by incitement."

The Science College Council, on December 9, 1968, authorized a subcommittee to draft a resolution which follows:

"Within an active academic community, there will be a difference of opinion on major issues that may be brought to its attention. The very nature of the community and the exercise of its functions demand that this be so.

"However, resort to violence, physical harassment, obstruction, or any action which infringes on the right of others, or impedes in any way the function of the University is never an acceptable tactic for expression of viewpoints. Such behavior is intolerable in an academic community."

At a special meeting on December 3, 1968, the Faculty of the College of Business Administration passed unanimously the following resolution:

"There are apparently at least three significances to the CIA-Dow demonstrations, all of which are important to the life of the university community:

"1. The two-way freedom-street concept which you have recognized so well in your letter, and the tyranny that results when any group attempts to impose personal convictions on others;

"2. The need for a community policy to prevent a recurrence of tyrannical action—one which incorporates penalties for students and/or faculty who involve themselves beyond the acceptable rights of peaceful protest.

"Both (1) and (2) above have been spoken of well in your letter. We suggest that a third significance of last Wednesday's actions might be corrected promptly:

"3. The need for an official apology to CIA (Dow probably needs none because the protest met was within the bounds of acceptability and respectability). Further, we feel that CIA should be extended an invitation to return soon to campus and be given a guarantee of safety to conduct interviews with interested students."

The faculty members of the Law School have generally approved and are preparing a statement supporting the President's letter of November 25, 1968.

Excerpts of a letter received February 12, 1969, from Mr. Leonard Skoglund, President of the Alumni Board, regarding the Board's discussion at their meeting of January 23, 1969:

"While most alumni concur with your philosophy that young people today be permitted, perhaps even encouraged to demonstrate their concern with the burning issues of our time, they cannot and will not support tactics which inhibit or disrupt the freedoms of others. . . . The Board was chagrined to learn that some administrative personnel were (by their own admission) uncertain as to the measures to be taken in the face of disruptive tactics. Although uninvited, we responded to your appeal to the community for support in dealing with such activities in the future. We also understand that you have now secured the backing requested from the Academic Council, the Faculty Senate, and the Student Life Council, and that the University now has in hand a firm policy regarding demonstrations, and responsive procedures in reaction to disruptive activities. We urge you to clearly publicize consequences which shall be faced by all who violate the established policy, and to prosecute to the limit any outsiders identified as participants. We feel that unless such measures and procedures are clearly defined and executed, the future of this University stands in jeopardy."

LETTER TO VICE PRESIDENT AGNEW ON CAMPUS UNREST

The following is the text of a letter to Vice President Spiro Agnew from Rev. Theodore M. Hesburgh, C.S.C., President, University of Notre Dame. It was dispatched from Bogotá, Colombia, where Hesburgh had been attending a meeting of the Council on Higher Education in the American Republics, and was released by his office at Notre Dame, Feb. 27, 1969.

Dear Mr. Vice President:

President Nixon has asked me to give you my views regarding campus unrest and possible action on the occasion of your meeting this week with the governors of the fifty states. The President most wisely states that any action must be "consistent with the vital importance of maintaining the traditional independence of American universities." In the concluding sentence of my recent letter to Notre Dame faculty and students I voiced my own central concern in the face of our current crisis:

"We rule ourselves, or others rule us, in a way that destroys the university as we have known and loved it."

Universities, like countries, can be equally destroyed from inside or from outside. The motivation may be different, to hurt or to help, but the result is the same—no more university: mob rule instead of civility, force substituting for reason, tyranny for persuasion, police state instead of the house of the intellect with all its glorious virtues exercised in freedom.

Writing from such a distance and in the midst of a busy conference, I shall make my comments as brief as possible.

1. The best salvation for the university in the face of any crisis is for the university community to save itself, by declaring its own ground rules and basic values and then enforcing them with the widest and deepest form of moral persuasion for the good life of the university, and consequent moral condemnation with academic sanctions for any movement against university life and values—especially violence, vandalism and mob action which are

the antitheses of reason, civility and the open society which respects the rights of each and all.

2. When moral persuasion and academic sanctions fail to deter those who show open contempt for the life-style and self declared values of the university community, there should be no hesitation to invoke whatever outside assistance is necessary to preserve the university and its values. However, it is the university that best judges its need for outside assistance and invokes this assistance, much as it would call for help in a three-alarm campus fire. Here the concern is survival against forces bent on destruction.

3. It is important to see and judge universities today as they really are, not as they appear to be. The bizarre and widely publicized antics of relatively few students and relatively even fewer faculty are accepted as the stereotypes of all students and all faculty, much to the disgust of this widely maligned majority of faculty and students. The vast majority of university and college students today are a very promising and highly attractive group of persons: they are more informed, more widely read, better educated, more idealistic and more deeply sensitive to crucial moral issues in our times, more likely to dedicate themselves to good rather than selfish goals than any past generation of students I have known. Many of them are bothered by some aspects of American and world society and current values or the lack of them—with good reason in most cases. They would work very hard, I believe, if given a real opportunity to participate in changing this world for the better. They would also find out how hard this is to do and would quickly discard some of their more naive present solutions to our problems. Even the most far-out students are trying to tell society something that may also be worth searching for today if they would only lower the volume so we could hear the message. Anyway, the great majority of our students need better leadership than we or the faculty have been giving them. In a fast changing society the real crisis is not one of authority but a crisis of vision that alone can inspire great leadership and create great morale in any society. A rebirth of great academic, civic and political leadership, a sharing of some of these youthful ideals and dreams (impossible or not) would be good for our universities and good for America too. It might also help us all remove some of the key problems that underline most of the unrest. The campus is really reflecting America and the world today in Hi-Fi sound and living color.

4. Part of the vision I have been speaking of must certainly include law and order. But curiously enough, one cannot really have law and order without another part of the vision: greater achievement of justice in our times, more compassion for all, real love between generations. All elements of the vision are interdependent. Moreover, the vision must be whole and real for everyone. Lastly, a measure of humor would help from time to time to break up the deathly seriousness of the present scene.

5. As to present action; I would make the following two suggestions:

A. Assume for a few months that the university community—faculty, students, administration and trustees—are capable, in most cases, laying down their own guidelines and effectively maintaining them in their usual free and independent university style. Things will be messy from time to time but we will make it as universities if we determine strongly to maintain our freedoms and our values. That determination is growing on every campus, everyday now. Give it elbow room in which to grow and operate in its own good way.

B. Where special help is needed, let all assume it will be asked for and given quickly, effectively and as humanely as possible, given the provocations that surround the need for such outside help, as a last alternative to internal self correction. But let it be understood that the university, and only the university, public or private, makes this determination.

If my two assumptions are correct, the crisis will pass without the further requirement of actions other than those contained in my assumptions, especially not repressive legislation, or over-reaction in its many forms.

May I conclude with a word of optimism? As Dickens wrote in *The Tale of Two Cities*, "It was the best of times and the worst of times." The worst, because many of our best traditions, as universities and as a nation, are under siege. The best of times, because we are going to win this battle, not by repressing the very values of rationality, civility and openness that we are trying to save, but by reinforcing them in our belief, in our lives, in our institutions and especially by using them, and hopefully youth's great vigor and idealism as well, to attack the deeper problems yet ahead of us in our age-long walk out of the jungle into the light.

My best personal regards, and prayers too, for you, Mr. Vice President and all the governors.

Devotedly yours,

Rev. Theodore M. Hesburgh, C.S.C., President
University of Notre Dame

PRELIMINARY REMARKS FOR A STATEMENT BY COLUMBIA UNIVERSITY FACULTY MEMBERS

These preliminary remarks by Fritz Stern, Seth Low Professor of History, Columbia University, accompanied the statement by 100 faculty members of the university, March 10, 1969, condemning force and disruptive activities on campus. The faculty members' statement immediately follows Prof. Stern's remarks.

I have been asked by some of my colleagues here to make an opening statement; let me say first of all that no one here can presume to speak for anyone but himself. We are colleagues with widely divergent views on many issues; we are fully agreed, however, on the principles set forth in our statement.

Universities today are facing a common challenge and a grave crisis: some universities may be more embattled than others, but none is safe from attack or disruption. From Berkeley to Berlin, a group of militant students, at war, as they put it, with their societies, have discovered the fragility of free, liberal universities; in exploiting that fragility they are threatening to wreck the traditional purposes and values of western universities. I have observed at close quarters the rapidity with which the ancient universities of continental Europe have been reduced to a state of intermittent chaos.

In the face of this still worsening crisis, we reaffirm our dedication to the principles of a free University. Teachers are called upon to defend not only their ideals of academic freedom but the rights of their students who entered academic institutions with clear expectations about their freedom to study. Universities thrive on controversy and benefit from dissent; we reject orthodoxy of any sort and we condemn the use of force instead of persuasion. The rights of dissent must be scrupulously protected; it is becoming clearer every day that the outside world will not forever put up with the present disruptions on campuses, but society's cure may be as damaging to universities as are the disruptions themselves. The universities may well be caught in the crossfire of rebellious students and reactionary politicians.

We freely admit that there are deficiencies and abuses in our academic institutions—most of us knew that before Berkeley erupted. We know that students can play an important role in calling these abuses to our attention and in correcting them. But idealism and nihilism have not infrequently been found together in the past, and student tactics today seem to belie the idealism of yesterday. There is an alarming discrepancy between the intensity of today's radicalism and its clarity of purpose.

For the last few months, a small group of us has met intermittently and informally, deeply troubled by the crises on this campus. Under the impact of recent events, we drafted a statement of principle which we circulated to a few colleagues. In three days, we collected over a hundred signatures. We are releasing that statement today and we are simultaneously appealing to all our colleagues on this campus to join us now in signing it. We appeal also to colleagues on other campuses to take similar counsel and above all we appeal to our students to protect their rights against all infringements. We wish to discuss with them our common concerns; we wish to collaborate with them in implementation of needed reforms. But these reforms can be achieved only if the orderly machinery for rational change remains intact. Violence and disruption paralyze all efforts at reform.

We hope that all members of this academic community will once again abide by the simple rules of self-restraint and mutual respect which make debate and controversy possible and productive. Should a small group of students persist in the tactics of disruption, the campus community must seek means to protect itself. We know that nothing is more pernicious to the life of a society than the passivity of its moderate majority. We are here today to say that we mean actively to fulfill our responsibilities as teachers and to protect the rights of our students. Together we mean to preserve and reform this university which commands our affection and our loyalty.

THE UNIVERSITY AS A SANCTUARY OF ACADEMIC FREEDOM

~~~~~~

This statement was signed and released by 100 Columbia University faculty members, March 10, 1969.

The tradition of the university as a sanctuary of academic freedom and center of informed discussion is an honored one, to be guarded vigilantly. The basic significance of that sanctuary lies in the protection of intellectual freedoms: the rights of professors to teach, of scholars to engage in the advancement of knowledge, of students to learn and to express their views, free from external pressures or interference. These freedoms can flourish only in an atmosphere of mutual respect, civility and trust among teachers and students, only when members of the university community are willing to accept self-restraint and reciprocity as the condition upon which they share in its intellectual autonomy.

Academic freedom and the sanctuary of the university campus extend to all who share these aims and responsibilities. They cannot be invoked by those who would subordinate intellectual freedom to political ends, or who violate the norms of conduct established to protect that freedom. Against such offenders the university has the right, and indeed the obligation, to defend itself. Nor does the sanctuary of the university protect acts violating civil or criminal law, which are illegal whether committed on or off the campus.

Current attempts to disrupt or prevent the holding of classes are a matter of urgent concern to us. These tactics are fundamentally inimical to university life. No genuine education can take place if teachers and students are cast in an adversary role. Disruptions deny students their right to an education and scholars their right to be heard.

The claim is false that only by disruptive tactics can criticism be made effective and university policies changed. In the past important policy and curriculum changes have been made through faculty and student action, in which rational discussion has been used to find constructive solutions to our problems. We recognize the need for further reforms and hope that all members of the university community will join in the process of orderly discussion leading to such changes, but we cannot accept force as a substitute for reasoned argument in deciding matters affecting the curriculum, instruction, and administration of the university.

In September of 1968 the faculty of this University adopted interim rules in order to insure the right to demonstrate peaceably and at the same time guarantee that the normal functioning of the university would not be impeded. It is desirable that university discipline be administered through bodies representative of the academic community, but this can be effective only if their members accept their responsibility to protect each other's rights and demonstrate the will to act. The argument that "justice delayed is justice denied" applies to the university community as well as to persons charged with violations of campus rules. Justice is denied the community if disciplinary cases go unresolved and all proceedings are subsequently abandoned.

We hope that present judicial bodies and any university-wide senate to be established will not shirk their responsibility in these matters. Teachers and students are entitled to meet their classes without interference, and the university is obliged to secure that freedom. We call upon all members of this and other universities to defend by example and by action the fundamental principles of a free university. It is our intention not to surrender the safeguards of freedom that men have erected at great sacrifice over several centuries.

[signed]
A. Doak Barnett
Jacques Barzun
Joseph Bauke
Malcolm W. Bean
Gary S. Becker
Jack Beeson
Daniel Bell
Sherman Beychock
Robert Branner
Ronald Breslow
Stuart Bruchey
Zbigniew Brzezinski
Phillip Cagan
Charles C. Cantor
Demetrios Caraley
James Clifford
Gerson D. Cohen
Lawrence B. Cohen
Stephen Cole
Robert Connery
L. Gray Cowan

Lawrence Cremin
B. P. Dailey
C. R. Dawson
Herbert Deane
Wm. Theodore de Bary
Donald Dewey
Sigmund Diamond
E. V. K. Dobbie
E. Talbot Donaldson
E. S. Donno
Nicholas England
William T. R. Fox
Julian H. Franklin
Charles Frankel
Fred W. Friendly
Eugene Galanter
John Garraty
Walter Gellhorn
Eli Ginzberg
Martin Golding
Henry Graff
William A. Hance

Elisabeth Hansot
Albert G. Hart
M. D. Hassialis
Richard Hofstadter
J. C. Hurewitz
Herbert H. Hyman
Graham W. Irwin
S. F. Johnson
Donald Keene
Peter Kenen
Paul Kristeller
Paul Henry Lang
Daniel J. Leab
William Leuchtenberg
Edward Lippman
Oliver Lissitzyn
Harvey C. Mansfield
Paul Marks
Joseph Mazzeo
Robert K. Merton
J. M. Miller
Jacob Mincer

Dwight Miner
Ivan Morris
Philip E. Mosely
John Mundy
Ernest Nagel
William Nelson
Walter Odajnyk
Yochanan Peres
Andre Racz
Michael Riffaterre
Paul Ritterband
Maurice Rosenberg

Joseph Rothschild
Alan Sachs
Wallace Sayre
Meyer Schapiro
Warner B. Schilling
Howard Shanet
David Sidorsky
Fritz Stern
Gilbert Stork
Wagner Thielens
William Y. Tindall
Lionel Trilling

N. J. Turro
H. Paul Varley
William Vickrey
Charles Wagley
Cheves Walling
Herbert Wechsler
Rudolf Wittkower
Carl Woodring
Howard Wriggins
James S. Young
Harriet Zuckerman

AN ENDORSEMENT OF THE COLUMBIA FACULTY'S STATEMENT

Andrew W. Cordier, as Acting President, Columbia University, issued the following statement, March 10, 1969, concerning the statement of the 100 faculty members of his institution. His position as President was made permanent on Aug. 20, 1969. Effective with the fall term, 1970, he assumed the deanship of Columbia's School of International Affairs.

I have noted with deep satisfaction the statement of a large group of faculty members regarding the University as a sanctuary of academic freedom. The substance of this statement deserves the support of the entire University community, the faculty, the student body and the administration.

On February 11th I indicated in my statement on disciplinary matters that: "The claims our institutional life make upon all of us are not satisfied by silence and indifference. They can only be met by conscious and articulate participation."

The statement issued by faculty members today is a demonstration of deep concern for the welfare and best interests of the University—interests that must be preserved by our collective will and action.

Thus far this year we have had 110,000 classes, seminars and laboratory sessions. Of this large number there have been approximately 25 reported disruptions; 9 of which have been of sufficient seriousness to cause the instructor to dismiss the class. Even if only one class had been disrupted, that action in itself would be unacceptable and contrary to the conditions and climate necessary for the carrying on of the main task of the University which is the instruction of its students.

FEDERAL LEGISLATION AND
STUDENT UNREST

~~~~~~

This letter from Robert H. Finch, Secretary of Health, Education, and Welfare, to the presidents of universities, colleges, and junior and community colleges was released on March 22, 1969.

It is my responsibility as the official chiefly charged with enforcement of Federal laws pertaining to education, to bring to your attention the recently enacted Federal laws relating to violations by students of criminal statutes.

The provisions enacted are included under Section 504 of the Higher Education Amendments of 1968 (P.L. 90-575) and Section 411 of the Department of Health, Education, and Welfare Appropriations Act, 1969 (P.L. 90-557). For your information, I am enclosing copies of these provisions as enclosures to this letter. [EDITORS' NOTE: The text of these provisions immediately follows Secretary Finch's letter.]

In view of the continued public debate over student unrest and the legitimate bounds of dissent, I ask that you bring to the attention of your students the applicable provisions of these laws and advise them of the procedures you intend to follow in complying with them.

It is important for all concerned to understand that Congress has spoken on this issue and that the law must be enforced. I hope at the same time that you will take the opportunity to review university policy and regulations with regard to student participation in campus affairs in order to guarantee that in maintaining order on the campus the right of legitimate and responsible dissent is fully protected.

I would suggest that these provisions be fully discussed by all parties at your institution—trustees, administrators, faculty members, students, and where possible, parents.

I hope that a thorough understanding of these provisions would enable you to better determine the ways and means by which your institution will deal with this legislation.

I am well aware that the implementation of the enforcement procedures established by Congress will require a reasonable amount of time, and that we are involved in areas fraught with tension and emotion.

Under this legislation, the burden of administration falls upon the institutions. We in DHEW will do our best to work with you in this difficult area.

Sincerely yours,

Robert H. Finch
Secretary

STUDENT UNREST PROVISIONS

DEPARTMENTS OF LABOR AND HEALTH, EDUCATION, AND WELFARE APPROPRIATIONS ACT, 1969
(PUBLIC LAW 90-557)

SEC. 411. No part of the funds appropriated under this Act shall be used to provide a loan, guarantee of a loan or a grant to any applicant who has been convicted by any court of general jurisdiction of any crime which involves the use of or the assistance to others in the use of force, trespass or the seizure of property under control of an institution of higher education to prevent officials or students at such an institution from engaging in their duties or pursuing their studies.

HIGHER EDUCATION AMENDMENTS OF 1968
(PUBLIC LAW 90-575)
Eligibility for Student Assistance

SEC. 504. (a) If an institution of higher education determines, after affording notice and opportunity for hearing to an individual attending, or employed by, such institution, that such individual has been convicted by any court of record of any crime which was committed after the date of enactment of this Act and which involved the use of (or assistance to others in the use of) force, disruption, or the seizure of property under control of any institution of higher education to prevent officials or students in such institution from engaging in their duties or pursuing their studies, and that such crime was of a serious nature and contributed to a substantial disruption of the administration of the institution with respect to which such crime was committed, then the institution which such individual attends, or is employed by, shall deny for a period of two years any further payment to, or for the direct benefit of, such individual under any of the programs specified in subsection (c). If an institution denies an individual assistance under the authority of the preceding sentence of this subsection, then any institution which such individual subsequently attends shall deny for the remainder of the two-year period any further payment to, or for the direct benefit of, such individual under any of the programs specified in subsection (c).

(b) If an institution of higher education determines, after affording notice and opportunity for hearing to an individual attending, or employed by, such institution, that such individual has willfully refused to obey a lawful regulation or order of such institution after the date of enactment of this Act, and that such refusal was of a serious nature and contributed to a substantial disruption of the administration of such institution, then such institution shall deny, for a period of two years, any further payment to, or for the direct benefit of, such individual under any of the programs specified in subsection (c).

(c) The programs referred to in subsections (a) and (b) are as follows:

(1) The student loan program under title II of the National Defense Education Act of 1958.

(2) The educational opportunity grant program under part A of title IV of the Higher Education Act of 1965.

(3) The student loan insurance program under part B of title IV of the Higher Education Act of 1965.

(4) The college work-study program under part C of title IV of the Higher Education Act of 1965.

(5) Any fellowship program carried on under title II, III, or V of the Higher Education Act of 1965 or title IV or VI of the National Defense Education Act of 1958.

(d) (1) Nothing in this Act, or any Act amended by this Act, shall be construed to prohibit any institution of higher education from refusing to award, continue, or extend any financial assistance under any such Act to any individual because of any misconduct which in its judgment bears adversely on his fitness for such assistance.

(2) Nothing in this section shall be construed as limiting or prejudicing the rights and prerogatives of any institution of higher education to institute and carry out an independent, disciplinary proceeding pursuant to existing authority, practice, and law.

(3) Nothing in this section shall be construed to limit the freedom of any student to verbal expression of individual views or opinions.

STATEMENT BY THE PRESIDENT

The following statement by President Richard M. Nixon was released on March 23, 1969.

This week the Secretary of Health, Education and Welfare has sent a letter to the presidents of the institutions of higher education in the nation calling attention to the provisions enacted in law by the 90th Congress which provide for the withdrawal of various forms of federal support to students found guilty of violation of criminal statutes in connection with campus disorders.

He did this in the exercise of his responsibility as the Cabinet officer chiefly charged with the routine enforcement of federal laws pertaining to education, however, the state of our campuses have for some time been anything but routine.

I should like to take this occasion to make some more general comments which I hope may be of some assistance in moderating the present turmoil.

First, a measure of perspective is in order with regard to the action of the previous Congress. The new regulations are moderate, and they are justified. It is one of the oldest of the practices of universities and colleges that privileges of various kinds are withdrawn from students judged to have violated the rules and regulations of their institution. Congress has done no more than to withdraw federal assistance from those students judged, not by university regulations, but by courts of law, to have violated criminal statutes. Almost by definition, given the present tactics of disruption, anyone so convicted may fairly be assumed to have been assaulting the processes of free inquiry which are the very life of learning. Any society that will not protect itself against such assault exhibits precious little respect for intellect, compared to which the issue of public order is very near to de minimis.

For there is a second issue, of far greater concern to me, and, as I believe, to the Congress, to the American people generally, and the faculties and students of American colleges and universities especially. That is the preservation of the integrity, the independence, and the creativity of our institutions of higher learning.

Freedom—intellectual freedom—is in danger in America. The nature and content of that danger is as clear as any one thing could be. Violence—physical violence, physical intimidation—is seemingly on its way to becoming an accepted, or at all events a normal and not to be avoided element in the clash of opinion within university confines. Increasingly it is clear that this violence is directed to a clearly perceived and altogether too conceivable objective: not only to politicize the student bodies of our educational institutions, but to politicize the institutions as well. Anyone with the least understanding of the history of freedom will know that this has invariably meant not only political disaster to those nations that have submitted to such forces of obfuscation and repression, but cultural calamity as well. It is not too strong a statement to declare that this is the way civilizations begin to die.

The process is altogether too familiar to those who would survey the wreckage of history. Assault and counter-assault, one extreme leading to the opposite extreme; the voices of reason and calm discredited. As Yeats foresaw: "Things fall apart; the centre cannot hold. . . ." None of us has the right to suppose it cannot happen here.

The first thing to do at such moments is to reassert first principles. The federal government cannot, should not—must not—enforce such principles. That is fundamentally the task and the responsibility of the university community. But any may state what these principles are, for they are as widely understood as they are cherished.

First, that universities and colleges are places of excellence in which men are judged by achievement and merit in defined areas. The independence and competence of the faculty, the commitment, and equally the competence of the student body, are matters not to be compromised. The singular fact of American society—the fact which very likely distinguishes us most markedly from any other nation on earth, is that in the untroubled pursuit of an application of this principle we have created the largest, most democratic, most open system of higher learning in history. None need fear the continued application of those principles; but all must dread their erosion. The second principle—and I would argue, the only other—is that violence or the threat of violence may never be permitted to influence the actions or judgments of the university community. Once it does the community, almost by definition, ceases to be a university.

It is for this reason that from time immemorial expulsion has been the primary instrument of university discipline. Those who would not abide the rules of the community of learning have simply been required to leave it, for any other form of coercion would cause that community to change its fundamental nature.

The difficulty of this moment, as of most times when fundamental principles are challenged, is that many of those posing the challenges, and even more of those supporting them, are responding to very basic problems. To reassert, in the face of student protest, the first principles of academic freedom, while ignoring the issues that are foremost in the minds of those students, is less than inglorious: it is slothful, and dishonest, and an affront to those principles and in the end futile.

Students today point to many wrongs which must be made right:

We have seen a depersonalization of the educational experience. Our institutions must reshape themselves lest this turns to total alienation.

Student unrest does not exist in a vacuum but reflects a deep and growing social unrest affecting much of our world today. Self-righteous indignation by society will solve none of this. We must resolve the internal contradictions of our communities.

There must be university reform including new experimentation in curricula such as ethnic studies, student involvement in the decision-making process and a new emphasis in faculty teaching.

I have directed the Department of Health, Education and Welfare to launch new initiatives toward easing tensions in our educational community.

This administration will always be receptive to suggestions for constructive reform. But the forces of separation and non-reason must be replaced by vigorous, persuasive and lawful efforts for constructive change.

A STATEMENT ON CAMPUS DISORDERS

A statement on campus disorders was released by the American Civil Liberties Union on April 3, 1969. The following letter from the organization to college and university presidents, heads of faculty councils and student governing bodies, and editors of campus newspapers introduces this official statement.

April, 1969

Dear _____

We recommend to your attention the enclosed statement on campus disorder which the American Civil Liberties Union has recently released to the public.

We feel the issues raised by student demonstrations are of such importance that we are taking the unusual step of writing directly to the presidents of colleges and universities, heads of faculty councils and student governing bodies and to editors of college newspapers.

We hope our warning will receive the widest possible consideration within the campus community and that our views will make a helpful contribution to the resolution of the issues at stake.

Sincerely yours,

Ernest Angell, Chairman
Board of Directors

John de J. Pemberton, Jr.
Executive Director

Samuel Hendel, Chairman
Academic Freedom Committee

Statement on Campus Disorders
April 3, 1969

Student protests and demonstrations in high schools, colleges and universities have mounted in volume, scope and intensity. Many of them have raised issues of fundamental importance about the nature and goals of our country and its institutions.

Student demonstrations have shown deep concern about the materialism of our society and the plodding pace toward desegregation and equal rights. They have raised questions about the moral bases of the Vietnam war, the power of the military-industrial complex, and the perversion of the university's purpose to serve military ends. They have sought a participatory role for faculty and students in the running of educational institutions and the revision of curricula to increase their relevance to the problems of life in our society.

On many college and university campuses there have clearly been grave violations of principles of sound academic governance. Administrators have denied to faculty and students a significant voice in the making of policy so vitally affecting them. Administrators and faculties both have frequently proved indifferent or slow to recognize the legitimate needs and aspirations of students. And, all too often, governing authorities have failed to give rigorous priority to academic, moral and human considerations over financial and organizational ones.

In general, whatever differences of opinion exist on how best to serve the causes of peace, equality, justice and freedom, it is well to recognize, too, that the student protests have in great degree been motivated by extraordinary selflessness, idealism and altruism. Speaking of a student demonstration in support of opening up opportunities for blacks in the construction of Buffalo campus buildings, Governor Nelson D. Rockefeller on March 21, 1969, said, "I think that students have assumed a share of social responsibility in the life of our community and I applaud them for it." So do we.

We are aware of the fact that student dissenters are handicapped by lack of funds and of direct access to media of mass communications as well as by stubborn and often recalcitrant resistance to desirable change. Many have used, therefore, dramatic forms of protest to call attention to their grievances.

We believe in the right and are committed to the protection of all peaceful, non-obstructive forms of protest, including mass demonstrations, picketing, rallies and other dramatic forms. However, we are deeply disturbed about some methods that some student activists have used in the attempt to achieve their ends; methods which violate and subvert the basic principles of freedom of expression and academic freedom. Protest that deprives others of the opportunity to speak or be heard, or that requires physical take-over of buildings to disrupt the educational process, or the incarceration of administrators and others are anti-civil-libertarian and incompatible with the nature and high purpose of an educational institution.

In December of 1968, students at New York University's Loeb Student Center stopped an address by Nguien Huu Chi, the South Vietnamese Permanent Observer at the UN, by draping a Nazi flag across him, hurling an egg and pouring a pitcher of water over him. They then invaded another room, seized the notes of James Reston, executive editor of the New York *Times,* and tore them to bits. He left without delivering his address.

In January 1969, at a symposium at Northwestern University on confronting change, student activists shouted down all but the most radical speakers.

In February at Harvard University, students disrupted a course whose focus they resented.

In March, Professor John H. Bunzel, of San Francisco State College, whose views are unpalatable to some student activists was drowned out in a flood of shouts and questions in his classroom.

At a conference on "World Problems and American Change" on March 22, 1969, Arthur J. Goldberg, former Supreme Court justice and United States ambassador to the United Nations, was shouted down by about 30 youngsters who dumped the head of a pig on the speaker's table.

Fundamental to the very nature of a free society is the conviction expressed by Mr. Justice Holmes that "the best test of truth is the power of the thought to get itself accepted in the competition of the market." When men govern themselves they have a right to decide for themselves which views and proposals are sound and which unsound. This means that all points of view are entitled to be expressed and heard. This is particularly true in universities which render great services to society when they function as centers of free, uncoerced, independent and creative thought and experience. Universities have existed and can exist without bricks and mortar but they cannot function without freedom of inquiry and expression.

For these reasons, the American Civil Liberties Union has from its very inception, defended free expression for all groups and all points of view, including the most radical and the most unpopular within the society and the university. To abandon the democratic process in the interests of "good" causes is to risk the destruction of freedom not just for the present but for the future, not just for our social order but for any future social order as well. Freedom, the world has learned to its sorrow, is a fragile plant that must be protected and cultivated.

We speak out of faith in our conventional wisdom—commitment to the principles of free expression embodied in the Bill of Rights—principles which are still essential, exhilarating, dynamic and even revolutionary. Free expression, academic freedom, habeas corpus, due process of law, and other liberties painfully won after centuries of struggle are worth preserving and extending.

It is well to remember, too, that violence and the threat of violence may be used in "bad" causes as well as "good" causes. They were employed by the Nazis in Germany and by Hungarian fascists to shut down universities or oust particular faculty members or students. They were used in the attempt to block the admission of James Meredith to the University of Mississippi and to block integration widely across the South. And there are those who today would use these methods to destroy our universities, not to reform them.

There are dangers, too, that violence and the threat of violence will breed a counter-violence and backlash that will defeat or set back the very objectives student activists seek to serve and lead to repressive counter-measures. Already under federal law enacted in 1968, any student convicted of a crime or regarded to have seriously violated college regulations, may be declared by the college authorities ineligible for two years to receive federal scholarships or loans. Under legislation enacted in 1969 any student convicted of a crime related to a campus disorder may not receive federal loans or scholarships.

In addition, no less than eighty bills are before the California legislature, and the New York legislature recently adopted a law intended to curb campus violence. At least 18 other states have campus control measures under consideration. Colorado has enacted a law which imposes fines of $500 and jail sentences of a year for those who interfere with the normal functioning of a college or university.

We are opposed to these measures. Their imposition is not likely to quiet down but rather to inflame further the unrest. Many of them are vague and would superimpose severe financial penalties in addition to punishment already provided by law. Their thrust often would be effective only against the poor. What is more, they threaten the traditional autonomy of academic communities to govern themselves. We are pleased that President Nixon has publicly recognized that the maintenance of order on campus "is fundamentally the task and responsibility of the university community." That function is more likely to be achieved if accompanied by orderly change.

We believe that the discussions between open-minded trustees and students which brought changes at the University of Pennsylvania set an admirable example. Similarly, we commend the experimentation in shared governance at Antioch College and Richmond College of the City University of New York. In general, we are convinced that universities must draw upon the whole academic community—trustees, administrators, faculties and students—to effect desirable changes. Where existing processes are inadequate or unrepresentative, creativity and imagination must be summoned to the task of developing new mechanisms for peaceful communication and decision-making that will prove responsive to just demands.

Let us recognize, finally, that some student activists have been moved by conscience to use extraordinary means in the belief that ordinary means have failed to build a just and equal society and secure peace. We in America have the burden of changing and adapting our social institutions and policies to demonstrate that we have the capacity and will to redress the evils of our social order.

A DECLARATION ON CAMPUS UNREST

The following statement, formulated by a group of prominent education-
al administrators, trustees, and foundation officers, was released by the
American Council on Education, April 18, 1969.

The unprecedented, comprehensive, and often unpredictable changes that
are taking place in this age both disturb and alarm large segments of our
society. Most of the changes and attendant alarms affect the operations of
our institutions of higher learning. They are also related to the values,
concerns, and behavior of our young people. In coming to grips with the
compelling issues, all who would think seriously about them must recognize
that present-day society—in America and in many foreign lands—is in
serious trouble on many fronts. We see around us racial conflict, continued
poverty, and malnutrition midst unparalleled prosperity and seemingly
unlimited promise. We are confronted by pollution of our environment,
decay of our cities, the continuation of wars and the threat of war, and
everywhere a vague but widespread discontent with the general quality of
life.

These problems affect all of society, not the university alone or the
young alone. We must all be concerned to deal intelligently and responsibly
with these problems that are neither the exclusive discovery, nor the sole
responsibility of the young. Yet the depth of feeling among young people in
many countries today about the issues, their general dissatisfaction with
the slow-moving ways of society, and the extreme behavior of a small
minority of students are evidence of the profound crisis that involves our
entire society and, specifically, the university community.

The university itself has often become the immediate target of student
discontent, sometimes couched as legitimate complaints about the deficiencies of the universities, sometimes devised as a softening-up exercise for
assault on the wider society.

How to deal with campus crises arising from the widespread protests has
become a major public issue and the cause of confused and angry debate.
That there should be deep anxiety about the course of the conflict and its

possible outcome is understandable. No social, racial, or age group that perceives itself and its values to be seriously threatened will fail to strike back. Increasingly there are backlash temptations to enact strong, often ill-considered, and largely futile measures to cope with a youth rebellion that none of us fully comprehends, not even the youth themselves.

Certain balanced judgments are proper to make, however, as we search for understanding and solutions:

1. It is important for the public to understand that, despite the nation-wide publicity given to student disorders, the great majority of American campuses have remained peaceful. On campuses where conspicuous disorders have occurred, educational programs generally have gone along their normal ways. Most students and faculty have continued to carry on their regular work. In the main, good teaching and good research, as traditionally defined, have been uninterrupted.

2. On the undisturbed campuses and among the majority of orderly students, however, there are widely shared discontents which extremists are at times able to manipulate to destructive ends. Moreover, even in the absence of violence, there has developed among some of the young a cult of irrationality and incivility which severely strains attempts to maintain sensible and decent human communication. Within this cult there is a minute group of destroyers who have abandoned hope in today's society, in today's university, and in the processes of orderly discussion and negotiation to secure significant change. Students and faculty are increasingly aware of the true nature of this group and are moving to deal with its destructive tactics. The necessity to deal with extremists, however, is placing an extraordinary burden upon the whole educational enterprise and upon those who man it. Consequently, universities are having to divert their energies and resources from central education tasks in order to deal with student unrest in its various forms.

3. The spectacular events precipitated by the extremists should not be allowed to obscure the recent accomplishments of those students, faculty, and administrators who have serious interest in constructive changes in society and in the university. They have broadened the curriculum and improved teaching. They have moved toward a more open and participating pattern for university governance. And they have begun to make the work of universities more meaningful in dealing with the problems of society. Those efforts must continue. Reform and self-renewal in higher education are ongoing imperatives.

4. Meanwhile, the speed and scale of social change have imposed many kinds of demands upon educational institutions for which their programs, their capabilities, and their funding are not always adequate. Moreover, universities are increasingly asked to perform functions for society, particularly in reshaping the behavior, values, and life-styles of the young, on

which the family and other social institutions have already had major influence—or lack of influence. Some of society's expectations for universities are quite unrealistic. Insofar as these expectations can be dealt with, they involve a sharing of responsibilities among diverse social institutions. Many of society's demands require new resources and fresh approaches to old and new problems.

5. Recognizing the right of and even the necessity for constructive dissent—and allowing for inevitable arguments over what is in fact constructive—certain axioms must be accepted as basic to the operation of any university:

a. Disruption and violence have no place on any campus. The academic community has the responsibility to deal promptly and directly with disruptions. If universities will not govern themselves, they will be governed by others. This elementary reality is increasingly becoming understood by all components of the university community. Student and faculty groups, including the American Association of University Professors and the National Student Association, have recently joined in efforts to improve disciplinary procedures and to formulate clear and realistic codes for dealing with misconduct, and more particularly with violence and disruption. Also, by involving students and faculty effectively in the governance of the university, it can be demonstrated that there are better ways of getting views considered and decisions made than by disruption.

b. The historic concern of the university community with academic freedom needs to be restated, reaffirmed, and vigorously defended against all, within or without the university, who would obstruct the right of scholars to investigate, teachers to teach, or students to learn. This reiteration is not to claim for the university special privileges that put it above the law or that free it from critical public appraisal—rather it affirms that the university must maintain a basic institutional integrity to function as a university.

c. Violations of criminal law must be dealt with through the ordinary processes of the law—and universities must attempt to deal with disruptive situations firmly before they reach the stage of police action. Governmental attempts to deal with these problems through special, punitive legislation will almost certainly be counter-productive. Meanwhile, students and faculty whose consciences demand that they express dissent through law violation must be prepared to accept the due processes and the penalties of the law. They should not be encouraged to expect amnesty from the effects of the law. Such an expectation would be the ultimate use of the *in loco parentis* concept against which many young activists passionately protest. Nor should they expect amnesty from academic discipline, which is the most effective sanction in disruptive incidents.

6. The education community needs to undertake a far more comprehen-

sive effort than ever before attempted to study the underlying bases of youthful discontent and alienation and the broad social problems to which they are related. As social critic, the university must help society understand and solve such problems.

7. All universities should give particular attention to a continuing search for ways, including new social inventions, by which the life of rationality and civility, shared concern, and mutual respect may be supported and strengthened within the university community. The survival of the university and its long-term contribution to society depend upon the ability of the institutions to make their everyday life reflect that spirit and pattern.

STATEMENT OF THE SECRETARY OF HEALTH, EDUCATION, AND WELFARE BEFORE A HOUSE EDUCATION SUBCOMMITTEE

Robert H. Finch, Secretary of Health, Education, and Welfare, made the following statement before the Special Subcommittee on Education of the Committee on Education and Labor, U.S. House of Representatives, April 18, 1969.

Madam Chairman, Members of the Subcommittee:

I am pleased to appear before your subcommittee in response to your letter of March 19, 1969. In that letter you requested my views on the "problems of student unrest on our campuses, the role that the Federal Government might play in regard to these problems and particularly in regard to Federal financial assistance to students under the various programs listed in Section 504."

Your letter also expressed the hope that some of my comments would be directed specifically to Section 504 of the Higher Education Amendments of 1968 and a similar provision in the Labor-HEW 1969 Appropriations Act.

As you know, the President issued a comprehensive statement on March 22, 1969, outlining the views of the Administration respecting the difficult and complex issues posed by the current student unrest. At the same time, I sent a letter to the Presidents of all Universities, Colleges, Junior Colleges and Community Colleges. My letter called their attention to recently enacted Federal laws and requested that they, in turn, inform their students, faculty, and governing boards both of the requirements of Congressional legislation on this subject and of the procedures that each plans to institute to comply with these provisions. Copies of the President's statement and my letter accompany this statement, and I offer them to you for the record.

The entire syndrome we now face—violence, disruption, confrontation—is a tragic development in the history of American higher education. All of us are agreed, I believe, that it is essential to maintain the integrity and autonomy of our educational community. Thus, we must guard against those few who employ the rhetoric and tactics of violence in order to destroy institutions for which they have no real understanding, institutions dedicated to the life of the mind.

These disorders are unquestionably serious. Still, I think we must keep them in balanced perspective. The problems involved are deep-seated and complex, and they vary from institution to institution. The line between legitimate dissent and intolerable disruption is hard to draw—sometimes, indeed, even within the life-cycle of a particular campus outbreak. I want to suggest three lines of thought in this connection:

First of all, as to present legislation on the termination of Federal assistance to students involved in campus disorders, we lack essential data. We have never maintained records of individual aid recipients and have no capacity to do so. Administratively, it is as difficult to catalog the 1.5 million students receiving benefits as it would be to lay down a uniform code of student conduct—and just as undesirable. We currently do not know much about the nature of those involved in disruptions, the numbers who receive Federal aid, or the numbers whose aid has been or will be terminated by the institutions charged with that responsibility. Both Section 411 and Section 504 (a) require court convictions before aid may be terminated, and this may mean months or even years before the legal issues are resolved. These provisions have only been in force since October 1968, and so it is far too early to expect precise data on their practical effect.

Furthermore, some institutions quite properly do not wish to prejudice their positions in pending criminal proceedings by premature disclosure of information. But we are instituting various inquiries and instructions—which I will specify below—and hope, in time, that these will provide us with the hard data we need.

Second, despite this lack of data, I think it *has* become clear that the serious problems are posed by a tiny minority of students. Many are children of the affluent, of the middle and upper-classes. Most aid recipients, on the other hand, are too busy maintaining grades and working to supplement their resources to spend much time on the barricades. Thus, we must focus on the hard-core extremists, not the vast majority of hardworking students, and adopt the appropriate instruments of policy. We want to solve the problem, not to wield an indiscriminate bludgeon.

Finally, I think it is also clear that the problems disturbing our student generation are not entirely those of the university, although this has become the field of battle. Rather, the problems embody many of those burning social and political issues which range at large throughout our society. We cannot realistically demand that our universities resolve those conflicts which our society as a whole has not resolved. Nor can we assume, out of hand, that campus conflict is simply conflict for its own sake: in many instances, it is solidly based in legitimate grievance.

All our attempts to address these problems—the President's statement, my letter, and the enforcement mechanisms embodied in the recently enacted Congressional legislation—have sought to maintain a deeply-felt tradition as to the proper relationship of the Federal Government to institutions of higher learning. Precisely because the issues and problems vary from campus to campus, these institutions are best equipped to invoke the enforcement mechanisms set forth in the legislation, in light of their own judgment and experience. We hold, and we have attempted to express, a true regard for academic freedom.

No one, I believe, contends that the instrument of terminating financial assistance will prove to be the entire answer to the problem of violence on our campuses. Only time and experience gained by implementing the laws enacted in late 1968 will be able to tell us how much of the answer this approach can provide. Congress has spoken on this subject, and I want to assure you of the determination of my Department to see that these laws are enforced. In addition to the President's statement and my letter to which I have referred, I want to outline for you the steps which we have taken in the weeks since January 20, 1969, when the new Administration took office:

1. On January 28, 1969, the Office of Education issued the Higher Education Reports to all institutions of learning. Included in this issue was an analysis of Section 504 as prepared by our Office of the General Counsel. We are currently reassessing this early analysis, in light of some additional experience, to see if we can provide more precise guidance to educational officials.

2. By a communication dated March 10, 1969, addressed to college and university presidents and coordinators of student financial aid, the Office of Education reiterated the requirements of Section 504 and explored the administrative implications of this legislation. It also called the attention of these institutions to the provisions of Section 411 of the Labor-HEW 1969 Appropriations Act.

3. On February 26, 1969, the Office of Education requested the Higher Education Representative in each of HEW's nine regions to contact at least three institutions of higher learning in their respective regions in which campus disturbances of a serious nature had taken place. Summaries that were received back by mid-March reflected considerable confusion and some dissatisfaction on the part of campus administrators with respect to the provisions of law they were expected to implement.

4. The Regional representatives were then asked to update their initial summaries to reflect campus activities as of April 10, 1969. These later summaries are now being received by the Office of Education and will be sent to you as rapidly as possible.

5. The communication of March 10, 1969, an informational memorandum on the implications of the 1968 legislation, requested also that the institutions administering aid to students under the affected programs specify in their annual reports to us detailed information on cases in which financial assistance had been terminated under Section 504. In addition, of course, under our routine procedures for auditing expenditures of Federal funds, we will check further as to compliance with Federal law.

6. We have every indication that institutions of higher education intend to comply promptly and fully with the provisions of these statutes. My office has already received in excess of 300 letters in response to the President's statement and my letter. These responses, which I offer now for the record, are convincing evidence that these institutions are aware of the requirements of the legislation and intend to implement it.

We are considering a number of proposals through which we might assist colleges and universities in resolving conflict. In my letter of March 22, I expressed concern that institutions of higher learning undertake a comprehensive review of their policies and procedures respecting the expression of dissent in order that the rights of responsible students to express their views be fully protected. We recognize, too, that many institutions are in the process of reexamining and restructuring the nature of the educational experience they offer to their students, and we want in every possible way to encourage and support such constructive efforts.

In addition to these steps, we have initiated or have under consideration, the following action:

(A) *Case Studies of Successful Dispute Resolution*

It is by no means the case that all instances of student unrest have resulted in outbreaks of violence. In many institutions, disputes arising among the various segments of that community have been resolved peacefully and constructively through procedures evolved by the community itself. The Office of Education is now collecting—and I have instructed it to disseminate widely to institutions of higher learning—information about models of successful dispute-resolution that might be adaptable to the particular circumstances of other institutions.

(B) *Projects Funded by Bureau of Research*
Under existing authority, the Bureau of Research of the Office of Education can respond to proposals by educational institutions or other groups which seek to develop new responses to questions of educational reform and institutional structure.

We know of several projects, one at the California Institute of Technology in particular, which have involved students actively and constructively in educational experiences which have, at the same time, contributed in a vital way to the needs of surrounding community. We hope we can, through research grants, stimulate such constructive projects and assist educational institutions in their own process of self-evaluation. We are exploring all such avenues of constructive response to the underlying causes of campus unrest.

(C) *Technical Assistance*
Finally, we are exploring the feasibility of applying funds for technical assistance under Title IV of the Civil Rights Act of 1964 for the resolution of conflict in which racial disturbances contribute to the basic unrest.

Legal Ramifications of the Present Statutes

You have asked me to comment in my testimony on Section 504 of the Higher Education Amendments of 1968 (P.L. 90-575) and Section 411 of the Departments of Labor and Health, Education, and Welfare 1969 Appropriations Act (P.L. 90-557). I have already outlined in detail the steps taken by my Department to call these provisions to the attention of local institutions and to see that they are enforced. I strongly reaffirm the position of the Administration, and of my Department, that the responsibility for enforcing these provisions properly lies with each educational institution. At the same time, I think it important to comment on some questions of interpretation that go to the practical application of these provisions.

For example, there is a question whether Section 504 (a) *obliges* an institution of higher education to institute a proceeding as to any individual attending or employed by the institution who appears to have engaged in conduct that warrants termination of his aid. The issue raised goes to the mandatory or discretionary nature of the law.

I have already observed that Section 504 is one of the tools the Federal government has provided to our institutions of higher learning to supple-ment—but not undermine—their own procedures for handling campus disor-ders. The law reflects, I believe, the judgment that the public interest in providing financial assistance also calls for terminating such assistance where there is an abuse of the opportunity provided. By an abuse, I mean the infringement of the rights of others who are part of the academic community, and of the institution's own right to conduct the business of higher education.

As with any provision of law, Section 504 demands compliance in good faith by those to whom it applies. So we expect that colleges and universi-ties will strive in good faith to implement its provisions for aid termination where the facts disclose the "abuse" has taken place. Compliance in this sense is mandatory and, as I have already indicated, we have every good reason to believe educational institutions genuinely intend to comply.

This is not to say, however, that an institution must invoke the determi-nation mechanism in all cases of campus agitation. Obviously, the school must exercise its best judgment whether the facts to be developed do or do not indicate the kind of abuse that would disqualify an individual for Federal aid. Under some especially explosive circumstances, it is even possible that the very institution of a hearing might aggravate campus tension. This does not mean Section 504 should *not* be implemented. It means simply, that there are risks involved, of which Congress should be aware.

I would call the attention of the subcommittee to the problems posed by the requirement, common to both statutes, that there be a "conviction." The problem arises with the age of the aid recipients who may be involved in campus disorders. Many, if not most of these are minors, and under applicable State law, may frequently be subject only to the juvenile court proceedings. In no state does such a proceeding result in a criminal conviction. However, the age at which students may be subject to the jurisdiction of juvenile courts varies widely from state to state, thus creating inequities in the application of the statute. This aspect of Section 504 (a) applicability came to our attention recently in a case involving a student at San Fernando Valley State College in California. While the student was involved in an act of arson on the campus, because of his age, criminal proceedings could not be brought. Additionally, of course, Section 504 (a) could not be a basis of termination of his Federal financial assistance.

The question has arisen whether the two Sections of law are compatible. I do not believe that Section 504 (a) of the Higher Education Act and Section 411 of the 1969 Appropriation Act are legally incompatible, and the Department is determined to see that both are enforced according to their terms. However, I think it is well to point out that these two Sections represent somewhat different policy approaches to the same problem. For example, under Section 504, before a student may be disqualified for assistance under the programs specified in that Section, the university must find that his crime was of a "serious nature" and "contributed to a substantial disruption of the administration of the institution." These particular findings are *not* required under Section 411. In this and other respects, Section 504 (a) confers somewhat greater discretion on institutions of higher education than Section 411.

A student against whom an adverse determination is made under Section 504 (a) is disqualified from receiving assistance under the relevant programs for a period of two years. Under Section 411, if the language of that Section is carried forward in future appropriations acts, disqualification (with respect to programs to which Section 504 applies, and certain additional programs) would be permanent. Moreover, the applicability of Section 411 may turn on the nature of the convicting court. Thus, a student subjected to a Section 504 proceeding may suffer somewhat different consequences than a student whose assistance is terminated under Section 411. This may be so, even though the participation of both students in a disorder, and their respective culpability, may be virtually identical. A uniform policy in this regard would be preferable.

There are technical and procedural differences between the two sections which may be a source of confusion for the universities that must administer these provisions. Under Section 504 a notice and hearing are required. Under Section 411, while notice and hearing are not expressly required, we believe that such notice and hearing would be required by due process considerations, as well as by the university's own disciplinary procedures. Thus, under certain circumstances, where both Section 504 and Section 411 apply to a particular case, the university might find itself obliged to make two determinations with respect to the same student.

In brief, I believe the problems involved are so important that the Congress should look again at the differences between Section 411 and Section 504 (a) and attempt to speak with one voice. I think too, that with time and experience in implementing these laws, there will be a much sounder basis for evaluating the relative efficacy of each approach. At the present time, however, I believe the approach of 504 is sounder and should be preferred to 411. It provides guarantees of due process of law, it allows for examination of student conduct in light of the institutions' own needs and interests, and it can be applied flexibly.

The current student unrest has posed grave questions for our university administrators. Having become accustomed to defending academic freedom against onslaughts from without, they now find themselves faced with an internal attack which is as new as it is virulent.

In all truth, many academic institutions have brought much of it on themselves. They have not always responded to the clear need of any viable institution for constant self-examination and self-renewal. In the quest for more and better research grants, they have not always attended to their primary objectives as teaching institutions. In attempting to serve many masters—government and industry among them—they have tended to serve none of them well. Now they are faced with extremist attempts to impose a new orthodoxy, and the only proper agents to insure bonafide academic pursuits within the context of order lie in the administration, faculty, governing boards and other segments of the university community itself.

Professor S. A. Tonsor, of the University of Michigan, recently delivered a speech in Washington which set many of our problems in thoughtful perspective. I would like to leave you with a few of his words:

"American education has become a single mechanism; its professors and students interchangable parts. Under these circumstances, even student riots are monotonously, repellently, alike. Among the most important functions of education is that of widening the options available to men in the solution of their problems and in the improvement of the quality of their lives, yet our universities steadily diminish and dilute the differences between themselves. Students are still able to choose the quality of their education; they are unable, however, to do much through their own choices about the kind of education they receive.

"The authority and the relevance of the university lies in its ability as an institution to explore systematically and rationally the problems men face. Its success is not dependent upon current fashions in ideas or current solutions to particular problems. Its success derives from its ability to take the long view and ask the hard questions, and the hardest of these is the question the professor asks of himself, of his colleagues and his society about the possibility of being wrong."

The university communities have asked for time to adjust their institutional procedures in response to these pressures, in response to legitimate demands for reform, and, indeed, to the very legislation before us. This is the approach supported by the Department of Health, Education and Welfare.

DISSENT ON THE CAMPUS:
REMARKS BY THE PRESIDENT

The following is an excerpt from an address that President Richard M. Nixon delivered at the 57th annual meeting of the United States Chamber of Commerce, Sheraton Park Hotel, Washington, D.C., April 29, 1969.

* * *

. . . I have decided to speak briefly on a subject of very great concern to all of you, of very great concern to me, and I will say to all Americans at this time. I refer to the problems of education in the very broadest sense in the United States.

I am not going to cover that subject in all of its ramifications. That is something that the Secretary of Health, Education and Welfare and Dr. Allen could do much more ably than I. But there are phases of it that I think do require, at this time, a statement by the President of the United States, amplifying a statement I made earlier on a problem that deeply concerns us all.

That is the problem of what I would call the new revolutionary spirit and new revolutionary actions that are taking place on the campuses of many of our colleges and universities and also that may begin to take place, and also are taking place, I understand, in some of the high schools of this country.

Now I am not going to speak to that problem in the way that you might usually expect. It is easy to be against some of the actions that have occurred. All of us are concerned by those actions. We are against them. The question is to refine our discussions to some simple issues and some simple principles. I am going to state some opinions now that are my own.

Some will not agree with me. But I think they are opinions that are in accord with the great traditions of free education in America. I think they need to be stated by the President of the United States and if you share them, I hope that when you go back to your communities you will state them and I would hope also to the extent that you have opportunities in official or other capacities, school boards, or as trustees, or faculty members, if you are that, you will be able, perhaps, to implement it.

First, with regard to that great problem of dissent on the college and university campuses, let us recognize that this is a very healthy force when we consider it at its best. We do not want, in America, an educational system which becomes in-grown, stultified, loses the ability to develop the new ideas to keep pace with the change in our very fast-changing society.

Consequently, we can be thankful today that we do have a younger generation, which is as I have often said, with all of the faults that we may see in it, the best educated younger generation that we have ever had; more deeply motivated than any that we have ever had; one that deeply cares about America, about our system, and about our educational system. We may not agree with them, but they do care.

Now having said that, I now indicate what I think are some principles in which dissent must properly be expressed. One is this: As far as our colleges and universities are concerned, I think that young people, students, are correct in asking that they have a voice; a voice in determining what the courses should be, a voice in determining what the rules should be. But then I say that while they should have a voice, under no circumstances should they be given control of the colleges and universities.

I suppose some could quarrel with that qualification. But I would suggest that we can always learn from history, not only the history of our own country, but the history of countries throughout the world who have gone through similar revolutions. Philosopher Santayana once wrote that, "Those who do not remember the past are condemned to repeat it."

Look to the countries to the south of us, our closest neighbors, our closest friends—very proud countries, many great and old universities. Those universities, most of them, went through a revolution similar to ours 100 years ago.

The students won. They won not only a voice, but they won control in many of those universities, the right to hire and fire the professors and to determine the courses. And the result is that the educational system as far as higher education is concerned, in Latin America generally, is one of the most inferior in the world. I say let us not let it happen here in the United States of America.

So our answer here is not to deny the voice. We must listen, and certainly where that voice expresses views that ought to be implemented, we should implement them. But on the other hand, remember that it is the responsibility of faculties, boards and trustees, to provide the leadership for educational institutions.

Then we come to the second point: That is the method of dissent. Here again, we have some fine lines that need to be drawn and some principles that we must have in mind.

There are those who believe that any means are justified, if the end is worthwhile. And all of us, again, if we remember the past, will, of course, agree that we can never adopt that principle, because when we adopt that principle of any means to the end, the end eventually becomes the means.

So we look at our college campuses and our university campuses today and we see some things which concern us. We see, first, the dissent. That we accept, we welcome, and we encourage, provided it is the peaceful kind of dissent within the rules of an institution and of our society.

And, second, we also—and I presently today proclaim as I have previously the principle that we do not want to have the Federal Government of this country running our institutions. We do not want them interfering with our colleges and our universities. It is their responsibility to provide education in an independent, free way in the American tradition.

But, third, we have another factor that we must face. That is this: When we find situations in numbers of colleges and universities which reach the point where students in the name of dissent and in the name of change terrorize other students and faculty members, when they rifle files, when they engage in violence, when they carry guns and knives in the classrooms, then I say it is time for faculties, boards of trustees and school administrators to have the backbone to stand up against this kind of situation.

What I am simply suggesting here is this: We do not want government control of our great educational institutions. We want to have that freedom which comes from the independence of a great university and college community. But as we look at the situation today, I think all of those who have a responsibility for providing educational leadership must recognize that there can be no compromise with lawlessness and no surrender to force if free education is to survive in the United States of America.

* * *

"WHAT KIND OF WORLD DO
YOU WANT?"

~~~~~~

*Attorney General John N. Mitchell delivered the following address at the
Annual Law Day Dinner, Detroit Bar Association, Raleigh House, Detroit,
Mich., May 1, 1969. Only his brief opening remarks have been deleted.*

<p style="text-align:center">*   *   *</p>

. . . I would like to talk to you about a serious threat to our system of
law, a threat which is as disturbing as the violence in our cities. It is the
violence and dissatisfaction on our college campuses.

Campus disorders are basically a local problem to be solved at the local
level and not by the federal government. But as Attorney General—as the
senior law enforcement officer in the nation—I believe that I have the
responsibility to comment on national problems which affect the administration of justice even though my legal jurisdiction may be limited.

I also come to you . . . as a fellow citizen, as a parent with two children
recently graduated from college and as a grandfather concerned about the
future.

An eminent Nobel laureate said last month in Boston: "What we are up
against is a generation that is by no means sure it has a future." I disagree
with that assessment.

I suggest that this generation has the most promising future world of any
generation of Americans.

But I must pose to them the query of Mr. Justice Holmes:

"Behind every scheme to make the world over lies the question, what
kind of world do you want?"

What kind of world do our students want? Do our university officials
want? Do our teachers want? Do our citizens want? And I must remind you
that when we talk about our students we are not talking about an alien
people—we are talking about our own sons and daughters and about the
type of nation we are making for them to inherit.

I. The Facts

Let me quote briefly to you a capsulized dispatch issued by the Associated Press at 10:15 a.m., EST, on April 24 [1969]:

Washington—Student militants seize buildings at American University and George Washington University.

Ithaca—Cornell University faculty members agree to demands of students who seized college buildings armed with guns.

Kent, Ohio—Kent college students create physical disturbances.

New Orleans—Southern University students lower the American flag.

Cambridge—Harvard professor resigns in the wake of police-student clash.

Princeton—Sixty students block doorways to a research facility.

New York—One hundred-fifty students and faculty stage a sit-in at Fordham University.

College Park, Maryland—University of Maryland protestors attempt to block entry to a science center.

New York—Two Brooklyn high schools forced to close after three days of student unrest.

That is one day of what kind of world some of our students have. In the current academic year, there have been demonstrations on over 200 college campuses throughout the nation. This has resulted in more than 2300 arrests and property damage in excess of an estimated $2.2 million.

Since January 1, 1969, the protest movement has escalated its tactics. For example, in the State of California:

At San Francisco State a bomb permanently blinded one student and a second bomb was discovered before it exploded.

At Pomona College in Claremont, a secretary was blinded in one eye and lost two fingers when a bomb exploded as she was removing it from a college mailbox.

At the University of California in Santa Barbara, a custodian at the Faculty Club died from burns when he picked up a firebomb.

At Berkeley, in the last eight months, there have been four arsons and two bombings, and $1.1 million in property damage.

This Administration has tried to be patient in the hope that students, faculty, and local officials, working together, would put an end to this chaos.

But the time has come for an end to patience. The time has come for us to demand, in the strongest possible terms, that university officials, local law enforcement agencies and local courts apply the law.

I call for an end to minority tyranny on the nation's campuses and for the immediate reestablishment of civil peace and the protection of individual rights.

If arrests must be made, then arrests there should be. If violators must be prosecuted, then prosecutions there should be.

It is no admission of defeat, as some may claim, to use reasonable physical force to eliminate physical force. The price of civil tranquillity cannot be paid by submission to violence and terror.

II. The Idea of the University

The American university educational system is one of our proudest achievements.

Perhaps, it is that our current generation does not appreciate the toil that has gone to build it. Starting with one small donated library in 1636, our university system now numbers more than 2,000 public and private institutions with 6.9 million students. The concept that we have in this nation that all who are qualified deserve an education, has been one of our unique contributions.

James Russell Lowell noted:

"It was in making education not only common to all, but in some sense compulsory on all, that the destiny of the free republics of America was practically settled."

Another cherished concept of our university is—as the Commission headed by former Solicitor General Archibald Cox reported—

"A university is essentially a free community of scholars dedicated to the pursuit of truth and knowledge solely through reason and civility . . . resort to violence or physical harassment, or obstruction is never an acceptable tactic for influencing decisions in a university."

III. The Student Movement

To date, we have had disturbances on more than 200 campuses—about nine per cent of the colleges in the country. In only a small number of such disturbances was there any severe physical violence and bloodshed reported. The total arrest rate, of 2300, is less than four-tenths of one per cent of all of our students.

While accurate statistics are not available, it is believed that less than two per cent of our students have engaged actively in any disruptions causing physical or property damage.

It might be convenient to look at these statistics and suggest that the situation has been exaggerated. I think not.

Society has a way of selecting symbols and it is no accident that some of the most violent demonstrations have occurred at some of our most highly regarded universities—California, Wisconsin, Harvard, Cornell, Duke, Columbia—the universities to which we point with pride as among the leaders of our higher educational system.

Furthermore, it is undeniable that, while violence-prone activists represent a small percentage of our students, some of their actions have struck a responsive chord to a whole generation: so responsive, in fact, that the activists receive at least tacit support or neutrality from many other students.

As Professor Freund said prophetically, a year ago, our students accuse us of hypocrisy: that our laws, while pretending to be equal, give preference to the rich; that our politics, while pretending to be honest, are tools for the influential; that our scientists, while pretending to be humanitarian, build machines of war; that our economic prosperity, while pretending to affluence, leaves some citizens hungry; that our religion, while pretending to be pious, is conveniently indifferent.

I would be less than candid with you if I did not admit that their accusations are sometimes true. I cannot deny that the world of my generation may appear hypocritical to the generation of our sons. Neither do I deny that my father's generation appeared hypocritical to me as his father's did to him.

What our sons must remember is that we have today in this nation more equality in the law, more honesty in politics, more ethics in science, more people employed and less people hungry, and more religious dedication to the problems of society than at any other period in our history and than in any other nation in the world. Our progress may be too slow for our sons. But it is good faith progress; and cautious advancement is no justification for destruction.

A decade ago we saw the "silent generation" going quietly from the university to earning a living. Today, we have the "involved generation" who are interested in the problems of our society. They are active in civil rights, in poverty, in hunger, in education for the poor, in job retraining, and in partisan politics. I welcome this generation's demand that the university not be an extraterritorial community removed from society, but that it and its members deeply involve themselves with the problems of the day.

But if they are to assume a role as adult activists in a community, they must also assume the obligations that go with adult citizenship. And one of the primary obligations upon which we exist is a simple maxim, carved above an entrance of the Justice Department in Washington, which says:

"Law alone can give us freedom. Where law ends, tyranny begins."

Campus militants, directing their efforts at destruction and intimidation, are nothing but tyrants. But there are others who share the blame by failing to act—university administrators must take firm and immediate action to protect the rights of faculty members to teach and of other students to learn. Faculty members should stop negotiating under the blackmail threat of violence. Apathetic students should stand up for the rights of those who wish to pursue civility and scholarship in the academic community. To the extent that they remain neutral or refuse to act, they are all accessories to the tyranny we are now witnessing.

IV. The Constitutional Right to Dissent

The genesis of our current student problems is thought to lie in our encouragement of lawful dissent.

The right to express disagreement with the acts of constituted authority is one of our fundamental freedoms. The First Amendment expressly protects "the freedom of speech" and "of the press" and "the right of the people peaceably to assemble, and petition the Government for a redress of grievances."

As one Supreme Court Justice has described it:

"The right to speak freely and to promote the debate of ideas is . . . one of the chief distinctions that sets us apart from totalitarian regimes."

Recognizing this, the Supreme Court has construed the First Amendment to protect the right of a citizen to speak, to write and to disseminate his ideas by peaceful methods.

Citizens have the right to use the streets and other public grounds, to conduct reasonable demonstrations, to distribute handbills and to quietly picket.

Furthermore, schools should be encouraged to abide by First Amendment principles.

As Mr. Justice Brennan has said:

"The vigilant protection of constitutional freedom is no where more vital than in the community of American schools. The classroom is particularly the 'market place of ideas'."

While this description was applied to the public, tax-supported school, it would seem to me that First Amendment ideas should apply equally to all universities, both public and private.

V. The Limits of Dissent

But there are definite limits beyond which these First Amendment guarantees may not be carried.

The Supreme Court has flatly rejected the argument "that people who want to propagandize protests or views have a constitutional right to do so whenever and however they please."

As Mr. Justice Goldberg has said:

"We also reaffirm the repeated decisions of this Court that there is no place for violence in a democratic society dedicated to liberty under law. . . . There is a proper time and place for even the most peaceful protest and a plain duty and responsibility on the part of all citizens to obey all valid laws and regulations."

The Supreme Court has explained that demonstrators do not have a constitutional right to cordon off a street, or to block the entrance to a building, or to refuse to allow any one to pass who will not listen to their exhortations.

The question remains, of course, whether the rights of students to protest on a university campus are to be greater or the same as the rights which the ordinary citizen enjoys under the First Amendment.

Only two months ago the Supreme Court ruled that the right of students to engage in peaceful protests does not include the right to disrupt the educational process.

If we are to be consistent, I believe that students on campus should enjoy at least the minimum protections for freedom of speech specified by the Constitution. In certain circumstances it may be appropriate for university authorities to offer additional rights. Exaggeration and bizarre behavior, romanticism and intellectual rebellion are traditional among our youth. The scope of these additional rights, if any, should be decided by each individual university authority.

But let me make one thing clear: students do not enjoy any special prerogative to interfere with the rights of other students or, as the Supreme Court has said: " . . . conduct by the student in class or out of it . . . is . . . not immunized by the constitutional guarantee of freedom of speech."

The right to be a student carries other fundamental rights than the right to dissent. Among these valuable rights which must also be protected, are the right to use research facilities, free from occupation by demonstrators; the right to use libraries free from seizure by dissidents; the right to consult with administrators free from having one's personal file and records destroyed; the right to study in an atmosphere of "reason and civility."

VI. The Moral Right to Dissent

In any honest discussion on student protests, one must meet the claim that civil disobedience is an accepted tradition in American society.

This is especially true among our student population who claim that their seizures of university buildings and imprisonment of university officials are legitimate acts of civil disobedience similar to their participation in the civil rights protests.

I disagree. First: traditionally, civil disobedience has involved an issue of universal or fundamental morality—such as the equality of the races. No such issue has been involved in the current student protests.

Second: organized disobedience in the civil rights movement has rarely involved violence or bloodshed. It has concentrated, rather, on non-violence and on symbolic action which offered no substantial deprivation of rights to anyone else. One can hardly equate a sit-in at a bus terminal with throwing a student out of a second story window.

Third: in this country, the historical key to civil disobedience has been its amenability to arrest and prosecution. Indeed, it has always been considered, as Thoreau told Emerson, that the moral righteousness of breaking a law was in the punishment that the law meted out.

Today's militants also reject that concept. They physically resist arrest and they are unwilling to submit the merits of their cause to any tribunal other than their own self-determination.

VII. What Should Be Done

Having defined the problem, I feel obligated to offer a few suggestions on what can and should be done to resolve it.

My jurisdiction, as you well know, is limited to the application of federal law. Our concept has always been that, unless we in the federal government have a clear mandate, we permit the states and the municipalities to deal with law enforcement problems. The clearest mandate we have, so far, is the anti-riot provisions of the 1968 Civil Rights Act. It prohibits persons from crossing state lines with intent to incite riots.

We have substantial information confirming the widely accepted belief that several major university disturbances have been incited by members of a small core of professional militants who make it their tragic occupation to convert peaceable student dissatisfaction into violence and confrontation.

These circumstances can only lead to the conclusion that this hard core is bent on the destruction of our universities and not on their improvement.

You can be assured that these violence-prone militants will be prosecuted to the full extent of our federal laws.

We are also collecting a great deal of information about student disorders and those who cause them.

We are offering this information to state and local law enforcement officials operating in jurisdictions where campus disorders may occur.

No society, including an academic society, can survive without basic agreement by a great majority of its members as to the fundamental precepts upon which it operates.

The first precept for any academic community must be to outlaw terror.

The second premise is that students, faculty and administration officials should all participate, in some measure, in the decision-making process. What this means, at a minimum, is that university administrators must offer a serious forum for responsible student criticism—and more than that, it must be clear to the students that their grievances will be honestly considered and will not be lightly dismissed under the procedural ruse of an artificial dialogue.

Third: universities must prepare for prospective violence. It is no longer acceptable for a university administration to claim, after the events of this year, that they were taken unawares—that they acted in panic and that their mistakes can be blamed on the alacrity with which the demonstration developed.

Here, too, the entire university community should be consulted since it is the censure or approbation of a majority of this community which will determine the course of student violence.

If, as has been done at some universities, the majority overwhelmingly rejects minority violence, the militants are left isolated except for brute physical power. Since the entire concept of confrontation is to attract the sympathy of the majority—and sometimes the sympathies may be forthcoming because of inappropriate reactions—this major avenue of support for violent demonstrators should be substantially diminished.

In any event, the university administrator should, in anticipation of the outbreak of a disturbance, consult with local law enforcement officials on the methods of handling various disturbances. Preparation and coordination by these parties may well eliminate the disturbance and will assure the timely application of any required counter-force.

Fourth: if all else fails and a disturbance does occur, university officials should consider applying immediately to a court for an injunction. This tactic has proved fairly successful in the past. It takes the university out of the law enforcement business, where it does not belong, and replaces it with the court which is better suited for this purpose.

Let me be specific: University officials are not law enforcement experts or judges. When a violent outbreak occurs, they should not take it upon themselves to decide how long the violence should endure and what rights should be trampled upon until local government is called in. For minor demonstrations, which involve no serious disruptions, the university should have the viability to decide for itself what the best solution may be.

But when people may be injured, when personal property may be destroyed, and when chaos begins, the university official only aids lawlessness by procrastination and negotiation. The university is not an extraterritorial community and its officials have the obligation to protect the rights of the peaceful students on its campus by use of the established local law enforcement agencies and the courts.

I should like to conclude this address by asking our sons and daughters to consider the words of Rousseau:

"If force creates right, the effect changes the cause: every force that is greater than the first succeeds to its right. As soon as it is possible to disobey with immunity, disobedience is legitimate; and the strongest being always in the right, the only thing that matters is to act so as to become the strongest. But what kind of right is that which perishes when force fails?"

Ladies and Gentlemen: "Behind every scheme to make the world over, lies the question: what kind of world do you want?"

AAUP ON LAW ENFORCEMENT AND ACADEMIC ORDER

The following statement was released at the 55th annual meeting of the American Association of University Professors, Minneapolis, Minn., May 3, 1969.

The Fifty-fifth Annual Meeting of the American Association of University Professors notes with grave concern press reports of a recent series of provocative statements by high federal officials which threaten "professional militants" allegedly responsible for disruption with prosecution for conspiracy, and which employ indiscriminate and dangerous phrases such as "ideological criminals" and "new barbarians." Such statements suggest a policy which is a direct threat to academic freedom and autonomy.

Academic life must be protected from both external and internal assaults. Having affirmed that the initiative in that protection must rest with properly constituted academic authorities, the Annual Meeting states its conviction that the present tragic season in our intellectual life must not be made the occasion for premature or punitive intervention by public officials or law enforcement officers. It calls upon administrative officers, faculty members, and students to exercise their obligations affirmatively so as to insure maintenance of institutional autonomy, academic order, and academic freedom.

AAUP STATEMENT ON CAMPUS DISRUPTION

The American Association of University Professors passed the following resolution at the 55th annual meeting, May 3, 1969, in Minneapolis, Minn.

The Fifty-fifth Annual Meeting of the American Association of University Professors recognizes that demonstrations and confrontations on campuses across the nation are frequently a manifestation of deep and sometimes profoundly moral discontent arising out of social injustice, public policy, and, in some cases, out of inefficiency, irresponsibility, and unresponsiveness within the institutions themselves. The Annual Meeting therefore calls on all members of the academic community to seek appropriate remedies, encourage necessary change, and discourage disruptive action.

American colleges and universities have long cherished a tradition of institutional autonomy. Disruptive actions of militant students and faculty can profoundly threaten that autonomy because those actions may provoke distrust and hostility and lead to countermeasures on the part of other students, government, and the public. The current crisis can thus only be compounded by vengeful reprisals, such as repressive legislation, punitive reduction of public and private financing of higher education that will penalize all students alike, or the withdrawal, on outside initiative, of grants from students alleged to have taken part in riots. Regular academic procedures, when utilized, can provide sufficient sanctions, and it is both unjust and destructive of institutional autonomy for additional punitive measures to be automatically imposed by outside authority as a consequence of institutional discipline.

Wherever possible, the maintenance of essential academic order should be the responsibility of the institutions themselves; breaches of that order by students should be judged by institutional tribunals, in accordance with the *Joint Statement on Rights and Freedoms of Students*, and breaches of students should be judged by institutional tribunals, in accordance with accepted professional standards. Academic due process, both procedural and substantive, must be guaranteed. Should the maintenance of academic order prove a task beyond the powers of regularly constituted institutional organs, and should it prove unhappily necessary to resort to the civil power, decisions as to its use should be made in the first instance by responsible administrative officers and faculty members in the service of academic criteria and not of political expediency. Thereafter every effort should be made to restore ordinary academic processes as quickly as possible.

THE STRUGGLE TO PRESERVE THE
RULE OF LAW

The following is an excerpt from an address on the rule of law in American society that Senator Edward M. Kennedy delivered before the NAACP Legal Defense and Educational Fund, Commodore Hotel, New York City, May 15, 1969.

* * *

Abraham Lincoln once said, "There is no grievance that is the fit object of redress by mob law." If rage replaces reason, if confrontation replaces argument and compromise; if every passionate interest must get what it wants, regardless of need, regardless of law, what kind of country will we become?

We will be a land where no one will be sure, where no one will be safe, where the majesty of the law is deposed by the passion of the moment and the tyranny of the mob.

No where is this danger more noticed today than in our colleges and universities, and I want for a few minutes to speak about this important aspect of our struggle to preserve the rule of law.

The aim of a liberal arts education is to stimulate free thought, intellectual restlessness, critical analysis of the status quo, and synthesis of new ideas, directions and values. To the extent that our young people have examined the status quo and have found it wanting, their education has succeeded. And this is so even if they cannot tell us what it is they would substitute. For they are young and are still learning. While we should be pleased that they have the questions, we cannot expect them to have all the answers.

Every student is a complex of different forces. Every campus is a complex of different students.

Students live with the general tension of growing up, the special tensions of university living, and the very direct kinds of tensions the larger society imposes on them. The draft hangs over them constantly. So do the need to

find a craft and ultimately to choose a calling, and the need to avoid or to
pick a political outlook, a set of social aspirations, a life style and an ethic.

For some of the more sensitive, the ironies of our nation—poverty and
hunger amidst plenty; unapplied cures for illness and ignorance; massive
destruction of nature's gifts; growing urban blight and suburban sprawl;
racism and hatred among men; the waste of war for the third consecutive
decade—convince them that the "establishment" as they see it has squand-
ered this nation's opportunities.

For black students there is a special tension—a need for pride and
identity, strength and confidence, and sometimes for expressing resentment
and anger over 200 years of bondage, 100 years of hypocrisy, 15 years of
procrastination, and day after day of inbred prejudice.

Depending on which of these tensions predominates in each student, his
approach to campus life can vary widely. He may be the residual adolescent, seeking thrills, following excitement wherever it leads, proving his
manhood by making childish judgments. He may be determined not to be
dehumanized by the giant university, dedicated to participating in its
processes and changing it until it is responsive to his needs and his sense of
priorities. He may be striking back at a society which imposes on him by
subjecting him to the draft, or offering him a good job only if he conforms
to its ethics. He may see his role as helping to cure the broader ills of society.
The massiveness of these ills may convince him that the university and
perhaps the entire society are unworthy of preservation and that the only
route to progress is destruction of existing institutions and a fresh start. Or
he may want only to have his racial identity recognized and respected by the
university and the community.

What ties them all together is a desire for change. Yet the same treatment
of them will produce different results. If we tell the "revolutionary" that
what he is doing threatens the viability of the university, he is pleased. To
him, it is an intimate part of the unacceptable array of institutions. But the
revolutionaries are few and far between. Only 2,300 arrests have been made
of a student population of almost 7 million, and most of these 2,300 are not
"revolutionaries." Obviously, the extreme militants cannot operate without the support of the mass of the moderates. Yet in most cases only if the
authorities cooperate can the revolutionaries lift themselves into a posture
attractive to the moderate mass. When the school or outside authorities
react to confrontation with dehumanizing repression, both groups join in
resisting it. As a result, the student body as a whole is radicalized.

I believe, however, that as this mechanism is understood and anticipated,
moderate students will break the chain by removing the occasion for
wide-scale repression before it arises. For most moderates begin opposed to
the methods of the extremists. And by now it is apparent to the moderates
that they are sometimes indiscriminately following leaders whose goals are

not their own. It should also be apparent that the goals of the many frequently conflict with the means of the few. For those pursuing humanistic values—individuality, participation, respect, dignity, freedom—the techniques of coercion and physical force just cannot be acceptable. To treat humans as objects, to call officers by animals' names, to deny others the right to fulfill their own needs and desires—these are dehumanizing activities. To those seeking an environment of peace and order and understanding, the confrontations and conflict we have seen on many campuses surely are not consistent.

And students are beginning to realize that if their demands are made through violence, the response is going to be reactionary repression. This is just what the destructive fringe wants, since it seems to prove their thesis of a decaying society. But sooner or later the moderates must weigh the price to be paid, whether in government support, alumni resources, police intrusion onto the campus, or increasing Federal or state control of education.

We cannot, however, rely only on the good sense of the student mass to break the unhappy cycle of conflict. For if they do so, and find that without conflict the incentives for change are absent, the appeal of the extremists will rebound to new heights.

Thus it is up to the universities themselves to reverse the trend. Government cannot do it for them. The universities must take two steps: they must recognize that they have serious shortcomings, and they must initiate accelerated reforms. They must provide an alternative route toward change besides the confrontation politics of the militants. And it must be real, substantial change—more student participation in decision-making, abolition of all vestiges of racial and economic discrimination, affirmative efforts to remove the present affects of past discrimination, more constructive participation of the university in the broader community, consideration of the community's needs and prerogatives in university planning, and the consideration of the extent to which participation in the national military effort might offend the standards of the university community.

There may be other issues which need exposure and response, but we should not have to wait for the students to find them. The faculty and the administrators must become the activists, seeking out opportunities for progress and providing the leadership and the example which the student body really wants. Every university, if it wishes to avoid turmoil, must decide to act as if it had just experienced violent campus turmoil and move accordingly. For no university needs to have turmoil if it can demonstrate, before turmoil comes, the kind of commitment to change and momentum toward progress which turmoil usually brings.

On those campuses where mass movements have already taken their toll, the same considerations apply. A student mass movement is usually a temporary thing—but the fact that the activists disappear is no reason to let the activism disappear. If the university goes back to business as usual, another confrontation is unavoidable. But if it chooses do-it-yourself activism, it can grow and improve, for it can change the equation of conflict.

This is the prescription for our universities: not threats and repression, but anticipation and action; not gimmicks and more laws, but reform and progress; not keeping one step ahead of the forces of repression in public life, but keeping one step ahead of the reasonable perception of intelligent students who seek to improve university life. Our focus must not be primarily on how to stop campus confrontations once they start. We can, and must, prevent them by removing the inertia, insensitivity and unresponsiveness that feeds the fires of conflict.

And even once conflict starts, we can de-fuse it with thought and experience, patience and care. Whenever the politics of confrontation gets out of hand and results in a serious threat to the safety or vital property of the university community, it may indeed be necessary for university officials to call for outside assistance. But even when this happens, the academic authorities have a continuing responsibility to assure that arrests are made only when arrests are necessary; and that force is used only when force is necessary. A "bust" should no more be an occasion for summary punishment in Harvard Yard than in Selma or Jackson. Those police forces which are not adequately trained to withstand the rigors of civil disturbance duty—the taunts and baiting and close quarters and physical strain—should not be used for such duty. It is not fair to them, and it can only exacerbate already difficult conditions.

The reason for reform and progress is not merely to head off conflict. The reason is to do what is necessary and right.

*   *   *

STATEMENT OF THE ATTORNEY GENERAL BEFORE A HOUSE EDUCATION SUBCOMMITTEE

Attorney General John N. Mitchell made the following statement before the Special Subcommittee on Education of the Committee on Education and Labor, U.S. House of Representatives, May 20, 1969.

Introduction

Madam Chairman and Members of the Subcommittee:

I appreciate the opportunity to appear before this Subcommittee to state my views on a matter of grave concern to all of us—violence on the campus.

At the outset, let me state that I shall confine my remarks to those aspects of the problem which fall within the ambit of my responsibilities and authority as Attorney General. I leave to others, including Secretary Finch, who has already appeared before this Subcommittee, those facets of the problem which relate to education itself and Federal financial assistance to the colleges and universities and to the students who attend them.

Also at the outset, I want to make clear that the problem to which we are addressing ourselves is one which involves a small fraction of our school population and an equally small fraction of our schools, but is, nevertheless, a most serious problem requiring attention at the highest levels of school administration, state and local government, and Federal government.

Most of our students at our colleges and universities across the country are of serious purpose in their quest for truth and knowledge. This great majority recognizes the bounds of permissible dissent and that violence and disruption are not the appropriate means to effect necessary or desirable reforms.

On the other hand, we have those relatively few violence-prone militants who seek only to destroy or who are misguided into believing that terror can lead to improvement.

Permit me to give you some of the factual background of campus disorders, which has come to the attention of the Justice Department, to illustrate what I consider to be the proper role of the Department, and to call to your attention existing federal criminal laws which are available to deal with various aspects of this grave problem.

The Problem

As I indicated in my recent Law Day speech, we have already had disturbances on more than 250 college campuses. These incidents have resulted in more than 3000 arrests and in property damage exceeding $2 million. The incidence of disorders has continued to increase in frequency and in the extent of violence. For example, in California alone:

At San Francisco State College a bomb permanently blinded one student, and a second bomb was discovered before it exploded.

At Pomona College in Claremont, a secretary was blinded in one eye and lost two fingers when a bomb exploded as she was removing it from a college mailbox.

At the University of California in Santa Barbara, a custodian at the Faculty Club died from burns when he picked up a package containing a bomb.

At Berkeley, in the last eight months, there have been four instances of two bombings, and $1.1 million in property damage.

In short, the wave of student disorders has brought personal injury, death, and millions of dollars of property damage. And it has disrupted the education of many earnest students. Further, the evidence indicates that this upswing in disorders is attributable, in some part at least, to planned and concerted action by certain small groups. One of these is the Students for a Democratic Society (SDS). I would like to highlight for the Subcommittee some of the activities of this militant student group.

The Militant Student Movement— Organization, Operation, and Goals

The militant student movement currently instigating and leading many campus disorders across the country involves several groups, consisting largely of students, many of them post-graduate students varying in age from 21 to 30 years, and a number of chronic demonstrators who join their ranks although they are no longer in college.

By and large these groups have no constructive objective; their sole aim is to disrupt. Their leaders brag about being revolutionaries and anarchists. They state their purpose to be to close the schools. They openly and brazenly profess a desire to destroy the establishment.

Most prominent in major campus disorders today is the Students for a Democratic Society, although many disorders have occurred in which its members have not been present and a good many disorders have been instigated by other groups such as the Black Student Union. Often, however, in such cases, members of the SDS soon join in and eventually assume a leading role in the demonstration, press statements, and negotiations.

The influence of the SDS cannot always be measured by the small number of its members that engage in any particular campus violence. On occasion SDS with less than 50 members has been able to capitalize on the issues and climate on the campus and obtain large numbers of allies who compound its disruptive influence.

The student allies of SDS are frequently law abiding students who many times have honest and indeed justifiable criticism about university administration and policies.

I recognize that the students of today are an "involved generation" who wish to tell us—as strongly as possible—that they are dissatisfied with many aspects of American life. I firmly believe that students on university campuses should enjoy the fullest and most vigorous debate guaranteed by the First Amendment. Indeed, it may even be advisable for some universities to permit even more dissent than the minimum guaranteed by the Constitution.

But I must draw the line at those actions which seriously disrupt a university and which involve a substantial denial of rights for those students who wish to pursue scholarship and civility.

The Students for a Democratic Society, despite a loose organizational structure, appears, through its local chapters, to carry out a national SDS policy keyed to widespread unrest among large segments of the otherwise peaceful student community. This organizational and operational relationship of the SDS leadership and some 250 local constituent chapters can best be illustrated by looking at the proposals and resolutions of the national leaders and the volume and frequency of the incidents following these national meetings.

For example, one of the resolutions approved at the SDS National Council meeting at Boulder, Colorado, in October, 1968, entitled "Boulder and Boulder," called for the organization of a national strike of high school and college students on November 4 and 5, 1968, and the mobilization of large militant SDS regional demonstrations in major cities to protest the elections. Typical of the planned responses to this resolution were the strikes at the University of Michigan on November 4, at the University of Denver on November 5, and the demonstration at the Lincoln Memorial here in Washington on November 5.

One of the highlights of the SDS National Council meeting at the University of Michigan in December 1968 was a panel discussion on the need for a nationwide coordinated attack on military activities on campuses—ROTC units and military research grants. Significant is the fact that in the four months prior to the meeting our records reflect only six violent actions directed at ROTC installations on campuses. For the four and a half months since, we record 22 such incidents.

The most recent SDS National Council meeting was held at Austin, Texas, in late March of this year. Since that meeting the tempo of campus disorders has substantially increased. Examples are:

(1) Harvard, April 9: Students, led by the SDS, forcibly ejected officials from an administration building.

(2) American University, April 23: A group of members of the SDS occupied the administration building.

(3) George Washington University, April 24: Members of the SDS occupied the Institute for Sino-Soviet studies.

(4) University of Washington, April 24: The SDS participated in a demonstration which succeeded in halting the operation of the Student Placement Center.

(5) Columbia University, April 30: Members of the SDS took over two university buildings.

(6) Stanford University, May 1: SDS members occupied an administration building.

(7) Northeastern University, May 13: Some 40 students led by the SDS took over a meeting room and lounge.

As distressing as the SDS campus activities are, and although not the subject of specific inquiry by this Subcommittee, I do want to note in passing the projected expansion of violent SDS activities into the labor field, our high schools, and even our armed forces.

While the foregoing examples of the involvement of SDS in campus disorders are ominous, it would be an oversimplification to blame all of the trouble on campuses today on the SDS. While the SDS often furnishes the aggressive leadership to exploit campus problems, there are many frictions and difficulties which would probably cause unrest even without the SDS. It is important for school authorities to recognize these frictions and difficulties and to maintain communication with the students concerning them. It is equally important, however, for school authorities and student bodies to recognize the basic intransigence of the militants and to understand the goals which these militants are pursuing. School authorities must take prompt and effective action to resist disruption by the militants.

Role of the Department of Justice

We must not lose sight of the fact that dealing with student unrest is, in the first instance, the responsibility of our college and university officials. When police authority is needed to restore law and order, the courts or the local police should be utilized immediately. The Federal Government does, however, have an important role and interest in the matter.

The fact that the student disorders are nationwide, that they disrupt Federally funded programs and that Federal criminal statutes may be violated gives the Federal government a substantial interest in the problem.

A facet of this interest falls within the area of my responsibilities as Attorney General.

As I see it, the role of the Department of Justice is threefold—preventive, investigative and prosecutive.

Prevention and Control Activities

As I have indicated, the first responsibility with respect to campus disorders rests with campus officials. When law enforcement authorities are required, these authorities should be state and local. On occasion, however, the Department of Justice Community Relations Service has been requested to send personnel to attempt to calm the storm. As you know, the Community Relations Service consists of persons skilled in establishing communication between conflicting factions. They are trained mediators, experienced in the art of dealing with emotionally charged situations which have racial overtones. Most recently, the Community Relations Service was called upon in connection with the Berkeley disorders last week.

Another element of the Department of Justice which is active with respect to campus disorders is the Law Enforcement Assistance Administration. As you know, this Administration was established by the enactment of the Omnibus Crime Control and Safe Streets Act of 1968. Insofar as campus disorders are concerned, the Law Enforcement Assistance Administration has been incorporating in seminars for police chiefs programs on campus disorders, their causes and control. The Administration is in the process now of planning a special conference on campus disorders to be held later this year. We expect that among approximately 300 conference participants, we will have college and university presidents and administrators, faculty members, state and local police and campus police.

Investigative Activities

Under its jurisdiction to investigate suspected violations of the Federal law, the Federal Bureau of Investigation is obtaining, and we are evaluating, information about campus disorders and those who cause them. Some of the background information stated earlier is the result of these efforts. In addition, we are making this information available to state and local law enforcement officials in jurisdictions where campus disorders may occur.

Through our investigative activities we hope to develop a full picture of the problem. We are looking for solid evidence to answer such vital questions as:

How serious is the problem and how best can responsible students, college authorities and government leaders deal with it?

Have those who lead or engage in student disorders violated Federal law and can they be successfully prosecuted?

Are existing Federal (and state) laws adequate to deal with the problem?

While our investigative efforts are intense, we must not be precipitous in our conclusions or actions. You may be assured, however, that these questions will be answered as quickly as our ability and resources permit. It would be inappropriate for me, of course, to discuss the specifics of our investigative activities.

Federal Criminal Laws—Prosecutive Powers

The prosecutive powers of the Attorney General are limited—quite properly—by the scope of Federal criminal law. Since most illegal activity on college campuses is in violation of state and local laws—such as trespass, illegal entry, assault and malicious destruction of property—I believe that current Federal laws are adequate. I therefore do not recommend to Congress that additional legislation be enacted at this time. However, should our investigations or congressional hearings reveal a need for some additional authority to deal with this problem, I will at that time recommend appropriate legislation.

I would like to briefly outline for the Subcommittee the scope of existing Federal criminal laws that are available, should our investigations warrant their use.

First, Section 2121 of Title 18 of the United States Code prohibits travel in interstate commerce, or the use of any facility of interstate commerce, by any person with the intent to incite, organize or promote a riot or to commit any act of violence in furtherance of a riot, or to aid or abet any person in furthering a riot. Violators are subject to a maximum fine of $10,000 and 5 years imprisonment.

Second, Section 231 of Title 18 prohibits the teaching or demonstrating of the use of firearms or explosive or incendiary devices or techniques with the intent that the same will be used in a civil disorder which may obstruct commerce or the conduct of any Federally protected function. It prohibits the transportation, or manufacture for transportation, of any such devices with the intent that they be used in furtherance of a civil disorder. The section also proscribes attempts to obstruct firemen or law enforcement officers in the performance of their duties during a civil disorder. A fine of $10,000 and imprisonment for 5 years may be imposed upon a violator.

Third, Section 245 of Title 18 is designed to protect the civil rights of persons participating in or receiving benefits from various Federally protected activities. Such activities include receiving Federal financial assistance, as is the case of most institutions of higher learning and many students. Interference by force or threat of force with these rights, carries a range of penalties extending to life imprisonment if death results. This law, of course, would only be utilized in an unusual case where local law enforcement could not act.

In addition to the statutes to which I have referred, there are some other Federal laws, one or more of which might well come into play during the course of campus disorders, depending upon the facts in each particular case.

Conclusion

In summary, I share the Subcommittee's concern about the violence now taking place on our college campuses. In the first instance responsibility rests with the college and university administrators. They must recognize the difference between dissent and disorder. When law enforcement assistance is necessary to quell disorder, it should come primarily from the states and communities involved. Federal law enforcement assistance, when appropriate, is the responsibility of the Department of Justice. In carrying out our role, we are working toward prevention and control, we are conducting investigations, and we will prosecute, when prosecution is indicated, those who seek to destroy our colleges and universities.

Let me close with a repetition of one optimistic observation I touched upon earlier—the vast bulk of our college youth know why they are in school and will not permit the minority to deprive them of their educational opportunities.

I would be pleased to answer any questions you may have.

STATEMENT OF A CONGRESSWOMAN
BEFORE A HOUSE EDUCATION
SUBCOMMITTEE

Representative Shirley Chisholm, who has the distinction of being the only black congresswoman at present, made the following statement before the Special Subcommittee on Education of the Committee on Education and Labor, U.S. House of Representatives, May 20, 1969.

Madam Chairman and Gentlemen:

I am grateful for the opportunity to testify before this special subcommittee as it considers what legislation dealing with higher education it will recommend to the 91st Congress. Although I have not been able to follow the previous testimony in detail, I am familiar with sections of it from newspaper stories, and I hope that there is something I can add.

As often as I can, I like to accept invitations to colleges. I have been to eleven this year—Georgetown, Howard, Trinity, Columbia, Notre Dame, Brooklyn College, Earlham, Bowdoin, Skidmore, Long Island University and Princeton. I have met many hundreds of students, and I want to say at the start that I like and admire today's college-age people. The breadth of their concern, the intensity of their moral outrage at injustice and the sincerity of their dedication to efforts to win real change and improvement in this society are amazing. They are probably the finest generation this country has ever produced.

I am sure some of you are dubious of this, and would like to ask me, "Is that why they are causing so much trouble?" Yes, to a great extent, that is why. I wish this subcommittee would make a greater effort to hear from students, and not so much from college presidents, state officials, psychologists and federal officials. Like too many of us older persons, they seem determined to misunderstand and oversimplify this "student unrest," as they call it, or this "student rebellion." This kind of jargon or cant is a method that is often used to avoid the pain of really coming in contact with and understanding the terrible problems that threaten the future of this country. I have heard similar phrases in other context—the "urban crisis," for instance. We use these phrases, and fool ourselves into believing that when we say them we understand what is happening.

But believe me, you do not know what you are talking about when you say "urban crisis," unless you have walked the streets of a neighborhood like mine, and lived there, and have known the people—the *people* who are the reality that we deny when we use some bureaucrat's catch-phrase.

Things are not always what they appear to us to be as we here in Washington watch them on television, or learn the inside dope from some syndicated columnist whose greatest skill is to conceal the fact that he is acting as a spokesman for someone with an axe to grind. Take the incident that has everyone so upset, the Cornell affair.

Who can help reacting with anger and fear at the picture of a band of young men, armed with rifles and shotguns, occupying a building at a great university and forcing its administration to give them whatever they demand? Was that the way it was? Why did it happen? Does this subcommittee intend to ask any of these young men, dispassionately and sympathetically, what drove them to this?

Their action seems inexplicable to most persons, because all they know is gleaned from television film clips and brief newspaper stories. Very few of these went into any of the background. Few mentioned the insults, the threats, the anonymous telephone calls that had frightened some of these students, or their friends. On the night before their occupation of Willard Straight Hall, a cross had been burned in front of a building where 11 black women students live.

A black American who sees a burning cross may be pardoned, I hope, for feeling that he may be in some danger. That burning cross is such an embarrassment to the good citizens of Ithaca that some of them have even tried to suggest that the black students did it themselves, to furnish an excuse for their violent action of the next day.

This proves, it seems to me, that there are no lengths to which some of us will not go to discredit these young people. What those boys did, in providing themselves with guns, may have been wrong. But they felt they were surrounded with enemies, and they knew some of those enemies had guns, and they knew they were the kind of people who would commit such a cowardly outrage as burning that cross. Put in this light, their action may still be reckless and mistaken—but it is no longer incomprehensible.

The Cornell incident illustrates another point I want to stress—that what is happening on our campuses cannot be understood without relating it to all the other problems of our society—to racism, to economic injustice, to the terribly mistaken war we are caught in. These students are the product of an unjust, racist society that spends more money on war than it does on education and medicine. They see the wrongness of this with a clarity that most of their elders have lost, if they ever had it. They are fighting back. Sometimes their goals may be obscure to us, and their tactics inadmissible, to our way of thinking. But perhaps we should criticize our own way of thinking more often. It might even be that we, ourselves, are the problem.

A Colgate University professor wrote a long article that the Washington Star reprinted May 4, and I think it tells a great deal more about what is wrong with our colleges than he intended. Let me read part of it. He said:

"Disaster first struck when we were compelled to educate, or try to educate, a great unwieldy mass of young men and women who had no definite objective in a system designed, organized, and operated with reasonable success for an intellectually elite or at least culturally oriented and carefully selected minority."

To this type of elderly scholar, accustomed to the children of the upper and middle class, it is apparently a mistake to open the doors of the universities to all sorts of people. They are an "unwieldy mass" that he can only "try to educate." His scorn of anyone who is not exactly like him and his friends is almost laughable:

"Barriers dropped or requirements lessened perceptibly. Students came without language equipment, without an ability to write intelligent English, without adequate preparation in subject matter, and worst of all without manners."

When students say that our institutions of higher education have become irrelevant to them and their concerns, and that the institutions are unaware of the need to change, and resistant to making changes when they are finally reluctantly made aware, here is the evidence that they are not imagining things.

Instead of focusing on the students, why do we not look to the root of the trouble? What is that? Suppose we look at the makeup of the boards of trustees that make the final decisions for the colleges. We will find them to be, typically, white male Protestant businessmen over 50 years old, with an income likely to be $30,000 a year or more.

Now, it is not a crime to be any of these things. But I think we will not be too unfair if we say that this type of citizen is not always in the forefront of social change. A little more variety in our colleges' governing bodies seems long overdue. How about electing some recent graduates, to break the monotony? Some members of racial minorities? Some plain working people? Even a few more women?

I was glad to read that Secretary Robert Finch made a very similar suggestion before this subcommittee, and I think he was exactly right when he said, "In truth, many academic institutions have brought much of it on themselves. They have not always responded to the clear need for constant self-examination and self-renewal."

What should they do? This is too long a subject to do more than suggest an answer. But briefly, our universities must begin to address themselves to community needs. They must begin to act, not remain aloof. They must descend from their traditional isolation and engage themselves in the fight for a just and rational society. Their own survival is at stake.

What can Congress do to help them? When this subcommittee began these hearings on February 3rd, the distinguished Chairman said she expected to hear testimony on the report of the Carnegie Commission on Higher Education. A member of this subcommittee has introduced a bill to carry out the recommendations of that commission, which are basically that the doors of our colleges should be open to every student, however poor, who is able to learn. What testimony has been heard on this most basic issue?

There was to have been consideration of whether cuts in appropriations for student financial assistance are making it impossible for the universities to carry out the congressional intent in passing student aid programs. There was to have been testimony on what the projected needs in buildings are. Have these things been considered?

Since these hearings opened, the President has proposed revisions in the fiscal 1970 budget that would cut $107 million from grants to build new college buildings, on the grounds that colleges should be encouraged to get their financing from non-federal sources. I think this subcommittee should be interested in this proposal.

The President claims that, by this method, about $220 million in loans for construction will be made in 1970, through the device of federal subsidies on interest on these private loans. I am highly skeptical of this claim, but I think it deserves to be looked into. I hope there will be testimony by the administration officials involved, and detailed questioning of how they propose to generate these loans in the face of our war-caused inflation and soaring interest rates.

Instead, all the attention has been on an investigation of whether the colleges are living up to two hastily-drawn amendments that the last Congress inserted in the Health, Education, and Welfare Department Appropriation Act of 1969 and the Higher Education Amendments of 1968. I want to say that I am strongly opposed to Section 504 of the Higher Education Act. I am nearly as strongly opposed to Section 411 of the HEW appropriation bill, although it does, at least, seem to offer the persons affected the protection of due process in a court of law.

Several Members of the House have proposed that all federal assistance be cut off to campuses that are beset by riots, and I was saddened to read that the Vice-President agrees with them. I am not merely opposed to this, I am shocked by the idea that someone be empowered to judge whether or not an institution has tried hard enough to put down dissident students so that it can keep its federal aid. Secretary Finch, I understand, called this suggestion unenforceable when he appeared before the subcommittee. The Secretary is certainly correct. The difficulty of deciding whether a given institution has satisfied the law's requirements would be insurmountable, and I hope that for this reason, if no other, the subcommittee will not consider such a scheme.

I am against the existing laws for several reasons. As they stand, they are not infringements of academic freedom. Congress certainly has the power to rule under what conditions the aid it offers shall be paid. But the existence of these paragraphs in the federal lawbooks shows, and the behavior of some elements in the Congress shows even more clearly, a regrettable and dangerous tendency on the part of some politicians to grab headlines by imposing harsh, uniform standards of conduct on citizens whose behavior they do not understand and of which they do not approve. Let me urge you to consider how un-American, in the strict sense of the word, such repressive actions would be.

Dr. Samuel Hayakawa, I think, disposed of the two sections involved with his remark that they put poor persons "in double jeopardy." They punish the poor, but not the rich. For the same action, a poor student will lose his chance to go to college, while a well-off student is hurt only in his father's pocketbook.

Dr. Hayakawa also pointed out that students receiving financial aid are not often those involved in rebellions on campus, so these laws are of little use in meeting the problem. It is for this reason that I called them hastily-drawn. They attack only the symptoms of trouble, and do not do an effective job even of that.

These two amendments seem to me to be as clear an indication as the article by a Colgate professor that I quoted earlier that there is a tragic lack of communication and sympathy between those who are in authority and the young who have begun to question the motives of those authorities, and the uses to which they put their power.

The best thing the Congress can do in this trying period is to continue to support the universities and their students, to fulfill our commitment to them, and then to increase that commitment. To intervene in campus disciplinary proceedings would constitute a serious over-reaction.

Local authorities should be left to deal with their problems as they see fit. No doubt, many of them will make mistakes of judgment or tactics, as they act under pressure. There is little that the federal government can do, and there is probably nothing that it should do, to prevent this. There is no uniform federal code of student conduct and discipline that we can impose and enforce without doing basic, perhaps irreparable harm both to our system of government and to our free universities. Each must solve its own problems, and in doing so move forward to an understanding and acceptance of its altered role in society.

We will not succeed in understanding what is happening if we act out of the ignorance that fear and anger produce. We will never be able to restore the status quo. We cannot, in the catch-phrase, "solve the problem of campus unrest." We should not, if we could. Instead, we should listen to what our children are saying. They are young, they are sometimes foolish, and they are sometimes ridiculous, but they are so often so much better than we were that we should feel humble, and give them the sympathetic hearing they deserve.

They are saying to us, "you do not practice what you preach," and they are right. They are saying they want real democracy now, not gradualism and tokenism. They are only asking us to live up to what we say we believe. If we do not listen, we run the terrible risk of leaving them prey to agitators, political mis-leaders who will find them easy to convince that the only way to achieve justice is with violence—bombs, bricks, and guns. The warning has become clear, and the time to avert such an outcome is very short.

INTERIM STATEMENT ON CAMPUS DISORDER

The National Commission on the Causes and Prevention of Violence, which President Lyndon B. Johnson created in 1968, released the following official statement on June 9, 1969. Members of the Commission are: Chairman, Milton S. Eisenhower, President Emeritus, Johns Hopkins University; Vice Chairman, Judge A. Leon Higginbotham, U.S. District Court for Eastern District of Pennsylvania; Rep. Hale Boggs (D-La.); Terence Cardinal Cooke, Archbishop of New York; Patricia Roberts Harris, Professor of Law, Howard University; Sen. Philip A. Hart (D-Mich.); Eric Hoffer, author; Sen. Roman Hruska (R-Neb.); Leon Jaworski, senior partner, Fulbright, Crooker, Freeman, Bate & Jaworski, Houston, Tex.; Albert E. Jenner, Jr., lawyer; Rep. William M. McCulloch (R-Ohio); Judge Ernest W. McFarland, Arizona Supreme Court; and Dr. W. Walter Menninger, psychiatrist.

The members of this Commission, along with most Americans, are deeply disturbed by the violence and disorder that have swept the nation's campuses. Our colleges and universities cannot perform their vital functions in an atmosphere that exalts the struggle for power over the search for truth, the rule of passion over the rule of reason, physical confrontation over rational discourse.

We are equally disturbed, however, by the direction of much public reaction to campus unrest. Those who would punish colleges and universities by reducing financial support, by passing restrictive legislation, or by political intervention in the affairs of educational institutions, may unwittingly be helping the very radical minority of students whose objective is to destroy our present institutions of higher education.

So threatening is the situation, so essential is the need for understanding and calm appraisal, that this Commission feels compelled to speak now rather than to remain silent until publication of its final report next fall. We offer our comments during the summer [1969] pause in the hope that they will contribute to constructive thought and action before the beginning of the new academic year in September.

The problem of campus unrest is more than a campus problem. Its roots lie deep in the larger society. There is no single cause, no single solution. We urge all Americans to reject hasty and simplistic answers. We urge them to distinguish between peaceful protest and violent disruption, between the non-conformity of youth and the terror tactics of the extremists. We counsel patience, understanding and support for those in the university community who are trying to preserve freedom and order on the campus. We do so in the conviction that our universities and colleges are beginning to learn how to achieve change without disorder or coercion.

I.

During the past year, many of America's universities and colleges have been seriously wounded. These wounds arise from multiple causes. One is the increasingly violent expression of widespread student discontent. Although much of this discontent often focuses on grievances within the campus environment, it is rooted in dissatisfactions with the larger society that the campus can do little about.

Students are unwilling to accept the gaps between professed ideals and actual performance. They see afresh the injustices that remain unremedied. They are not impressed by the dangers that previous generations have overcome and the problems they have solved. It means little to them that the present adult generation found the way out of a major depression to unparalleled heights of economic abundance, or that it defeated a massive wave of vicious totalitarianism and preserved the essential elements of freedom for the youth of today. To students, these triumphs over serious dangers serve primarily to emphasize other problems we are just beginning to solve.

Today's intelligent, idealistic students see a nation which has achieved the physical ability to provide food, shelter and education for all, but has not yet devised social institutions that do so. They see a society, built on the principle that all men are created equal, that has not yet assured equal opportunity in life. They see a world of nation-states with the technical brilliance to harness the ultimate energy but without the common sense to agree on methods of preventing mutual destruction. With the fresh energy and idealism of the young, they are impatient with the progress that has been made but seems to them to be indefensibly slow.

At a time when students are eager to attack these and other key problems, they face the prospect of being compelled to fight in a war most of them believe is unjustified. This traumatic experience has precipitated an unprecedented mass tension and frustration.

In assessing the causes of student unrest, it would be a mistake to assume that all causes are external. There are undoubtedly internal emotional pressures and internal value conflicts in many students which contribute to their own dissatisfaction and thus to the tension and turmoil of campus life.

Students attribute the shortcomings they see to the smugness of their elders and the weaknesses of social institutions. They see the university, guardian of man's knowledge and source of his new ideas, as an engine for powering the reform of the larger society, and as the first institution they are in a position to reform.

We emphasize that most students, despite their view of society's failures, accept as valid the basic structure of our democratic system; their main desire is to improve its ability to live up to its stated values. Their efforts to do so are welcome when they take the form of petitions, demonstrations and protests that are peaceful and non-violent. Although many persons are unsettled by these activities (which are often of a bizarre nature), we must all remember that peaceful expression of disturbing ideas and petitions for the redress of grievances are fundamental rights safeguarded by the First Amendment of our Constitution. Methods of dealing with "campus unrest" must not confuse peaceful protest and petition with violent disruption. To do so will aggravate rather than solve the problem.

A small but determined minority, however, aims not at reform but at the destruction of existing institutions. These are the nihilists. They resort to violent disruption as the means best suited to achieve their ends. By dramatic tactics of terror, they have focused widespread public attention upon themselves and have often induced university authorities either to surrender or to meet force with force. When they have managed on occasion to provoke counter-force to an excessive degree, they have succeeded in enlisting the sympathies of the more moderate campus majority.

They are the agent that converts constructive student concern into mindless mob hysteria. They are the chief danger to the university and its basic values.

There is also a minority of students who are not nihilists, but who feel that violence and disruption may be the only effective way of achieving societal and university reform.

II.

Forcible obstruction and violence are incompatible with the intellectual and personal freedom that lies at the core of campus values. In its recent *Declaration on Campus Unrest*, the American Council on Education noted that "there has developed among some of the young a cult of irrationality and incivility which severely strains attempts to maintain sensible and decent human communications. Within this cult is a minute group of destroyers who have abandoned hope in today's society, in today's universi-

ty, and in the processes of orderly discussion to secure significant change."
These "destroyers" seek to persuade more moderate students that verbal
expressions of grievance go unheeded, while forcible tactics bring affirmative results.

Despite some eloquent and subtle rationalizations for violent methods of
protest, the record of experience is incontrovertible. While violent protest is
sometimes followed by the concessions sought, it more often produces a
degree of counter-violence and public dismay that may gravely damage the
cause for which violence is invoked.

Even when violence succeeds in achieving immediate social gains, it tends
frequently to feed on itself, with one power group imposing its will on
another until repressive elements succeed in reestablishing order. The
violent cycles of the French and Russian revolutions and of the decade
resulting in the Third Reich are stark summits of history to ponder. All
history teaches that as a conscious method of seeking social reform, violence
is a very dangerous weapon to employ.

That is why our nation has sought to avoid violent methods of effecting
social change, and to foster instead the principles of peaceful advocacy
proclaimed in the Bill of Rights and the rule of law. As the President has
just reminded us:

> "The purpose of these restraints is not to protect an 'establish-
> ment,' but to establish the protection of liberty; not to prevent
> change, but to insure that change reflects the public will and
> respects the rights of all."

The university is the citadel of man's learning and of his hope for further
self-improvement, and is the special guardian of this heritage. Those who
work and study on the campus should think long before they risk its
destruction by resorting to force as the quick way of reaching some
immediate goal.

Father Theodore Hesburgh of Notre Dame has observed that the university, precisely because it is an open community that lives by the power of
reason, stands naked before those who would employ the power of force. It
can survive only when the great majority of its members share its commitment to rational discourse, listen closely to those with conflicting views, and
stand together against the few who would impose their will on everyone
else.

Kingman Brewster of Yale has persuasively articulated this policy:

> "Proposition one is the encouragement of controversy, no matter
> how fundamental; and the protection of dissent, no matter how
> extreme. This is not just to permit the 'letting off of steam' but
> because it will improve [the university] as a place to be educated.
> Proposition number two is a convincing intention to deal speedily
> and firmly with any forcible interference with student and faculty

activities or the normal use of any [university] facilities. . . . I see no basis for compromise on the basic proposition that forcible coercion and violent intimidation are unacceptable means of persuasion and unacceptable techniques of change in a university community, as long as channels of communication and the chance for reasoned argument are available."

Several attitudes held by members of the university community have often interfered with the application of these sensible standards. One is the belief of many that the civil law should not apply to internal campus affairs. They feel that the academy is an enclave, sheltered from the law, that the forces of civil authority may not enter the campus, save by invitation. This is a serious misconception—a residue of the time when the academy served *in loco parentis*, making and enforcing its own rules for students' behavior and protecting them from the law outside, save for such extreme crimes as murder and arson. Now that students themselves have firmly discarded school authority over their personal lives, they must logically accept the jurisdiction of civil authority. They cannot argue that of all Americans they are uniquely beyond the reach of the law.

At the same time, the university is ill equipped to control violent and obstructive conduct on its own. Most institutions have few campus police; most of these are not deputized and thus do not possess true police power. Few schools have explicit rules either defining the boundaries of permissible protest or stating the consequences if the boundaries are crossed. Some have very loose rules for disciplinary proceedings; others have diffused disciplinary power so widely among students, faculty and administration that effective discipline is difficult to impose, and is seldom imposed quickly enough to meet an emergency. And in most institutions the ultimate internal disciplinary sanction of suspension or expulsion lies unused because the campus community shrinks from its probable consequence—exposure of dismissed students to the draft and what students call the "death sentence" of Vietnam.

III.

Out of many discussions with faculty members, students and administrators, and with full appreciation that no two institutions are the same, we offer the campus community the following specific suggestions:

(1) A broad consensus should be achieved among students, faculty and administration concerning the permissible methods of presenting ideas, proposals and grievances and the consequences of going beyond them. Excellent guidelines have been provided by the American Council on Education's recent Declaration on Campus Protest. These could usefully be supplemented by more detailed statements developed by representatives of

the American Association of University Professors, the American Association of Universities, the American Council on Education, the Association of Land Grant Colleges and State Universities, the National Student Association, and possibly others. Where agreed upon and explicit codes of student conduct and procedures for student discipline are lacking, they should be adopted; where they already exist they should be reviewed and, if necessary, improved.

Students have the right to due process and to participate in the making of decisions that directly affect them, but their right of participation should not be so extensive as to paralyze the disciplinary process itself. Codes for campus conduct should place primary reliance on the power of the institution to maintain order in its own house, and on its courage to apply its own punishment when deserved. These codes should also recognize the universal duty to obey the civil and criminal laws of the larger society, and the right of the civil authorities to act when laws are violated.

(2) Universities should prepare and currently review contingency plans for dealing with campus disorders. Advance plans should be made to determine, insofar as possible, the circumstances under which the university will sue (i) campus disciplinary procedures, (ii) campus police, (iii) court injunctions, (iv) other court sanctions and (v) the civil police. A definite plan, flexibly employed at the moment of crisis, is essential. There have been enough violent and obstructive incidents on enough campuses to permit institutions to assess alternative courses of action and to anticipate both the varieties of disorder which might occur and the most appropriate response.

Most importantly, university authorities should make known in advance, that they will not hesitate to call on civil police when circumstances dictate, and should review in advance with police officials the degrees of force suitable for particular situations. It is a melancholy fact that even in cases where the need for calling the civil police has been generally recognized, the degree of force actually employed has frequently been perceived as excessive by the majority of the campus community, whose sympathies then turned against the university authorities. Indeed, there is reason to believe that a primary objective of campus revolutionaries is to provoke the calling of police and the kinds of police conduct that will bring the majority over to their side.

(3) Procedures for campus governance and constructive reform should be developed to permit more rapid and effective decision-making. There is great misunderstanding and confusion as to where ultimate authority for campus decision-making lies. The fact is that the authority is shared among several elements.

By law, trustees are granted full authority over colleges and universities. But trustees cannot supervise the day-to-day affairs of a university; hence they delegate power to the president. The president, however, in addition to being the agent of the trustees, is the leader of the faculty. His effectiveness derives as much from campus consensus of faculty and students as it does from the power delegated to him by the trustees.

In the American system of higher education, the faculty plays the primary role in determining the educational program and all issues directly relevant to education and faculty research. Unlike the systems of some other countries, educational control in the American system is faculty-oriented; anything else is a deviation from the norm.

Faculty control of education and research is the best guarantee we have of academic freedom. It is a precious asset that must not under any circumstances be sacrificed. Most student demands for change pertain to educational and research matters and too often their efforts have been directed toward administrative officers who usually do not have the power which students assume they possess. And often, too, some faculty members have mistakenly joined with students in using coercive force against administrative officers when it is the faculty itself that should deal appropriately and effectively with the issues in question.

Most other powers in the university are diffused. For most purposes, shared power is an asset. But to prevent disorders, universities must be able to respond quickly. Campus protests are sometimes escalated to the level of force because legitimate grievances, peacefully urged, have been referred to university committees which were slow to respond. Scholars have the habit of examining any hypothesis, debating it exhaustively, deferring decision to await more evidence, and when something must be decided, shunning a consensus in favor of subtle shades of disagreement and dissent. For the process of education, these are admirable qualities. But for dealing with naked force, they can be a prescription for disaster. Faculties therefore have a special obligation to organize themselves more effectively, to create representative groups with power to act, and to maintain constant and systematic lines of communication with students. They should be ready to meet every challenge to the educational integrity of the institution. If this integrity is compromised, it will be the faculty that suffers the most.

Students should, of course, have a meaningful role in the governance of all non-educational, non-research functions. They should serve, too, on committees dealing with educational and related questions, exercising their right to be heard on these subjects, so long as the faculty remains paramount.

(4) Faculty leaders and administrative officers need to make greater efforts to improve communications both on the campus and with alumni and the general public. Campus difficulties are constantly aggravated by misinformation and misunderstanding. On campus, large numbers of faculty and students often act on the basis of rumor or incomplete information.

Alumni and the general public receive incomplete, often distorted, accounts of campus developments. The communications media, on and off the campus, concentrate on controversy. Much of the peaceful progress of our colleges and universities is never communicated to the outside world. Campus authorities have the responsibility to see to it that a balanced picture is portrayed.

IV.

To the larger society, we make these suggestions:

(1) The majority of the American people are justifiably angry at students who engage in violent and obstructive tactics. While the public varies widely in its desire for social change, it shares a common belief in the value of social order. It also regards university students as among the most privileged in society—among those who should understand best the importance of freedom and the dangers of anarchy. One outlet for this public resentment has been the support of legislation withholding financial aid both from the students who engage in disruption and from colleges and universities that fail to control them.

There has also been a steady weakening of public sentiment in favor of the additional public funding that higher education so badly needs. Current appropriations for new facilities and for annual operating costs have been insufficient. Some private universities have faced a reduction in individual and corporate gifts.

Existing laws already withdraw financial aid from students who engage in disruptive acts. Additional laws along the same lines would not accomplish any useful purpose. Such efforts are likely to spread, not reduce the difficulty. More than seven million young Americans are enrolled in the nation's colleges and universities; the vast majority neither participate in nor sympathize with campus violence. If aid is withdrawn from even a few students in a manner that the campus views as unjust, the result may be to radicalize a much larger number of convincing them that existing governmental institutions are as inhumane as the revolutionaries claim. If the law unjustly forces the university to cut off financial aid or to expel a student, the university as well may come under widespread campus condemnation.

(2) We believe that the urge to enact additional legislation should be turned into a channel that could assist the universities themselves to deal more effectively with the tactics of obstruction. State and municipal laws against trespass and disorderly conduct may not be wholly effective means of dealing with some acts of physical obstruction. They were not written to deal with such conduct, and they do not cope with the central issue—forcible interference with the First Amendment rights of others. We are presently considering whether there is a need for statutes authorizing universities, along with other affected persons, to obtain court injunctions

against willful private acts of physical obstruction that prevent other persons from exercising their First Amendment rights of speech, peaceable assembly, and petition for the redress of grievances. Such laws would not be aimed at students exclusively, but at any willful interference with First Amendment rights, on or off the campus, by students or by non-students. They would also be available to uphold the First Amendment rights of students as well as other citizens.

(3) Finally, we urge the American people to recognize that the campus mirrors both the yearnings and weaknesses of the wider society. Erik Erikson, a renowned student of youth, has noted that young and old achieve mutual respect when "society recognizes the young individual as a bearer of fresh energy, and he recognizes society as a living process which inspires loyalty as it receives it, maintains allegiance as it extracts it, honors confidence as it demands it."

One effective way for the rest of us to help reduce campus disorders is to focus on the unfinished task of striving toward the goals of human life that all of us share and that young people admire and respect.

RESOLUTION ON RIGHTS AND RESPONSIBILITIES

The following interim statement, drafted by the Committee of 15 at Harvard University, consisting of 10 faculty members and five students, was passed by the university's Faculty of Arts and Sciences on June 9, 1969.

The central functions of an academic community are learning, teaching, research and scholarship. They must be characterized by reasoned discourse, intellectual honesty, mutual respect, and openness to constructive change. By accepting membership in this community, an individual neither surrenders his rights nor escapes his fundamental responsibilities as a citizen, but acquires additional rights as well as responsibilities to the whole University community. They do not require him to be silent and passive. But they do require him to see how easily an academic community can be violated, knowingly or unknowingly—whether by actual violence or by lack of responsiveness to widely perceived needs for change; whether by impatience or by insensitivity; or by failure in a process of decision to make sufficient effort to consult those who have to live with the results of the decision.

We believe it timely to state explicitly what certain of these rights and responsibilities are, and to establish procedures for their protection and enforcement. The present formulation is an interim statement, limited to activities that touch on the essential functions of a university. We recognize the need to formulate, in the near future, a document that will emerge from the widest discussion within and will reflect a wide consensus of all members of the Harvard community. This statement shall apply equally to students, to officers of instruction, and to officers of administration.

All individuals or groups within the University community have the right to express, advocate and publicize their opinions. They also have the right to press by appropriate means for action on any matter on which they believe that the University can and should act, and they have the right to be given a full and fair hearing and prompt response. To be appropriate the means must respect both the need to preserve the essential commitment of the University and the right of individual or collective expression of opinion or dissent. We have taken and will continue to take measures aimed both at dealing with issues and grievances raised by members of the community and at improving and broadening the procedures by which such matters can be resolved and decisions made. We welcome participation of all members of the community in this endeavor.

We regard the following activities as unacceptable because they would prevent or impede the performance of the essential tasks of the University and are incompatible with the shared purposes of an academic community:

a. violence against any member or guest of the University community;
b. deliberate interference with academic freedom and freedom of speech (including not only disruption of a class but also interference with the freedom of any speaker invited by any section of the University community to express his views);
c. theft or willful destruction of University property or of the property of members of the University;
d. forcible interference with the freedom of movement of any member or guest of the University;
e. obstruction of the normal processes and activities essential to the functions of the University community.

Any such activity shall subject the violator to discipline by an appropriate agent.

In case of any violation of any of the subparagraphs *a* through *e* by a student, he shall be subject to appropriate discipline within the full range of possible disciplinary measures by the Faculty or by a committee or agent to which the Faculty may have delegated disciplinary power. Appropriate discipline for a student who violates subparagraph *a* will ordinarily be expulsion, dismissal, separation, or requirement to withdraw. In cases of violations of subparagraphs *c*, *d*, and *e*, discipline will ordinarily be initiated upon complaint by a member of the University community adversely affected, or on a determination of probable cause by a committee or agent to which the Faculty may have delegated disciplinary power.

In cases of violation of any of the subparagraphs *a* through *e*, a student found to be engaging in unacceptable activities may be warned to stop. If, despite the warning, the student persists in the unacceptable activity, he may be suspended summarily from the University by a committee or agent to which the Faculty may have delegated disciplinary power, pending completion of a regular disciplinary proceeding.

Occasions may arise that may require the appropriate University authorities to use other proper means to control or terminate unacceptable activities. It is the sense of the Faculty that the appropriate authorities should attempt whenever possible to deal with such occasions through the disciplinary measures described in the preceding paragraphs. The Faculty also urges that appropriate University authorities consult with representative student and faculty bodies to the maximum extent practicable in devising and implementing ways to invoke other proper means of control.

While this Interim Statement is in effect, the disciplinary authority over students engaging in the activities listed above shall be delegated to the Committee of Fifteen or a designated successor. The power of summary suspension shall be delegated jointly to the Dean of the Faculty of Arts and Sciences and the Committee of Fifteen (or its designated successor), who are authorized to establish appropriate working arrangements to give effect to this power.

We further affirm that an officer of instruction or administration who engages in the unacceptable activities listed above should also be considered subject to discipline by the appropriate agencies of the University.

RESOLVED:

That the Faculty of Arts and Sciences approves the Interim Statement of Rights and Responsibilities for the College and the Graduate School of Arts and Sciences.

LESSONS TO BE DRAWN FROM A YEAR'S EXPERIENCE OF CAMPUS DISRUPTION

This statement was the result of a conference of nine college and university presidents at The John LaFarge Institute, New York City, June 11-12, 1969. The participants were: Dumont F. Kenny (Chairman), York College of The City University of New York; William G. Caples, Kenyon College; James A. Colston, Bronx Community College; Arthur O. Davidson, Wagner College; James B. Donovan, Pratt Institute; J. Osborn Fuller, Fairleigh Dickinson University; Clifford Lord, Hofstra University; Joseph P. McMurray, Queens College; and Gregory Nugent, F.S.C., Manhattan College.

While it is still too early to assess the long-term effects of the disturbances and challenges faced by so many American universities and colleges during the academic year just ended, immediacy is of help when attempting to ascertain some of the lessons to be drawn from a year of campus unrest. With details and impressions still fresh in their minds, nine college and university presidents spent the better part of two days at this task. They reflected the experiences of campuses large and small, public and private, religious and non-sectarian, those marked by violence and those which remained peaceful. Speculation on the causes of the current campus unrest, although highly interesting and important, was put aside for the more practical task of finding guidelines for action in the immediate future.

Several points of consensus emerged during the discussions and provided a backdrop for the lessons drawn. First, each campus situation is unique. The complexity and variety of details in individual situations, despite superficial similarities, cannot be underestimated when searching for rules generally applicable. Second, accidental and irrational factors play a considerable role in nearly all campus disorders. Third, because of differences and variables, no college president would feel comfortable in criticizing a colleague at another institution for taking a course of action different from the one he would follow under similar circumstances on his own campus. Fourth, reexamination of college governance, and resulting justifiable changes—generally in the direction of a tri-partite (student-faculty-administration) structure—are marks of a forward looking administration. Fifth, violent and disruptive actions strike at the very heart of constructive dissent, academic freedom, and due process in the accomplishment of reform, all of which are the earmarks of a free university, and cannot be countenanced. Sixth, since members of the academic community are subject to the same civil and criminal laws as every other citizen, imposition of repressive legislation designed as campus control measures which tend to single out students for special restrictions are unfair and have no validity in principle or in practice. On the contrary, because many problems of the social order tend to show up earlier and be more visible in educational institutions, a helpful focus for legislative efforts would be attempts to deal directly and positively with the social roots of these problems rather than with their campus manifestations. Finally, a year of campus disorders has taken its toll in the colleges in instructional effectiveness, retention of able administrators and public support. One of the casualties of this experience is open and frank communication which becomes more and more difficult when everyone is playing roles.

Practical lessons drawn from a year's experience:

1. Clear-cut policies and procedures to be followed in case of campus violence or disorder must be thought through, established and published.
2. There should be no negotiation of demands under duress, i.e., when personnel are detained or buildings occupied. It must be made clear to all that there can be no amnesty for civil or criminal lawbreakers.
3. Students should be reminded of the major stake they have in answering and implementing a basic question of college governance, "Who represents the students?" When student governments are representative and legitimate, college administrations should support them against the challenges of "coalition" and "ad hoc committees," generally a tiny minority purporting to speak for all the students.
4. University faculties must face up to their responsibilities in dealing with unprofessional and irresponsible conduct of those few faculty members who have engaged in such practices as manipulating and agitating students for their own partisan and political goals.
5. Since sensational press coverage and mass media exposure are goals of the more militant activists, media representatives must be made to realize that mass media exploitation of a campus disturbance has always exacerbated it, while restrained and responsible coverage has caused many campus disturbances to fade quickly.

Additional lessons drawn from the year's experience:

6. Student confidence in their faculty and administration can be enhanced by giving responsible students a chance to "carry the ball."
7. Student actions must be assessed against their needs for personal recognition, status and partisan interests. Administrators must listen very carefully to what students really mean when stating "demands."
8. The methods and instrumentality for responding to student demands or disorders should be appropriate and proportional, e.g., the printed page versus verbal message, a large assembly versus a small, representative group.
9. Faculty involvement and support must be gained by involving faculty members early enough so that "the problem" is also their problem.
10. "Layers" of response should be prepared to prevent escalation of issues and help defuse crises. Since trivial or imaginary issues may grow into major demonstrations and disorders, it is important that faculty and administrators respond to all situations quickly in order to dispel rumors, correct misinformation, or provide time to take the steam out of irrational urges or inventions.
11. With much of campus structure and function politicized and stereotyped, informal occasions and events should be provided to bring together faculty, students, and administrators in non-formal and unofficial ways.
12. Channels of continuing communication must be maintained and care taken to "fill-in" each incoming freshman class so that they have some understanding of the antecedents of current situations.

Selected References

STUDENT ACTIVISM IN HISTORICAL, INTERNATIONAL, AND CONTEMPORARY PERSPECTIVES

WILLIAM W. BRICKMAN

The following is a selection of publications in Danish, Dutch, English, French, German, Russian, Spanish, and Swedish. These furnish background information on student discipline, dissent, and disorder throughout history in various parts of the world. Brief annotations are provided for works in foreign languages. (Most of the titles in Russian were taken from Lewis S. Feuer, *The Conflict of Generations.*) Stanley Lehrer contributed a few items in English.

I. Historical

Altbach, Philip G. *Student Politics in Bombay*. New York: Asia Publishing House, 1968.

Altbach, Philip G., ed. *Turmoil and Transition: Higher Education and Student Politics in India*. Bombay: Lalvani, 1968.

Bärnstein, A. P. von. *Beiträge zur Geschichte und Literatur des deutschen Studententhums*. Würzburg, 1882. History of German student life.

Battistini, L. H. *Postwar Student Struggle in Japan*. Tokyo: Tuttle, 1956.

Bevis, A. M. *Diets and Riots: An Interpretation of the History of Harvard University*. Boston: Marshall Jones, 1936.

Bristed, Charles A. *Five Years in an English University, 1840-1844*. New York: Putnam, 1851

Bruchmüller, Wilhelm. *Der Leipziger Student, 1409-1909*. Leipzig: Teubner, 1909.

Brügmann, A. *Zucht und Leben der deutschen Studenten, 1648-1948*. Berlin: Limpert, 1941. Three centuries of German student life and behavior.

Buy, François. *Les étudiants selon Saint-Marx en Europe et en Afrique*. Paris: Les Editions Municipales, 1967. Critique of Communist influence on European and African student activism.

Cabanès, Docteur. *Moeurs intimes du passé (Quatrième série): La vie d'étudiant*. Paris: Albin Michel, n.d. Student customs of earlier periods.

Capes, W. W. *University Life in Ancient Athens*. New York: Harper, 1877.

Cheng, Wen-han. *The Chinese Student Movement*. New York: King's Crown Press, 1948.

Chow Tse-tsung. *The May Fourth Movement: Intellectual Revolution in Modern China*. Stanford: Stanford University Press, 1960.

Compayré, Gabriel. *Abelard and the Origin and Early History of Universities*. New York: Scribner, 1892.

Der Göttinger Student. Göttingen: Vandenhoeck & Ruprecht, 1913. Reprint of edition of 1813.

DeVrankrijker, A. C. J. *Vier eeuwen Nederlandsch studentenleven*. Voorburg: Boot, n.d. Four centuries of Dutch student life.

Dolch, Oskar. *Geschichte des deutschen Studententhums von der Gründung der deutschen Universitäten bis zu den deutschen Freiheitskriegen: Ein historischer Versuch*. Leipzig, 1858. Reprint—Graz: Verlag für Sammler, 1968. German student life from the 14th to the early 19th century.

Emmerson, Donald K., ed. *Students and Politics in Developing Nations*. New York: Praeger, 1968.

Engel, G., and Gorohov, V. *Iz istorii studencheskago dvizheniya, 1899-1906*. St. Petersburg, 1906. The Russian student movement during the early 20th century.

Feuer, Lewis S. *The Conflict of Generations: The Character and Significance of Student Movements*. New York: Basic Books, 1969.

Fournière, Michel de la, and Borella, François. *Le syndicalisme étudiant*. Paris: Seuil, 1957.

Gabriel, A. L. *Student Life in Ave Maria College, Mediaeval Paris: History and Chartulary of the College*. Notre Dame, Ind.: University of Notre Dame Press, 1955.

Georgievsky, Aleksander I. *Materialy po istorii studencheskago dvizheniya v Rossi*. 2 vols. London, 1906. Documents on the history of the Russian student movements.

Griewank, Karl. *Deutsche Studenten und Universitäten in der Revolution von 1848*. Weimar: Böhlau, 1949. The role of German students in the 1948 revolution.

Hart, James H. *German Universities*. New York: Putnam, 1874.

Haskins, Charles H. *The Rise of Universities*. New York: Holt, 1923.

Hofstadter, Richard, and Metzger, Walter P. *The Development of Academ-*

ic Freedom in the United States. New York: Columbia University Press, 1955.

Jahnke, Karl Heinz. *Niemals vergessen: Aus dem antifaschistischen Widerstandskampf der Studenten Europas.* Berlin: Neues Leben, 1959. Anti-Fascist resistance by European students.

Jato (Miranda), David. *La rebelión de los estudiantes (Apuntes para una historia del alegre S.E.U.).* Madrid: [Cies,] 1953. Historical background and analysis of student revolt in Spain.

Keil, Richard, and Keil, Robert. *Geschichte des Jenaischen Studentenlebens (1548-1848).* Leipzig: Brockhaus, 1858. History of German student life during the first half of the 19th century at the University of Jena.

Kibre, Pearl. *Scholarly Privileges in the Middle Ages.* Cambridge, Mass.: Mediaeval Academy of America, 1962.

Kibre, Pearl. *The Nations in the Mediaeval Universities.* Cambridge, Mass.: Mediaeval Academy of America, 1948.

Kiss, Gabor. *Die gesellschaftspolitische Rolle der Studentenbewegung im vor-revolutionären Russland.* Munich: Heller, 1963. The impact of the student movement on the tsarist Russian society.

Klose, Werner. *Freiheit schreibt auf Eure Fahnen: 800 Jahre deutsche Studenten.* Hamburg, 1967. An historical survey of German students' struggle for freedom since the Middle Ages.

Lund, H. C. A. *Studentenforeningens Historie, 1820-70: Dansk Studenterliv i det 19. aarhundrede. I del.* Copenhagen: Gyldendal, 1896. Danish student life in the 19th century.

Mathes, William L. "The Origins of Confrontation Politics in Russian Universities: Student Activism, 1855-1861," *Canadian Slavic Studies,* II, Spring, 1968, pp. 28-45.

Meijer, Jan M. *Knowledge and Revolution: The Russian Colony in Zürich (1870-1873).* Assen: Van Gorcum, 1955.

Orlov, V. I. *Studencheskoe dvizhenie Moskovskogo Universiteta v XIX stolyetii.* Moscow, 1934. The student movement at the University of Moscow in the 19th century.

Oudin, Bernard. *Les corporations allemandes d'étudiants.* Paris: Pichon & Durand-Auzias, 1962. German student fraternities.

Petry, Christian. *Studenten aufs Schafott: Die Weisse Rose und ihr Scheitern.* Munich: Piper, 1968. The student opposition to Nazism in Germany.

Rait, R. S. *Life in the Medieval University.* Cambridge: University Press, 1912.

Rashdall, Hastings. *The Universities of Europe in the Middle Ages.* New edition, Vol. III, pp. 339-464. London: Oxford University Press, 1936.

Sack, Saul. "Student Life in the Nineteenth Century," *Pennsylvania Magazine of History and Biography,* LXXXV, July, 1961, pp. 255-288.

Schachner, Nathan. *The Mediaeval Universities*. Philadelphia: Lippincott, 1938.

Schulze, Friedrich, and Ssymank, Paul. *Das deutsche Studententum von den aeltesten Zeiten bis zur Gegenwart*. Leipzig: Voigtländer, 1910. History of German student life

Seale, Patrick, and McConville, Maureen. *Red Flag/Black Flag: French Revolution 1968*. New York: Ballantine Books, 1968.

Sheldon, Henry D. *Student Life and Customs*. New York: Appleton, 1901.

Smith, Cyril E. *The University of Toulouse in the Middle Ages*. Milwaukee, Wis.: Marquette University Press, 1958.

"Studencheskoe dvizhenie v Rossii," in I. A. Kairov and N. K. Goncharov, chief eds., *Pedagogicheskii slovar*, Vol. II. Moscow: Izdatelstvo Akademii Pedagogicheskikh Nauk, 1960. Pp. 445-446.

Studentengewerkschaft Bonn, ed. *150 Jahre Klassenuniversität: Reaktionäre Herrschaft und demokratischer Widerstand am Beispiel der Universität Bonn*. Bonn, 1968. Historical analysis of student activism at the University of Bonn in behalf of democracy.

Suchlicki, Jaime. *University Students and Revolution in Cuba (1920-1968)*. Coral Gables, Fla.: University of Miami Press, 1969.

Tholuck, A. *Das akademische Leben des 17. Jahrhunderts mit besonderer Beziehung auf die protestantisch-theologischen Fakultäten Deutschlands*. 2 vols. Halle, 1853-54. Student life in the 17th century in Protestant theological faculties in Germany

Van Maanen, G. H. O. *Geschiednis van de internationale studentenbeweging, 1945-1965*. The Hague: S.I.D.I.C. (Interdoc), 1966. History of the international student movement since World War II.

Van Maanen, Gert. *The International Student Movement: History and Background*. The Hague: International Documentation and Information Centre (Interdoc) [, 1966]. Translation of the previous title.

Vydrin, Rafail. *Osnovnye momenty studencheskogo dvizheniya v Rossi*. Moscow, 1908. Foundations of the student movement in Russia.

Walter, Richard J. *Student Politics in Argentina: University Reform and Its Effects, 1918-1964*. New York: Basic Books, 1968.

Wechsler, James. *Revolt on the Campus*. New York: Covici-Friede, 1935.

Wedekind, Eduard. *Studentenleben in der Biedermeierzeit*. 3d edition. Göttingen: Vandenhoeck & Ruprecht, 1927. Student life in mid-19th century Germany.

Zweig, Ferdynand. *The Student in the Age of Anxiety: A Survey of Oxford and Manchester Students*. London: Heinemann, 1963.

II. International Scene in the 1960's

Califano, Joseph A., Jr. *The Student Revolution: A Global Confrontation*.

New York: Norton, 1970.

Cockburn, Alexander, and Blackburn, Robin, eds. *Student Power: Problems, Diagnosis, Action.* Baltimore, Md.: Penguin Books, 1969.

Cohn-Bendit, Daniel and Gabriel. *Obsolete Communism: The Left-wing Alternative.* New York: McGraw-Hill, 1969.

Comparative Education Review, June, 1966.

DiBona, Joseph E. *Change and Conflict in the Indian University.* Detroit, Mich.: Cellar Book Shop, 1969.

Ehrenreich, Barbara and John. *Long March, Short Spring: The Student Uprising at Home and Abroad.* New York: Monthly Review Press, 1969.

Ghosh, S. K. *The Student Challenge around the World.* London: Eastern Law House, 1969.

Hermann, Kai. *Die Revolte der Studenten.* 2d edition. Hamburg, 1967. Analysis of student revolts.

Kidd, Harry. *The Trouble at L.S.E.* [London School of Economics]. London: Oxford University Press, 1969.

Lipset, Seymour M., ed. *Student Politics.* New York: Basic Books, 1967.

Ross, Aileen D. *Student Unrest in India: A Comparative Approach.* Montreal: McGill-Queen's University Press, 1969.

Rüegg, Walter. *Die studentischen Revolte gegen die bürgerliche Gesellschaft.* Erlenbach-Zürich, 1968. A Swiss view of the challenge of the student revolts to middle-class society.

Schoeps, H., and Dannermann, Ch., eds. *Die rebellischen Studenten: Elite der Demokratie oder Vorhut eines linken Faschismus.* Munich, 1968. Analysis of the nature of student rebels—democratic élite or vanguard of a left Fascism.

Schönbehn, Wulf, Runge, Jürgen B., and Radunski, Peter. *Die herausgeforderte Demokratie: Deutschlands Studenten zwischen Reform und Revolution.* Mainz: V. Hase & Koehler Verlag, 1968. The challenge of students to the democratic society of West Germany.

Survey: A Journal of Soviet and East European Studies, October, 1968.

III. U.S. Scene in the 1960's

American Scholar, Autumn, 1969.

Avorn, Jerry L., *et al. Up against the Ivy Wall: A History of the Columbia Crisis.* New York: Atheneum, 1969.

Bell, Daniel, and Kristol, Irving, eds. *Confrontation: The Student Rebellion and the Universities.* New York: Basic Books, 1969.

Draper, Hal. *Berkeley: The New Student Revolt.* New York: Grove Press, 1965.

Frankel, Charles. *Education and the Barricades.* New York: Norton, 1968.

Gerzon, Mark. *The Whole World Is Watching: A Young Man Looks at Youth's Dissent.* New York: Viking, 1969.

Howe, Irving, ed. *Student Activism.* Indianapolis: Bobbs-Merrill, 1967.

Journal of Social Issues, July, 1967.

Kennan, George F., *et al. Democracy and the Student Left.* Boston, Mass.: Little, Brown, 1968.

Kunen, James S. *The Strawberry Statement: Notes of a College Revolutionary.* New York: Random House, 1969.

Miller, Michael V., and Gilmore, Susan, eds. *Revolution at Berkeley.* New York: Dell, 1965.

Peterson, Richard E. *The Scope of Organized Student Protest in 1964-1965.* Princeton, N.J.: Educational Testing Service, 1966.

Peterson, Richard E. *The Scope of Organized Student Protest in 1967-1968.* Princeton, N.J.: Educational Testing Service, 1968.

School & Society, Oct. 26, 1968.

Schwab, Joseph J. *College Curriculum and Student Protest.* Chicago: University of Chicago Press, 1969.

Smith, G. Kerry, ed. *Current Issues in Higher Education, 1968: Stress and Campus Response.* San Francisco, Calif.: Jossey-Bass, 1968.

Taylor, Harold. *Students without Teachers: The Crisis in the University.* New York: McGraw-Hill, 1969.

Vaccaro, Louis, and Covert, James T., eds. *Student Freedom in American Higher Education.* [New York:] Teachers College Press, 1969.

Walterstein, Immanuel. *University in Turmoil: The Politics of Change.* New York: Atheneum, 1969.

Williamson, E. G., and Cowan, John L. *The American Student's Freedom of Expression: A Research Appraisal.* Minneapolis: University of Minnesota Press, 1966.

IV. Source Collections

Cohen, Mitchell, and Hale, Dennis, eds. *The New Student Left: An Anthology.* Revised and enlarged edition. Boston, Mass.: Beacon Press, 1967.

Cohn-Bendit, Daniel, *et al. The French Student Revolt: The Leaders Speak.* New York: Hill and Wang, 1968. (Translation from the French.)

[Cox, Archibald, *et al.*] *Crisis at Columbia.* New York: Vintage Books, 1968.

Gamby, Erik, ed. *Studentliv i Uppsala fran 1600-talet till vara dagar: En memoarantologi.* Uppsala: Bokgillets Förlag, n.d. Selections from the memoirs of students on life at the University of Uppsala from the 17th to the early 20th century.

Georgievsky, Aleksander I. *Materialy po istorii studenscheskago dvizhheniya v Rossii.* 2 vols. London, 1906. Documents on the history of the Russian student movements.

Hammond, William G. *Remembrance of Amherst: An Undergraduate's Diary, 1846-1848.* New York: Columbia University Press, 1946.

Haskins, Charles H. "The Life of Medieval Students as Illustrated by Their Letters," *American Historical Review,* III, January, 1898, pp. 203-229.

Jacobs, Paul, and Landau, Saul. *The New Radicals: A Report with Documents.* New York: Vintage Books, 1966.

Jacobsen, Hans-Adolf, and Dollinger, Hans, eds. *Die deutschen Studenten: Der Kampf um die Hochschulreform, Eine Bestandsaufnahme.* Munich: Verlag Kurt Desch, 1968. Chronology and documentary collection on university reform and student unrest in West Germany.

Katope, Christopher G., and Zolbrod, Paul G., eds. *Beyond Berkeley: A Sourcebook in Student Values.* Cleveland, Ohio: World Publishing Co., 1966.

Lipset, Seymour M., and Wolin, Sheldon S., eds. *The Berkeley Student Revolt: Facts and Interpretations.* Garden City, N.Y.: Doubleday, 1965.

Mazo, Gebriel del, ed. *La reforma universitaria.* 6 vols. Buenos Aires, 1926-27.

Munro, Dana C., ed. *The Mediaeval Student.* Philadelphia: Department of History, University of Pennsylvania, 1899.

Norton, Arthur O. *Readings in the History of Education: Mediaeval Universities.* Cambridge: Harvard University, 1909.

Ocampo, Tarsicio, comp. *México: Huelga de la UNAM, Marzo-Mayo, 1966; Documentos y reacciones de prensa.* Cuernavaca: Centro Intercultural de Documentación, 1967. Documents relating to the student strife at the National Autonomous University, Mexico City, in 1966.

Seybolt, Robert F., trans. *The Manuale Scholarium: An Original Account of Life in the Mediaeval University.* Cambridge: Harvard University Press, 1921.

Thorndike, Lynn. *University Records and Life in the Middle Ages.* New York: Columbia University Press, 1944.

Walden, J. W. H. *The Universities of Ancient Greece.* New York: Scribner, 1909.

V. Bibliographies

Altbach, Philip. *A Select Bibliography on Students, Politics, and Higher Education.* [Cambridge, Mass.:] Center for International Affairs, Harvard University, 1967.

Altbach, Philip G. *Student Politics and Higher Education in the United States: A Select Bibliography.* Cambridge, Mass.: Center for International Affairs, Harvard University, 1968.

NOTE

Much information may be obtained by consulting histories of individual universities, *e.g.,* J. Bass Mullinger, *The University of Cambridge,* 2 vols. (Cambridge: University Press, 1873-84); Charles E. Mallet, *A History of the University of Oxford,* 3 vols. (London: Methuen, 1924); Samuel E. Morison, *Three Centuries of Harvard, 1636-1936* (Cambridge, Mass.: Harvard University Press, 1936); Merle Curti and Vernon R. Carstensen, *The University of Wisconsin: A History,* 2 vols. (Madison: University of Wisconsin Press, 1949) .

Index

Academia, affronted by behavior and costumes of student hippies and radicals, 94; constitutional revolution in, 57; functions of, 20; and industry, 68-69; place of political activism in, 20; *see* Higher education

Academic, anarchy, inevitability of, 22; anti-, attitudes in America, 76-77; apologists, abundance of, in higher and secondary education, 21; authority, erosion of traditional structure of, 59; authority, need to readjust to new realities, 57; authority, structure of, 57; community, functions of, 477; community, law as safeguard for, 299; community, laws threatening traditional autonomy of, 423; community, need for due process in, 286-290; community, responsibility of, in dealing with dissent, 305-307; community, rights and responsibilities of, 301-302, 477-479; departments, call for student role in decision-making of, 245-246; evaluation, protecting students against improper, 371; governance, need for student participation in, 201-202; governance, problem of creating more representative, 62; institutions, dropouts' attitudes toward, 72; institutions, reasons for existence of, 370; justice, requirement of, 24; leaders, misinterpretation of true nature of student unrest by, 59-60; life, student's, educators need to learn more about, and non-academic life, 217; order, AAUP statement on law enforcement and, 448; procedures, reform of, as result of student activism, 17; program, need for student participation in development of, 316; records, student, minimizing risk of improper disclosure of, 371; rejection of, as irrelevant by student activists, 75-76; way of life, American, need to accept controversy as part of, 124; world, resistance in, to abandoning old forms of authority, 58

Academic freedom, of Amish in Iowa, 196-197; basic principles of, student demonstrations as violation of, 395; changing character of, 262-263; in classroom, need for, 31; in classroom, responsibilities of professor toward, 370-371; defined, 310; demonstrations in name of, 20; extremism cloaked as, 274-276; freedom to teach and freedom to learn as facets of, 370; as *sine qua non* of higher education, 23-24; state legislature's interference with, in California, 96; student attempts to prevent government officials from expressing viewpoints on campus, 19-20; and student dissent, conflict between, 208; students', maintaining standards for, 371-374; in university, need to maintain, 427; university neutrality as prerequisite for, 208-209; *see* Censorship *and* Freedom

Activism, cerebral, 107-109; existentialist, affect on administrator and scholar, 212-213; in high schools, 182-189; inherent, in students with intellectual curiosity, 238-239; nihilistic, condemnation of, 315; *see* Student activism

Activists, alienation of, from concept of future, 187-188; American, described, 186; contrasted with black power advocates and hippies, 183-184; demands, administration acceptance of, results of, 185-186; obsessed with ends, 188; personality, described, 186-187; *see* Student activists

Administration, acceptance of activists' demands, results of, 185-186; affect of existentialist activism upon, 212-213; college and university, political pressures on, 172; concern with "good public image," 264-265; concern with restricting deviant student, 218; concern with student behavior outside of classroom, student activists' opposition to, 224-225; Conference of Rectors of the Universities, Germany, 347; as conflict resolution expert, 100; confrontation between students and, over use of marijuana, 85; decision-making, growing role of college students in, 215; decision-making, justice vs. efficiency in, 256-257; dogmatism of, 33; -faculty relationship, 57, 266-267; functions of, need to reexamine, 24; high school, student resentment of, as cause of unrest in college, 191-192; inactivity of, 20; leadership, need for resolute, 242; of Mexico's schools, students' dissatisfaction with, 334; need for, to eschew role of adversary in coping with student unrest, 213; need for reasonable rules of, 20; neglect of noncognitive and nonverbal aspects of student behavior, 217-218; ongoing task of, 99-100; participation in joint disciplinary committee at Columbia, 387, 390; release of power to students, as cause of student activism, 188; resistance to student demands for participation in decision-making, 166; rigidified and politicized structure of, forcing students to political activism, 234; student communication, need for better, 190-191, 239-240, 480; students as pawns of, 102; -student relationship, 57, 202, 235; sympathizing with student activists, 21; uni-

versity, Japanese, reluctance to call in police to quell student riots, 364; university, need to develop corporate procedures, 200; *see* Educators; Presidents (s); and Trustees

Admission (s), automatic, of high school students into Latin American universities, 328; of black students, as issue of student unrest, 59, 194-195; Japan's university entrance examination system, 365; need for reasonable regulations of, 21; policies, in higher education, 370; re-, of students rejecting draft, 377-378; standards, student demands for voice on, 89; *see* Enrollment (s)

Adolescents, ambivalence of, 122; disruptive and violent action by, 21; *see* Boys; Girls; *and* Youth

Adult (s), -hood, proposal to give full, at age of 18, 125; reaction to student activism, 184; upset over Berkeley student movement, 167; upset over students' use of drugs, 167; world, sexual hypocrisy of, 56; *see* Parents

Affluence, as cause of student unrest, 130-131

Africa, 13, 19; *see* Black studies; History, African *and* South Africa

Agnew, Spiro, 465; Father Hesburgh's letter to, on campus unrest, 405-407

Alabama, Dixon vs. State of, 263

Alameda County, Calif., 164

Albion College, 33

Alexander the Great, 155

Allen, James E., Jr., 437

Alumni, dismay at change on campus, 95; Notre Dame, response to Father Hesburgh's plan for dealing with campus disruptions, 404

America (n), academic way of life in, need to accept controversy as part of, 124; activists, described, 186; Afro-, curriculum, black power advocates' demand for, 184; anti-academic attitudes in, 76-77; anti-intellectualism in, 67; campus, race relations on, 88-89; classical, college, role of, 44-47; colleges, role of student activism in modernization of, 108-109; colleges and universities,

ance to reforms in, 94

Existentialism, 39; appeal of, to youth, 209; characteristics of, 209-210; effect of, activism on administrator and scholar, 212-213; vs. essentialism, 209-211; influence of, on student militants, 146

Existential psychotherapy, 86

Experimental Collegiate Program, at Berkeley, 228-229

Expulsion, consequences of, 472; as penalty for campus disruptions, 60-61, 399; as primary instrument of university discipline, 418

Extracurricular activities, emergence of organized, as significant educational development of 19th century, 107; *see* Athletics *and* Student newspapers

Extremism, cloaked as academic freedom, 274-276; compromise with, or concession to, as open invitation to graduated repetition, 24; need to deal with, 426

Facilities, campus, institutional control of, not to be used as censorship device, 372; library and student union, lack of, instrumental in keeping Latin American students away from campus, 329; university, lack of, in France, 351

Faculty, -administration relationship, 57, 266-267; authority to create new courses, stricter controls on, in California, 96; authority, growth of, 57-58, 82; collaboration with military-industrial establishment, 56; collective bargaining, AAUP support of, 90; collective bargaining, AFT support of, 91; Columbia, statement condemning force and disruptive activities on campus, 408-413; contrasting role of, in U. S. and Latin American universities, 329; criticism, of amnesty in campus disruptions, 284; failure, as cause of student unrest, 273; functions of, need to reexamine, 24; inactivity of, 20; involvement in off-campus affairs, in Latin America, 322; locals vs. cosmopolitans, 65-66;

militant, threat to autonomy of American colleges and universities, 449; need to bring, back into main flow of university life, 238; need to discipline fellow faculty members participating in campus disruptions, 481; need for, to eschew role of adversary in coping with student unrest, 213; number of, enrollments explosion increasing, 102; opposition to war in Vietnam, 387; participation in campus governance, extending, 98; participation in decision-making, 446; participation in joint disciplinary committee at Columbia, 387, 390; participation, rating colleges on basis of, 90; part-time nature of, in Latin American universities, as stimulus to student unrest, 322; position of, dramatic rise in relative, 74; power, growth of, in university, 82, 273-274; power, heightened, 73; power, recognition of, 75; power, resistance to, in commuter colleges, 75; radical, criticism of role of university in American society, 90; radical, role of, in student protest in France, 357; resistance to educational reform, 85; resistance to student demands for participation in decision-making, 166; resistance to student power in area of curriculum, 254; responsibility, need to stimulate, 274; responsibility for present state of American universities, 291-292; role of, in classical American college, 44; role in selection of presidents, need for, 241; salient identifications of, 65-66; selection, student demands for voice in, 89; self-determination, in California state colleges, 91; social status of, 51; strikes, AAUP position on, 90; -student communication, need for better, 190-191, 239-240, 480; -student confrontations, 123; -student efforts to improve disciplinary procedures, 427; -student relationship, 134-135, 216, 228-230, 235, 266-267; support of New Left, 274; support of student protests, 21, 91-92, 102; tradition-minded, vs. reform-minded students, 94; -trustee

ADDENDUM

After the printing of most of the pages of this book, both of the following individuals resigned their positions. James E. Allen, Jr., and Robert H. Finch were, respectively, U.S. Commissioner of Education and Secretary of Health, Education, and Welfare. As of June 10, 1970, Dr. Allen no longer holds the post noted on p. 113. Mr. Finch, on June 8, 1970, became Counsellor to the President, and no longer holds the post noted on pp. 414 and 429.